*China's Quest for Independence:*
*Policy Evolution in the 1970s*

edited by Thomas Fingar and
the Stanford Journal of International Studies


ERRATUM


*On page 177, the last seven lines should read:*

    In mid-1979, the Chinese published selected budget figures. Out of a total state expenditure of 112,000 million yuan in 1979, 18 percent was to be spent on national defense and "preparations against war." The Finance Minister explained that such spending would reach 20,230 million yuan in 1979 because of added costs associated with the conflict in Vietnam and other border defense needs. Since the figure of 20,230 million yuan would convert to about $12.8 billion at 1979 exchange rates

# China's Quest for Independence:
# Policy Evolution in the 1970s

## Other Titles in This Series

*Women in Changing Japan*, edited by Joyce Lebra, Joy Paulson, and Elizabeth Powers

*The Chinese Military System: An Organizational Study of the People's Liberation Army*, Harvey W. Nelsen

*Mineral Economics and Basic Industries in Asia*, K. P. Wang and E. Chin

*Huadong: The Story of a Chinese People's Commune*, Gordon Bennett

*China's Oil Future: A Case of Modest Expectations*, Randall W. Hardy

*A Theory of Japanese Democracy*, Nobutaka Ike

*Perspectives on a Changing China: Essays in Honor of Professor C. Martin Wilbur on the Occasion of His Retirement*, edited by Joshua A. Fogel and William T. Rowe

*Technology, Defense, and External Relations in China, 1975–1978*, Harry G. Gelber

*Encounter at Shimoda: Search for a New Pacific Partnership*, edited by Herbert Passin and Akira Iriye

*The Problems and Prospects of American–East Asian Relations*, edited by John Chay

*The Politics of Medicine in China: The Policy Process, 1949-1977*, David M. Lampton

*Intra-Asian International Relations*, edited by George T. Yu

*Chinese Foreign Policy after the Cultural Revolution, 1966-1977*, Robert G. Sutter

*China's Four Modernizations: The New Technological Revolution*, edited by Richard Baum

*Military Power and Policy in Asian States: China, India, Japan*, edited by Onkar Marwah and Jonathan D. Pollack

## Westview Special Studies on China and East Asia

*China's Quest for Independence: Policy Evolution in the 1970s*
edited by Thomas Fingar and the Stanford Journal of International Studies

This examination of policy developments in the People's Republic of China since the Cultural Revolution addresses two central questions: (1) how durable were foreign and domestic policies during the 1970s; and (2) what is the relationship between foreign and domestic policy and between both of these policy areas and internal political maneuvering? Studies of five broad policy areas reveal that most policies were very stable during this period and that foreign policy was linked to domestic issues and political competition only to the extent that it impinged on domestic interests.

The studies trace the evolution of policies on specific issues such as education, foreign trade, and military doctrine, but they also evaluate these policies and decisions in the larger context to which they belong. Key decisions at the start of the decade affected the evolution of policy in all areas and largely shaped the change from adherence to precepts of the Cultural Revolution to the conviction that economic and technical emphasis must displace efforts to achieve social equality in the short run if China is to become a secure and independent nation.

Thomas Fingar is the assistant director of the United States–China Relations Program, Stanford University. His publications include *China's Energy Policies and Resource Development* (editor) and *Developments in PRC Science and Technology* (co-editor).

# China's Quest for Independence:
# Policy Evolution in the 1970s

edited by Thomas Fingar and the
Stanford Journal of International Studies
(Paul Blencowe, Editor in Chief)

Westview Press / Boulder, Colorado

*Westview Special Studies on China and East Asia*

All rights reserved. No part of this publication may be reproduced or transmitted in any form or by any means, electronic or mechanical, including photocopy, recording, or any information storage and retrieval system, without permission in writing from the publisher.

Copyright © 1980 by the Board of Trustees of the Leland Stanford Junior University

Published in 1980 in the United States of America by
  Westview Press, Inc.
  5500 Central Avenue
  Boulder, Colorado 80301
  Frederick A. Praeger, Publisher

Library of Congress Catalog Card Number: 79-5499
ISBN: 0-89158-570-2

Printed and bound in the United States of America

# Contents

Preface, *Thomas Fingar and Paul Blencowe* . . . . . . . . . . . . . . . . . . . . . . . . . . . . ix

Introduction: The Quest for Independence, *Thomas Fingar* . . . . . . . . . . . . 1

1. Domestic Policy and the Quest for Independence,
   *Thomas Fingar* . . . . . . . . . . . . . . . . . . . . . . . . . . . . . . . . . . . . . . . . . . . 25

2. The Domestic Politics of China's Global Posture,
   1973-78, *Harry Harding* . . . . . . . . . . . . . . . . . . . . . . . . . . . . . . . . . . . 93

3. China's Military Doctrines and Force Posture,
   *John Wilson Lewis* . . . . . . . . . . . . . . . . . . . . . . . . . . . . . . . . . . . . . . 147

4. Chinese Foreign Trade Policy and the Campaign
   Against Deng Xiaoping, *Ann Fenwick* . . . . . . . . . . . . . . . . . . . . . . . 199

5. Sovereignty at Sea: China and the Law of the Sea
   Conference, *Victor H. Li* . . . . . . . . . . . . . . . . . . . . . . . . . . . . . . . . . 225

Index . . . . . . . . . . . . . . . . . . . . . . . . . . . . . . . . . . . . . . . . . . . . . . . . . . . . 247

# Preface

This volume is the product of unusual, and in some ways unique, collaboration. A joint research project on change, continuity, and linkages in Chinese policy was launched in 1976, but the core group of Stanford China specialists (Thomas Fingar, Harry Harding, John Lewis, Victor Li, and Douglas Murray) already had been sharing insights and information for several years. Under the auspices of Stanford's United States–China Relations Program, and with partial support from the Office of External Research, U.S. Department of State, the group set out to examine the stability and predictability of China's domestic and foreign policies. Building upon their different interests and disciplinary backgrounds, the participants proposed to study changes in selected issue areas and, more importantly, to examine how policy debates and policy changes in one area shaped, and were shaped by, developments in other areas.

Two Stanford graduate students (David Bachman and Frank Hawke) joined the project as research assistants and colleagues who contributed far more to the final product than the prodigious amount of material they helped to collect. Their observations, together with those of Ann Fenwick who joined the group somewhat later, were woven into each of the separate studies. Over time, the interchange became so extensive that we now would be hard put to say precisely who had contributed what ideas.

Collaboration entered a new stage in 1978 when Stanford's United States–China Relations Program joined forces with the *Stanford Journal of International Studies* to prepare the papers for publication. Draft chapters were checked and edited by members of the *Journal* staff whose suggestions helped the authors to resolve remaining problems before the final papers were sent to Westview Press—the third partner in this cooperative venture. As a result, the papers in this collection have been published simultaneously in a Westview edition and in the *Stanford Journal of International Studies*.

Mr. Fingar would like to thank all those who participated in the project seminars and otherwise contributed to this volume. He especially acknowledges the patience and support of the editors and staff of the *Stanford Journal of International Studies*, the many contributions of Douglas Murray, and the special assistance of Andrew Andreasen, Helen Morales, and Gerry Bowman. Mr. Blencowe, on behalf of the *Stanford Journal of International Studies,* would like to thank Victor H. Li for bringing to the *Journal* the opportunity to work on this project and Dean Joseph E. Leininger, Stanford Law School, for his unfailing support. He also would like to thank the senior staff members of the *Journal* who gave much time and effort to this volume: Andy Williams, Gwen Griffith, Jack Gillman, Dave Temin, and Lee Cort.

The support provided by Stanford's United States–China Relations Program and the Department of State's Office of External Research (contract number 1722-620241) was critically important, but the views expressed in this volume do not necessarily reflect those of either organization. Similarly, the contributions of many individuals greatly enhanced the final product, but the editors and authors alone are responsible for the analysis presented here.

*Thomas Fingar and Paul Blencowe*

# China's Quest for Independence:
Policy Evolution in the 1970s

# Introduction:
# The Quest for Independence

*Thomas Fingar*

In certain respects, the 1970s were years of tremendous change in the People's Republic of China. To rank developments in order of significance would be foolish and futile, but even a partial list must include the deaths of Mao Zedong, Zhou Enlai, Zhu De, Li Fuchun, and other founding fathers of the PRC; the bungled coup and purge of Lin Biao; the rise and fall of the "gang of four"; and the improbable fate of Deng Xiaoping. To this must be added President Nixon's journey to Peking; "normalization" of relations with the United States; campaigns to criticize Lin Biao and Confucius, *Water Margin*, "Taking the Three Directives as the Key Link," and Deng Xiaoping; and the conspicuous changes of the post-Mao era.[1] Despite all of these changes, however, there has been a strong element of continuity and stability in Chinese policy.

Conventional wisdom and much scholarly writing have characterized China and Chinese policy as convulsive and ever-changing.[2] Such assessments contain more than a grain of truth, but by focusing on what was novel or dramatic, they have often obscured much that was prosaic and relatively unchanging. Moreover, they suggest that the only prudent prediction about the future international behavior of the PRC is continued flux and uncertainty. Predictions of that sort may be safe for the seer, but they are not particularly helpful to those who must make commercial or foreign policy decisions. Are China and Chinese policy really so unstable, or has fascination with rhetoric and change blinded us to reality and continuity? Posing the question somewhat differently, have PRC policies changed as often and as dramatically as suggested by Chinese commentators and many foreign analysts, or is there an underlying stability that endures despite leadership changes and the vicissitudes of politics?

To answer the questions posed above, contributors to this volume have focused on policy and political maneuver rather than on personalities. The objective was to establish a policy baseline and thence to ascertain where, when, and why changes occurred. This approach revealed that many policies remained relatively unchanged during the 1970s and that the most intense debates and inflammatory rhetoric often resulted in only minimal shifts of policy. In short, there appears to have been considerable stability or policy continuity throughout the decade.[3]

An interest in the stability and predictability of PRC policy was at the heart of the studies that led to this volume, but so too were a number of other questions: To what extent do Peking's foreign policies determine or derive from domestic policies? How sensitive to domestic politics are China's foreign policy and international behavior? How and under what conditions do questions of foreign policy become contentious political issues in China? Do certain domestic developments portend changes in foreign policy? Does policy continuity tend to outweigh shifts in political rhetoric?

The papers in this collection provide only imperfect answers to these and the many additional questions they examine, but together they constitute an impressive case for the basic stability of PRC policy in the 1970s. By comparing rhetoric to behavior and examining specific policy shifts against the background of the total policy package, the contributors demonstrate that most policies evolved in a linear fashion after 1969. At times evolutionary progress and implementation were temporarily thwarted by opponents of the emerging program, but policies were not repealed or reversed; they were simply put on "hold" for a time.

Political maneuver and personal rivalries played influential roles in the evolution of policy, but so too did such factors as bureaucratic inertia, technological imperatives, and events beyond China's borders. Efforts to effect dramatic or systemic change met with minimal success in each of the policy areas examined in this volume. Failures were due, in part, to the errors and political weakness of those who opposed the program that took shape in 1970-71,[4] but, as the papers demonstrate, they were also due to inherent structural and political limitations that severely inhibited major policy shifts. One implication of this assessment is that the factors that made dramatic change difficult during the 1970s will continue to operate into the 1980s and that policy changes could become even more conservative.

Three themes are central to the papers in this collection. One is "the quest for independence," i.e., the ranking of objectives and evaluative criteria that has shaped PRC policy since the Cultural Revolution. The priorities established in 1969-70 set the terms for discourse and largely predetermined the outcomes of specific policy debates. Each of the papers examines the efforts of Chinese political leaders to work within—or in some cases to change—the parameters set at the beginning of the decade.

The second general theme concerns the interconnection of internal and external policies. Linkages (budgetary, functional, political, etc.) among policy areas both constrain and require certain kinds of change.[5] For example, the budgetary linkage between defense and civilian expenditure required Chinese officials to limit military procurement in order to increase investment in industry and agriculture during the 1970s. Planners and policymakers in the PRC are acutely aware of the importance of such linkages and their awareness has shaped the course of political debate. Moreover, the existence of issue and policy linkages adds to the stability and predictability of PRC policy.

This brings us to the third common theme—the durability and predictability of foreign and domestic policy. The interconnection of policy (conceptually, economically, and politically) effectively precludes major shifts in one area without corresponding change in all others to which it is linked. The more difficult it is to change policy, the more likely that programs will continue in effect with only marginal adjustments to enhance performance or solidify political coalitions. Similarly, the interconnection of policy makes it possible to anticipate certain kinds of change on the basis of shifts in either the underlying approach (now the "quest for independence"), or in critical areas such as military expenditure or intellectual policy. Each of these themes is discussed more fully in the pages that follow.

## I. The Quest for Independence

Although they have repeatedly disagreed on tactical questions and short-term objectives, PRC leaders have generally espoused the same long-range goals: (1) national independence (*guojia de duli* or *guomin duli*) or national security (*guojia anchuan*); (2) modernization (*xiandaihua*); and (3) socialist transformation (*shehuizhuyi gaizao*). A fourth objective—deemed essential for realizing the first three—is effective leadership and Party control.[6] The long-range goals are compatible and mutually reinforcing, but officials have learned that specific policies designed to realize one objective often impede or delay attainment of others. It proved necessary, therefore, to rank objectives and to clarify the extent to which attainment of one is predicated on progress toward the other two. The ranking is extremely important because it specifies the "weighting" and evaluative criteria to be used in the selection of both general and specific policies. The ranking or set of priorities adopted in 1969-70 shaped policy decisions throughout the seventies and will likely remain in force well into the next decade.

The first and, since 1969, the highest objective is national independence.[7] In the Chinese view, for a nation to be truly independent, it must be both politically *and* economically independent. According to Deng Xiaoping, "In the final analysis, political independence and economic independence are inseparable."[8] Deng did not include the third and fourth components of national independence (i.e., military strength and cultural independence) in his 1974 address to the United Nations General Assembly, but he and other officials have noted their importance in numerous articles and speeches.[9] In other words, true independence requires political independence, economic independence, a strong national defense, and cultural independence.[10]

Two concepts underlie Chinese commentaries on attaining national independence, namely, sovereignty (*zhuchuan*) and self-reliance (*zili gengsheng*). Sovereignty, according to Chinese formulation, subsumes both the *right* and the *ability* to determine what is done within a specified realm. It is more than a legal construct or abstract "right"; it presupposes the capacity to exercise specified prerogatives in a meaningful way. For example, political sovereignty requires that a country and its leaders be immune to pressures and blandishments from abroad. Under this view, Israel lacks sovereignty to the extent that the United States can pressure its leaders to negotiate with its Arab opponents.

Chinese statements sometimes imply that sovereignty is a scalar concept and that a state can be more or less sovereign in a particular area such as economic development or military strength. At other times or when referring to different policy areas, commentators employ sovereignty as a nominal concept. Under this formulation, either a state enjoys total control over matters at issue (absolute sovereignty), or it is by definition deprived of sovereignty. The implication is that anything less than total control is unacceptable.[11] The internal affairs of a country, including the rights of its citizens, generally fall into the latter category.

Most PRC commentators argue that sovereignty can be attained (or increased) only through self-reliance, but the definition of self-reliance has changed over time and from one situation to another. Some officials have advocated extreme forms of self-reliance that border on autarky; others have endorsed substantial imports of equipment and technical know-how.[12] The key seems to be that the extent to which a nation takes advantage of external opportunities (e.g., to purchase plant and equipment, obtain scientific information, or benefit from tacit alliances) is less important than maintaining absolute control over all decisions. So long as a country—China—can control its own destiny and make the critical decisions affecting its well-being, it is, by definition, self-reliant. Regardless of differences over time and among policy areas, and notwithstanding the fact that PRC policymakers have often disagreed about whether specific measures satisfied the requirements of self-reliance, there has been a general consensus that national independence entails and requires maintaining sovereignty through a policy of self-reliance.

The second objective, modernization, is viewed as an essential prerequisite for security and national independence. Without modernization of agriculture, industry, national defense, science and technology, and all other sectors, it is argued that China will remain weak and vulnerable.[13] Modernization, like its predecessor "socialist construction," is a very broad objective.[14] Representatives of many different bureaucratic and factional interests can readily endorse the general concept while disagreeing sharply over priorities and allocation of scarce resources. Zhou Enlai specified in 1975 that economic plans should reflect the following order of priority: agriculture, light industry, and heavy industry.[15] National defense was presumably assigned an even lower priority. But it is not clear that this ranking did much to resolve allocational disputes or to simplify the task of deciding what to modernize first. Much of the debate in the 1970s centered on precisely such questions. How much money and how many skilled researchers should be assigned to military research and development? Should metallurgy or electronics be accorded priority in the distribution of investment and research funds? Should advanced equipment and technologies be imported to modernize the petrochemical industry? The list of questions faced by China's leaders is almost endless. Even where general decisions were reached (e.g., to import complete plants and accept foreign credits, and to improve the education system), innumerable details remained to be specified through political consultation and economic calculation.

"Socialist transformation" is another of those broad amorphous terms that bedevil students of China. It generally refers to measures designed to increase social equity and reduce the "three major differences"—between industry and agriculture, town and countryside, and mental and manual labor. Whereas socialist construction refers primarily to changes in the economic base (the "forces of production"), socialist transformation has generally been applied to changes in the "superstructure" ("relations of production"). During the Cultural Revolution, commentators emphasized the changing of relationships, on the theory that advances in the superstructure could "pull" the economic base to higher levels of performance. In other words, traditional Marxism had been reversed; changes in the relations of production were to precede rather than follow from modernization of the economic base.[16]

About 1969-70, a decisive group of senior leaders apparently concluded that the need and opportunity to increase the country's long-term security and independence was so great that "modernization" warranted a higher priority than socialist transformation. Concerns of social equity and justice were not to be ignored, but they were relegated to secondary importance.

Similarly, efforts to preserve ideological and cultural purity were not to be denied, but they were most certainly not to take precedence over the "requirements" of modernization.

The definition and ranking of objectives in effect since 1969 is noteworthy for two reasons. One is the importance attached to economic independence as an attribute of sovereignty and security. Briefly, sovereignty, in the Chinese view, includes the right to control one's economic destiny. To the extent that a nation surrenders the ability to control its own economic development, it loses the capacity to act as a sovereign state.[17] Similarly, a nation that does not control its own economy or is dependent on external suppliers for critical products, technologies, or raw materials is, by definition, vulnerable and insecure.[18]

Acute sensitivity to the immanent dangers of diminished economic sovereignty is the direct and understandable result of China's humiliation and restricted development in the century preceding 1949.[19] The extent of actual exploitation by foreign firms and the final balance between harmful and beneficial effects are matters of dispute among Western scholars, but unquestionably China's leaders interpret the experience in the worst possible light. This presently does not preclude the possibility of foreign borrowing, substantial imports, or even joint ventures, but it does mean that China has become extremely careful in negotiating the terms of its economic dealings with other nations or transnational corporations.

National independence ranks as the highest ultimate objective of PRC leaders, as it has since before 1949, but decisions reached in 1969–70 elevated modernization to first priority as an instrumental goal. A dominant group of officials evidently concluded that comprehensive modernization was the necessary prerequisite for independence and security. Zhou Enlai first articulated this view in his 1975 address to the Fourth National People's Congress, but pursuit of the "four modernizations" (agriculture, industry, national defense, and science and technology) did not become a major slogan or develop into a mass campaign until after the death of Mao and the purge of the "gang of four."[20] The ranking adopted in 1969–70 (but subsequently redebated)[21] accorded differential priority to the four components of national security. Throughout the 1970s, economic security has been defined as the *sine qua non* for political, military, and cultural security. The argument is that if a nation is not strong and sovereign in the economic sphere, it cannot possibly retain its political independence or cultural integrity, nor can it obtain or sustain military security. Some commentators have gone even further by insisting that economic development is essential for maintaining Party rule and the "dictatorship of the proletariat."[22] The net and probably inevitable result of this ranking of priorities, as demonstrated in the chapters by Fingar, Harding, Lewis, and Fenwick, is that policy debates have been resolved in ways that correspond to the order of priorities outlined above.

The relationship between priorities and policy decisions can be demonstrated by three examples. John Lewis and Harry Harding each deal with certain aspects of the military procurement vs. economic construction issue. Forced to choose between increased expenditures on the military and expansion and modernization of economic capacity, officials decided, albeit only after intense debate and political maneuver, to concentrate resources for expansion of economic capacity in the short-run so that defense procurement could be accomplished more easily and be better suited to the requirements of modern warfare in the future.

The second example is drawn from my own paper. Opponents of policies adopted in 1970–71 argued that equity and social justice (elements of socialist transformation) were more important than maximum rates of growth or optimally efficient development. They were repeatedly defeated by advocates of rapid economic development who maintained that without growth and steadily increasing opportunities, socialist transformation would be either impossible to achieve or would be completely meaningless.

Ann Fenwick's chapter on the role of foreign trade in the campaign to criticize Deng Xiaoping provides the third example, namely, that economic development in the short-run took (and still takes) precedence over cultural security. Arguments that importing advanced technologies and complete plants would undermine the confidence and capabilities of Chinese scientists and technicians were simply not persuasive to the dominant leadership coalition, which asserted the need to import selectively in order to strengthen the economy and to provide PRC scientists with the tools and experience that would enable them to work up to advanced world levels. Her study also illustrates the willingness of senior officials to make short-term concessions and incur short-term costs in the areas of economic, cultural, and perhaps even political security in order to hasten the advent of greater national security.

Leadership willingness to extend the definition of self-reliance to permit substantial imports, foreign loans and investment, overseas training of scientists and engineers, and the export of natural resources raises important questions concerning the viability of Peking's strategy of development. As I argue in my paper, officials have taken a variety of steps to insure that policies are implemented and that short-term disadvantages do not undermine the entire program. However, one must question whether it is possible to retain the desired level of cultural and ideological identity amidst growing contact with foreigners and imported technologies. The leadership asserts that it is possible, and that the benefits of current policies will quickly become apparent and alleviate the concerns of those who are presently disadvantaged by these policies. This assessment may be correct, but the question is still open, as is the question of whether China can achieve its vision of security and independence in an increasingly interdependent world. The chapter by Lewis strongly suggests that Peking has already lost a degree of independence in the military area and that nuclear weapons and advances in conventional warfare will compel China to surrender some measure of sovereignty in order to attain greater international stability and hence greater Chinese security. As China becomes more deeply involved in international affairs, it appears doubtful that it can avoid the constraints that bind other major powers.

## II. Policy and Political Linkages

One of the most common observations about policy in China is that when changes occur, they generally seem to fit together into a more or less integrated package.[23] Shifts in educational policy, for example, are almost invariably accompanied by complementary changes in science policy and the treatment accorded intellectuals. Organizational, industrial, agricultural, military, and certain aspects of foreign policy have repeatedly changed in tandem or in patterned sequences. Why is this? What is there about policymaking or policy linkages in China that produces patterned transmutations? Are all linkages of equal significance, or do some exist with little relevance to political maneuver and policy formulation? How do linkages become important and what is their role in policy change? The papers in this collection suggest tentative answers to these and related questions.

Policy linkages in China take many forms and derive from at least five related but analytically distinct origins: (1) structural; (2) operational; (3) budgetary; (4) functional; and (5) political. All are important, but their importance varies over time and from one issue or issue cluster to another.[24] Although they have not employed this terminology, all contributors to this volume have examined one or more of these linkage mechanisms and their consequences.

### Structural Origins

It is an obvious but nonetheless important fact that China is a highly centralized polity. Although limited authority has been delegated to subordinate units, policymaking is still concentrated in Peking. Numerous individuals and organizations contribute to the policymaking process, but broad policy decisions are made by a very small number of people. Whether one defines the relevant group as including only the Standing Committee of the Politburo or as including all Politburo members plus the full State Council, the result is essentially the same: issues are resolved by the same small group. Issues—and hence policies—become linked because they are decided in the same meetings by the same group of officials. Individual and collective memories reduce the likelihood that inherently contradictory policies will be adopted. In other words, the situation is quite different from polities where policymaking authority is dispersed among numerous legislative bodies, functional bureaucracies, and regulatory agencies.

More individuals and organizations are involved in the formulation of detailed provisions, but the fact that specific measures must conform to a reasonably well integrated set of policy guidelines enhances the likelihood that resultant policies will mesh into a mutually supportive program. The system does not always function as efficiently as suggested in this summary, but even when it is working rather badly, there is still a strong tendency toward policy integration.

My study of domestic policy illustrates some of the consequences of structurally based linkage mechanisms. Even though members of the post–Cultural Revolution leadership assumed or were assigned specific areas of responsibility (e.g., Yao Wenyuan was in charge of propaganda work and Li Xiannian specialized in economic matters), policies were decided by the group as a whole. This prevented the "radicals" from putting into effect their own policy preferences even in those areas where they had principal responsibility. By the same token, it facilitated and legitimized their right to participate in decisions on the entire spectrum of issues facing the leadership. The integration and compatibility of policies during the 1970s resulted, at least in part, from the fact that decision making was highly centralized. The "majority viewpoint" prevailed, therefore, in all policy areas, including those administered by members of the minority.

*Operational Origins*

Policymaking in the PRC is not only concentrated in the hands of a small number of officials, it is also based on tenets of comprehensive planning. As a result, fortuitous linkages created by consideration of the major issues in the same forum are supplemented by the purposeful meshing of policy alternatives that occurs in the planning process. Central planning has failed to eliminate waste and duplication or to ensure rapid development, but it has caused policymakers to consider measures in relation to one another and to the "Plan" as a whole. The planning process forces staffers to consider the impact of every proposal and to harmonize the demands and requirements of separate bureaucracies and geographic regions. In addition, bureaucratic rivalries and internal procedures aggregate and integrate proposals as a normal part of both the planning and the policymaking process.

In short, routine procedures create and underscore policy overlap and interconnection.

During the Cultural Revolution, policies were not carefully integrated and ad hoc arrangements resulted in confusion and inefficiencies. Determined to overcome these defects and to promote rapid development, senior officials decided to restore comprehensive planning and carefully meshed policies. My chapter describes how this was accomplished in the early 1970s and provides numerous illustrations of policies considered together because of the way in which they moved from the planning to the policymaking agenda.

*Budgetary Origins*

Budgetary linkages are similar to those derived from operating procedures followed in the PRC, but they are also important in polities that do not rely on comprehensive planning. In China, as in most countries, the demand for scarce resources (human, fiscal, and other) far exceeds the available supply. As a result, the process of budgetary allocation is inherently a "zero-sum" game. Since resources apportioned by one policy decision are unavailable for use elsewhere, all policies are linked by bonds of mutual competition. A decision to allocate ten *yuan* for national defense means that ten fewer *yuan* (or skilled engineers, or production lines, etc.) are available for schools, agricultural research, railroad construction, and all other policy areas.

Since most policy areas are assured at least some resources, the actual situation is less Hobbesian than implied in the preceding paragraph. However, participants in the policymaking process must recognize the budgetary impact of their decisions and think about the consequences of every decision for all subsequent policy choices. Moreover, the "zero-sum" nature of the process compels all participants to pay attention to all decisions. Even if a given official has responsibility in only one area (e.g., agricultural policy), that official must follow the debate on other policies lest decisions be taken that foreclose later options and jeopardize programs of direct importance to his "constituents." Structural and operational features enable all participants to become involved in all policy decisions; budgetary linkages require that they do so.

Budgetary linkages figure prominently in the discussions by Lewis and Harding of the relationship between military policy and economic construction. Although they examine the problem from different angles, both make it clear that budgetary considerations are one of the principal sources of policy linkage in the PRC. Additional examples are provided in my discussion of domestic policy, and Fenwick's chapter illustrates the budgetary connection between foreign trade and domestic expenditure (in this case in the shipbuilding industry based in Shanghai).

*Functional Origins*

Issues and policies sometimes become linked because they are inseparably or functionally connected. For example, it is virtually impossible to consider science policies without also considering policies governing the treatment of intellectuals and the operation of schools and research institutes. Scientists are trained in universities and research organs and they are, by Chinese definition, intellectuals. A decision to undertake major research efforts in electronics or metallurgy would be senseless unless there were supporting decisions to train more metallurgists, applied physicists, and electrical engineers. Similarly, if technical specialists are to play a major role in priority research projects, they must be permitted to devote sufficient time to professional work and be relieved of the burden of "bad class background" that has often stigmatized and disheartened intellectuals in China.

Functional linkages are almost the converse of budgetary linkages. Whereas budgetary linkages are essentially negative (i.e., policy areas are linked because the decision to do X precludes or complicates a decision to do Y and Z), functional linkages are positive (to do X, Y and Z must also be done). Policy clusters bound together by functional linkages tend to be smaller than those joined for budgetary reasons, but the linkages appear to be stronger. As societies become more complex and more policy areas become functionally interconnected, the size and strength of policy clusters is likely to increase. As will be discussed below, this entails significant consequences for the ease and magnitude of future policy change.

During the 1970s, both supporters and opponents of the program that emerged in 1970–71 treated policy areas bound by functional ties as unbreakable sets rather than collections of discrete issues. Sets discussed in this volume include: science, education, and intellectual policy (Fingar); trade, technology acquisition, and resource development (Fenwick); and military doctrine, advanced weaponry, and industrial technology (Lewis). In contrast to the situation during the 1950s when there were repeated efforts to disaggregate and recombine policies governing functionally related areas, the past decade was marked by disputes over one or another set of policies dealing with essentially the same sets of issues.[25]

Some policy clusters involve only domestic matters (e.g., commodity prices, peasant incentives, rural organization, and farmland improvement); others are solely or primarily concerned with external affairs (e.g., the set of law of the sea issues discussed by Victor Li). Still others—and the number appears to be growing—involve both domestic and foreign policy issues. The chapters by Harding, Fenwick, and Lewis all deal with policy sets that contain functionally linked internal and external policies. One finding to emerge from the five studies in this collection is that the strength of the linkage or the extent of the overlap between domestic and foreign policy issues is a significant determinant of whether and how foreign policy questions enter into domestic politics.

*Political Origins*

In addition to the linkage mechanisms outlined above, issues and policies may be linked through deliberate political maneuver. Such maneuver can take many forms and can result from very different motivations. For example, the structure of the system enables senior leaders to champion or oppose certain policies in order to undercut the strength of political rivals. Issues and policies may be joined simply as part of individual or factional struggles. Significantly, however, no examples of this type of linkage were presented in the papers collected here.

Both budgetary and functional linkages are conducive to formation of political bonds. The zero-sum nature of budgetary competition combined with the existence of functionally related clusters, is conducive to formation of coalitions comprised of individuals (or bureaucratic organs) with particularistic interests. For example, there is a natural affinity between advocates of sophisticated scientific or industrial research and champions of high quality education and increased contacts with foreign specialists. Coalitions forged around particular clusters of issues and policies seem to endure over time and to lend stability to the policymaking process. In addition, as new issues arise or old issues acquire greater salience, participants are likely to draw upon the support of existing coalitions in order to secure adoption of particular policies. As a result of bargaining (at times accompanied by threats, side payments, pressure, and other familiar political tactics), initially discrete policies or clusters become linked in ways that produce a more or less coherent program.

Political linkages can take other forms as well. Issues or policies that bear no relationship to one another other than their simultaneous consideration by decision makers may give rise to logrolling strategies and the resulting relationships. As certain issues, especially those related to national security, become highly salient, politicians attempt to hitch their own particular policy preferences to the bandwagon of the preeminent question facing the leadership. My chapter describes how policies on a wide range of domestic matters were justified on the basis of their purported ability to hasten greater economic and hence national security.

# The Quest for Independence

With the exception of Victor Li, all of the contributors have described policymaking during the 1970s in terms of competition between rival coalitions. The coalitions seem to be held together by a combination of budgetary, functional, and political bonds. Although they exhibit a degree of permanence, there are defections and realignments as issues change and politicians adopt new tactics. Harding's study demonstrates this particularly well.

One of the central questions guiding the studies in this collection concerns the relationship between domestic and foreign policy and the interplay of foreign policy and domestic politics. Answers to the question of whether and how foreign policy matters become linked to domestic policy debates depend very much on which policies or policy clusters are examined. Three of the studies focus on foreign policy issues that have direct and immediate consequences for domestic policy. Harding's study of China's global posture and Lewis's chapter on military doctrine demonstrate that military issues—which are defined as primarily matters of foreign policy in their studies—are closely linked to domestic matters. Budgetary and functional bonds appear to be the most important linkage mechanism binding these policies to domestic issues, but political maneuver is also a factor. Fenwick's chapter on foreign trade as an issue in the *Pi Deng* campaign examines another case of strong links between foreign and domestic policy arising from the fact that trade policy necessarily entails specific budgetary and functional consequences for numerous internal policies. These studies suggest that the more directly foreign policy issues impinge on domestic interests, the greater the likelihood that those issues will become embroiled in domestic politics.

Victor Li's chapter on law of the sea issues illustrates cases at the opposite extreme. Law of the sea questions and PRC policy on those questions are almost completely unrelated to domestic issues or to most other matters of foreign policy. China's position evolved gradually over several years in virtual isolation from the policy debates and political rivalry of the 1970s. Since the issues involved did not impinge upon domestic concerns and were highly esoteric from the point of view of most officials, formulation of policy was left to specialists who seem to have operated autonomously or with only *pro-forma* supervision by political leaders. It is questionable whether or not there are many other issues so completely divorced from internal policy, but if there are, they might well be handled in the same way as the law of the sea.

Between these two extremes lie a number of foreign policy issues that have weak or variable ties to domestic issues. My own chapter illustrates several instances in which political figures asserted the importance of linkages between their domestic policy preferences and realization of foreign policy objectives, but there is at least a measure of opportunism in their arguments. Statements about the Soviet threat often fall into this category. Proponents of everything from tighter managerial authority to rapid exploitation of China's energy reserves justified their approach on the grounds that the threat from the Soviet Union was increasing daily and hence made it imperative to act with dispatch to maximize the rate of economic growth. Such linkages probably did not affect foreign policy since they were asserted after basic foreign policy decisions had been made. They did, however, have a pronounced effect on the course of domestic policy debate.

The primacy of foreign policy and its impact on domestic politics is one of the clearest findings to emerge from the studies. There is, of course, reciprocal influence between foreign and domestic policy, but during the 1970s the dominant line of causality appears to have flowed from the international to the domestic arena. Throughout the decade, China's policies were shaped by a single, relatively unchanging perception of the international situation. Harry Harding demonstrates that this interpretation—sloganized as the "theory of three worlds"—was challenged in the media and presumably in leadership meetings, but the challengers lost and policies continued to be based on an assessment of the world adopted in 1970-71. Subsequent developments—some of which have been characterized by Western scholars and officials as substantial changes—such as the fitful evolution of U.S.-Soviet détente; American withdrawal from Vietnam; communist victories in Vietnam, Laos, and Cambodia; the emergence of energy and resource supplies as major security concerns; and the gradual normalization of U.S.-China relations were all fitted into the interpretive framework devised shortly after the Cultural Revolution. The genesis of that framework is described in my study; its subsequent elaboration is the subject of Harding's chapter. Once the overall assessment had been made, proponents of different policy alternatives found that they had to work within that framework. They also learned that the framework largely predetermined the outcome of debates. Unable to change derivative policies, opponents of the new program attempted first to redefine the international situation (described in Harding's chapter), and then to obstruct implementation of formally adopted policies (examined in the chapters by Fingar and Fenwick).

It was argued above that policy clusters have grown in size and strength over the years and that linkages between foreign and domestic issues seem likely to increase in the future. If this is correct, it suggests that effecting major shifts of policy will become increasingly difficult. It also suggests that domestic *and* foreign policies are unlikely to change very much unless there is perceived change in the international situation.

## III. Durability and Predictability of PRC Policy

Despite considerable evidence to the contrary, Chinese policy is generally thought of as unstable and subject to extreme change at any time. The five contributors to this collection disagree with such an assessment, and hold that both domestic and foreign policies were quite stable during the 1970s and that the policy debate and political maneuver were characterized by competition between a dominant coalition supporting the program devised in 1970-71 and a smaller, less powerful group of opponents. They do not agree completely on the prospects for continued policy stability. Potential sources of instability will be discussed below; first I wish to make the case for policy durability in the years ahead.

As outlined in section I, the objectives and priorities shaping PRC policy since 1969 are similar to those of other nations—and even to the "models" in standard textbooks on international politics. National security, broadly defined, and economic development are among the most salient concerns of political leaders around the globe. The fact that China fits the general pattern would be a trivial observation were it not for the widespread belief that the PRC is somehow radically different from other countries. Ideology, commitment to "revolution," and continuous struggles for power are among the explanations that have been advanced to account for China's purportedly unique approach to policymaking. Under close scrutiny, these explanations do not hold up very well, even for the period before 1970; the studies in this collection reveal them to be of little utility in the present decade.[26]

Similarities between the "determinants" of PRC policy in the 1970s and those shaping policy decisions elsewhere can be traced to two factors. One is simple and straightforward: China is part of the international system and must respond to challenges, opportunities, and agendas over which it has little control. In a world of many actors (nations, international organizations, transnational corporations, and the "market," among others), China is subject to the same proddings and limitations that affect other nations. Peking's susceptibility to external stimuli increased in the 1970s as a result of both deliberate decisions and fortuitous developments that led to greater involvement in international affairs. To cite just one example, when the PRC replaced the Republic of China at the United Nations in 1971, Peking had to address numerous issues that, in the past, could be ignored or dealt with from the perspective of an outsider with no responsibility for the outcome.

Deliberate—and contentious—decisions to increase imports of equipment and technologies; to improve relations with the United States, Japan, and Western Europe; and to break out of the self-imposed isolation of the

Cultural Revolution inevitably exposed the country and its leaders to new and competing pressures. The quest to transform China into a major power, willing and able to influence developments ranging from the creation of a new economic order to the international rules governing environmental pollution or the testing of new pharmaceuticals, has introduced new constraints as well as new opportunities for PRC policymakers.

Relegation of "socialist transformation" to secondary or even tertiary priority is the second factor producing similarities between policymaking in the PRC and in other countries. During the Cultural Revolution, official rhetoric — and what passed for formal policy — placed a premium on closing income, status, and other differentials, often by leveling downward. This may have resulted in slower economic growth, diminished scientific capabilities, and even reduced military strength, but at least some leaders were willing to pay that price in order to accelerate socialist transformation. By the early 1970s, however, a decisive group of senior officials had become convinced that the costs and risks of those policies were too high. The decision to accord lower priority to equity and social justice had the effect of making China's policy considerations more like those of other countries than they had been in the late 1960s.

Although PRC policy considerations have become increasingly similar to those found in textbook examples and real-world states, it remains to be seen whether this will lead to significant convergence in the sense predicted by Brzezinski and Huntington and other analysts of industrial society.[27] China's leaders have adapted to new constraints and opportunities in ways conditioned by the country's special history, cultural endowment, political system, resources, and current objectives. In some policy areas, such as higher education and industrial organization, adaptation has produced policies that appear quite similar to those of other countries at comparable or higher stages of development and with similar short-term objectives. Policies in several other areas (e.g., personal freedoms, military procurement, and avoidance of international dependencies) indicate that China does not always accept the same "logic" of the situation as do other countries, for example the Soviet Union or Mexico.

The chapters in this volume suggest that policies on a wide array of domestic and international matters were formulated on the basis of a particular assessment of the "overall international situation." Even when individuals and coalitions expressed opposition to the prevailing interpretations or to policies derived therefrom, they did not challenge the propriety — indeed the necessity — of basing programs on such a comprehensive evaluation. Consensus on this point has contributed to the increasing durability of PRC policy by reducing the likelihood of knee-jerk reactions to external developments or the destabilizing consequences of domestic events. In other words, unless it is established to the satisfaction of a decisive group within the leadership that a *fundamental* change has occurred, policy changes are likely to be characterized by marginal adjustments rather than dramatic new departures. Discrete events seldom weigh heavily in the overall calculus; perceptions of fundamental change are more likely to rest on cumulative developments and discernment of clear trends. Unless and until a fundamental change occurs, policymaking in China will probably continue to exhibit a strong conservative bias.[28]

Stability and conservatism certainly do not mean the end of politics. Chinese leaders evinced substantial and continuous disagreement throughout the 1970s and there is every indication that debate and political maneuver will continue. The character of politics and the "rules of the game" have changed, but honorable officials will continue to disagree over appropriate courses of action and disputes will have to be resolved, at least in part, through political means. Economic and technical efficiency have become more important, perhaps even more decisive criteria in the seventies, but economic and technical rationality are inappropriate for deciding questions that are inherently political. Almost every policy advantages some and disadvantages others. "Representatives" of particular regions, bureaucracies, or other groupings must compete in a series of zero-sum games. Ambitious officials seek to further their own careers, and political rivals seek to undercut their opponents by deriding policy stands, apportioning blame for difficulties, and stealing issues or supporters. "Winners" must preserve their victories and maintain their coalitions; "losers" must reopen debate and recruit supporters. Politics is omnipresent, but more than that, it is recognized as an essential and entirely appropriate means of dispute resolution.

Political maneuver can take many forms (e.g., logrolling, compromise, blackmail, character assassination, manipulation of the media and efforts to curry favor with powerful officials) and most of them have been employed in the PRC. The chapters by Harding, Fingar, and Fenwick illustrate both the variety and the changing efficacy of tactics adopted in the 1970s. Tactics that had served the "gang of four" and other defenders of the Cultural Revolution well in the late sixties proved rather ineffective in the changed circumstances of the seventies. Efforts to seize the initiative and set the terms of debate with sloganized appeals to "go against the tide" or to "defend the socialist new-born things of the Cultural Revolution," for example, were rather easily countered or co-opted by political opponents. Mao's failure to intervene on the side of the "radicals" probably doomed this tactic by denying its users the kind of authority they had enjoyed a few years earlier. Similarly, manipulation of the media proved less effective because other channels of control—principally those of democratic centralism and

Party discipline — had supplanted the media as vehicles for conveying and enforcing central directives.

Those who emerged victorious from the major political conflict of the 1970s — the conflict between defenders of the Cultural Revolution and efficiency maximizers eager to increase China's security and independence as rapidly as possible — concluded that politics had gotten out of hand in the decade after 1965 and took immediate steps to correct the situation. In typical Chinese fashion, they did so through a combination of positive and negative examples. The "gang of four," which by early 1977 had become something of an ideal type rather than a simple reference to Jiang Qing, Wang Hongwen, Yao Wenyuan, and Zhang Chunqiao, was denounced for a wide variety of illegitimate political behavior. Examples of their resort to "unprincipled political struggle" included efforts to discredit policies by stigmatizing their supporters, refusing to permit free discussion of alternatives, and attempting to forge voting blocs through intimidation and side payments.[29]

Positive examples took the form of calls to "return to the fine traditions of the Party," and commentaries on "democratic" decision making. Doctrinal authority was provided by the first official publication of Mao's 1962 address entitled "Talk at an Enlarged Working Conference Convened by the Central Committee of the Communist Party of China."[30] The following excerpt illustrates the mode of politics sanctioned by Mao's successors.

> If unity is to prevail throughout the Party and the nation, we must give full play to democracy and let people speak up. This holds both inside and outside the Party. . . . All leading members of the Party must promote inner-Party democracy and let people speak out. What are the limits? One is that Party discipline must be observed, the minority being subordinate to the majority and the entire membership to the Central Committee. Another limit is that no secret faction must be organized. We are not afraid of open opponents, we are only afraid of secret opponents. . . . As long as a person does not violate discipline and engage in secret factional activities, we should allow him to speak out and should not punish him if he says wrong things. If people say wrong things, they can be criticized, but we should convince them with reason. What if they are still not convinced? They can be allowed to reserve their opinions. As long as they abide by the resolutions and decisions taken by the majority, the minority can reserve their opinions.[31]

Two points in the passage quoted above merit additional comment. One is that renewed emphasis on the principles of democratic centralism was designed, in large part, to overcome one of the most troublesome problems of 1970–76, namely, cadre disobedience and deliberate obstruction of policy decisions. Opponents of the policies that began to emerge in 1970–71 used their control of the media and the convocation of special meetings to create confusion and otherwise block implementation of formal policies. These actions violated Party discipline, but they also proved to be a source of confusion and paralysis impeding realization of objectives considered prerequisites for true independence. This tactic has again been denounced as illegitimate and concrete steps (e.g., reestablishment of the Central Commission for Inspecting Discipline)[32] have been taken to insure compliance.

The second noteworthy point is the injunction against formation of secret factions. Descriptions of "bourgeois factionalism" have been quite vague, probably by design, but the implied definition is sufficiently broad to include virtually all forms of coalition building. Officials apparently are to interact as individuals committed only to finding the best possible solutions to problems on the policymaking agenda. Prearranged deals and "voting blocs" based on political maneuver or factional loyalty seem to be proscribed. In theory, this should produce "better" decisions and more effective policies, but in practice it is likely to prove unworkable. Regardless of how well it works, however, the fact that such an injunction has been issued signals both a reaction against the kind of politics operating through most of the 1970s, and an effort by the dominant group to structure the rules of the game in ways that enhance their position.[33] To the extent that they are successful and the new rules are observed, policymaking should become more conservative, and policies should continue to be shaped in accordance with the ranking of objectives outlined above. This, in other words, makes it even more likely that the quest for independence will continue into the 1980s and that the main contours of PRC policy will continue to resemble those of the late 1970s.

Although several factors—structural, developmental, political, and even technological—suggest that policies will exhibit durability and predictability into the next decade, the analyses in this collection caution us not to be overly sanguine. Continued policy stability could be jeopardized in at least three ways. Since the program developed after 1969 was predicated on a particular assessment of the international situation, it is reasonable to conclude that policies could change substantially if PRC leaders perceive that major change has occurred in the "overall situation." It is, however, impossible to predict with confidence exactly what changes might lead to such a perception. Dramatic improvement in U.S.-Soviet relations accompanied by Western refusal to aid China's developmental effort would presumably qualify as a major change, but this hardly seems likely in the foreseeable future. The fact that we cannot predict what would trigger a major reinterpretation of the international situation does not mean that reassessment is impossible or even unlikely. In the end, the decision to redefine the global situation will be made by the PRC officials who view the world through lenses colored by ideology, personal ambition and responsibility, and political pressures. The factors outlined above reduce the probability of redefinition resulting from internal political causes, but they do not eliminate it entirely.

The second possible cause of policy instability is internal. PRC developmental plans are extremely ambitious and almost certainly unattainable within the specified number of years. In addition, the post-Mao leadership has staked its claim to legitimacy on its ability to outperform its predecessors. The central elite has raised expectations and thus taken substantial political risks. As the developmental program runs into difficulties and people begin to demand promised benefits, pressure will mount to find scapegoats for shortcomings and ways to buy more time. Personnel changes at the top of the system appear inevitable, and this may lead to policy change. The critical element would seem to be the speed at which things begin to come apart and the skill of the leadership in deflecting criticism and making necessary adjustments. If all else failed, the leadership might resort to radical policy change in order to preserve its power and prerogatives.

The third possibility seems unlikely in the 1980s, but could become more important at the end of the century. Briefly, policy could change substantially if China realizes its objectives and attains a high degree of security. If the PRC succeeds in its effort to modernize without dependency or the constraints of interdependency, it might adopt a more aggressive military or economic posture, but such a development seems highly unlikely. There appears to be a dynamic at work in the international system that drives all nations toward certain types of behavior. Technological imperatives and the "logic" of specialization in the modern world are at the heart of this process, but so too is the spectre of nuclear war. China denies that it is or will be subject to this dynamic and its constraints, but there is little reason to acquiesce in this assessment.

Weighing the factors leading to continued policy stability and the likely sources of major change leads to a cautious prediction that PRC policy will remain basically the same into the 1980s. Marginal adjustments will be necessary and policy debates will continue to be a major part of political life in China, but basic stability appears more likely than dramatic change.

## Notes

1. The campaign to criticize Lin Biao and Confucius (1973–74) was essentially a polemical debate between defenders of the Cultural Revolution and advocates of the

policies adopted in 1970-71. The campaign to criticize the classical novel SHUIHUZHUAN [WATER MARGIN] began in August 1975; it has since been described as an effort by the "gang of four" to undermine the persons and policies of Zhou Enlai and Deng Xiaoping. *Taking the Three Directives as the Key Link* refers to an instruction given by Deng Xiaoping. The campaign to criticize this directive eventually was transformed into the campaign to criticize Deng (1976).

2. The following titles are illustrative: Michel Oksenberg, *China: The Convulsive Society,* HEADLINE SERIES, No. 203, 1970; RICHARD BAUM, ed., CHINA IN FERMENT: PERSPECTIVES ON THE CULTURAL REVOLUTION (1971); and HAROLD C. HINTON, CHINA'S TURBULENT QUEST (1970).

3. As used here, stability subsumes both durability and consistency. A policy is stable if it remains in effect over time and retains a basic consistency even though marginal adjustments may be made.

4. Chinese sources have never referred to policies adopted in the early seventies as the "1970-71 Program," but, as I argue in the next chapter, the measures adopted at that time do appear to constitute a well-integrated program.

5. Linkage is a difficult and complex concept. As used here, it refers to both interaction and interdependence. Problems, issues, positions, and policies are considered to be linked if they evidence even a small degree of interdependence, or if they appear to interact at any time. Some linkages are derivative, *i.e.,* they exist because of earlier policy decisions, the nature of the planning and allocational system, or because of a natural or functional connection such as that between an expanding work force and the need to create more jobs. Linkages constitute a part of the process that shapes both politics and policymaking. Officials must either work within the constraints or seek to change them in some way. Efforts to bring about change (by breaking old links and/or forging new ones) can take several forms, but they invariably affect the policymaking process—even if they are unsuccessful. In addition to derivative and deliberately forged linkages, there are others which come into being purely by chance. Perhaps the simplest example of chance linkage is that which frequently occurs solely or primarily because two or more items happen to arise at the same time.

6. Leadership and Party control are not examined in this introduction because they are discussed in the next chapter.

7. The ranking presented here refers to ultimate objectives. Modernization has higher priority than independence as an instrumental objective because PRC leaders assume that independence and security are impossible without first achieving modernization. Socialist transformation ranks third as both an ultimate and an instrumental objective.

8. Deng Xiaoping, *Speech at the Sixth Special Session of the United Nations General Assembly* (April 9, 1974), Renmin Ribao [People's Daily, hereafter RMRB], April 11, 1974.

9. On military strength and national independence, *see, e.g.,* Xu Xiangjian, *Heighten Vigilance, Be Ready to Fight,* HONG QI [RED FLAG, hereafter HQ], No. 8, 1978, at 42-50. On the importance of cultural independence, see Deng Xiaoping, *Speech at the Opening Session of the National Science Conference* (March 18, 1978), RMRB, March 22, 1978.

10. The Chinese word for culture (*wenhua*) subsumes education and science as well as literature, music, and art. To be culturally independent means to retain distinctive artistic traditions, but it also means to be strong and independent in respect to scientific and technical knowledge and the ability to increase and transmit such knowledge. In the Chinese view, unless a nation has a strong science establishment and an educated populace, it will always be dependent on others. For example, unless a country's engineers understand the basic science and engineering that goes into a particular piece of machinery or industrial process, imported equipment and know-how cannot be completely absorbed and the recipient will remain dependent on the supplier for spare parts, repairs, and design modifications. Cultural independence also means the ability to preserve core values and ideological principles in the face of increased contact with other cultures. The trick is to be able to borrow selectively from other cultures without losing that which makes one distinct.

11. As John Lewis notes in his chapter of this volume, Chinese unwillingness to be constrained by arms control agreements is, in part, attributable to the belief that acceptance of such controls amounts to surrendering the "sovereign right" to employ military forces as the leadership desires.

12. Differences on this issue gave rise to the trade-related components of the campaign to criticize Deng Xiaoping, discussed by Ann Fenwick in her chapter. For contrasting views of self-reliance, see Fang Hai, *Criticize the Philosophy of Slavishness to Foreign Things,* HQ, No. 4, 1976, at 21-26; Mass Criticism Group of the Ministry of Light Industry, *Relying on Our Own Efforts, Making Foreign Things Serve China,* RMRB, Nov. 16, 1976; and the untitled article by the Theoretical Group of the Research Institute on Questions of International Trade, Peking Foreign Trade College broadcast by New China News Agency on Dec. 10, 1976, translated in FOREIGN BROADCAST INFORMATION SERVICE, DAILY REPORT: PEOPLE'S REPUBLIC OF CHINA [hereafter FBIS], Dec. 15, 1976, at E7-9.

13. *See, e.g.,* Hua Guofeng, *Report on the Work of the Government Delivered at the First Session of the Fifth National People's Congress* (February 26, 1978), RMRB, Feb. 27, 1978.

14. Socialist construction (*shehuizhuyi jianshe*) was the term used in the 1950s and early 1960s. It has now been replaced by modernization or "the four modernizations" as a rallying and descriptive slogan.

15. Zhou Enlai, *Report on the Work of the Government* (January 13, 1975), RMRB, Jan. 21, 1975.

16. Defenders of the Cultural Revolution certainly never claimed that they had stood Marx on his head. Nevertheless, their preoccupation with the relations of production stands in sharp contrast to the approach of those supporting the 1970-71 Program. Compare Yu Dajiang, *"Everything for Modernization" is a Slogan for the Theory of Productive Forces,* Guangming Ribao [Guangming Daily, hereafter GMRB], Feb. 11, 1976; and Jin Yan, *The "Gang of Four's" Sinister Intentions in Wielding the Big Club of the "Theory of Productive Forces,"* HQ, No. 4, 1977, at 62-67.

17. This view is very similar to that expounded in writings on "dependency theory." *See, e.g.,* ROBERT I. RHODES, *ed.,* IMPERIALISM AND UNDERDEVELOPMENT (1970); and K. T. FANN AND DONALD C. HODGES, *eds.,* READINGS IN U.S. IMPERIALISM (1971).

18. For an interesting commentary on the loss of independence by COMECOM

members as a direct result of Soviet efforts to exercise economic control, *see Inside that "Community,"* PEKING REVIEW, Oct. 10, 1975, at 17-19.

19. *See, e.g.,* Stephen C. Thomas, The Effects of Foreign Intervention on Chinese "Self-Strengthening" Efforts: The Case of the Kaiping Coal Mines, 1870-1912 (unpublished Ph.D. dissertation, Stanford University, 1979).

20. Mao Zedong died on September 9, 1976; the principals in the "gang of four" were arrested on October 6, 1976.

21. Portions of this debate are examined in Harry Harding's chapter in this volume.

22. *See, e.g., "On the Ten Major Relationships" is a Powerful Ideological Weapon to Criticize the "Gang of Four,"* Peking Radio (Feb. 1, 1977), *in* FBIS, Feb. 10, 1977, at E2-7 (second in a series of sixteen commentaries on *On the Ten Major Relationships*).

23. *See, e.g.,* Richard P. Suttmeier, *Science Policy Shifts, Organizational Change and China's Development,* CHINA QUARTERLY, June 1975, at 207-241.

24. An issue cluster is a set of contentious matters that are treated as a unit rather than individually. Similarly, a policy cluster is a set of policies that are treated as a unit and covary over time.

25. On the 1950s, *see* Thomas Fingar, Politics and Policy Making in the People's Republic of China, 1954-1955 (unpublished Ph.D. dissertation, Stanford University, 1977).

26. For an earlier study that discounts the "revolutionary" aspect of PRC foreign policy, *see* PETER VAN NESS, REVOLUTION AND CHINESE FOREIGN POLICY (1971).

27. ZBIGNIEW K. BRZEZINSKI & SAMUEL P. HUNTINGTON, POLITICAL POWER USA/USSR (1964). *See also* the discussion of convergence in FREDERIC J. FLERON, JR., *ed.,* TECHNOLOGY AND COMMUNIST CULTURE (1977).

28. Conservative is used in its original rather than its political meaning. Conservative policymaking tends to preserve as much of the old program as possible and to make only those minor adjustments thought necessary to cope with new problems or overcome deficiencies.

29. Articles criticizing "gang" political behavior include: Gao Zhi, *What Kind of Party did the "Gang of Four" Seek to "Rebuild"?*, RMRB, July 12, 1977; *Thoroughly Bury the Fallacy of "Dynastic Changes"—The People of Sichuan Scathingly Criticize the Counterrevolutionary Political Program of the "Gang of Four,"* RMRB, Oct. 8, 1977; and Shi Qiao, *The Gang of Four Sought to Subvert the Dictatorship of the Proletariat by Inciting Anarchism,* HQ, No. 5, 1978, at 38-44.

30. This speech was published in HQ, No. 7, 1978, at 2-16; and in RMRB, July 1, 1978. Unofficial versions of the speech were circulated during the Cultural Revolution and a full translation of that earlier version can be found in STUART SCHRAM, *ed.,* MAO TSE-TUNG UNREHEARSED (1974).

31. The excerpt is taken from the translation published in FBIS, June 30, 1978, at E1-18; excerpts are from E15.

32. The Central Commission for Inspecting Discipline was established at the Third Plenum of the Eleventh Central Committee which met between December 18 and 22, 1978. This commission is patterned on the Central Control Commission established on March 31, 1955. There are a great many similarities between the steps taken in 1977-78 and those taken in 1955 after the so-called "Gao Gang Affair."

33. These themes are developed at greater length in Fingar, *supra* note 25.

# 1
# Domestic Policy and the Quest for Independence

*Thomas Fingar*

## I. Introduction

Beginning in late 1976, Chinese leaders announced a series of carefully integrated policies designed to transform the People's Republic of China (PRC) into a modern and powerful socialist country by the year 2000.[1] Western observers and many Chinese cadres were skeptical about the longevity of the new program.[2] Three separate perspectives on PRC politics and policymaking underlay this reaction.

Adherents of one perspective have interpreted developments since late 1976 as constituting a sharp break with the policies of the preceding period and with fundamental tenets of "Maoism." In their view, PRC policies have little inherent continuity or structural foundation and can therefore be changed quickly and extensively if the Politburo has a change of heart or power shifts to a different faction or coalition. Specific policies are generally depicted as independent of structure, precedent, and political memory. In short, PRC policies can, have, and presumably will continue to change dramatically.[3]

A second group of analysts has characterized recent policies as little more

---

Partial support for this research project was provided by the Department of State under Contract 1722-620241. Additional support was provided by the Rockefeller Brothers Fund. Views or conclusions contained in this study should not be interpreted as representing the official opinion or policy of either the Department of State or the Rockefeller Brothers Fund.

The author wishes to acknowledge the research assistance of David Bachman and Frank Hawke, and the critical comments of Douglas Murray, Victor Li, Harry Harding, John Lewis, and Ann Fenwick who helped to formulate ideas over the many months of this project. A special word of thanks is due Dorothy Solinger and John Lewis, whose incisive and helpful comments on an earlier draft added greatly to the quality of this manuscript.

Thomas Fingar is the assistant director of the United States–China Relations Program, Stanford University. He earned his A.B. at Cornell University in 1968, his M.A. at Stanford University in 1969, and his Ph.D. at Stanford University in 1977.

than the reincarnation of programs attempted with mixed success in earlier periods, specifically the mid-1950s and early 1960s.[4] Subscribers to this view imply that PRC policies have alternated between two more or less unchanging and diametrically opposed approaches and prescriptions.[5] Attitudes, policies, and individuals are assumed to cluster into just two coalitions, and policy change is interpreted as merely a shift from one comprehensive "package" to the other. "Oscillation" between these two poles is posited to be a permanent feature of Chinese politics.[6]

Those adopting the third perspective have focused on the senior elite and have interpreted developments in China in terms of intra-elite conflict. Factions of various types (e.g., clientalist, generational, and regional) are seen to vie for power, and policies are treated as either pawns in what is essentially a struggle for power and prestige, or as the objects of such a struggle. Personnel changes, particularly at the Politburo level, are generally equated with changes in policy.[7]

Regardless of which perspective is adopted the implication is the same; namely, that the current web of foreign and domestic policies is likely to be transient and problematic. The accuracy of such an assessment is a matter of considerable importance to policymakers around the world as they ponder China's role in the international system. A well-founded assessment of leadership and policy stability is critical to decisions on whether to enter into long-term trade agreements with China; whether to forge explicit or tacit security agreements with Peking; and how to respond to specific overtures or warnings from the PRC. A major objective of this chapter is to provide an alternative perspective and interpretation of policy change in the PRC so that analysts and government officials will have a firmer basis for anticipating future developments in Chinese foreign policy. To achieve that objective, this chapter will examine changes and trends in PRC domestic policy since 1970 and will comment briefly on the relationship between domestic and foreign policy.

## II. Policymaking in China

There has been a marked tendency on the part of Western analysts to predict shifts of PRC foreign policy on the basis of changes in domestic programs.[8] Although the track record for such predictions is not impressive, it is reasonable to examine the domestic roots of foreign policy because of the integrated character of PRC policies. Part of the problem in the past has been the failure to properly distinguish among three types of policy.

The first type (or highest level) is that of formal or intended policy. Such policies refer to those measures that have been adopted in accordance with specified rules and procedures. They are often, but not always, promulgated as explicit and authoritative directives that explain official policy and the reasons behind its adoption.

The second type might be called "rhetorical policy." Rhetorical policies exist in all polities, but they are particularly important and troublesome in the case of China. Basically, they consist of the exaggerated and distorted interpretations presented by both supporters and opponents of official policies. Supporters and beneficiaries exaggerate the advantages and successes of particular policies; opponents resort to hyperbole and outright falsification to discredit measures they hope to change.[9]

Actual or implemented policies may resemble either of the first two types, but they may also differ from both. While there is likely to be just one official policy at any particular time, the distortions introduced at the level of rhetorical policy frequently lead to considerable variation at the level of actual policy. It follows that policies may be "made" (through formal procedures, willful distortion, or unconscious modification) at all three levels.

Unlike agricultural, educational, investment, and many other measures, China's foreign policies are implemented by a professional bureaucracy with tight controls on all stages of the process. As a result, actual foreign policies generally differ very little from formal ones.[10] By observing behavior, one can be reasonably certain what the formal foreign policy is in specific areas. If comparisons and parallels are to be drawn between domestic and foreign policy, they should therefore be made at the formal level. Attempts to predict foreign policy or PRC behavior in the international arena on the basis of rhetorical or even actual policies in the domestic arena are likely to fail because formal external policies tend to remain in effect even when policies at other levels seem to vary. Unfortunately, many analysts have deduced foreign policy from rhetorical statements about domestic programs and have been misled on two counts: what actually happened domestically and what inferences should be drawn about future international behavior.

As will be discussed below, China's present leaders have made a determined effort to minimize disparities among formal, rhetorical, and actual policies. They have done so precisely because such differences proved to be a major problem during the previous six years. The analysis that follows will examine the magnitude, causes, and consequences of these differences. It will focus on the formal policy level, however, on the assumption that formal domestic policies adopted (or reiterated) since 1970 provide the best guide to formal—and therefore actual—PRC foreign policy.

The approach employed in this paper grew out of an earlier study of politics and policymaking in the mid-1950s.[11] That study generated the following propositions:

1. Policymaking in China is a continuous process subdivided into a series of debates, decisions, and derivative actions (rounds) in which the events and outcomes of one round are significantly shaped by what took place in preceding rounds.
2. Policymaking in China normally involves the formation and realignment of coalitions built around common or compatible stands on a number of policy issues. Over time, coalitions become larger, fewer in number, and more permanent. In addition, the requirements of coalition maintenance and recruitment of new members (partly by inducing defection from other coalitions) reduce both the magnitude of difference between the policies advocated over time by any one coalition, and the magnitude of prescriptive differences between rival coalitions.
3. Policymaking and national planning in China are intertwined in a way that transfers the conservatism of planning to the larger process of policymaking. Because planning is essentially an incremental exercise, policymaking tends to become a matter of adjustments at the margin.
4. Political maneuver designed to maintain or bolster coalitions, and the requirements of comprehensive planning, combine to insure that issues will be handled simultaneously rather than sequentially, and that policies in different areas will be extensively and explicitly interconnected.

Taken together, these propositions suggest that policymaking in China should become gradually but increasingly conservative unless there is a fundamental or systemic change in the "rules of the game,"[12] as occurred during the Cultural Revolution (1966–68). They also suggest that persons dissatisfied with specific policies or the general trend toward analytic and incremental change will have ever greater difficulty "reversing" those policies or bringing about dramatic changes.[13]

These tendencies are reinforced at the level of actual policy by another noteworthy characteristic of the Chinese political system. Over the past thirty years, informal "arrangements" have provided a kind of glue, or grease, enabling the system to work relatively well despite structural flaws, deficient policy guidelines, and politically motivated interference. Cadres throughout the system have forged alliances and devised irregular, even extra-legal arrangements to accomplish essential tasks. Both the system as a whole and all of its myriad subsystems have almost assuredly functioned better than would have been the case in the absence of these informal arrangements. Over time, many of these arrangements—especially the most successful ones—have been institutionalized.[14] As argued below, institutionalization and the clarification of tasks generate increased conservatism of a type that facilitates implementation of certain policies and impedes actualization of others.

The propositions listed above all deal with the internal dynamics of politics and policymaking, but analysts of national policies, both domestic and foreign, also must assess the relative impact of internal and external events on the formulation and execution of policy decisions. For example, to what extent are domestic policies tailored to respond to challenges and opportunities in the international system? Similarly, are foreign policies an outgrowth of domestic political contests and policy decisions, or are they shaped primarily by ideological considerations or developments beyond China's borders? This chapter will argue that the set of policies formulated in 1970-71 derived from a specific perception and projection of the global situation, and that both foreign and domestic policies were tailored to take advantage of that situation. It will also argue that internal changes—in leadership, economic performance, the salience of particular issues, etc.—had minimal impact on PRC foreign policies after 1970, and that external events such as détente between the United States and the Soviet Union and the fall of the Saigon regime had relatively little effect on China's domestic policies and politics.

To state that external developments did not have a pronounced effect on China's policies in the 1970-78 period is not to suggest that this always has been or will be the case. On the contrary, events beyond the PRC's borders strongly shaped the decisions that culminated in the "1970-71 Program"[15]—as they had in earlier periods. However, perceptions of events are generally more important than are the events themselves, and throughout the 1970s, most—or certainly the dominant—senior leaders did not perceive any fundamental changes in the international situation. Adjustments had to be made, but key officials saw no need to reformulate either their earlier view of the world or the policies predicated on that interpretation.

## III. Genesis of the 1970-71 Program

With the partial exception of the Great Leap Forward (1958-59), policymaking in the period before the Cultural Revolution was predicated on the assumption that Chinese Communist Party (hereafter CCP or Party) leadership and comprehensive national planning were essential prerequisites for rapid economic growth, enhanced national security, and ultimate realization of communist objectives. This fundamental tenet was challenged, discredited, and temporarily discarded during the late 1960s. A variety of alternative "models" was attempted, but their social and political advantages were generally outweighed by their economic and security costs.[16] If the new organizational forms and economic programs of the Cultural Revolution had achieved the promised results (e.g., more rapid economic growth with greater social and economic equality), officials imbued with the doctrines of prior years might have become enthusiastic supporters. Unfortunately, many of the innovations did not work very well, and by 1968 it was becoming increasingly clear that something had to be done to improve the system's performance.

Domestic critics initially included those displaced by the Cultural Revolution who had vested interests in restoring elements of the pre-1966 system. Eventually, however, many who had been willing to experiment with dramatically different policies and policymaking procedures joined the ranks of the critics. We will not here assess the reasons key leaders became disenchanted, but it is necessary to note two factors of crucial importance to the decision to phase out the largely unstructured policymaking procedures of the Cultural Revolution, and to restore much of the old order.

First, the collective memory of both leaders and subordinate functionaries supported comprehensive planning and relatively tight central control. Despite the efforts of PRC publicists and sympathetic foreign scholars to trace Cultural Revolution innovations to practices in base area governments before 1949, the fact is that most cadres had only dim or second-hand memories of Yan'an, the Jiangxi Soviet, or other bases. For almost two decades, they had been taught that organizational forms of earlier periods were inappropriate for later stages of the Revolution. In short, many of the experimental programs and organizational forms had begun without a firm theoretical or experiential base, and would have had to be immediately and dramatically successful in order to overcome the skepticism with which they were viewed. This they failed to do.[17]

The second factor in the decision to restore centralized policymaking was the consensus that the international situation had undergone fundamental changes.[18] Events such as the Soviet invasion of Czechoslovakia, proclamation of the Brezhnev Doctrine, Lyndon Johnson's decision not to seek reelection, deescalation of the Vietnam War, military clashes along the Sino-Soviet border, the first steps toward détente between the Soviet Union and the West, and signals from Washington of a new willingness to improve relations with the PRC posed new challenges and opportunities for Peking. However, the existing machinery put China in a poor position to respond to or influence international developments.

External developments heightened concern about China's security and sparked renewed debate on the relationships among the military, economic, political, and cultural elements of national security. Perceived

## Domestic Policy and the Quest for Independence

changes in the international balance of forces and shifts in United States, Soviet, and other foreign policies persuaded at least some Chinese leaders that the likelihood of attack and efforts to "blackmail" China politically or economically would increase unless effective steps were taken without delay.[19] Policies had to be devised and implemented to achieve rapid growth in all areas, especially those most clearly related to national defense.[20]

Senior political figures were concerned about the emerging mix of problems and opportunities facing China. Although these leaders agreed that the domestic and international situations were in flux, they did not concur on how to respond. Those political figures who saw the need for major structural and policy changes faced three separate but closely related problems.[21]

One problem was to formulate an alternative set of policies and institutions that would facilitate rapid and efficient growth and meet the requirements of the new international context. To simplify the search for and evaluation of alternatives in a climate of great urgency, officials turned first to familiar and proven "models" from the period before 1965: (1) a dominant role for the Communist Party, (2) relatively tight central control, (3) comprehensive national planning, and (4) emphasis on economic and technical efficiency.

Another problem was to devise a program that would win the support of key leaders, particularly Mao. In devising these programs, officials also attempted to satisfy some of the demands of those leaders most interested in preserving the status quo. In other words, they sought to prevent a sharp split between "advocates of change" and "defenders of the old order." As a result, most so-called "radicals" apparently decided to live with proposed changes, at least for a while.

The third problem was how to deal with those who argued against major modifications of Cultural Revolution policies. Direct attacks probably would have been counterproductive. Mao would not have tolerated a frontal assault on the "new born things" of the Cultural Revolution or the individuals he had elevated to positions of power. As experienced politicians, organizers of the emerging coalition sought to include as many of the radicals as they could without jeopardizing the chance to make fundamental changes in both policies and the policymaking process.[22] Most of the radicals gave at least grudging support to the first such changes. Initially the changes did not constitute a comprehensive or integrated package with clearly articulated policies in all areas. On the contrary, individual policies emerged in somewhat piecemeal fashion over a period of several months and only gradually acquired the coherence of an overall program.

## IV. Evolution of the 1970-71 Program

Although prior debates and pre-1966 policy sets influenced the course of events in 1969-71, political maneuver and the internal "logic" of the emerging strategy for security and independence were the more direct determinants. Renewed emphasis on speed and economic efficiency set the terms of debate and shaped decisions, but policy outcomes were determined more by political skill and will in manipulating the new rules of the game than by any sort of mechanistic process. This section will sketch the developments of 1970-71 and their immediate consequences in four policy areas: (1) political and organizational, (2) economic, (3) cultural, and (4) military. An approximate chronological sequencing of key decisions in these areas will be followed.[23]

*Political and Organizational Policies*

Both logically and chronologically, the first step in creating a substitute for Cultural Revolution policies and procedures was to restore the authority and organizational integrity of the CCP. Leninist theories of organization and the earlier vanguard role of the Party had a pronounced influence on the thinking of senior leaders, especially those who had risen to positions of power before 1966. Theoretical teachings ingrained in countless "study sessions" were reinforced by direct personal experience before as well as after Liberation: when and where the Party was weak, policy success was uncertain and setbacks more common. The experience and "lessons" of the previous two to three years provided additional reinforcement; many of the problems besetting the country at the time could be—and were— blamed on Party weakness.

Restoration of Party authority involved several more or less simultaneous processes. One process was to restore the stature and authority of the CCP as an organization. Having been reduced to essentially coequal status with a variety of mass organizations, the Party *qua* organization could not play the leading role in society.[24] Efforts to "correct" that anomolous situation began in early 1969 with preparations for the Ninth National Party Congress—the first since 1958.

The fact that the Congress took place, together with contemporary articles in the PRC press, indicated that the Party was to play a more significant role in national and local affairs. However, the precise nature of that role remained ambiguous. For example, documents from the Congress, including the new Party constitution, failed to spell out the Party's role. This probably reflected continued debate within the elite.[25] Advocates of a more effective role for the Party as a Leninist organization continued to press their case. In the months that followed, their arguments became more specific and increasingly forceful.[26]

Concurrent with the drive to reassert and reestablish the legitimacy of Party authority, there was a concerted but highly contentious effort to rebuild CCP committees at all levels. This part of the rebuilding process began with the election of the Ninth Central Committee and a new Politburo, and worked its way downward through provincial and other subordinate levels. Each stage of the year-long process was marked by controversy and competition as individuals and groups jockeyed for positions and power in the new committees. Multiple and cross-cutting cleavages were activated (e.g., veteran vs. new cadres, advocates of tight central control and comprehensive planning vs. exponents of extensive local autonomy) in the course of debate over the procedures and criteria used to select members of each committee.[27]

The campaign to restore the CCP to the dominant position in China's hierarchy of organizations also required changes in the composition of the Party and the attitudes of Party members. This was the most complex of the processes since it involved not only the enrollment of new members from the ranks of the army and mass organizations, but also the rehabilitation of once discredited cadres and the (re)inculcation of norms and values that had been neglected or denounced during the Cultural Revolution. Several million former Red Guards, peasant activists, and model workers and soldiers joined the CCP during the late 1960s, but according to later and probably correct charges leveled at the "gang of four," prescribed recruitment procedures were often ignored, and the composition of the Party changed substantially.[28] Many new members had been admitted to the Party without adequate ideological indoctrination, and beginning in 1970, those distressed by the state of the CCP launched a campaign to strengthen Party discipline and to inculcate common values and operational norms.[29]

This was an interesting and important campaign. Although it will not be examined in detail, two elements should be noted: (1) the admonition to avoid "leftist" as well as "rightist" errors, and (2) the renewed emphasis on the study of Marxism-Leninism and works by Chairman Mao.

In the final quarter of 1970, a number of articles were published in *Renmin Ribao* and *Hong Qi* on the dangers of "leftist" errors and "false Marxism." These articles demanded the study of theoretical writings by Mao and other giants of Marxism, and dictated avoidance of rash attempts to transform society without regard for objective conditions. The message was clear: cadres were no longer authorized to change policies at will, disregard the opinions of "experts" and veteran officials, or ignore directives in the name of "going against the tide."[30] Later articles were even more specific.

For example, they elaborated "proper" modes of behavior and stressed the importance of (1) correctly distinguishing between the "two types of contradictions" (i.e., among the people and between the people and their enemies), (2) observing democratic centralism, and (3) implementing the mass line.[31] There was also a marked decline in emphasis on knowing slogans from Mao and increased attention to reading complete essays by Marx, Lenin, Engels, and the Chairman.[32] Advocates of change evidently hoped to reform and reeducate those in positions of responsibility in 1970–71 (especially those who had entered the Party during the previous five years), and to remove those who could not or would not change their attitude or behavior. However, since strengthened discipline and central control conflicted with the objectives and policies of some political leaders, there was substantial resistance to the new rectification campaign. Resistance and opposition in both national and local units was so effective that rectification was thwarted for six years. Advocates of substantial change were not able to carry out extensive Party rectification until after the downfall of the "gang of four."

While steps were being taken to rebuild Party committees and restore effective command and communication within the CCP, a series of less publicized efforts were undertaken to restore the state bureaucracy. Ministries, bureaus, and commissions that had been understaffed for several years were gradually brought up to strength, and units that had essentially ceased to exist during the Cultural Revolution were slowly and selectively re-created. As Party committees assumed functions that had been performed by revolutionary committees, many revolutionary committees were transformed into administrative organs and incorporated into the state structure. Few changes were announced with great fanfare, but contemporary materials make it clear that gradual rebuilding was in fact taking place.[33] As with the restoration of Party committees, rebuilding seems to have taken longer and generated more controversy at lower levels of the system.

The rebuilding of Party and state organs was accompanied and facilitated by the rehabilitation of veteran cadres and various specialists who had been discredited during the Cultural Revolution. Lower ranking cadres generally returned to the scene earlier than more senior officials, and the most controversial figures typically had to wait longest for reinstatement. By mid- to late 1971, however, the tide was clearly running in the direction of rehabilitation. Concomitantly, few cadres were removed or reassigned. That is, many who had been elevated to positions of power and responsibility during the Cultural Revolution retained their jobs. Consequently, bureaucratic ranks swelled, and "new" and "veteran" cadres were forced to work in tandem. Whether the decision not to make rehabilitation a "zero-sum" game resulted from political astuteness on the part of those advocating restoration or from the necessity to make concessions to those favoring the status quo, it did manage to defuse — temporarily — what could have been a highly explosive issue. At the same time, it created tensions and inefficiencies that ultimately had to be reduced if national objectives were to be realized. Conflict between efforts to improve efficiency and efforts to preserve the "new born things" of the Cultural Revolution engendered substantial political controversy over the next six years.

The most dramatic event during the 1970-71 period was the demise of Lin Biao. Once touted as Mao's "closest comrade-in-arms and chosen successor," Lin allegedly died in a plane crash while attempting to flee to the Soviet Union after an unsuccessful attempt to seize the reins of government in a military coup.[34] Thereafter, many alleged supporters of Lin were removed from their posts, and many policies associated with the former vice chairman were openly discredited. These purges and policy critiques weakened the position of those defending the status quo.

*Economic Policies*

The economic policies of 1970-71 reveal a mix of Cultural Revolution innovations and approaches reminiscent of the 1950s and early 1960s.[35] Although these policies generally stressed technical and economic efficiency, they also reflected compromise between efficiency maximizers and those more concerned about social justice and local self-reliance. The discussion presented here will note examples of compromise, but its primary objective is to provide a policy synopsis that will serve as a baseline for comparison when analyzing subsequent developments. To facilitate comparison, policies will be divided into three general areas: (1) planning and control; (2) industry, incentives, and enterprise management; and (3) agriculture and rural policy.

*Planning and Control.* Whereas the rhetoric and de facto policies of 1966-69 had emphasized local initiative and self-reliance, commentaries published in 1970-71 revived the proposition that swift, smooth, and socially desirable development could only be achieved with comprehensive planning and effective central control.[36] Articles extolling the benefits of better planning initially focused on specific industries or sectors of the economy, but gradually broadened their focus to include manpower, research, investment, and other types of coordination.[37]

While restoration of the state bureaucracy facilitated both planning and control, the principal vehicle of control was to be the revived network of Party committees. Party members and committees were instructed to carry out central plans; failure to do so would be regarded as a breach of Party discipline. There was thus an operational link between planning, rebuilding Party committees, and studying Party doctrine.

Recentralization of control over the economy proved to be a difficult and divisive issue in 1970-71. Officials who placed high value on the capacity of communities to decide local matters opposed the drive for greater central control.[38] In the ensuing debate, some commentators emphasized the "democracy" side of democratic centralism and stressed the importance of using the mass line to gauge popular sentiment.[39] Others, in contrast, stressed "centralism" and obedience to higher-level organs.[40] Over time, the emphasis on "centralism" grew more pronounced.

*Industry, Incentives, and Enterprise Management.* Debate in this area centered on the scale of facilities and the proper balance between centrally and locally controlled enterprises. As in the mid-1950s, China's leaders decided to foster both large, capital-intensive enterprises, and small, labor-intensive factories. But in 1970-71, "walking on two legs" favored large, centrally funded, and centrally controlled establishments. This emphasis was fully consistent with the general quest for efficiency and rapid growth. Small facilities had certain advantages (e.g., they required less capital and generally lower skill levels), but they could not produce goods as efficiently as larger, more highly integrated industrial complexes. Accordingly, policies called for consolidation of existing factories and concentration of new facilities.

The goals of efficiency and rapid economic growth were also used to justify the reinstatement of "rational" rules and regulations and the restoration of technical and managerial authority.[41] This aspect of 1970-71 policies provoked sharp and specific criticism from defenders of the Cultural Revolution.[42]

Reinstitution of rules and regulations, and efforts to improve worker discipline and managerial effectiveness were expected to produce a sudden spurt in industrial production followed by sustained growth. Sustained growth that would assure China's security and permit improvement of material and cultural life required expansion and modernization of the country's industrial capacity. Investment funds were to be channeled into industries, sectors, and geographic regions according to expected rate of return and relative contribution to economic independence. Within these parameters, however, there was considerable latitude for disagreement and political maneuver over allocation of funds, equipment, skilled manpower, and other scarce resources.[43]

The emphasis on speed that marked all policy discussions in this period led officials to pay renewed attention to the possible benefits of foreign trade, and to imports of prototypes and complete industrial plants. A concomitant concern not to become dependent on external suppliers shaped decisions on what to buy and with whom to trade; the rule of thumb was to

*Domestic Policy and the Quest for Independence*  37

minimize the degree of dependence in all transactions.[44] Changes in the international arena made it possible for China to enter the world market in ways that would have been impossible a few years previously. For example, the decision to improve relations with the United States and word of President Nixon's impending visit were quickly followed by improved access to the markets and technologies of Japan, West Germany, and other U.S. allies, as well as by potential access to advanced U.S. technology. In other words, China could reach out for complete plants and technical assistance with better prospects for success than at any time since the 1950s.[45] A second example was the development of the PRC petroleum industry which provided a commodity offering much higher rates of return than such traditional exports as textiles and processed foods. The Arab oil embargo was still two years in the future, but China's planners seem to have begun thinking about using oil to pay for imports of plants and industrial know-how as early as 1970-71.[46] At precisely the point when China was prepared to enter the international marketplace on a larger scale, its prospects were improved significantly by the rise in crude oil prices and fear of future supply shortages fostered by the embargo of late 1973.

*Agriculture and Rural Policy.* Agriculture and rural policies appear to have been of only secondary interest to most senior leaders in 1970-71. Whether they placed higher priority on accelerating the pace of economic development and attainment of greater national security, or on preserving the status quo that had emerged from the Cultural Revolution, officials viewed questions of rural policy largely in terms of how they related to other policy and political objectives. In addition, there seems to have been a general consensus that investment capital for the countryside would have to be largely self-generated if industrial capacity was to be modernized and expanded as rapidly as desired.

As a result of the decision to concentrate investment funds in other sectors, exhortations to increase agricultural production generally emphasized measures requiring minimal infusions of capital. Mechanization, chemization, improved use of water, and development of better seed strains were to be accomplished by relying on local resources. For example, small-scale research activities were encouraged, and local manufacture of equipment was heralded as an important way to modernize Chinese agriculture. In addition to these programs for long-term growth, production was to be raised in the short run through better planning, opening new areas to cultivation, and greater productivity on the part of individual peasants.[47]

To increase individual productivity, remunerative incentives supplemented and then all but supplanted the normative appeals of the Cultural Revolution. The 1970-71 Program called for an end to excessive egalitarianism in the distribution of year-end profits. Instead, adherence to the socialist principle of "to each according to his work" was stressed. The Program also affirmed the importance of private plots and demanded that more consumer goods be made available to the peasantry as an incentive to strive for higher individual earnings. Likewise, diversification of production was encouraged to enable collective units and individual households to increase income by growing more profitable crops.[48]

*Cultural Policies*

Debates over cultural policy have been among the most visible and vitriolic in the PRC. Passions run high when changes in cultural policies are discussed because those policies have a direct impact on the lives of the entire populace. To understand why, it is important to bear in mind that culture (*wenhua*) is a much broader and more integrated concept in China than it is in the United States and many other countries. For example, whereas Western societies distinguish between scientific and technical matters, on the one hand, and "cultural" activities (literature, art, music, drama, etc.) on the other, the Chinese view them as part of a single whole.[49] In addition, cultural issues have frequently been used as surrogates in debates centered on other policy questions. In 1970-71, cultural policy was both an issue in and of itself, and the battleground for debate on the emerging approach to national development.[50]

In 1970-71, and for the next several years, debate over cultural policy focused almost exclusively on three areas: science, education, and treatment of the country's intellectuals. This focus (rather than a stress on literary policy, freedom of expression in the plastic and performing arts, or other "cultural" areas) was the logical corollary of the emerging strategy of development that assigned high priority to science and technology as prerequisites to modernization.

Science and technology acquired greater salience in the early 1970s because they were perceived to be essential for rapid and sustained modernization. As they surveyed the world, China's leaders concluded that nations were powerful, respected, and independent in direct proportion to the strength and achievements of their scientific establishments.[51] Although there was a broad consensus on the *importance* of improving China's scientific and engineering capabilities, this consensus broke down on the question of *how* to strengthen research and development.

Most 1970-71 articles on science and technology policy emphasized principles from the Cultural Revolution (e.g., concentration on solving practical problems, the breakdown of distinctions between professional scientists and ordinary researchers, and the importance of combining scientific research with production). Toward the end of 1971, however, there were slight shifts toward according greater respect and responsibility to science professionals, toward more theoretical and basic research, and toward revitalizing university and institute laboratories. These announced changes accorded with the emphasis on quality, efficiency, concentration, and other characteristics of the emerging national program. Changes in science policy seem to have preceded those in education, but this perception may simply be the product of the kind of information available to foreign observers. Then again, these changes may reflect a decision by the efficiency maximizers that it was more urgent to rehabilitate and reassign veteran scientists and engineers than to begin training successors. There is a certain logic to formulating science policies before education policies. The way in which scientific research is restructured could significantly shape the way the educational system will be fashioned. Moreover, advocates of change may well have felt that they had greater power and fewer political entanglements in the sciences than in education. By deciding science policy questions first, they effectively made an end run around the radicals and potentially hostile public sentiment. By late 1971 there were clear indications that scientists would be restored to positions of respect and that professional science would receive more support than it had since 1966. This was true even though general science. and technology policy remained somewhat fluid and ambiguous.[52]

To achieve sustained economic growth and increased national security based on scientific and technical advances, China unquestionably needed more engineers, research personnel, teachers, and intellectuals. China also needed to raise the academic and technical competence of the entire populace. Officials disagreed on the means to achieve these ends. Those who placed a premium on quality and efficiency generally extolled the virtues of formal education and pressed for major changes in the school system. They saw the classroom and the laboratory as more effective than on-the-job training for the cultivation of successors who could lead the revolution to higher stages. These views were challenged as elitist and at variance with the lessons of the Cultural Revolution. In education, as in other policy areas, there was a confrontation between advocates of change and defenders of the status quo.

Although most primary and middle schools had reopened, the quality of instruction was uneven and generally poor due to the dismissal of experienced teachers during the Cultural Revolution, the withdrawal of standard textbooks, and the failure to adopt new curricula to replace those abolished in 1966. University education was largely confined to the various "new" colleges run by factories, and to the small numbers of undergraduate and graduate students—albeit not labeled as such—who continued to study in major universities and research institutes. Having made the decision to reopen the universities, Party leaders had to confront a Pandora's box of emotion-laden questions. The list of issues included the criteria to be used in admitting and promoting college students, the content of specific courses and curricula, and the relationship between colleges and units of production. In retrospect, it seems likely that the balance in education was tipping in the direction of higher academic standards, more rigorous curricula, and greater emphasis on theoretical instruction. Contemporary materials, however, did not clearly set forth explicit policies; rather, most articles focused on the virtues of integrating practical and classroom instruction, the dangers of elitism in education, and other defenses of the existing educational system.[53]

The staunch defense of the existing educational system can be interpreted in a number of ways. For example, the preponderance of articles defending the status quo might be viewed as evidence that the radicals had triumphed in the educational portion of the 1970–71 policy debates. It might also be interpreted, however, as a deliberate attempt to use the media to distort and subvert policy decisions. Charges leveled against the "gang of four" in 1977–78 are consistent with the latter interpretation. Nevertheless, educational issues seem to have been only partially resolved in 1971 and, for a variety of reasons, other leaders apparently were willing to indulge the position of those defending the Cultural Revolution. Educational policies do not appear to have been decided until mid- to late 1972; when they were resolved, they were fully consistent with the thrust of the 1970–71 Program (see below).

Policy developments dealing explicitly with the role of intellectuals were foreshadowed by decisions about reviving the economy, strengthening scientific research, and education. Beginning in 1971 there was a pronounced move to rehabilitate scientists, engineers, and other technical personnel discredited during the Cultural Revolution. As new policies in science, education, and the arts were clarified throughout 1971 and early 1972, commentators began to devote more attention to the proper role of intellectuals in achieving socialist development.

To implement the kind of policies outlined above, the Party leaders recognized that they must make optimal use of the existing pool of skilled professionals. That required not only the rehabilitation of those who had been removed from their posts for alleged ideological errors, but also a redress of the imbalance between professional work on the one hand, and productive labor and political study on the other. In short, teachers, technicians, accountants, etc., were to be utilized in their professional capacities. Proposals to accord special treatment to intellectuals provoked opposition and debate.

As in other areas, the legacy of the Cultural Revolution made intellectual policy a sensitive issue. For example, the role of specialists had to be defined in a way that minimized the appearance — and the danger — of elitism. The rhetoric that accorded a dominant role to the masses of "ordinary" workers, peasants, and soldiers had set the tone of discussion and had raised expectations that could not be ignored. Moreover, even those leaders who were anxious for change were also eager to avoid creating the kind of privileged technocratic elite that, in their view, was dominant in the Soviet Union. In short, China's intellectuals were to be both red and expert. Various means to achieve this goal were discussed in 1970-71, but by the close of this period, decisions in other policy areas had made it imperative to rehabilitate discredited professionals immediately and to tip the balance fairly far in the "expert" direction. The 1970-71 Program envisioned an active and responsible role for China's intellectuals; efficiency maximizers were prepared to make substantial concessions to this group to obtain their active support and cooperation in the drive for development and security.[54]

*Military Policies*[55]

One of the most striking developments of 1970-71 was the diminution of the political power of the People's Liberation Army (PLA). Called in to restore order and provide a channel of communication and control in the later stages of the Cultural Revolution, the PLA emerged as perhaps *the* predominant political force in the late 1960s. Members of the PLA assumed positions of leadership in schools, factories, government bureaus, and virtually all facets of society. They sat on, and in many cases dominated, the newly formed revolutionary committees. For a time the military was the only viable organization that was truly national in scope.

The role of the PLA *qua* organization began to change at the very time that the power of individual PLA members was affirmed by appointment to important positions in the Party.[56] Some analysts have pointed to the sizeable jump in the number of PLA members on the Ninth Central Committee and on the revived Party committees at subnational levels as evidence of the strong and increasingly influential role of the military in Chinese politics.[57] Arguably, precisely the opposite was the case. By drawing individual members of the PLA into the Party while Party doctrine and leadership were being reasserted, senior leaders were taking steps to insure that the Party would be superior to individual commanders and to "the military" as a rival political organization. Restoration of Party authority necessarily entailed a reduction in the power of the military. Rather than PLA members dominating the CCP from the outside or the inside, the situation after 1969-70 was one of increasing compliance with Party discipline and Party authority.[58]

A second notable development concerns the apparent shift in resources from military procurement to economic construction and military research and development. There was a sharp decrease in military expenditures in 1971; the result of prior decisions to channel more money into economic construction and to stop producing weapons and other hardware that were obsolete by international standards.[59] This shift is further evidence of the seriousness with which political leaders pursued rapid economic growth and the nonmilitary elements of national security.

*Political Consequences of Policy Debates and Decisions*

The debate and political maneuver sparked by perceived changes in the international situation and by shortcomings in the program that had evolved during the Cultural Revolution produced a number of important political changes beyond mere shifts in individual policy areas. These changes largely set the parameters of debate, and structured the political and policy competition for the next five years. They also helped determine the outcome of that competition. The major political consequences were:

1. Decisions made very early in the reassessment of Cultural Revolution policies established the "rules of the game" that have prevailed to the present and will continue to shape policy debates unless there is a "systemic" change in Chinese politics.[60]
2. The "rules of the game" adopted in 1969–70 precluded all but minor or temporary victories by defenders of the status quo. If the "conservative-radicals" were to influence policy significantly, they would either have to change the rules or effect changes in the course of implementation.[61]
3. The program that emerged in 1970–71 was the product of a consensus within the dominant leadership subgroup (the efficiency maximizers), but it was not a detailed prescription for the future. Specific policies remained to be formulated. This would involve competition and political maneuver within as well as between subgroups of the elite.
4. The primary factors influencing political and policy developments of 1972–76 were the attitude and actions of the "conservative-radical" opposition.
5. Policies incorporated into the 1970–71 Program continued to evolve, albeit at different rates, over the next five years. Although progress was uneven and implementation was at times seriously impeded, the overall process was one of evolution rather than oscillation between two dramatically different approaches and policy sets.

Although there was considerable ambiguity in some policy areas, the dominant theme of the 1970–71 Program stressed economic and technical efficiency at the expense of equity and social justice. Although many details had not been finalized by the end of 1971, it was clear that much of the program that had evolved during the Cultural Revolution was to be replaced by updated models from the pre-1966 period. In short, the defenders of the status quo (the conservative-radicals) had lost the critical policy debates of the period. The losers had but three options: to accept defeat and work for the new program; to oppose and subvert policies in the hope of reopening the debate; or to launch a coup to bring about a fundamental change in the rules of the game.

## V. Political Maneuver, 1972-76: Stages and Developments

### January 1972-August 1973

January 1, 1972, is the appropriate starting point of a political period or stage that lasted until early the following year. After the recent trauma of the Lin Biao affair and two years of nearly continuous debate, senior leaders were determined to close ranks and preserve what was left of elite solidarity. Lin's death had reopened the succession question and jockeying for position intensified during this period, but the dominant mood seems to have been one of determination to limit political infighting in order to concentrate on responding to new challenges and opportunities.

The new year opened with an authoritative editorial about the new international situation and the hectic developments of the past year.[62] This editorial, while stressing Party leadership, ideological study and observance of Party discipline, focused on the need for unity and avoidance of unprincipled struggle. A pithy quotation from Mao expressed this key idea: "Practice Marxism, and not revisionism; unite, and don't split; be open and above board, and don't intrigue and conspire."[63]

Although the editorial mentioned certain policy changes of the previous twelve months, it also implied that many issues remained to be resolved. Widespread use of the above quotation from Mao and other contemporary material suggest that all participants, including defenders of the Cultural Revolution, expected the debates to continue. More important, all parties seem to have assumed that the outcome of those debates was far from certain. Democratic discussions were to illuminate the different aspects of problems, issues, and contradictions and thereby enable participants to find the "best" policy for the current situation. In essence, the editorial called for returning to a slightly romanticized version of policymaking in China during the mid-1950s.[64]

For the next fourteen months (i.e., until March 1973), Chinese politics seems to have been comparatively calm. Senior leaders were adjusting to the catharsis of the Lin Biao episode and were involved with the appointment of personnel to fill positions vacated by recently disgraced officials. This situation, along with political maneuver at the apex of the system, diverted attention from policymaking per se. There was some elaboration of policies implicit in the 1970–71 Program, but the overall situation was one of minimal change and little public debate. Neither exponents of the 1970–71 Program nor defenders of the Cultural Revolution seemed eager to continue the dispute over policy and policymaking procedures.

Supporters of the new program were in a very different position than they had been a year or two earlier. Since they had "won" the policymaking round of 1970–71, those who had previously argued for major change now stood to benefit most from preservation of the status quo. On the whole, policies were evolving in the direction they desired, and the predominant attitude seems to have been that things were on the right track and it was best not to risk upsetting either the course of events or the precarious balance within the elite. The sense of urgency that had been so pervasive just a few months earlier dissipated rapidly once the balance had tipped in favor of the efficiency maximizers.

There were other reasons for the lack of vigorous effort toward resolution of policy questions in 1972. Perhaps the most important reason was the need to regroup after the purge of Lin and his cohorts. While this episode redounded to the advantage of those who endorsed the 1970–71 Program, members of the victorious coalition recognized the need to preserve the system and to restore its legitimacy and ability to function. Therefore, they had to give temporary priority to restoring confidence and rebuilding the elite. This entailed working out an accommodation with their opponents; a task that was simplified by their exercise of restraint in promoting additional, more specific policy changes.

Lin's downfall also left the radicals with a serious political problem. Many members of this group had risen to power with Lin and had championed essentially the same policies and structural changes during the Cultural Revolution. Their immediate problem was to extricate themselves from the stigma of those past associations. In addition, they too saw the need to restore cohesiveness and elite credibility. Toward that end, they seem to have been willing to leave policy questions in abeyance.

From January through December 1972, the leadership gradually resolved the immediate problems created by the Lin Biao incident and increasingly turned attention to policy issues that had not been addressed since late 1971. As the debates resumed, defenders of the Cultural Revolution realized that they were at a severe disadvantage under the existing rules of the game. Finding that they could not "win" on specific issues (e.g., material incentives, enterprise management, rules and regulations) because the criteria used to evaluate competing policy alternatives were heavily weighted in favor of economic efficiency, they apparently concluded that the best way to regain more than a modicum of influence over policy decisions was to change the rules, that is, to reorder priorities and redefine evaluative criteria. Their efforts to do so led to the next stage of political competition.

In the first quarter of 1973, supporters of 1966–69 practices launched a minor campaign to defend the achievements of the Cultural Revolution. One of the first articles in this campaign appeared in the March issue of *Hong Qi*.[65] The author argued that even though the policies that emerged from the Cultural Revolution were imperfect, they should not be discarded merely because they had shortcomings. This was, in essence, a plea to give Cultural Revolution policies more time to prove that they could indeed produce rapid growth and greater national strength. The article also asserted that the errors of Lin Biao and Chen Boda were "ultra-rightist," not "ultra-leftist." Among other objectives, redefining the errors of Lin and Chen was apparently designed to put more ideological distance between those purged and the coalition of "conservative-radicals." Finally, the article stressed that the "socialist new born things" of the Cultural Revolution were still supported by official policy. In the months that followed, both supporters of the new program and preservers of the old order emphasized continuity with the Cultural Revolution. These groups differed, however, in what they chose to emphasize and in how liberally they interpreted the notion of continuity.

Efforts to reassert the virtues of Cultural Revolution innovations and the concomitant criticism of specific policy developments forced supporters of the 1970–71 Program to devote relatively more attention to propaganda and image building in 1973, but the general trend of policy evolution continued much as it had in 1972. There were no major new departures, but marginal changes across almost the entire policy spectrum (e.g., the redefinition of the Dazhai model to place greater emphasis on science and technology,[66] and a call for more variety in literature and the performing arts)[67] signaled the steady decline of "radical" influence.

## August 1973–June 1974

Having suffered a series of major and minor policy defeats, the radicals changed their tactics and intensified public (and presumably intra-elite) criticism of the emerging program in the autumn of 1973. The primary target of the assault, at least initially, was the trend of developments in education policy. Two separate and completely consistent reasons seem to have underlain selection of both the target and the tactics of the new campaign.

First, education policy had figured prominently in the early stages of the Cultural Revolution and remained a matter of considerable importance to the entire populace. Consequently, it was an issue that aroused strong passions and on which there was a ready constituency of supporters for the policy changes made during the Cultural Revolution.

The second reason for focusing attention on education policy was a matter of timing and opportunism. Enrollment for the new academic year was in progress, and a number of important decisions had just been made on admissions standards, curricula, and the role of rehabilitated teachers and other professional educators.[68] Education policy was thus an issue ripe for exploitation by those displeased with the trend of recent developments. Moreover, the specific changes taking place in education were such that unless opponents acted quickly, new policies would be implemented and thus become more difficult to reverse. The radicals therefore launched a media campaign to denouce excessive emphasis on "cultural" (*i.e.*, academic) standards in the selection of university students, and to extoll actions such as those of a young candidate in Liaoning who had submitted a blank examination paper.[69]

What began as a narrowly focused critique of specific developments in education quickly broadened into a harsh attack on virtually all policies growing out of the 1970-71 Program. The transition from the specific to the general was first made in a signed commentary published in *Renmin Ribao* on August 16, 1973. Entitled *The Spirit of Going Against the Tide,* the commentary cited the case of Zhang Tiesheng to illustrate both the errors of recent policies and the need for concerted and heroic opposition to current trends.[70]

Policy critiques increased in scope and intensity on the eve of the Party's Tenth National Congress (convened on August 24, 1973), raising interesting but unanswerable questions of cause and effect. For example, was the level of criticism increased to strengthen the arguments and positions of radicals so that they could play a more decisive role at the Congress, or did intensification signal that defenders of the Cultural Revolution had already regained a portion of the influence they had lost during the preceding thirty-six months? In view of what had transpired since 1969, the apparent strength of the radicals evidenced in the assignment of leadership positions and in the tone of Congress documents was somewhat surprising. Thus, the campaign to reverse or slow the pace of policy developments may have influenced, or been influenced by, the decisions of Mao or other key figures. If this was the case, the propaganda efforts of 1973 proved to be partially successful.

Other interpretations are consistent with available information, however. For example, one can argue that radical strength was more apparent than real at the Tenth Party Congress, and that the distribution of offices and prestige did not reflect the balance of power within the elite. The

Tenth Party Congress was, in fact, strikingly unexceptional. Personnel changes aside (and even here the rehabilitation of former officials was probably more significant than the elevation of radicals Wang Hongwen and Zhang Chunqiao), the Congress is most noteworthy for what it did not do. Although it provided a perfect forum for announcing bold new programs and specific guidelines for the future, the Congress did neither.[71] Explanation and condemnation of the Lin Biao affair dominated the published speeches and subsequent commentary, and vague statements substituted for clear policy directives. Internal debate and a perceived need to maintain the facade of unanimity, if only on such abstract principles as the need to continue the Cultural Revolution, may have precluded further clarification or repudiation of the 1970-71 Program. Whatever the reasons, the Congress's only real impact on policy was an indirect one. The ambiguity of formal documents and the prominence of leading radicals enabled those opposed to evolving policies to speak out with greater authority than they had been able to command during the previous year and a half.

The next stage in the drive to alter the trend of policy development began in September 1973 with the opening of the anti-Confucian campaign. This campaign soon became linked to the ongoing campaign to criticize Lin Biao.[72] Three aspects of this campaign merit special attention because they are important to an understanding of politics and policymaking in China and because they have generally been misinterpreted by foreign analysts.

First, although differences in coverage and tone had often been observed in comparisons of various PRC media, the campaign to criticize Lin and Confucius evidenced particularly clear splits between *Hong Qi*, on the one hand, and *Renmin Ribao* and the new Shanghai journal *Xuexi yu Pipan,* on the other. These organs differed in their treatment of the errors committed by those who were the targets of their criticism as well as in their treatment of broader issues such as the legitimacy of "going against the tide" and the need to observe Party discipline. The radicals appear to have controlled *Renmin Ribao* and hence commanded more press space for their views. One consequence is that foreign, and doubtless many Chinese, readers deduced that radical strength was greater than was actually the case.

The second noteworthy feature of the campaign is that while opponents of evolving policies denounced the new rules of the game for spawning revisionism, supporters repeatedly called for unity, subservience of the minority to the majority, and strict observance of Party discipline.[73] In addition to attacking the rules, the radicals employed veiled *ad hominem* attacks and strongly implied that current policymaking procedures were revisionist and hence proper objects of struggle.

Third, the radical offensive criticized existing policies and practices, but it did not result in formal repudiation or reversal of the 1970-71 Program.

This distinction is important to note because many analysts have confused rhetoric and substance. Defenders of the Cultural Revolution managed to denounce, defame, and block implementation of evolving policies, but they did not succeed in displacing those policies.

It is impossible to discern and disentangle motives, but members of the radical coalition apparently hoped not merely to forestall policy implementation, but to reorient the policymaking process. They achieved, however, little more than temporary obstruction of policies supported by the majority of senior leaders. Supporters of the 1970-71 Program responded to the polemical challenge and shifted their attention from policy formulation and implementation to ideological defense of their program. The confusion engendered by the media war and resultant lack of clear guidance for subordinate officials led to partial paralysis and great diversity in the way programs were implemented. Depending on which article or publication is consulted, one can find evidence of very different "policies" in 1973-74.[74] Nevertheless, the momentum of the system resulted in continued but imperfect implementation of the 1970-71 Program.

Even though the radicals failed to reopen the issues that had been "resolved" in 1970-71, and did not change the "rules" of policymaking, they did manage to block implementation of certain policies. By pressing their case in the media and calling upon their supporters at all levels of the system, they effectively distorted formal policies, engendered confusion on the part of lower level functionaries, and greatly complicated the task of policy implementation. As noted above, their "success" in this regard was uneven; some administrators carried out formal policy guidelines despite the media campaign, others did not.

Imperfect communications, tremendous variations over time and space, and preoccupation with the "ideological debate" being waged in the media combined in a way that disinclined the architects of the 1970-71 Program to press for additional changes or even for better implementation of current policies. For several months, they engaged their opponents on the propaganda front, pressed their demand for observance of Party discipline and the rules of the game, and seemingly put most policies on "hold" pending resolution of the broader debate. To have launched a major counterattack as soon as the assault began, or to have used their preponderant strength within the elite to destroy the opposition totally would have been unwise. In retrospect, supporters of the 1970-71 Program appear to have played the situation just about right.

Mao's support was critical to the success of any program or coalition in the early 1970s. Many analysts have speculated that the chairman aligned himself with the radicals during this period.[75] However, it seems almost certain that Mao endorsed, or at least acquiesced in, the decisions that culminated in the 1970-71 Program. From what we know of his approach to politics, as expressed in his writings and published speeches, it is likely that he also insisted on including radicals on all policymaking bodies even after most of the Cultural Revolution program had been rejected. He probably did so in the name of unity and to insure that there would be a conscience and counterweight to prevent policies from veering too far in the direction of pure economic efficiency. If this assessment is correct, he is certain to have insisted that the radical "minority" be given a fair hearing in 1973-74. Moreover, he certainly would have tolerated some bending and breaking of the "rules" if that was necessary to overcome the biases and constraints inherent in the prevailing rules of the game.

To the extent that this analysis of Mao's attitude is correct, it would have been impolitic for supporters of the 1970-71 Program to have acted other than they did during the period from September 1973 through June 1974. In presenting their case to Mao, they could legitimately claim, by mid-1974, that their opponents had had ample opportunity to argue their views and, perhaps more importantly, that those views had been taken seriously by proponents of greater economic efficiency.

*Mid-1974–Early 1975*

Supporters of the 1970-71 Program seem also to have taken a more forceful position in mid-1974 due to performance-related considerations. Concern about both the problems of policy implementation and the failure to achieve hoped-for rates of development was exacerbated by fear that the external environment was becoming more dangerous. Détente between the United States and the Soviet Union seemed to be progressing, and some PRC leaders responded with a sense of urgency reminiscent of that which had prompted the policy review and system restructuring of 1969-71.[76] In sum, the conclusion that the time had come to put an end to public debate, cadre confusion, and imperfect implementation of previously agreed upon policies was reinforced by political, economic, and security-related developments.

The decision to clamp down on diversionary and obstructionist behavior was apparently made in June of 1974. Evidence for this derives from the joint editorial published on July 1 (Party Day) which made it clear that willful disobedience of Party policies and Party discipline would no longer be tolerated. Entitled *The Party Exercises Leadership in Everything,* the editorial stressed unity, discipline, and the importance of carrying out Party policies even though criticism of certain aspects of those policies was appropriate under the rules of intra-Party debate.[77] This last point apparently was intended to end the propaganda war and return discussion of policy differences to the confines of Party committees. In the words of the editorial:

Only when Party leadership is strengthened is it possible to organize the forces in various fields and attain unity in thinking, policy, plan, command, and action on the basis of Chairman Mao's proletarian revolutionary line. In the course of the movement, it is normal in Party life *to wage struggles inside Party committees for the correct line against the erroneous line and for correct ideas against mistaken ideas, and to make criticism of the shortcomings and mistakes in one's work in line with the principle of "Practice Marxism, and not revisionism; unite, and don't split; be open and aboveboard, don't intrigue and conspire."* . . . *"Obey orders in all our actions, march in step to win victory."*[78]

Subsequent articles and commentaries reiterated the injunction to carry out policy directives even though certain aspects of those policies or even the underlying approach to China's problems might be objectionable. In contrast to earlier radical articles implying that cadres should disobey or modify directives with which they disagreed ("going against the tide"), authoritative statements now admonished cadres to implement formal policies even though they might question the wisdom of those policies. Criticism of specific policies was still sanctioned, indeed, it was encouraged, provided that it was presented in accordance with the requirements of democratic centralism.[79]

In addition to increased stress on unity and discipline *within* the Party, commentaries published between mid-1974 and early 1975 emphasized "uniting" with all who could contribute to the cause of socialist development. The number of articles expressing this theme increased from month to month, and commentators became increasingly specific in terms of the groups with which unity was possible. At first, the emphasis was on (re)uniting with cadres who had made mistakes but now recognized their errors and were ready to resume positions of responsibility. Gradually, however, it became clear that scientists, teachers, factory managers, and many others were considered suitable alliance partners by exponents of the 1970–71 Program.[80]

The emphasis on working with all who could serve the cause of rapid development led to further rehabilitation of officials discredited during the Cultural Revolution. The pace of rehabilitation had slowed somewhat during the radical offensive of late 1973, but by mid-1974 it returned to approximately the level of 1971–72. Symbolic of the emphasis on rehabilitation was the fact that Deng Xiaoping was especially prominent during this period.

Contemporary materials provide little evidence of the kind of debates and political maneuver that occurred behind closed doors, but competition and tradeoffs are certain to have taken place in late 1974 as preparations were made for the upcoming Fourth National People's Congress (NPC).

## Domestic Policy and the Quest for Independence

Competition doubtless took place within as well as between the two major coalitions as participants scrambled for positions and for influence over policy decisions relating to the ambitious development program announced by Zhou Enlai.[81] Although Zhou's address to the Fourth NPC (January 1975) was generally quite vague, officials must have begun thinking about policy specifics and implementation even before the Congress convened. After all, the basic program was already four years old.

Zhou's report explicated many of the assumptions and considerations that underlay the 1970–71 Program. Indeed, his discussion of the necessity for realizing the "four modernizations" was the first public statement to that effect.[82]

Convocation of the Fourth NPC, adoption of a new State Constitution, formal appointment of senior government officials, and proclamation of the intent to make an all-out effort to achieve significant advances in economic and military development within the next half decade seemed to herald redoubled efforts to flesh out the details of, and put into effect, policies of the 1970–71 Program. The intent was clear, but disgruntled radicals immediately began to challenge and criticize fundamental aspects of the newly reaffirmed program.

During the next six months, the media carried remarkably few items about the new State Constitution or Zhou's report to the NPC. One would have expected a long series of commentaries extolling and explaining such "important new developments," but there was little publicity and almost no explanation as to how Zhou's declared goals were to be realized.[83] Within a matter of days after the close of the NPC, discussion of Congress documents completely disappeared from the media. Instead of including detailed commentaries on the newly announced Program, press and broadcast reports focused on studying the "dictatorship of the proletariat." The prominence of this new campaign in media largely dominated by the radicals, as well as the tone and focus of most articles, indicate that opponents of the 1970–71 Program were not prepared to accept defeat. At the same time, efficiency maximizers apparently felt compelled to respond to the charges and theoretical interpretations of the radicals. The result was a public debate which closely paralleled that of 1973–74.

There was an important difference, however. The propaganda war of 1973–74 involved more or less equal presentation of both sides of the dispute: that of 1975 was heavily slanted in the direction endorsed by defenders of the Cultural Revolution. Subsequent charges leveled at the "gang of four" would maintain that Jiang Qing and her allies manipulated the media and denied their opponents the "right" to present their case to the public.[84] These accusations appear to have more than a little basis in fact. The "gang" apparently attempted to change policy and policymaking by appealing to the "masses" and various special constituencies over the head of the dominant group in the central leadership. One can question, however, whether the radicals could have dominated the media during this period if the "majority" had really wanted to control the organs of communication.

This question suggests a number of propositions about the conduct of politics in the PRC. It is possible, for example, that the position of the efficiency maximizers had become so strong, and that internal lines of communication and control had become so effective that the media ceased to be a major factor in either the formulation or implementation of national policy. There is considerable indirect evidence to support the assertion that, despite the vehemence and volume of media criticisms and *ad hominem* attacks in 1975-76, many policies of the 1970-71 Program were implemented as intended and principal targets of criticism retained much of their former stature in the eyes of subordinate functionaries and ordinary citizens.[85] In short, members of the dominant group may well have been relatively unperturbed by the media campaign launched by their opponents and may have made only perfunctory efforts to resume the propaganda war of 1973-74.

There are two other explanations for the lack of effort on the part of the "majority" to oppose the radicals' media campaign. One is that the dominant coalition had concluded that Mao's support could be imperiled by another direct attack on the radicals. This is pure conjecture, but since we know that the chairman's health was failing, it seems plausible that the dominant group decided to play it safe and wait for Mao to improve or to die. The second explanation is that members of the dominant group were largely preoccupied with the difficult task of devising detailed plans and policies to realize the goals proclaimed in Zhou's report to the Fourth NPC. With the radicals reduced to the status of gadflies and nay-sayers, proponents of optimally efficient development could—and did—concentrate on what they regarded as more important problems.

While the radicals were filling the media with articles decrying the persistence of "bourgeois rights" and the need to prevent the emergence of a new bourgeoisie, the dominant group prepared to make difficult choices on a wide range of policy issues.[86] The tempo of activity increased in late spring and early summer as participants worked to meet "deadlines" for preparation of the Fifth Five-Year Plan (1976-80). We have since learned that a series of conferences and high-level meetings was convened in 1975 to draft realistic assessments of the situation and to prescribe concrete steps to overcome problems impeding realization of the "four modernizations." Toward this end, there were separate meetings on industry, national defense, and science and technology.[87]

While exponents of greater economic efficiency debated details and specific appropriations, the radicals shifted to a new strategy of opposition. Although their diversionary measures and theoretical debates had failed to block the overall formulation of more specific policies, they had achieved a measure of success in obstructing implementation of agricultural policy. Evidence is limited, but it appears that the disagreements at and following the First National Dazhai Conference were so intense, and the appeal of radical arguments to certain constituencies was so strong that much confusion was engendered. As a result, the media and official statements described a variety of different and partially contradictory Dazhai "models." Basic level cadres were understandably confused, and policies (on mechanization, consolidation of small-scale industrial enterprises, distribution of year-end profits, adherence to planned targets, etc.) were only imperfectly implemented. Given the crucial role of agriculture in China, confusion and policy distortion threatened realization of targets in a host of related policy areas and were therefore matters of vital concern to the leadership.

*Late 1975–September 1976*

Having achieved only limited successes in the ideological offensive of early 1975, the radicals apparently decided to concentrate future efforts in the area of cultural policy where they had the largest and most secure constituency, and where they could hope to reactivate passions of past years. Accordingly, they launched a new offensive in late 1975 with a frontal attack on policies governing education and science and technology. One of the first articles in the new propaganda offensive charged that the renewed emphasis on science and professional competence was merely a smoke screen to mask reintroduction of educational practices criticized and abolished during the Cultural Revolution.[88] In February, the campaign was broadened to include science policy.[89] Cutting right to the heart of the entire 1970–71 Program with its emphasis on economic and technical rationality, the radicals charged their opponents with using the name of "scientific necessity" to justify a series of revisionist policies.[90]

Zhou Enlai was seriously ill when the radicals launched their final offensive in late 1975; his death in January seemingly enhanced their prospects for success. The premier was virtually unassailable—as they had learned in the anti-Confucian campaign—but his closest deputy, Deng Xiaoping, was clearly more vulnerable. The short-lived and rather confusing campaign to criticize the classical novel *Water Margin* included allegorical attacks on Zhou and Deng, but the radicals had only minimal success in their efforts to discredit the principal targets.[91] Following Zhou's death in early 1976, however, defenders of the Cultural Revolution launched a new and more vitriolic campaign to vilify Deng and the 1970-71 Program.

As part of the campaign against Deng, distorted excerpts from three of the draft proposals prepared the previous summer and fall—the "Three Big Poisonous Weeds"—were denounced in media controlled by the "gang of four."[92] Critics resorted to *ad hominem* attacks; pressing the point that if Deng was a "representative of the bourgeoisie," policies formulated under his guidance and direction must of necessity be "erroneous" or "revisionist." One objective of this campaign was to stigmatize policies adopted since 1969 by linking them to a tainted individual. Radicals called upon all cadres to dissociate themselves from Deng and his policies in order to prove their fealty to Mao and the Cultural Revolution.

Eventually, the radicals did succeed in removing Deng from office, but the policies he helped formulate remained intact. Following the still mysterious Tiananmen Incident of April 5, 1976, Deng was removed "from all posts inside and outside the Party" and Hua Guofeng was named first vice-chairman of the Party and premier of the State Council.[93] Whether Deng stepped down voluntarily or was persuaded to do so by others in his coalition, he served as a shield deflecting criticism from the policies he had helped to formulate. Deng became the scapegoat and efficiency-based policies remained in effect.

Although Deng's removal did not result in the changes desired by the radicals, this victory—magnified by their control of the media—engendered confusion about China's policies both inside and outside of the country. Those eager to strengthen all components of security before the international situation deteriorated further grew increasingly impatient with the obstructionist behavior of their radical opponents and became convinced that the obstructionists had to be removed. Moreover, the bellicosity of the "gang of four" began to appear increasingly dangerous to military leaders charged with defense of the country, economic planners eager for imports of advanced technology and essential equipment, and intellectuals who saw the need to broaden international contacts and strengthen the educational system even further if China was to become and remain strong and independent. Mao's death in September 1976 eliminated the last reason for preserving the pretense of elite solidarity and continued indulgence of uncooperative oppositionists. The inevitable finally happened a month later when the ringleaders of the opposition were arrested. Politics entered a new stage in October 1976, and so too did the evolution of policies. Before looking briefly at developments since Mao's death, however, it will be useful to illustrate the basic continuity of most policies throughout the 1972-76 period.

## VI. Policy Evolution, 1972-76

Changes in important areas of PRC foreign policy (i.e., China's global posture, military doctrine and force posture, international trade, and the law of the sea) are discussed in the companion chapters of this volume. The overall pattern of these changes is one of gradual evolution—albeit at times by fits and starts—in the direction implicit in the 1970-71 Program. These are excellent case studies and there is no need to summarize their findings here. Note, however, that in all instances, foreign policies developed in accordance with the dictates of economic and technical rationality. Radical opposition and obstruction occasionally diverted the evolutionary path, but there was never a return to the policies of 1966-69. In short, PRC foreign policy has exhibited a pattern of evolution, rather than oscillation.[94]

The pattern of development of PRC domestic policies since 1970-71 has also been evolutionary.[95] That pattern may be summarized as follows:

1. No fundamental changes occurred at the level of formal policy, therefore policies adopted or foreshadowed in 1971 were still in effect at the time of Mao's death.[96]
2. Rhetorical policies appeared to change substantially during this period. However, recognizing that there was considerable spatial and temporal variation, it appears that implemented policies generally conformed more closely to formal policy decisions than to the distortions and hyperbole found in PRC media.[97]
3. Policies evolved in the direction of greater specificity as central officials acquired more information and resolved more inter- and intracoalition disputes.[98]

To illustrate the pattern of changes that occurred in domestic policy, developments in three closely related subsets of cultural policy will be briefly examined. The three areas (education, science and technology, and treatment of intellectuals) have been chosen because they were among the most prominent issues in the public "debates" of 1972-76, and because they are at the heart of the 1970-71 blueprint for China's future.

Only one aspect of the interconnection of education, science and technology, and intellectual policy will be considered in the synopsis presented here, even though there are in fact many linkages. Those who saw the need to take immediate and far-reaching steps to enhance China's security concluded that it was imperative to build a modern infrastructure of scientific and technical research.[99] To strengthen China's science base, proponents of greater speed and efficiency wanted to rehabilitate, reassign, and provide logistical support for the existing corps of scientific and technical personnel. They also saw the need to improve the education system in order to train future generations of skilled professionals. These perceptions formed the basis for the cultural policies of the 1970–71 Program.

Programmatic statements about education, science, and treatment of intellectuals began to be translated into concrete policies in 1972. For example, most colleges and universities had reopened by the end of the first quarter. In addition, although political criteria were to be considered in the selection of new students, academic qualifications ("cultural level") were given greater weight.[100]

At all levels of the school system, particularly at the university level, curricula were redesigned to emphasize basic scientific and mathematical principles.[101] The interrelationships among education, science, and national development were clearly articulated by Zhou Peiyuan (vice chairman of the Peking University Revolutionary Committee) in October 1972.

> Only when one has mastered the laws of nature, that is, deeply understood the internal relations of objective things, can one put forward one's views on analyzing and solving practical problems. . . . This is to say that the task of the science faculty is to train working personnel versed in the theories of natural science who are required by current production as well as theoretical workers required by the country in its future development of production and science. . . . Successful conduct of science education and raising the level of the basic sciences will play a great promotional role in the development of industrial and agricultural production, medical and health work, and national defense.[102]

To train young scientists and technicians and to tackle the formidable technical problems confronting China in its drive to modernize *and* avoid dependence on foreign countries, the existing group of skilled professionals had to be persuaded and enabled to engage in research work directed toward accomplishing these goals.[103] Veteran scientists were to return to reequipped laboratories, and experienced teachers were to return to the classroom.[104]

The importance of science and technology to the renewed drive to transform China into a modern socialist country was reiterated in numerous articles published during the first half of 1973. Following a national conference early in the year on scientific and technological work, provincial meetings were held to discuss the current line on treatment of intellectuals, science education, and the conduct of scientific research. While professionals were still admonished to reform themselves and to spend time in productive labor, the need to unite with all who could serve the cause of development received greater stress. Party committees were instructed to "include scientific and technical work on their agendas," and to play the leading role in assuring that policies were implemented properly.[105]

As discussed above, the radical offensive of late 1973 focused on evolving practices in education. Specifically criticized were the criteria for selecting students and the displacement of "political study" and "practical work" by more traditional courses in mathematics, natural sciences, and technical specialties. The resultant campaign had some impact on the evolution and implementation of policies governing education, science, and the treatment of intellectuals, but it is extremely difficult to measure that impact with precision. For example, despite the extreme example of Zhang Tiesheng's blank examination paper, critics do not appear to have claimed that academic qualifications should be eliminated entirely. Rather, they argued that tests of "cultural knowledge" should not be the predominant criteria for selection of new students.[106] Regardless of whether or not there were *formal* entrance examinations—and there apparently were not at most institutions—there *was* academic screening of potential applicants. One of the most important safeguards employed to assure that students would be competent was the stipulation that most would return to their original place of work. Given the key role that educated young people were to play in increasing the productivity of individual units, university authorities could be relatively certain that local units would nominate relatively well-qualified applicants. If the student did poorly, not only would the unit be discredited, but it would be stuck with the incompetent when he or she returned.

As for admonitions to combine theoretical study with practical work, we need only point out that there had never been a complete separation of the two. Rather, there had merely been differing opinions on how to combine them most effectively. Linking university-based research to the needs of industrial or agricultural production was a noncontroversial proposition, and virtually every institution of higher education worked out a cooperative arrangement with production enterprises. Some institutions required students and teachers to spend many hours on the production line; others did so on a purely perfunctory basis. Likewise, tremendous variation occurred from one institution to another with regard to time spent on political study.[107] Overall—and this is admittedly a highly subjective judgment—the radical offensive during the autumn of 1973 probably had relatively little impact on education policies.[108]

During the period 1972–76, professional researchers were faced with a rather awkward situation. On the one hand, they had been rehabilitated in order to foster rapid national development. Official policy supported concerted efforts to raise the level of science and technology. On the other hand, media criticism of professionals trained prior to the Cultural Revolution and exhortations to give full play to the role of the masses made it difficult for scientists to conduct research. The situation differed from place to place, but in some institutions, radical rhetoric was co-opted by science professionals and their administrative supporters. For example, experienced technicians and foreign trained scientists were called "veteran science workers," recent university graduates assigned to research institutes for additional (graduate) training were designated "young scientists" or "young people," and other technicians and paraprofessionals were classified as "research workers." In short, nominal changes reflected the prevailing rhetoric of the time, but the complex, esoteric nature of scientific research often allowed professional researchers to work pretty much as they wanted to during this period.[109]

Comparison of the statements made about education in general and enrollment policy in particular in 1972, 1973, and 1974 reveals two interesting developments. Perhaps the most striking was that there was great consistency in selection criteria from one enrollment period to the next. Radicals had raised a great hue and cry in the media over enrollment during the interval between selection of incoming students in 1973 and admission of the next class in 1974. However, when it came time to actually select new students, the procedures differed only slightly from those of a year earlier.[110] In other words, the criteria used to select incoming students in 1974 were essentially the same as they had been the two previous years.

The second noteworthy development concerned the extent to which radical rhetoric was co-opted by advocates of higher academic standards. For example, although a major commentary on enrollment work adopted many of the themes and slogans used previously by defenders of the Cultural Revolution, the author drew very different conclusions about the meaning of the slogans and the status of the enrollment procedures than had radical articles:

> The proletariat openly declares that "education must serve proletarian politics and must be integrated with productive labor." This dictates our placing proletarian politics in command, placing awareness of the line and political performance above all else and giving full attention to practical experience when selecting students. Our stressing these two aspects does not mean that we do not want culture. A cultural test of the recommended objects of education is necessary. The key lies in under which line this is carried out. The chief aim of a cultural test is to find out the ability of the person recommended to analyze and solve problems. . . . It is necessary to adhere to the four links of the student enrollment method, namely, voluntary registration, mass recommendation, leadership approval, and school reexamination.[111]

Further evolution of educational policy was impeded by radical opposition. For example, Mao Zedong Thought Propaganda Teams comprised of veteran workers were sent to some colleges in early 1975 to supervise administration of both academic and nonacademic activity. Alternative "models" were promoted to emphasize the virtues of nontraditional schools. Zhaoyang Agricultural College was singled out for special praise and attention by the radicals, as were various "July 21 Workers' Universities" and other part work–part study arrangements.[112] Efficiency maximizers were prepared to support the irregular alternatives suggested by the radicals if the "models" were seen as *supporting* rather than *replacing* the regular school system. Nevertheless, the existence of competing "models" complicated the situation and impeded further restructuring of university curricula. Again, the radicals were moderately successful in the use of diversionary and obstructionist tactics.

Those eager to raise the quality of China's professionals had managed to modify admissions standards, but experienced less success with attempts to change curricula. The problem they faced was not simply one of overcoming radical opposition; it also involved restructuring curricula to strengthen the base for sustained scientific and technical progress in the future.[113] By 1975 some members of the elite apparently concluded that existing policies were too short-sighted; i.e., they were training people to solve current problems and copy existing technologies, but they were not paving the way for independent development in the future. The psychological, economic, military, and security consequences of the situation were troublesome, and so a major reassessment was begun in the summer of 1975. This reassessment produced the "Outline Report" on the work of the Academy of Sciences, but it seems probable that there was also a detailed critique of existing educational policy with concrete proposals for change.[114]

Radical criticisms of emerging policies, together with subsequent denunciations of these criticisms by exponents of greater economic efficiency, present a reasonably clear picture of the kind of policy changes under active consideration in 1975. Briefly, curricula at all levels of the school system were to place greater emphasis on scientific theory, the natural sciences, and competence in foreign languages. The quality of instruction was to be raised at all levels as rapidly as new teachers could be trained and old instructors could be reassigned to classrooms. Classroom discipline was to be restored—students would learn and teachers would teach. Multitrack education would be utilized in the name of speed and efficiency. Resources would be concentrated in key schools, and de facto elitism would be tolerated as the price of rapid development.[115]

Several factors account for the highly variegated pattern of policy implementation in 1975–76. The lack of clear, formal guidelines enabled scientists and science administrators sympathetic with the emerging program to anticipate and execute policies that were not actually adopted until several months later. At the same time, the absence of specific policies exposed exponents of greater technical rationalization to charges of "bourgeois" behavior. Such charges were leveled with increasing ferocity by members of the radical opposition. Their targets consequently had to divert their attention from scientific research to self-defense.

Organizational shortcomings aggravated the confusion engendered by the lack of explicit policy guidelines. The problem was further compounded by the failure of efficiency maximizers to carry out the kind of Party rectification they deemed necessary to restore discipline and control. Disruptive tactics by radical politicians effectively prevented this kind of rectification.

Despite the variation and mixed results of policy implementation, de facto policies toward education, science, and treatment of intellectuals were becoming increasingly specific and antagonistic to radical objectives. The radicals realized that their opponents were steadily gaining ground and that further delay could be politically fatal as well as detrimental to realization of their own vision of China's future. As a result, they launched a frontal assault against evolving policies in education and science. Both efficiency maximizers and their radical opponents agreed that policies affecting education, science, and treatment of intellectuals were *the* central political issues of the time. Efficiency maximizers viewed prompt resolution of these issues and faithful implementation of economically and technically rational policies as crucial to the realization of China's security objectives. Meanwhile, the radicals recognized that defeat on these issues would not only greatly diminish their political power, but also would allow further policy "development" along lines largely dictated by economic and technical considerations. The radicals' partial success in blocking formal policies convinced the dominant coalition that the only way to insure realization of its objectives was to put an end to deliberate distortion and obstruction of efficiency-minded policies.

## VII. Politics and Policy Evolution, 1976-78

Chinese politics entered a new era in the mid-1970s. The death of Mao, Zhou Enlai, Zhu De, and other "founding fathers" altered power relationships and forced participants in the policymaking process to adopt new tactics. However, personnel changes and the long-deferred transfer of authority to the successor generation did not lead to major shifts in policy. Nor are such personnel changes likely to generate dramatic reorientations or reformulations in the future. As argued previously, the rebuilding and restoration that occurred during 1970-76 were predicated on specific perceptions and assessments of the international situation and China's position therein.

## Domestic Policy and the Quest for Independence

Barring significant changes in the international order—or perceptions that such changes have occurred—the assumptions, organizations, and procedures of policymaking are not likely to change dramatically. Rather, further evolution will occur along the lines of the 1970-71 Program.

Prediction of relative policy constancy—but not necessarily leadership stability—over the next decade is based on the argument that there is increasing continuity and conservatism in the policymaking process. This argument is elaborated in the Introduction to this volume. To provide additional support for that interpretation, brief commentary on events since Mao's death and the "gang of four's" downfall follows. For ease of presentation, developments are divided into four topical areas: (1) assumptions, principles, and guidelines; (2) personnel and organizations; (3) planning and economic policy; and (4) cultural policy.

### Assumptions, Principles, and Guidelines

After an initial wave of articles denouncing the ringleaders and principal supporters of the "gang of four,"—best described as an exercise in character assassination—commentaries began to contrast the errors of the "gang" with the "correct" approach and policies of the dominant coalition.[116] At first these comparisons were more specific in their treatment of "gang of four" errors than they were in their elaboration of more appropriate policies, but by late March, the negative examples of the "gang" were less prominent than were positive affirmations of official policy. Although the progression from denunciation to positive affirmation was marked by considerable overlap, it is useful to look at the way commentaries changed over time.

Litanies expounding "gang" errors began to appear shortly after the arrest of Jiang Qing and her cohorts. For succinctness and clarity, we will excerpt a speech delivered five months later, in March 1977.[117]

> Under the pretext of grasping class struggle, going against the tide and supporting the new things of the Cultural Revolution, the gang incited bourgeois factionalism, stormed Party committees at all levels, disrupted the Party's unified leadership over enterprises, and confused enemies and comrades in a fundamental way during the historical stage of socialism. Under the pretext of placing politics in command and criticizing the theory of productive forces, it opposed making all-out efforts to do great things, opposed grasping production and doing well in construction and disrupted and undermined the socialist economic base. Under the pretext of supporting the mass movement to oppose controlling, checking and suppressing the workers, it incited nihilism, denied the need for reasonable regulations and systems and disrupted enterprise management. Under the pretext of criticizing the

philosophy of servility to foreign things, the gang distorted Chairman Mao's policy of maintaining independence, keeping the initiative in our own hands and relying on our own efforts; opposed studying and importing advanced foreign science and technology; and opposed quickly developing our country's industry.[118]

In this and similar passages, "correct" policies were revealed only indirectly. Thus, for example, if the gang had opposed "making all-out efforts to do great things" and "opposed studying and importing foreign science and technology," the implication was that "correct" policies would do the opposite. Such an interpretation was, in fact, supported by positive declarations of future policies, but until the spring of 1977, such declarations were limited to a relatively few areas.[119]

Discussions of the approach and policies of the victorious coalition became more specific following publication of Mao's 1956 speech entitled *On the Ten Major Relationships*.[120] The previously unpublished speech was used to justify evolving policies by demonstrating that Mao had developed the underlying logic twenty years earlier. That logic was explained in numerous press and radio commentaries on the speech, and in meetings convened explicitly to study the lessons and guidelines formulated by the late chairman.[121]

The approach to policymaking endorsed by the Hua Guofeng leadership was neatly encapsulated in one of the first commentaries on *On the Ten Major Relationships*.

> In his work *On the Ten Major Relationships*, Chairman Mao set forth basic ideas about the general line of building socialism. . . . "*We must do our best to mobilize all positive factors, both inside and outside the party, both at home and abroad, both direct and indirect, and build China into a powerful, socialist country.*"
>
> *Building socialism with greater, better and more economical results and developing our social productive forces at high speed are very important conditions for the proletariat to triumph over the bourgeoisie and to consolidate the socialist system.*
>
> To mobilize all positive factors means to whip up the enthusiasm of the people throughout the country and arouse all the people in the nation to aim high. This is *to fully use all the manpower and material resources available in socialist construction and make the best and most effective use of them* so that all the people are used to their full capability and all the material resources are used to the full extent.[122]

These excerpts highlight several interconnected elements in the leadership's approach to policy, namely, the emphasis on speed and economic efficiency, the importance of uniting with intellectuals and all others who can contribute to the drive for modernization, and the need for comprehensive planning and effective control to make maximum use of available resources. Similarities between this approach and that embodied in the 1970-71 Program are not coincidental. Coalitions forged in 1969-70 remained more or less intact over the years, and a single coalition dominated policymaking—at least at the formal level—throughout the period. With the removal and disgrace of leading radicals, advocates of greater efficiency could press their arguments more openly, and articulate policy details that had earlier been muted in the name of continued elite solidarity. As a result, policy statements of 1977-78, although fundamentally the same as those of 1970-71, were more specific and more forceful in their defense of economic and technical efficiency.

The sense of urgency surrounding policy discussions in 1970-71 returned to public statements about China's requirements for the future in the spring of 1977. For example, speed and efficiency were emphasized in the major published speeches delivered at the National Conference on Learning from Daqing in Industry.

> On the whole, our country is still relatively backward industrially and economically and our material base is not powerful enough. It is the urgent desire of the people of the whole country to change this state of affairs as soon as possible. . . .
>
> The question of the speed of construction is a political rather than a purely economic question. When viewed in the light of the international class struggle, the political nature of this question stands out still more sharply. By their very nature, imperialism and social-imperialism mean war. We must definitely *be ready for war*. We cannot afford to let time slip through our fingers, as it waits for no one. Every Communist, every revolutionary and every patriot should be clear about the situation, seize the present opportune moment, strive to work well and make our country strong and prosperous as soon as possible.[123]

> The question of speed in industry concerns the victory of the proletariat over the bourgeoisie and of socialism over capitalism, and concerns the future and destiny of our country. The factors for revolution and war are both increasing in the world today and the contention between the two hegemonic powers—the Soviet Union and the United States—is becoming ever more acute. A world war is bound to break out some day. Soviet revisionism has not given up its wild ambition to subjugate China. With the wolf and tiger confronting us, we must never lower our guard. As far back as over half a century ago, Lenin sharply pointed out: *"Either perish or overtake and outstrip the advanced countries economically as well."* We have already achieved great victories in the socialist revolution and socialist construction, and the dictatorship of the proletariat in our country is being strengthened and consolidated day by

day. But, generally speaking, our economic capacity and national defense capabilities are not yet strong enough; the question raised by Lenin in his day confronts us in all its sharpness. We must fully understand this and never waste time which is so precious to us. We must seize every minute and second, work with tremendous exertion, strive with the greatest determination to make up for the losses caused by the "gang of four" and exert every ounce of energy to accelerate the rate of industrial growth.[124]

Recapitulating briefly, the approach and policies endorsed by the post-Mao leadership were essentially the same as those embodied in the 1970-71 Program. Economic rationality and efficiency criteria were to play a decisive role in the formulation of general guidelines and, insofar as possible, specific policies. Unity, stability, predictability, and production were accorded high priority in the name of enhancing China's security as quickly as possible.

*Personnel and Organizations*

Authoritative statements about personnel and organizational issues reaffirmed or expanded upon policies incorporated into the 1970-71 Program. To illustrate the continuity between the policies of 1971 and those of 1978, we will focus first on two subissues involving personnel, and then on two involving organizations.

Rehabilitation and reassignment of veteran cadres had been part of the 1970-71 Program from its inception. As was noted in the section surveying developments in the 1972-76 period, many persons discredited during the Cultural Revolution were restored to positions of responsibility and assigned major roles in the developmental effort. The pace and degree of rehabilitation varied, but the overall trend was toward complete rehabilitation of all but a handful of former officials.

Recent pronouncements have gone beyond the policies of 1970-71 by calling not merely for the reinstatement and rehabilitation of veteran cadres, but for their complete exoneration.[125] This is being done not merely to satisfy the wishes of those purged earlier, but also to enhance their stature as effective leaders at a time when there is a high premium on leadership.[126]

A second subissue involves the role of specialists and non-Party cadres. The 1970-71 Program had called for uniting with scientists, engineers, and intellectuals more generally to insure that their talents were used to the full. The objective was to accelerate the pace of development and increase the degree to which China could develop without becoming dependent on foreign states, corporations, or specialists.

As with the policy toward veteran cadres, the guidelines and directives governing specialists have been reaffirmed and made more specific since 1976. Mao's essays on joining with all those willing and able to serve the cause of socialist construction have again been commended for study, and numerous articles and speeches have proclaimed the importance of implementing Party policy toward the intellectuals.[127] Specific directives on the treatment and utilization of specialists have mandated, for example, that scientists and research personnel be enabled to devote five-sixths of their working time to professional work, that teachers be reassigned to classrooms, that salaries be raised and titles restored, and that persons with professional competence be installed as directors of research facilities.[128]

In the area of organizational policies, recent announcements have reaffirmed the leading role of the Party. One of the most publicized developments has involved reassertion and revitalization of Party control. Party committees at all levels of the administrative system (regional, provincial, municipal, county, etc.) have been restructured ("rectified") and ordered to monitor and guide all activities within their areal purview.[129] Similarly, Party committees in industrial enterprises, research units, and other functionally specific organizations have been revived with instructions to insure that official policies are properly implemented in their respective units.[130]

In addition to emphasizing the leading role of Party committees, post-1976 articles have stressed the importance of discipline and proper understanding of Party doctrine. Cadres have been admonished to abjure "bourgeois factionalism" and to engage in serious study and self-criticism. Party schools have been re-established to train cadres and provide refresher courses for veteran Party members—including those who joined during and after the Cultural Revolution. The content of these articles and directives differs slightly from those of the early 1970s, but only in terms of greater specificity; the thrust and intent of the policies are the same.[131]

The final development to be noted in the area of personnel and organizational policy concerns the continued reform of governmental, functional, and mass organizations. Rebuilding of organizational units began even before adoption of the 1970–71 Program and proceeded somewhat erratically throughout the 1970s. Following the purge of the obstructionists, however, central leaders launched a renewed effort both to clarify organizational relationships and to "rationalize" lines of authority and communication.

Organizational reform—other than that involving Party organs—has had wide-ranging impact, affecting everything from military units and supraprovincial bodies to schools and research institutes. Revolutionary committees, once proclaimed among the list of "new born things" to emerge from the Cultural Revolution, have now been abolished in all types of units (e.g., universities, factories, and laboratories). Mass organizations such as the Youth League, the Women's Federation, and the trade unions have been revitalized after years of limited activity. Specialized coordinating bodies such as the State Commission for Science and Technology and supraministerial committees under the State Council have also been revived. In short, the rebuilding effort launched in 1969-70 has been brought much closer to completion.[132]

The foregoing discussion has, of necessity, left many interesting points unexplored and has passed quickly over events and policy developments worthy of deeper analysis. Nevertheless, the summaries presented above do demonstrate the extent of continuity and evolutionary progression reflected in the policies of 1970-71, 1972-76, and the post-Mao period. In the area of personnel and organizational policy, as with the guiding principles of policymaking processes, contemporary developments represent the extension and refinement of earlier policies, not a sharp break with the past or a return to programs of an earlier period.

*Planning and Economic Policy*

Comprehensive central planning and the need for strong central control have figured prominently in recent discussions concerning China's quest for independence and security. The following excerpts from 1977-78 pronouncements illustrate the interconnection of the myriad economic policies involved in this planning:

> Socialist economy is a planned economy. This is a basic characteristic that distinguishes if from the capitalist economy. Chairman Mao said: "To build a powerful socialist country it is imperative to have a strong and unified central leadership, and unified planning and discipline throughout the country; disruption of this indispensable unity is impermissible."
>
> Concentration of power in the hands of central authorities and distribution of power to local authorities, centralization and decentralization, are a unity of opposites and a contradiction among the people. We must proceed from the concrete situation and handle it properly to benefit the development of productive forces. We should oppose rigid and all-inclusive control by the central authorities or "dictatorship by the ministries" which stifles the local initiative, as well as departmentalism and decentralism in the interests of this or that locality and department and ignoring the interests of the whole nation. *Centralization should be exercised whenever possible and necessary.* . . .
>
> We must insure an overall balance in the distribution of funds and material, in planning the use of the labor force, and developing all fields of work. *We should meet the needs of key projects, that is, concentrate our efforts* on fighting battles of annihilation. . . .
>
> Chairman Mao long ago said: "In the last analysis, the impact, good or bad, great or small, of the policy and the practice of any Chinese political par-

*Domestic Policy and the Quest for Independence*  67

ty upon the people depends on whether and how much it helps to develop their productive forces, and on whether it fetters or liberates these forces." . . . *[I]ncreasing or decreasing production is an important criterion to judge whether a revolution is successful or not.*[133]

The second excerpt is from an address by Yu Qiuli, chairman of the State Planning Commission:

> We must redouble our efforts and go forward courageously and at a faster speed to catch up with the advanced [nations.] *Neither the international situation nor the domestic situation at present permit us to go slowly. We have to quicken our pace to counter the threats of aggression by social-imperialism and imperialism and get prepared against war. We have to quicken our pace too to increase our economic strength,* reinforce the material base of the dictatorship of the proletariat, and continue to improve the material and cultural life of the people. . . .
>
> [E]conomic work must be consolidated. The crux of the matter is better management of plans and strengthening the planning of work. The "gang of four" undermined our planned economy so seriously that for the past few years the national economy was in fact developing in a semi-anarchical fashion. A significant proportion of economic activities was not included in the unified plan; even some included did not function strictly according to plan. *In order to put our national economy on the proper footing, we must stress planning.* . . . *A plan that has been approved by the state must be carried out strictly.* . . . There is a need to strengthen the system of responsibility from top to bottom and put an end to the situation of no person accepting responsibility.[134]

To discuss adequately the full range of economic policies announced or reaffirmed since 1976 would require far more space than is permitted here. Nonetheless, a brief summary of these economic policies is appropriate.

The post-Mao leadership advocated reinstitution of rational rules and regulations in industrial, mining and other enterprises;[135] affirmed the necessity for material incentives and multigrade wage scales;[136] and stressed the importance of running enterprises profitably.[137] Agricultural policies stressed mechanization (but without large input of funds from the central government),[138] consolidation of commune and brigade run enterprises,[139] and strict observance of national plans.[140] Technologies and equipment from abroad were depicted as playing an important, but not decisive, role in China's development,[141] and military procurement was accorded lower priority than economic construction.[142] In short, policies articulated since Mao's death represent extensions and elaborations of those developed in 1970–71.

*Cultural Policy: Science and Education*

Though radical influence was most pervasive in literature and the performing arts, machinations by the "gang of four" were allegedly most disruptive in the areas of education and science policy.[143] More specifically, followers of the "gang" were said to have willfully distorted and blocked implementation of Party policies governing schools, teachers, examinations, research, laboratory equipment, and virtually every other aspect of science and education.[144] These critiques of "gang" malfeasance consistently stressed that even though there were no dramatic revisions of formal policy (as implied by media under radical control), distortion at the level of rhetorical policy in 1972–76 impeded realization of developmental objectives.

Although many policy subsets were considered more or less simultaneously, during 1976–78 officials and the media seem to have focused on constituent areas in roughly the following sequence. Science policy, including guidelines on the treatment of professional researchers and technicians, rose to the top of the policymaking agenda almost immediately after the arrest of Jiang Qing and her fellow obstructionists. Discussions of the appropriate role and treatment of technical specialists gradually broadened to include virtually all intellectuals. Intellectual policy did not displace science policy as the most salient topic of discussion, but it did become an important correlate.

As the decision process moved forward in the areas of science and intellectual policy, leaders began to turn their attention to another correlate, namely, education. Education policy reached the agenda by two routes. One was via discussions of science policy and the role of university-based research and training. The other route was dictated by the approach of a new academic year and the need to revitalize the education system at all levels. Within months of the "gang's" downfall, commentaries and policy guidelines had begun to treat science, education, technical innovation, intellectual policy, and even management techniques as parts of an integrated whole. Interestingly, other areas of cultural policy such as the performing arts were of much lower priority and generally were treated as discrete issues. They reached the policymaking agenda somewhat later and were handled separately from the issues listed above.

Beginning in early 1977, commentaries on science and technology (including imports of technology and advanced equipment) cited the need for speed and efficiency. In addition, leading scientists invoked the memory of the country's preeminent political figures (Mao, Zhou Enlai, and Hua Guofeng) to legitimize implementation of policies that gave science professionals better working conditions and increased political influence. The message was simple and straightforward: Mao, Zhou and Hua recognized the importance of science and technology to China's quest for security and material well-being.[145]

Science policy was subsequently discussed in terms of its relevance to attainment of the "four modernizations." The argument advanced in virtually all commentaries published since early 1977 has been that appropriate science and technology policies (elaborated below) are essential to the realization of high priority objectives. The following excerpt is typical:

> [W]ithout modernized science and technology, it is impossible to have modernized agriculture, industry, and national defense, and we cannot build a powerful socialist state. Therefore, to grasp science and technology well is not only an economic issue but also a political issue. To develop our country's social productive forces and build our country into a modernized, socialist and powerful state, we must fight well the battle of science and technology.[146]

One of the most striking features of commentaries on science and technology policy is the degree of specificity regarding major decisions in the 1970–76 period. To buttress claims that the "gang of four" distorted and obstructed Party guidelines, commentators have provided detailed chronologies and specific declarations of policy evolution since adoption of the 1970–71 Program. These post hoc accounts are consistent with available contemporary material and with the interpretation presented in earlier sections of this chapter. Moreover, virtually every explication of science policy since late 1976 has claimed to be a reiteration or clarification of decisions made earlier in the decade rather than a bold new departure.[147]

Many of the current policies in the area of science and technology have been on the books for years, but were revitalized and elaborated only after removal of obstacles created by radical opponents. Specific developments in this regard have been examined and documented elsewhere; we will focus on the formal statements of policy issued in September 1977 and March 1978.[148] Though far from a complete list of policies endorsed in the past year, the summary presented below does touch upon a sufficient number of points to show the extent of policy continuity since 1970–71.

The guiding principle underlying contemporary science policy was captured in Deng Xiaoping's opening speech to the National Science Conference; i.e., policies should produce results and advance the cause of socialist development. The following excerpt illustrates this point:

> The basic task of scientific research institutes is to produce scientific results and to train competent people. They must show more scientific and technical achievements of high quality and train scientific and technical personnel who are both red and expert. The main criterion for judging the work of the Party committee of a scientific research institute should be the successful fulfillment of this basic task. . . . The leadership given by Party committees is primarily political leadership, that is, to ensure the correct political orientation and the

implementation of the Party's line, principles and policies and to bring out the initiative of all concerned. At the same time, leadership is exercised through the plan. . . . In order to follow out the plans and push forward our scientific research, it is also necessary to guarantee the supporting services and supplies and to provide the necessary working conditions for scientific and technical personnel. . . . We should give the director and the deputy directors of research institutes a free hand in the work of science and technology according to their division of labor.[149]

To realize the objectives stated in Deng's address, a number of specific policies was proclaimed in both the September 18 Circular and Fang Yi's discussion of the "Outline National Plan for the Development of Science and Technology, 1978-1985 (Draft)." A partial list of the announced policies includes: consolidating and revitalizing research institutes and university laboratories;[150] placing greater emphasis on basic and theoretical work;[151] and raising the status and improving the working conditions of research personnel.[152] Still other policies confirmed the leading role of the Party committee and Party responsibility for the success of logistical work,[153] reactivation of professional societies and frequent convocation of academic conferences,[154] publication of specialized professional journals,[155] and increased contact with foreign scientists and research facilities.[156] In short, the evolution of science policy since October 1976 conforms to the guidelines implicit in the 1970-71 Program. The major differences between the post-1976 situation and the preceding five years are that policies have been articulated more clearly, implementation has been accorded higher priority, and obstruction of formal policies seems to have been reduced considerably.

Similarly, commentaries on education during 1977-78 referred to key decisions and periods of debate earlier in the decade. The impression conveyed, however, is that education policies had not been as fully articulated as science policies. The reason — if this impression is correct — may be that education issues were more contentious and the strength of the radicals was greater in this area than it was in science and technology.

As noted above, education has frequently been discussed in the context of science and the country's requirements for skilled professionals. The following excerpt illustrates both this connection and the tenor of current policy:

> The basis of scientific training is education. It takes ten years to train a good man so we must not delay any longer. We must manage primary schools, middle schools, and universities well, do a very good job in carrying out revolution in education and improve the quality of teaching. We must restore

*Domestic Policy and the Quest for Independence* 71

order in teaching, strictly enforce school discipline, improve teaching materials and methods, and strive to educate young people in modern scientific knowledge. Universities must strengthen teaching in basic science and vigorously develop scientific research. All areas and departments must select a number of schools where such work will be carried out.[157]

Policies in education, like those in science, were being implemented—or in many cases reimplemented—before they were formally adopted. The sources noted below illustrate specific developments in education and should be read in conjunction with the speeches delivered at the National Conference on Education Work held in May 1978.[158] Briefly, the education policies enforced since the purge of the "gang of four" have struck a balance between quality and quantity, with somewhat greater emphasis on attaining high quality even at the cost of temporary inequities.

Specific policies enunciated during the period after Mao's death include: enrollment of university students on the basis of competitive national examinations;[160] reinstatement of teachers and improved status for the teaching profession;[161] increased stress on maintenance of classroom discipline;[162] and adoption of standardized teaching materials.[163] Other developments include designating key schools at all levels of the system to provide high quality instruction;[164] resumption of graduate instruction;[165] and raising the quality of supplemental schools such as July 21 Universities and May 7 Colleges.[166]

Education policy has been articulated in a draft plan for the 1978–85 period. The plan has not been published, but, as summarized by Liu Xiyao, it calls for improving schools at all levels and preparing curricula that will train people for positions in a modernizing society. Science and technology will receive special attention since they are regarded as critical to success in the quest for independence.[167]

In summary, therefore, science and education policies announced or implemented without formal announcement since 1976 reflect basic continuity with the program of 1970–71 and policies formally in effect since 1972. They have been made more specific, and concrete steps have been taken by members of the central leadership to assure that they are implemented as intended, but continuity and evolution are more evident than dramatic change.

## VIII. Conclusion

By tracing policy-related developments since 1969, the foregoing analysis has attempted to demonstrate that, contrary to Chinese rhetoric and the interpretations of many foreign scholars, policy change in China has been essentially linear and evolutionary over the entire nine-year period.[168] A variety of reasons were advanced to account for both policy continuity and employment of particular political tactics. The data and analysis presented above suggest the following conclusions.

First, although internal as well as external developments induced Chinese leaders to seek policy changes in 1969–70, the precise nature of those changes appears to have been determined primarily by the way officials interpreted the international situation. By 1969–70, key leaders (including Mao and Zhou) had concluded that changes in Soviet and U.S. policies, and in the international order more generally, posed new dangers to China's security as well as new opportunities. In response to what was perceived to be a new situation, officials formulated a set of policies on the basis of past experience and assessments of the relative "costs" associated with alternative courses of action. The result was the approach and policy guidelines referred to here as the 1970–71 Program. That there have been no fundamental changes in policy since 1970 can be explained, in large measure, by the fact that the leaders' perception of the international situation has remained the same. Developments subsequent to 1970–71 were interpreted as confirming the correctness of the earlier assessment and hence of the program adopted at the time. Moreover, it appears that the nature of the international situation has not been a matter of debate since 1970 even though officials have disagreed over how to respond to that situation.

Second, during the last eight years, despite torrid rhetoric and intervals of distortion and nonimplementation of policy directives, the basic pattern in virtually all policy areas has been one of evolution along the lines implicit in the 1970–71 Program. The evidence and analysis presented above refute the contention that policies have "oscillated" between two more or less fixed and contradictory poles or orientations. Different policy preferences clearly coexisted throughout the 1970s, and the dynamics of politics resulted in repeated bifurcation, but one policy set predominated throughout the entire period. That program was challenged, and at times denounced in the media, but at no time were policies reversed or made to correspond to the wishes of the minority coalition, at least not at the level of formal policy. Regional and temporal variation existed (in some places and at some times official policies were obstructed or even reversed in the course of implementation), but at the level of *formal* policy the pattern has been one of stability and gradual evolution in the direction of greater specificity and better integration.

Third, policymaking in China is essentially a conservative process. Once the rules of the game have been established (i.e., organizational units are in place, and procedures have been regularized), the same set of issues rises to the top of the policymaking agenda, and problems and solutions tend to be

## Domestic Policy and the Quest for Independence

viewed basically as they had been in previous rounds. Power is distributed according to the rules and changes little as long as the system remains intact.

With the establishment of a "new" policymaking system in 1969-70, evaluative criteria, power distributions, and other structural conditions were set and have continued to shape debate and policies up to the present. The rules of the game largely determine the range, content, and utility of different political strategies. The rules of the game established in 1969-70 strongly favored those who placed a premium on economic and technical efficiency, and were disadvantageous to those eager to preserve the "system" that emerged from the Cultural Revolution. Unable to "win" according to the rules, defenders of the Cultural Revolution employed a variety of tactics to obstruct implementation of policies they disliked. In addition, they attempted to change the system to secure adoption of rules more favorable to their own policy preferences and political aspirations. Moderately successful in the short run, their tactics ultimately proved to be inadequate to secure dramatic changes.

What does the foregoing analysis suggest about the future of politics and policy in China? To begin with, it suggests that the approach and program adopted in 1970-71 will continue to shape PRC policy unless leaders perceive that fundamental changes have taken place in the international situation. Current assessments by China's leaders caution that such change is possible at any time, but the underlying expectation seems to be that, in the foreseeable future, major changes are unlikely to occur. At a minimum, this implies that officials in Washington, Moscow, and other major capitals should consider the possible impact of their statements and actions on perception in Peking.

Officials at all levels of the system will continue to disagree over the details of policy, and political maneuver will continue to play an important role in the allocation of resources, rewards, and responsibilities. Removal of radical opponents has made it easier for the dominant coalition to secure implementation of formal policies, but it has not ushered in a new era of unanimity. Individuals and institutions will continue to compete for scarce resources and to perceive problems and proposals through lenses colored by parochial (e.g., regional, functional, and personal) concerns. Perceptual and preferential differences will spark debate, but they will also provide grist for political mills. Coalitions will dissolve and reform in slightly different ways, individuals and organizations will gain and lose power depending on the relative success of particular policies, and efforts will be made to settle old scores. Politics is far from dead, but participants are likely to abide by the rules of the game—most of the time.[169]

Even under the rules of the game, however individuals and administrative units are likely to be criticized for real and imagined shortcomings. The fact that proclaimed objectives are extremely ambitious and that so much has been promised to all segments of society virtually assures that some goals will not be attained and some groups will be dissatisfied with regime performance. Scapegoats will be found, incompetents will be removed, and political rhetoric will intensify to discredit thoroughly those who have erred. High-ranking officials may be dismissed and disgraced, but basic policies will not change dramatically as a result.

**Notes**

1. Representative articles and developments in the renewed drive for rapid modernization include: Mass Criticism Group of the Ministry of Light Industry, *Relying on Our Own Efforts, Making Foreign Things Serve China,* Renmin Ribao [hereafter RMRB], Nov. 16, 1976; Mass Criticism Group of the State Planning Commission, *The "Gang of Four" are the Chief Culprits in Undermining Socialist Modernization in the Four Fields,* HONG QI [hereafter HQ], No. 12, 1976, at 43–48; *The Basic Policy for Building a Powerful Socialist Country is to Mobilize all Positive Factors,* Peking Radio Broadcast (Jan. 31, 1977), *translated in* FOREIGN BROADCAST INFORMATION SERVICE, DAILY REPORT: PEOPLE'S REPUBLIC OF CHINA [hereafter FBIS], Feb. 9, 1977, at E6–10 (first of sixteen Peking Radio commentaries on Mao's *On the Ten Major Relationships*). *See also* Hua Guofeng, *Speech at the Second National Learn from Dazhai in Agriculture Conference,* RMRB, Dec. 28, 1976; Hua Guofeng, *Speech at the National Learn from Daqing in Industry Conference,* RMRB, May 13, 1977; and Hua Guofeng, *Report at the Fifth National People's Congress,* RMRB, Mar. 6, 1978.

2. *See, e.g.,* Jürgen Domes, *China in 1977: Reversal of Verdicts,* 18 ASIAN SURVEY 1–16 (No. 1, 1978); Allen S. Whiting, *China After Mao,* 17 ASIAN SURVEY 1028–35 (No. 11, 1977).

3. This seems to be the implication of Kenneth Lieberthal, *The Politics of Modernization in the PRC,* PROBLEMS OF COMMUNISM, May–June 1978, at 1–17.

4. The sense of *déjà vu* is heightened by the publication and study of reports by Mao Zedong [Mao Tse-tung] dating from these periods, and by the rehabilitation of individuals denounced during the Cultural Revolution for having played central roles in the formulation of policies in 1955–56 and 1960–63. Perhaps the two most important of the recently published Mao documents are *On the Ten Major Relationships* (Apr. 25, 1956), RMRB, Dec. 26, 1976, and *Talk at an Enlarged Working Conference Convened by the Central Committee of the CCP,* RMRB, July 1, 1978.

5. Generally identified as "radical" and "moderate" in analyses written since the Cultural Revolution, the alternative approaches have also been labeled "ideological" and "pragmatic," "radical" and "conservative," and simply "left" and "right."

6. For discussion and a useful critique of this perspective, *see* Andrew J. Nathan, *Policy Oscillations in the People's Republic of China: A Critique,* CHINA QUARTERLY, Dec. 1976, at 720–33.

7. See, e.g., Ting Wang, *Leadership Realignments*, PROBLEMS OF COMMUNISM, July-Aug. 1977, at 1-7; and Jürgen Domes, *China in 1976: Tremors in Transition*, 17 ASIAN SURVEY 1-17 (No. 1, 1977). For an earlier discussion of this perspective, *see* Thomas W. Robinson, *Political Succession in China*, WORLD POLITICS, Oct. 1974, at 1-38.

8. See the excellent discussion in Harry Harding, Linkages Between Chinese Domestic Politics and Foreign Policy (Aug. 12-14, 1976) (paper presented at the Workshop on Chinese Foreign Policy sponsored by the Joint Committee on Contemporary China, Ann Arbor, Michigan).

9. Media campaigns in China, especially during the period covered by this study, occasionally give a highly distorted view of both official policies and those actually implemented. This is a very serious problem for analysts of PRC policy. Much of the data used by foreign scholars comes from the media—one of the least reliable sources. Many analysts have confused rhetoric and reality by failing to distinguish between what policies were, what they were said to be, and what actually happened. Increased opportunities to speak with officials and technical specialists in and from China have made it easier to draw proper distinctions. Much of the analysis presented here is based on such conversations in conjunction with reconstructions based on close readings of extensive materials.

10. This is an overstatement meant only to contrast domestic and foreign policies. Whereas foreign policies frequently impinge directly on a country's security and hence have a certain priority in the minds of national leaders, few domestic policies are seen as critical in the short run. Moreover, there are fewer levels of bureaucracy intervening between formulation and execution of foreign policy. The process is therefore more susceptible to control by the central leadership.

11. Thomas Fingar, Politics and Policy Making in the People's Republic of China, 1954-55 (unpublished Ph.D. dissertation, Stanford University, 1977).

12. On fundamental, or systemic, change, see CHALMERS JOHNSON, REVOLUTIONARY CHANGE (1966), and Scott C. Flanagan, *Models and Methods of Analysis*, in GABRIEL A. ALMOND, SCOTT C. FLANAGAN·& ROBERT J. MUNDT, eds., CRISIS, CHOICE AND CHANGE 46-57 (1973).

13. On the magnitude of change, see DAVID BRAYBOOKE & CHARLES E. LINDBLOM, A STRATEGY OF DECISION (1963).

14. THOMAS FINGAR & JOHN W. LEWIS, THE CHINESE POLITICIAN (forthcoming).

15. The reference to a "1970-71 Program" is in quotes because the term has never been used by the Chinese to describe policy changes made during the period. I believe, however, that those changes qualify for the title of "program."

16. Such models included the short-lived "Paris Commune" experiment undertaken in Shanghai, and numerous extreme versions of local autarky and near autonomy.

17. One reason the experiments failed was that they disrupted, often deliberately, the informal arrangements between individuals and institutions that might have assured success. The policy and planning practices of earlier years had many shortcomings. Over time, however, cadres and other individuals had learned how to

overcome these problems. The effectiveness of these arrangements varied but they often precluded complete collapse or serious dysfunction. Even during the most radical stages of the Cultural Revolution, such arrangements continued to function, especially in the countryside where the impact of new policy departures was either minimal or generally favorable. Those involved in such arrangements, whether as cadres or as advisors to those who replaced them, continued to act and operate largely as they had previously. The result was considerable conservatism amidst great calls for radicalism. To the extent that informal arrangements were prevented from operating, however, informal correctives and substitutes for the vague and often ill-conceived policies of China's temporary leaders could not be effective. All policies were thus less effective than they might otherwise have been.

18. There seems to have been a general consensus that significant changes had occurred in the international arena, but there was sharp disagreement as to how to respond to the perceived changes. *See* Linda D. Dillon, Bruce Burton, and Walter C. Soderlund, *Who Was the Principal Enemy?: Shifts in Official Chinese Perception of the Two Superpowers, 1968-69,* 17 ASIAN SURVEY 456-73 (No. 5, 1977).

19. The sense of urgency injected into nascent discussions on restructuring the system reinforced other conservative inclinations, and officials turned to the familiar solutions of the past. This is not to suggest that they attempted to re-create the system in effect before the Cultural Revolution. On the contrary, they recognized that each of the permutations tried previously had inherent problems and elements that were no longer appropriate. They also recognized that the organizational arrangements and policymaking procedures of earlier years had, on the whole, produced respectable, and at times remarkable, achievements. On balance, the rebuilding effort launched in 1969-70 apparently took the centralized, Party-dominant, economic efficiency-minded model of the past as its starting point.

20. *See* THOMAS GOTTLIEB, CHINESE FOREIGN POLICY FACTIONALISM AND THE ORIGINS OF THE STRATEGIC TRIANGLE (1977).

21. Not all leaders favored major changes. One need not question their belief in the efficacy of existing programs to note that those who had risen to prominence during the Cultural Revolution had a considerable personal stake in the preservation of policies and organizational forms they had helped create.

22. The term "radical" is actually something of a misnomer during this period since the group labeled "radicals" by Western analysts were, in fact, defenders or conservers of Cultural Revolution practices. "Conservatives" would be a misleading substitute; "conservative-radicals" would be more accurate, but too cumbersome.

23. While there was discussion of many issues and sub-issues during this period, the order of presentation here merely reflects the relative salience of problems discussed in the media during 1969-71 and, probably, the sequence in which they were formally "resolved." Unfortunately, the kind of data available does not permit reconstruction of precise chronologies and policy agendas. The order in which issues were considered is important because sequence (or "agenda") often shapes the outcome of the debate. On this point, see ROGER W. COBB & CHARLES D. ELDER, PARTICIPATION IN AMERICAN POLITICS: THE DYNAMICS OF AGENDA BUILDING (1972); and E. E. SCHATTSCHNEIDER, THE SEMISOVEREIGN PEOPLE (1960).

24. See JOHN W. LEWIS, ed., Introduction, PARTY LEADERSHIP AND REVOLUTIONARY POWER IN CHINA 1-31 (1970).

25. For speeches and documents of the Ninth National Party Congress, see HQ, No. 5, 1969, at 7-52; PEKING REVIEW [hereafter PR], Apr. 30, 1969, at 16-49. Lin Biao and the "conservative-radicals" retained control of the still emasculated Party in 1969, but post-1976 commentaries on the relationship between Lin and the "gang of four" support the view that there was an unsuccessful effort at the time of the Ninth Party Congress to restore the CCP to its former role. See, e.g., Shen Daosheng, The "Gang of Four" and Lin Biao, RMRB, May 18, 1978.

26. See Editorial Departments of Renmin Ribao, HONG QI, and Jiefangjun Bao, Long Live the Communist Party of China, RMRB, July 1, 1969, and Continue the Revolution, Advance from Victory to Victory, RMRB, Oct. 1, 1970; and Communiqué of the Second Plenary Session of the Ninth Central Comm. of the Communist Party of China, PR, Sep. 11, 1970, at 5-7.

27. The first provincial committee was announced in December 1970, RMRB, Dec. 14, 1970; the last was announced in August 1971. Completion of this stage of the process was marked by a major editorial entitled Our Party is Advancing Vigorously, RMRB, Aug. 27, 1971. In light of subsequent developments, it is interesting to note that the first of the newly elected provincial First Secretaries was none other than Hua Guofeng.

28. For one indication of the change, see ROBERT A. SCALAPINO, ed., The Transition in Chinese Party Leadership: A Comparison of the Eighth and Ninth Central Committees, ELITES IN THE PEOPLE'S REPUBLIC OF CHINA 67-148 (1972).

29. For a description of the importance of shared norms and the observance of specified procedures to the Chinese Communist concept of leadership, see JOHN W. LEWIS, LEADERSHIP IN COMMUNIST CHINA (1963).

30. See, e.g., Diligently Study Chairman Mao's Philosophical Works, RMRB, Oct. 30, 1970; Xue Shengping, Be Conscious, HQ, No. 12, 1970, at 10-12; see also Victory of Chairman Mao's Line in Party Building, RMRB, Jan. 31, 1971.

31. E.g., Editorial Departments of Renmin Ribao, HONG QI, and Jiefangjun Bao, Commemorate the 50th Anniversary of the Communist Party of China, RMRB, July 1, 1971; Writing Group of the Liaoning Provincial Comm. of the CCP, A Powerful Ideological Weapon for Knowing and Changing the World: Study "On Practice," HQ, No. 5, 1971, at 11-19; Writing Group of the Hubei Provincial Comm. of the CCP, A Strong Weapon to Unite the People and Defeat the Enemy: Study "On Policy," HQ, No. 8, 1971, at 10-17.

32. See, e.g., Diligently Read the Works of Marx, Lenin, and Chairman Mao, RMRB, Apr. 4, 1971; Read the Works of Marx and Lenin Conscientiously, Diligently Study the Writings of Chairman Mao, RMRB, Apr. 6, 1971; CCP Comm. of the Peking No. 3 Commercial Works, Read Books Seriously and Persist in the Firm and Correct Political Direction, HQ, No. 7-8, 1971, at 68-73.

33. The restoration of state organs is more difficult to chronicle than is the rehabilitation of the Party. One of the best sources of information is the sequence of name lists released by national and local organs on major holidays such as May 1, July 1, and Oct. 1. Over time, the number of people and positions identified in-

creased considerably. Tangential evidence comes from the fact that China embarked upon its Fourth Five-Year Plan in 1971. Preparation and execution of the Plan would have been difficult without a viable state apparatus.

34. For details on Lin's downfall, see MICHAEL Y. M. KAU, ed., THE LIN PIAO AFFAIR (1975).

35. Two reasons can be advanced to explain this development: (1) the necessity to compromise with defenders of the status quo, and (2) the inability of advocates of change to agree on a single strategy of development.

36. See, e.g., Writing Group of the Jilin Provincial Revolutionary Comm., Class Struggle in the Field of Socialist Construction and Economics, HQ, No. 2, 1970, at 52-63; Writing Group of the State Planning Commission, Launch a Penetrating Movement to Increase Production and Practice Economy on the Industrial Front, HQ, No. 2, 1971, at 39-47.

37. Commentators stressed the importance of compiling accurate and complete statistics in order to make realistic plans and facilitate monitoring of the results. See Gong Xiaowen, It Is Necessary to Have a Head for Figures — Refuting the Theory that Statistics Are Useless, RMRB, Oct. 29, 1971. One of the reasons for rehabilitating cadres disgraced during the Cultural Revolution was to strengthen capabilities in this area.

38. In particular, this opposition was manifested in efforts to prevent raising the level of accounting from the team to the production brigade, and to strengthen *xian* [county] administrative bodies. See Jürgen Domes, New Course in Chinese Domestic Politics: The Anatomy of Readjustment, 13 ASIAN SURVEY 633-46 (No. 7, 1973).

39. See, e.g., Writing Group of the Hunan Provincial Comm. of the CCP, Go One Step Further in Strengthening the Party's Democratic Centralism, HQ, No. 1, 1971, at 38-42; Our Party is Advancing Victoriously, RMRB, Aug. 27, 1971.

40. E.g., Editorial Departments, supra note 31; Xiang Hui, Conscientiously Implement the Party's Economic Policies for Rural Areas, HQ, No. 13, 1971, at 30-34.

41. See Writing Group of the State Planning Commission, Advance in Triumph Along the Road of Daqing Indicated by Chairman Mao, RMRB, Sep. 10, 1971.

42. E.g., Rely on the Working Class to Institute Rational Rules and Regulations, HQ, No. 12, 1970, at 57-62; and Suo Gang, We Must Establish a New Production Order — Refuting the "Theory that Systems Are Useless," RMRB, Aug. 29, 1971.

43. Evidence of the emerging trend in industrial policies comes primarily in the form of criticisms, rather than positive statements about the new program, e.g., Mass Criticism and Repudiation Group of Plant No. 5751 of Hongwei District, Carry Out Revolution on the Revisionist Line of "Big, Foreign, and Complete" Plants in Designing, RMRB, Mar. 26, 1971.

44. On the development of trade policy, see Ann Fenwick's chapter in this volume; Kent Morrison, Domestic Politics and Industrialization in China: The Foreign Trade Factor, 18 ASIAN SURVEY 687-705 (No. 7, 1978).

45. On the development of earlier import policies, see Robert F. Dernberger, Economic Development and Modernization in Contemporary China, in FREDERIC J. FLERON, JR.,ed., TECHNOLOGY AND COMMUNIST CULTURE 224-64 (1977); see also Nai-Ruenn Chen, China's Foreign Trade: 1950-74, Joint Economic Comm., 94th Cong., 1st sess., CHINA: A REASSESSMENT OF THE ECONOMY 617-52 (1975).

46. This is largely conjectural, but it is fully consistent with the fact that China began to purchase oil exploration and extraction equipment in 1972 and began construction of pipelines and port facilities (which could be used to export petroleum) the following year. Given the lead times involved, it seems likely that preliminary decisions were made in 1970-71.

47. *See, e.g., Build a Three-Level Repair and Manufacturing Network to Expedite Agricultural Mechanization,* Peking Radio Broadcast (Aug. 17, 1971), *in* FBIS, Aug. 30, 1971, at B6-9; Writing Group of the First Ministry of Machine Building, *Advance Along Chairman Mao's Line on Agricultural Mechanization,* RMRB, Sep. 17, 1971; and *Red Banner in Developing a Mountain Region,* PR, Jan. 29, 1971, at 17-19.

48. *See, e.g.,* Writing Group of the Ministry of Agriculture and Forestry, *Advance from Victory to Victory Along the Brilliant Road of Learning from Dazhai [Ta-chai] in Agriculture,* RMRB, Apr. 13, 1971; *Investigate, Research, and Seriously Implement the Party's Economic Policy in the Countryside,* RMRB, Feb. 24, 1971; *Grasp Well the Production of Minor Commodities,* Peking Radio Broadcast (June 12, 1971), *in* FBIS, June 18, 1971, at B9-11; *Actively Develop the Diversification of Our Economy,* Sian Radio Broadcast by Hua Jianwen (Apr. 8, 1971), *in* FBIS, Apr. 13, 1971, at H1-2.

49. *See* JOSEPH R. LEVENSON, THE PROBLEM OF INTELLECTUAL CONTINUITY, CONFUCIAN CHINA AND ITS MODERN FATE, VOL. I (1958).

50. A unique feature of the policy debates throughout most of the 1970s was the extent to which the media were dominated by the opponents of emerging policies. Possessing relatively little political resources in other areas, this group (now subsumed under the label "gang of four") sought to maximize their strength by focusing the debate on issues where they enjoyed certain advantages. One of the central theses of this chapter is that the series of media campaigns involving cultural issues represented concerted efforts by those who wanted to preserve the Cultural Revolution system to reverse or obstruct policy changes designed to dismantle the system that had enabled them to rise to power.

51. Such a conclusion was based on objective considerations of military and economic strength, but it also seems to have rested on presumptions about the almost magical spillover effects of scientific research. *See* Thomas Fingar, Pursuit of Political Interest: Scientists, Policy Makers, and Policy-Making in the PRC (August 10-17, 1977) (unpublished paper prepared for the Workshop on the Pursuit of Political Interest in the People's Republic of China sponsored by the Joint Committee on Contemporary China, Ann Arbor, Michigan).

52. To trace the changes and ambiguity of science policy, see, *e.g.,* Mass Revolutionary Criticism and Repudiation Writing Team of the Chinese Academy of Sciences, *Scientific Research Must be Combined with Production Practice,* RMRB, Jan. 6, 1971; Revolutionary Mass Criticism Group of Shenyang Metals Research Institute, *Thoroughly Repudiate the Idea of "Private Ownership of Knowledge,"* RMRB, Mar. 19, 1971; Guangzhou Steel Factory Worker's Revolutionary Mass Criticism Writing Group, *Make Strenuous Efforts to Master Science and Technology for the Purpose of Building Socialism,* Guangming Ribao [hereafter GMRB], Oct. 6, 1971; and Ke Yen, *Strive to Make a Success of Scientific Research for the Revolution,* HQ, No. 11, 1971, at 61-66.

53. *See, e.g., Special Issue on the Proletarian Revolution in Education,* HQ, No. 8, 1970;

Gao Ge, *Build a Socialist University in the Practice of Struggle,* HQ, No. 3, 1971, at 56–59; and *Special Issue on the Proletarian Revolution in Education,* HQ, No. 6, 1971.

54. For articles that illustrate the evolution of intellectual policy, see, *e.g., Employ Them in the Course of Educating Them, Intensify Their Education in the Course of Employing Them,* RMRB, Apr. 21, 1970; Tang Aoqing, *Obey Chairman Mao's Word, Resolutely Take the Road of Integration with Workers, Peasants, and Soldiers,* GMRB, Oct. 9, 1970; *Persevere in the Re-education of Scientific and Technical Personnel,* GMRB, Apr. 24, 1971; *Intensify the Re-education of Intellectuals and Let Technical Personnel Play Their Parts to the Full,* GMRB, Sep. 6, 1971; and Revolutionary Committee of the Fushun Coal Research Institute, *Seriously Carry Out the Party's Policy Toward Intellectuals, Fully Arouse the Enthusiasm of Scientific Research Workers,* GMRB, Oct. 6, 1971.

55. Changes in China's military doctrine and force posture have been analyzed by John Lewis and there is no need to retrace the ground he has covered so well in his contribution to this volume. Here, I will indicate how military policies fit into the larger policy package that took shape in this period, and comment briefly on the domestic elements of the new military policies.

56. One of the earliest indications of the changing relationship of the military to the Party was the unheralded change in the nature of the "three-in-one" combinations on Party committees. Revolutionary committees and, apparently, Party committees had been comprised of representatives of the PLA, revolutionary cadres, and mass organizations. Beginning in late 1970, however, press reports began to refer to the "three-in-one" combination of "old, middle-aged, and young people." *See, e.g., Third Kiangsi [Jiangxi] Provincial Congress of the CCP Held, Third Kiangsi Provincial Party Committee Elected,* New China News Agency [hereafter NCNA] (Dec. 31, 1970), *in* SURVEY OF THE CHINA MAINLAND PRESS [hereafter SCMP], No. 71-01, at 151–54.

57. *See, e.g.,* Stephen A. Sims, *The New Role of the Military,* PROBLEMS OF COMMUNISM, Nov.–Dec. 1969, at 26–32; and Ellis Joffee, *The PLA in Internal Politics, id.* Nov.–Dec. 1975, at 1–12.

58. *See Politics Should Really Play its Role in Commanding Military Affairs,* Sichuan Radio Broadcast (Dec. 26, 1971), *in* FBIS, Dec. 29, 1971, at E1; and Editorial Departments of Renmin Ribao, HONG QI, and Jiefangjun Bao, *Commemorate August 1st, Army Day,* RMRB, Aug. 1, 1971.

59. *See* Sydney I. Jammes, *The Chinese Defense Burden, 1965–74, in* JOINT ECONOMIC COMMITTEE, 94TH CONG., 1ST SESS., CHINA: A REASSESSMENT OF THE ECONOMY, 459–66 (1975).

60. *See generally* material cited notes 12 and 13, *supra.*

61. On the importance of the "rules of the game," *see* T. Fingar, *supra* note 11; and ROGER W. COBB & CHARLES D. ELDER and E. E. SCHATTSCHNEIDER, *supra* note 23.

62. Editorial Departments of Renmin Ribao, HONG QI, and Jiefangjun Bao, *Unite to Win Still Greater Victories,* RMRB, Jan. 1, 1972.

63. This quotation was used by advocates of the 1970–71 Program to criticize and discourage the obstructionist activities of their opponents. Since adherents of the 1970–71 Program were in the dominant position, they were able to use the "rules of the game" to their advantage. If they could compel or intimidate their opponents to abide by the rules, they could guarantee their own success.

64. *See generally* T. Fingar, *supra* note 11.
65. Ji Ping, *It is Necessary to Examine Problems According to their Basic Nature*, HQ, No. 3, 1973, at 7–10.
66. Jiang Hong, *Conscientiously Sum Up Experience and Accelerate Agricultural Development*, HQ, No. 3, 1973, at 29–34.
67. Zheng Lei, *Do a Better Job in Publication Work*, HQ, No. 5, 1973, at 44–48.
68. Education policies in China are generally formulated and promulgated during the late summer. *See, e.g.*, Revolutionary Committee of Huaiyin Administrative District, Jiangsu Province, *Do a Good Job in the Enrollment of University Students*, RMRB, June 20, 1973; and *Give Priority to Selecting Educated Young People with Practical Experience for College*, GMRB, Sep. 25, 1973.
69. *A Thought-Provoking Test Answer*, RMRB, Aug. 10, 1973, *reprinted from* Liaoning Ribao, July 19, 1973, (the note and letter on the case of Zhang Tiesheng). *See also* Zhu Yan, *The Significance of Reforming College Enrollment*, HQ, No. 8, 1973, at 9–13.
70. Yang Pu, *The Spirit of Going Against the Tide*, RMRB, Aug. 16, 1973. In a representative passage, the article stated:

> What attitude did Comrade Zhang Tiesheng adopt in the face of the force of old ideas and old habits? Having been steeled for five years in the countryside and now serving as a production team leader, this educated youth adopted the attitude of going against the tide: He handed in a "blank" answer paper in the examination of physics and chemistry and wrote on the back of this paper "a thought-provoking answer." Going against the tide is a Marxist-Leninist principle.

71. Documents from the Tenth Party Congress can be found in HQ, No. 9, 1973, at 5–36.
72. For details on this campaign and the way it became linked to criticism of Lin Biao, *see, e.g.*, Merle Goldman, *China's Anti-Confucian Campaign, 1973–74*, CHINA QUARTERLY, Sep. 1975, at 435–62; Peter R. Moody, Jr., *The New Anti-Confucian Campaign in China: The First Round*, 14 ASIAN SURVEY 307-24 (No. 4, 1974); Chou Tzu-Ch'iang, *Observations on the Chinese Communists' Anti-Confucian Campaign*, ISSUES AND STUDIES, Feb. 1974, at 18–43; Wang Hsueh-wen, *The Development of the Maoists' Criticism of the Confucius Movement*, *Id.*, Mar. 1974, at 32–54; Wang Hsueh-wen, *The Maoists' Deepened Struggle to Criticize Lin Piao and Confucius*, *Id.*, June 1974, at 2–18; and Wang Hsueh-wen, *The Maoists' Criticism of Mencius*, *Id.*, July 1974, at 29–45.
73. The list of articles on both sides of this issue is extremely long. *See, e.g.*, Li Qinglin, *On Going Against the Tide*, HQ, No. 11, 1973, at 65–67; Zhai Jiang, *To Have the Revolutionary Spirit of Going Against the Tide is Essential*, RMRB, Nov. 7, 1973; Fang Yanliang, *Going Against the Tide is a Marxist-Leninist Principle*, HQ, No. 12, 1973, at 23–26; and Fang Hai, *We Must Have a Lively Political Situation*, XUEXI YU PIPAN [STUDY AND CRITICISM, hereafter XXYPP], Dec. 1973, at 3–6.
74. *Cf., e.g.*, Fang Hai, *supra* note 73, and Hong Yuan, *Communist Party Members Should Strengthen Their Sense of Discipline*, HQ, No. 1, 1974, at 28–32.
75. *E.g.*, Henry S. Bradsher, *China: The Radical Offensive*, 13 ASIAN SURVEY

989-1009 (No. 11, 1973); and Parris H. Chang, *Mao's Last Stand*, PROBLEMS OF COMMUNISM, July-Aug. 1976, at 1-17.

76. Although precise figures are lacking, production grew more slowly in late 1973 and early 1974 than it had in the previous eighteen months. This slowdown must have disturbed leaders who were eager to strengthen China as rapidly as possible during the temporarily opportune situation afforded by the international arena. Urgency was heightened by changes in U.S.-USSR trade relations (the great grain sales), by arms control developments (the protocol to the ABM treaty and preparations for the Vladivostok summit), and by the approaching end of America's combat role in Indochina.

77. Editorial Departments of Renmin Ribao, HONG QI, and Jiefangjun Bao, *The Party Exercises Leadership in Everything*, RMRB, July 1, 1974.

78. *Id.* (emphasis added).

79. *E.g.*, Qi Li, *Persist in Revolutionary Unity, Deepen the Criticism of Lin Biao and Confucius*, HQ, No. 9, 1974, at 8-10; Zhu Gongyan and Liu Yongqing, *Criticize Lin Biao's Criminal Acts in Sabotaging the Attack Against Jinzhou [Chinchou]*, GMRB, Aug. 13, 1974; Zhan Shipu, *Obey Orders in All Your Actions — A Criticism of Lin Biao's Criminal Act in Opposing Party Leadership in the Beiping-Tianjin [Peiping-Tientsin] Campaign*, RMRB, Sept. 13, 1974; and Li Xin, *Correctly Handle the Relationship Between Unity and Struggle*, HQ, No. 11, 1974, at 14-17.

80. *See, e.g.*, Qi Xin, *Be Promoters of Revolutionary Unity*, HQ, No. 8, 1974, at 8-12; *Foster Revolutionary Unity and Win New Victories in the Criticism of Lin Biao and Confucius*, RMRB, Sep. 5, 1974; Party Committee of the Dalian Red Flag Shipyard, *It is Necessary to Firmly and Unswervingly Unite with the Great Majority*, GMRB, Sep. 13, 1974; and Zhi Heng, *Master the Dialectical Method of One Dividing into Two*, HQ, No. 11, 1974, at 5-8.

81. Chou En-Lai [Zhou Enlai], *Report on the Work of the Government*, Speech Delivered to the First Session of the Fourth National People's Congress (January 13, 1975), in RMRB, Jan. 21, 1975.

82. The "four modernizations" are agriculture, industry, national defense, and science and technology. *See also* Deng Xiaoping's [Teng Hsiao-p'ing's] Speech at the Sixth Special Session of the U.N. General Assembly, *reprinted in* PR, Apr. 12, 1974 (Supp.), at I-V. In retrospect, this speech can be read as setting parameters and criteria for use in formulating plans for China's development that complement those in Zhou's report, *supra* note 81.

83. Examples of the few commentaries in national media include Gan Wen, *Cardinal Law for Consolidating the Dictatorship of the Proletariat*, RMRB, Jan. 24, 1975; Liu Yinggong, *The Dictatorship of the Proletariat is a Magic Weapon for Defeating the Enemy and Protecting Ourselves*, RMRB, Jan. 26, 1975; and Zhong Wen, *Strengthen the Leadership of the Party Over the State Under the Dictatorship of the Proletariat*, GMRB, Jan. 25, 1975. Short commentaries broadcast by provincial radio stations can be found in relevant sections of FBIS during the last week of January 1975.

84. *See* Mass Criticism Group of HONG QI, *A Record of Troublemaking, Failure, and Destruction — Exposing and Criticizing Yao Wenyuan's Crimes in Using* HONG QI *to Create Counterrevolutionary Public Opinion*, RMRB, Mar. 25, 1977.

85. Indirect evidence includes statements by Chinese scientists indicating that their work continued even during the "dark days" of interference by the "gang of four." These personal accounts are supported by 1978 articles extolling the achievements of individual scientists and research facilities. These panegyrics praise researchers who pursued professional work despite "illegal" orders to the contrary by followers of the "gang." *See, e..g.,* An I-chao [An Yizhao], *He Aspires for Great Achievements — on Professor T'ang Ao-ch'ing [Tang Aoqing], a Quantum Chemist,* Peking Radio (March 10, 1978), *in* FBIS, Mar. 14, 1978, at E6-8. Deng Xiaoping is the best example of someone castigated in the media for months but still able to retain considerable prestige and political influence.

86. The two most famous articles in this campaign were Yao Wenyuan, *On the Social Basis of the Lin Biao Anti-Party Clique,* HQ, No. 3, 1975, at 20-29; and Zhang Chunqiao, *On Exercising All-Round Dictatorship Over the Bourgeoisie,* HQ, No. 4, 1975, at 3-12. Other important articles appeared in Renmin Ribao under pseudonyms such as Liang Xiao and Luo Siding.

87. Although it seems likely that there was also a conference on the problems of agriculture, subsequent discussions of the period have not confirmed such a meeting or indicated that draft proposals were considered. That there was a high level conference with draft proposals is virtually certain, however, in view of the fact that the First National Learn from Dazhai in Agriculture Conference was held in September-October 1975. Preparatory meetings to set the agenda and recommend specific courses of action must have taken place. It is interesting and puzzling that, in view of the way other draft proposals were distorted and discredited in media controlled by the radicals, no mention has been made of the conference agenda or Deng's address to that forum.

Unofficial versions of working papers prepared in and for conferences on industry, and on science and technology, have been released by sources in Taiwan and Hong Kong. The versions obtained by these sources are consistent with the excerpts quoted in critical articles published by Xuexi Yu Pipan. The draft on industrial problems, entitled *Some Problems in Speeding Up Industrial Development* (also known as *The Twenty Points*), can be found in Issues and Studies, July 1977, at 90-113. The major critique of this program is *Criticism of Selected Passages of "Some Problems in Speeding up Industrial Development,"* XXYPP, Apr. 1976, at 28-35. Science and technology were discussed in *Several Questions Concerning the Work of Science and Technology* (also entitled *Outline of a Briefing on the Work of the Academy of Sciences,* hereafter *Outline Report*), Issues and Studies, Sep. 1977, at 63-70. Criticisms include Kang Li and Yan Feng, *The Circumstances Surrounding the Appearance of the "Outline Report,"* XXYPP, Apr. 1976, at 20-27.

Military matters were discussed at an enlarged session of the Military Affairs Commission. Documents are said to have been discussed and approved, but they have not been released. For information on the meeting, see Editorial Department of Jiefangjun Bao, *A Struggle Concerning the Major Issues of Right and Wrong on the Military Front,* RMRB, Jan. 30, 1978; Theoretical Group of the Headquarters of the PLA General Staff, *Persevere in Grasping the Key Link in Running the Army Well and Speed Up the Building of Our Army — Criticizing the "Gang of Four's" Crimes in Opposing the 1975 Enlarged Meeting of the Military Affairs Commission,* HQ, No. 2, 1978, at 2-11.

There was also a draft on the role of the Party and overall strategy for the period ahead. *See On the General Program of All Work of the Party and the Country (The General Program),* ISSUES AND STUDIES, Aug. 1977, at 77-99.

88. Mass Criticism Groups of Beijing and Qinghua Universities, *The Orientation of the Revolution in Education Brooks No Alteration,* HQ, No. 12, 1975, at 5-12. *See also* Fang Hai, *Learn to Look at Problems from All Sides,* XXYPP, Nov. 1975, at 62-65.

89. Mass Criticism Groups of Beijing and Qinghua Universities, *Hit Back at the Right Deviationist Wind of Reversing Previous Verdicts in Science and Technology Circles,* HQ, No. 2, 1976, at 3-11. This article is a prime example of inflammatory writing based on an accurate assessment of the situation.

90. The tone of much of the argument is summed up in the following sentence: "Historical experience demonstrates that revisionists often stage their offensives against Marxism by making use of the position of natural science." *Id.* at 7.

91. The campaign to criticize WATER MARGIN began on August 31, 1975. *See* for example, *Attach Importance to the Commentary on* Water Margin, RMRB, Aug. 31, 1975; Editorial, *Promote Criticism of* Water Margin, RMRB, Sep. 4, 1975; and Fang Yanliang, *Let Everyone Know the Capitulationists,* HQ, No. 9, 1975, at 8-12.

92. *See, e.g.,* Editorial, *Grasp the Key, Deepen Criticism of Deng Xiaoping,* RMRB, Aug. 23, 1976; and Liang Xiao, *Grasp the Question of Line and Deepen Criticism of Deng Xiaoping,* GMRB, Aug. 26, 1976.

93. The initial account of the Tiananmen Incident can be found in RMRB, Apr. 8, 1976. For the subsequent reinterpretation of the incident, *see Long Live the People—On the Revolutionary Mass Movement in Tiananmen Square,* RMRB, Dec. 21, 1978.

94. A major article published by supporters of the 1970-71 Program during the counteroffensive of late 1974 contains an interesting discussion of policy development. Among other arguments, it asserts that programs and political conflicts neither should nor could revert to the forms of earlier periods. *See* Hong Yu, *History Develops in Spirals,* HQ, No. 10, 1974, at 8-14.

95. Limited space precludes detailed analysis of policy changes in each of the areas of domestic policy outlined in part IV of this chapter. However, developments have been traced in each area and, with the partial exception of policies governing literature and the performing arts, the patterns of development are similar.

96. Only one policymaking round took place after that of 1970-71. This round had not been completed at the time of the arrest of the "gang of four."

97. As mentioned previously, however, rhetorical policies may not accurately reflect changes in formal or implemented policies. For example, media reports suggest (1) that policies adopted pursuant to the 1970-71 Program were more "revisionist" than was actually the case, and (2) that radical policies were adopted in 1973 and 1976 when they really were only being trumpeted by the press. This, together with the penchant of PRC spokesmen to employ both hyperbole and bipolar categories, produces a misleading view of the actual situation.

98. Although few formal policy directives were published during this period,

developments suggest that increasingly detailed instructions were being transmitted to cadres at lower levels of the system.

99. Advanced munitions, guidance systems, automated machinery, precision equipment, high-yield agriculture, and myriad other prerequisites of great power status rest on a modern science establishment. This point has been made in several commentaries published after the fall of the "gang of four." *See, e.g.,* Commentator, *Get Mobilized and Accelerate the Modernization of Science and Technology,* HQ, No. 7, 1977, at 3-5; and Qian Xuesen, *Science and Technology Must Catch and Surpass Advanced World Levels Before the End of the Century,* HQ, No. 7, 1977, at 14-18.

100. *See, e.g.,* Educational Revolution Group of Beijing University, *Insist on the Unity of Politics and Vocational Work, Have a Complete Grasp of Conditions for Enrollment,* RMRB, Mar. 4, 1972; and *Selecting and Sending Outstanding Young People to College,* RMRB, Mar. 4, 1972.

101. Educational Revolution Group of Beijing University, *Make a Success of Teaching Fundamental Theoretical Subjects of Natural Science,* HQ, No. 9, 1972, at 51-54.

102. Zhou Peiyuan, *Some Views on the Educational Revolution in University Science Faculties,* GMRB, Oct. 6, 1972. After the fall of the "gang of four," it was claimed that this article had been written at the express request of Zhou Enlai. *See Education Ministry on Gang's Sabotage of Research,* NCNA (Jan. 30, 1977), *in* FBIS, Jan. 31, 1977, at E11-13; Zhou Peiyuan, *Infinitely Cherish the Memory of Premier Zhou and Wrathfully Denounce the "Gang of Four,"* Peking Radio (Jan. 7, 1977), *in* FBIS, Jan. 12, 1977, at E12-14.

103. This theme and guidance for realizing Party objectives were expressed in several important articles. *See, e.g., Conscientiously Carry Out Education on the Line Toward Scientific and Research Personnel,* GMRB, Mar. 27, 1972; CCP Committee of the Jilin Medical College, *Arouse the Enthusiasm of Intellectuals in Carrying Out Scientific Research for the Revolution,* GMRB, Nov. 5, 1972.

104. *See CCP Committee of the Jilin Normal University Conscientiously Implements the Party's Policy Toward Intellectuals — Give Full Play to the Role of Veteran Teachers,* GMRB. May 10, 1972.

105. Examples include the March 10, 1973, Heilongjiang Radio broadcast reporting on the provincial conference to discuss scientific and technical work, *in* FBIS, Mar. 22, 1973, at G1-3; the Guangdong Radio report of April 14, 1973, on a similar conference; and *Party Committee of the Dalian Institute of Physics and Chemistry Thoroughly Implements the Victorious Line of Unity of the Ninth Party Congress — Strengthen the Unity of New and Old Research Workers, Push Forward the Development of Research Work,* GMRB, Apr. 19, 1973.

106. The radicals' insistence on the need to recruit students from the ranks of workers, peasants, and soldiers was designed purely for political effect since by 1973 there were very few other candidates available. The only partial exceptions were the children of the Party and state bureaucrats who enjoyed the benefits of access to better urban schools, but who should also have been more attuned to the current political line.

107. Such variation depended on the caliber of the school, faculty, and students, the disciplines being taught, distance from Peking and other administrative centers,

the political inclinations and ties of school administrators, and so forth.

108. Noteworthy articles and reports dealing with education policy during this period include: *A Thought Provoking Test Answer,* RMRB, Aug. 10, 1973; Zhu Yan, *The Significance of Reforming the System Used to Enroll College Students,* HQ, No. 8, 1973, at 9-13; *Give Priority to Selecting Young People with Practical Experience for College,* GMRB, Sep. 25, 1973; Revolutionary Committees of Qinghua and Beijing Universities, *Consolidate and Further Develop the Achievements of the Revolution in University Education,* HQ, No. 1, 1974, at 53-58; Revolutionary Committees of Qinghua and Beijing Universities, *The Movement to Criticize Lin Biao and Confucius Pushes the Educational Revolution to Greater Depths,* HQ, No. 5, 1974, at 65-69; and the collection of materials in American Consulate General, Hong Kong, CURRENT BACKGROUND [hereafter CB], No. 74-09.

109. Similarly, the topics of research often changed less dramatically than suggested by either contemporary articles or subsequent critiques of policy distortions by the "gang of four." These and similar tactics are discussed in Thomas Fingar, Pursuit of Political Interest: Scientists, Policy Makers, and Policy-Making in the PRC, *supra* note 51; and Thomas Fingar, Science Policy in the PRC: Priorities and Distinctions (December 1975) (unpublished paper prepared for the United States-China Relations Program, Stanford University).

110. Or at least they did at the level of formal policy. What actually happened differed from place to place.

111. Gao Yang, *Take the Criticism of Lin Biao and Confucius as the Driving Force in Conscientiously Conducting Student Enrollment Work of Institutions of Higher Learning,* GMRB, July 15, 1974. The article also stresses the leading role of the Party, and other themes of the counteroffensive launched by supporters of the 1970-71 Program in mid-1974. *See also* CCP Committee of the Shanghai Municipal Lixin Shipyard, *Deepen the Criticism of Lin Biao and Confucius and Do a Good Job in the Enrollment of Students for Institutions of Higher Learning,* GMRB, Aug. 6, 1974.

112. For discussions of alternative models in the educational realm, see *Consolidate the Dictatorship of the Proletariat and Run Well the Spare-Time University for Peasants,* GMRB, Mar. 14, 1975; CCP Committee of Zhaoyang Agricultural College, *School Should be a Tool for the Dictatorship of the Proletariat,* HQ, No. 5, 1975, at 64-69; Xu Ming, *Train New Men Who Will Fight to Consolidate the Dictatorship of the Proletariat,* RMRB, June 5, 1975; and the collection of articles on "Socialist Universities" in CB, No. 75-01.

113. Zhou Peiyuan had referred to this problem in his famous 1972 article on the differences between science and engineering. *See supra* note 102.

114. On the *Outline Report,* see *supra* note 87. For scathing criticism of nascent educational policy proposals, see Mass Criticism Groups of Beijing and Qinghua Universities, *supra* note 88.

A defense of these proposals can be found in Mass Criticism Group of the Ministry of Education, *A Big Poisonous Weed Which Opposed the Party and Created Chaos in the Schools — Criticizing the Article Entitled "The Orientation of the Revolution in Education Brooks No Alteration,"* RMRB, Oct. 21, 1977.

115. *See, e.g.,* the report on the meeting of the Chinese Academy of Sciences to

discuss the work of the Chinese Scientific and Technical University broadcast by Peking Radio on Aug. 18, 1977, *in* FBIS, Aug. 24, 1977, at E4-5; Lin Jinran, *We Must Push Education Forward,* HQ, No. 8, 1977, at 45-47; Editorial, *Build Up a Contingent of Scientists and Technicians of the World's First Rank,* GMRB, Sep. 25, 1977; Yuan Ding, *The Faithful Stand Firm in Times of Danger and Confusion — Thoroughly Settle Accounts With the Gang of Four for Their Crimes in Making False Charges Against and Persecuting Comrade Zhou Rongxin [Chou Jung-hsin],* RMRB, Sep. 15, 1977; Theoretical Group of the Ministry of Education, *It is Imperative to Run a Group of Key Schools Well,* GMRB, Jan. 13, 1978; Shanxi Provincial Education Bureau, *Correctly Handle Several Problems of Relationships in the Current Development of Education,* GMRB, Jan. 23, 1978. *See also* THOMAS FINGAR & GENEVIEVE DEAN, DEVELOPMENTS IN PRC SCIENCE AND TECHNOLOGY POLICY, JULY-SEPTEMBER 1977 (1977).

116. Articles in the category of character assassination include: Editorial Departments of Renmin Ribao, HONG QI, and Jiefangjun Bao, *A Great, Historic Victory,* RMRB, Oct. 25, 1976; Wei Jin, *Zhang Chunqiao Was a Trumpeter for Jiang Jieshi [Chiang Kai-Shek],* RMRB, Nov. 13, 1976, and *Jiang Qing is a Political Pickpocket Who Glorified Herself to Hoodwink the Public,* RMRB, Nov. 22, 1976.

Provincial leaders singled out for special condemnation included Ma Tianshui in Shanghai, and Weng Senhe in Zhejiang. The character of many commentaries during this period is captured in the first sentence of a broadcast denouncing Weng Senhe: "As already pointed out by our great leader and teacher Chairman Mao, Weng Senhe is a bad person." Zhejiang Radio (Dec. 31, 1976), *in* FBIS, Jan. 3, 1977, at G3-8.

117. For a typical early list of "gang of four" errors, *see* Zhu Jinping, *The Basic Principles for Socialist Revolution and Construction,* HQ, No. 1, 1977, at 91-95.

118. From a March 7, 1977, address by Xian Henghan [Hsien Heng-han], First Secretary of the Gansu Provincial CCP Committee, *Under the Banner of Chairman Mao, Closely Follow Chairman Hua, Deeply Expose and Relentlessly Criticize the Gang of Four, and Advance the Mass Movement to Learn from Daqing in Industry to a New Stage,* Gansu Radio (Mar. 8, 1977), *in* FBIS, Mar. 16, 1977, at M1-11, excerpt at M3.

119. One area in which specific declarations of intent were announced was foreign trade, particularly the export of raw materials and the import of equipment and technology. *See* Mass Criticism Group of the Ministry of Light Industry, *Relying on Our Own Efforts, Making Foreign Things Serve China,* RMRB, Nov. 16, 1976; *A Grave Step for Usurping Party and State Power — Exposing the Towering Crimes of the "Gang of Four" in Rampantly Opposing Chairman Mao and the Party Central Committee and in Viciously Attacking Premier Zhou in Foreign Trade,* Peking Radio (Jan. 13, 1977), *in* FBIS, Jan. 14, 1977, at E1-8.

120. Mao's speech was published in Renmin Ribao on December 26, 1976. Unofficial versions appeared during the Cultural Revolution, and comparison indicates that there was some, but not major, rewriting prior to official release — assuming that the earlier versions were accurate. *See* Stuart R. Schram, *Chairman Hua Edits Mao's Literary Heritage: "On the Ten Great Relationships,"* CHINA QUARTERLY, Mar. 1977, at 126-35.

121. Peking Radio broadcast sixteen commentaries, and Shanghai Radio carried

eleven. Translations of both series are available in FBIS, Feb. 7–Mar. 14, 1977. Typical directives on studying the speech include the text of a December 26 circular by the Qinghai Provincial CCP Committee, Qinghai Radio (Dec. 27, 1976), *in* FBIS, Jan. 4, 1977, at M1–2; and Anhui Radio (Dec. 29, 1976), *in* FBIS, Jan. 6, 1977, at G3–5.

122. *The Basic Policy for Building a Powerful Socialist Country is to Mobilize All Positive Factors,* Peking Radio (Jan. 31, 1977), *in* FBIS, Feb. 9, 1977, at E6, E8–9 (emphasis added). *See also The Basic Policy for Socialist Revolution and Construction,* Shanghai Radio (Feb. 8, 1977), *in* FBIS, Feb. 11, 1977, at E1–4.

123. *Chairman Hua Guofeng's Speech At the National Conference on Learning from Daqing in Industry,* PR, May 20, 1977, at 7, 12–13 (emphasis in original).

124. Yü Chiu-li [Yu Qiuli], *Mobilize the Whole Party and the Nation's Working Class and Strive to Build Daqing-Type Enterprises Throughout the Country: Report at National Conference on Learning from Daqing in Industry,* PR, May 27, 1977, at 5, 17–18 (emphasis in original).

125. One of the earliest charges leveled at the "gang of four" was that of equating veteran cadres with capitalist roaders. Several articles published since 1976, however, have proclaimed the fallacy of such an assertion and have stressed the importance of restoring experienced cadres to positions of respect and authority. The fact that frequent emphasis on the importance of rehabilitating cadres has been necessary suggests that implementation has been difficult. One reason for this difficulty may derive from opposition by persons elevated to cadre posts since 1966 who fear displacement by rehabilitated veterans. To assuage their concerns the regime proclaimed that people assigned to cadre posts in the past decade will not be removed automatically and will be given every opportunity to demonstrate that they are capable of handling assigned tasks.

*E.g.,* Xiang Qun, *The Fundamental Reversal of the Relationship Between Ourselves and the Enemy — Criticizing the Gang of Four's Serious Distortion of Chairman Mao's Directive that the Bourgeoisie is "Right Inside the Communist Party,"* RMRB, Mar. 14, 1977; Yang Fengzhun, Ye Yang, and Chen Zhong, *Correct the "Gang of Four's" Topsy-Turvey Interpretation of Right and Wrong in the Line on Cadres,* RMRB, Oct. 7, 1977; and Huo Shilian, *Continue to Firmly Grasp and Implement the Party's Policy on Cadres,* HQ, No. 5, 1978, at 19–23.

126. On the importance of leaders and leadership, see *Those in Positions of Leadership Should Do Leaders' Work,* RMRB, May 27, 1978.

127. The works by Mao singled out for special attention are *On the Correct Handling of Contradictions Among the People,* and *Speech at the Chinese Communist Party's National Conference on Propaganda Work.* Both works date from 1957 and are included in Volume 5 of SELECTED WORKS OF MAO TSE-TUNG (1977) edited under the direction of Hua Guofeng.

On Party policy toward intellectuals, *see, e.g.,* Xiang Ping, *Intellectuals are an Important Force in Socialist Revolution and Construction,* Peking Radio (May 27, 1977), *in* FBIS, May 31, 1977, at E7–9; Shen Keding, *Refuting the Gang of Four's Theory of "The Stinking Ninth Category,"* HQ, No. 7, 1977, at 55–62; Mass Criticism Group of Sha'anxi Normal University, *Intellectuals Must be Treated Correctly — Criticizing the Gang of Four for Equating Intellectuals with the Bourgeoisie,* HQ, No. 7, 1977, at 63-67; and *Deng Xiaoping's Opening Speech to the National Science Conference,* RMRB, Mar. 22, 1978.

128. *See, e.g.,* CCP Central Committee, *Circular on Holding a National Science Conference,* PR, Sep. 30, 1977, at 6-11; Fang Yi, *A New Stage in the Development of China's Socialist Cause of Science and Technology,* RMRB, Mar. 29, 1978; Lin Pinglan, *Sichuan Resolutely Implements Party Policy on Intellectuals,* RMRB, Mar. 12, 1978; and those sources cited with commentary in GENEVIEVE DEAN & THOMAS FINGAR, DEVELOPMENTS IN PRC SCIENCE AND TECHNOLOGY POLICY, OCTOBER-DECEMBER 1977 (1978).

129. *E.g.,* Shi Qiao, *By Inciting Anarchism, [the Gang of Four] Aimed at Subverting the Dictatorship of the Proletariat,* HQ, No. 5, 1978, at 38-44; and *Liu Xiyao's [Liu Hsi-yao's] Report to the National Education Conference,* Peking Radio (June 10, 1978), *in* FBIS, June 15, 1978, at E6-17. *See also* Hua Guofeng, *Political Report to the Eleventh National Congress of the Communist Party of China,* PR, Aug. 26, 1977, at 23-57.

130. *See* Editorial, *The Work of Expanding Agricultural Scientific Research Brooks Not a Moment's Delay,* RMRB, May 7, 1978; *The NCNA Report on the Closing of the National Education Work Conference,* Peking Radio (May 16, 1978), *in* FBIS, May 18, 1978, at E1-4; and CCP Central Committee, *Circular on Holding a National Science Conference, supra* note 128.

131. On cadre policy and Party schools, see the *Central Committee Decision on Running Party Schools at Various Levels* and the related speeches by Hua Guofeng and Ye Jianying *in* RMRB, Oct. 10, 1977. *See also* the eighteen lectures on Party building broadcast by Peking Domestic Service in July 1977, and rebroadcast in early 1978. The lectures are translated in issues of FBIS between July 7 and July 27, 1977. On the rebroadcast of these lectures, see Peking Radio (Dec. 31, 1977), *in* FBIS, Jan. 19, 1978, at E6.

132. A large number of sources treat this topic. *E.g.,* CCP Central Committee, *Circular on Holding the Tenth National Congress of the Chinese Communist Youth League (May 4, 1978),* Peking Radio (May 3, 1978), *in* FBIS, May 4, 1978, at E1-6; All-China Federation of Trade Unions, *Circular on Convening the Ninth National Trade Union Congress (May 1, 1978),* Peking Radio (Apr. 30, 1978), *in* FBIS, May 5, 1978, at E15-19; and Fang Yi's Report at the National Science Conference (Mar. 28, 1978), RMRB, Mar. 29, 1978.

133. State Planning Commission, *Great Guiding Principle for Socialist Construction,* RMRB, Sep. 12, 1977 (emphasis added; paragraph order altered).

134. Yu Qiuli, *The Situation with Regard to the Development of Our Country's National Economy,* RMRB, Oct. 25, 1977.

135. Typical articles include: Mass Criticism Group of the Ministry of Petroleum and Chemical Industries, *Bury the Big Stick of "Control, Check, and Suppress" Together with the "Gang of Four,"* RMRB, Feb. 15, 1977; and Mass Criticism Group of the State Planning Commission, *A Counterrevolutionary Force of Usurping Party and State Power—Commenting on the "Gang of Four's" "Criticism" of "The Twenty Points,"* RMRB, July 16, 1977.

136. Theoretical Group of Beijing Normal University, *The Gang of Four's Betrayal*

of Chairman Mao's Instructions on the Question of Theory, Peking Radio (Feb. 21, 1977), in FBIS, Feb. 23, 1977, at E1-5; and Xue Muqiao, Criticize the "Gang of Four's" Reactionary Fallacies on the Question of Bourgeois Rights, HQ, No. 11, 1977, at 35-42.

137. Theoretical Group of the Ministry of Finance, *Accumulate More Funds to Build a Powerful Socialist Country,* HQ, No. 8, 1977, at 70-73; and Mass Criticism Group of the Ministry of Finance, *The Maggots Within Socialism—A Criticism of the Crimes of the "Gang of Four" in Sabotaging Socialist Accumulation and State Finances,* Peking Radio (Jan. 26, 1977), in FBIS, Feb. 1, 1977, at E3-5.

138. Mass Criticism Group of the First Ministry of Machine Building, *Penetratingly Expose and Relentlessly Criticize the "Gang of Four," Accelerate the Realization of Agricultural Mechanization,* HQ, No. 1, 1977, at 102-107; and Chin Hechen, *Develop Agricultural Mechanization on the Basis of Self-Reliance* (Speech at the Third National Conference on Agricultural Mechanization), Peking Radio (Jan. 5, 1978), in FBIS, Jan. 9, 1978, at E1-11. See also *Report on the National Financial and Banking Conference,* Peking Radio (Mar. 25, 1977), in FBIS, Mar. 28, 1977 at E8-11.

139. Editorial, *It is Necessary to Greatly Develop Commune and Production Brigade Run Enterprises,* RMRB, Apr. 4, 1978. Articles have also stressed the importance of sideline production by households, see, e.g., *It is Necessary to Develop Sideline Occupations on a Large Scale in Rural Areas,* RMRB, Mar. 29, 1978.

140. Guangdong Provincial CCP Committee, *Grasp the Main Theme, Persist in Education in the Basic Line,* HQ, No. 5, 1977, at 64-69. On this and other points relating to rural policy, especially economic policy, see the collection of delegates' speeches at the Second National Conference on Learning from Dazhai in Agriculture prepared as a supplement to the Jan. 21, 1977 edition of FBIS.

141. Li Qiang, *Distinguish Between Right and Wrong in Line and Actively Develop Socialist Foreign Trade,* HQ, No. 10, 1977, at 31-38; and Wu Lü, *Speaking of "Importism,"* RMRB, Nov. 14, 1977.

142. See the companion chapter by John Lewis, and *It is Necessary to Strengthen Defense Construction on the Basis of Developing Economic Construction,* Peking Radio (Feb. 5, 1977), in FBIS, Feb. 7, 1977, at E5-9.

143. *See, e.g.,* Mass Criticism Group of the Ministry of Education, *A Big Poisonous Weed Which Opposed the Party and Created Chaos Among Schools,* RMRB, Oct. 21, 1977; and Deng Xiaoping, *Speech at the National Education Work Conference (Apr. 22, 1978),* RMRB, Apr. 26, 1978.

144. Examples include: Liu Xiyao's report at the National Education Work Conference (Apr. 22, 1978), FBIS, June 15, 1978, at E6-17; and Theoretical Group of the Chinese Academy of Sciences, *To Know the Pine's Great Moral Fortitude, One Must Wait Until the Snow Melts—Reverse the Gang of Four's Slander of the "Outline Report,"* RMRB, June 30, 1977.

145. *See* Science and Technology Commission for National Defense, *Premier Zhou Made Painstaking Efforts to Develop Advanced Technology for National Defense,* Peking Radio (Jan. 20, 1977), in FBIS, Jan. 21, 1977, at E1-4. For a more extensive discussion of this strategy and approach, see Thomas Fingar, *supra* note 51, at 22-25.

146. Mao Chiyong, *Respond to Chairman Mao's Call and Modernize Science and Technology as Soon as Possible,* Hunan Ribao (July 22, 1977), in FBIS, July 29, 1977,

at H1-2. Other examples include: Theoretical Group of the Chinese Academy of Sciences, *Scientific Research Should Advance Ahead of Production and Construction*, Peking Radio (May 18, 1977), *in* FBIS, May 26, 1977, at E11-17.

147. Examples include Fang Yi, *Report on the Situation in Science and Education*, RMRB, Dec. 30, 1977; and Theoretical Group of the Chinese Academy of Sciences, *A Shocking Struggle in Scientific and Technical Circles*, RMRB, Mar. 9, 1977.

148. For specific developments, assessment, and documentation, see the quarterly summaries entitled DEVELOPMENTS IN PRC SCIENCE AND TECHNOLOGY POLICY prepared by Thomas Fingar and Genevieve Dean since the autumn of 1976. The summaries are published by the United States-China Relations Program, Stanford University. The major policy statements of 1977 and 1978 are the Central Committee's *Circular on Holding a National Science Conference*, RMRB, Sep. 23, 1977; and the speeches and reports of Deng Xiaoping and Fang Yi at the National Science Conference in March 1978. Deng's address was published in Renmin Ribao on Mar. 22, 1978. Fang's report, entitled *A New Stage in the Development of China's Socialist Cause of Science and Technology*, appeared in Renmin Ribao on Mar. 29, 1978.

149. Deng Xiaoping, *Opening Address at the National Science Conference*, RMRB, Mar. 22, 1978.

150. All of the policies here can be found in the Central Committee's September 18 circular and/or published documents of the National Science Conference. Sources indicating that the policies were already implemented will be listed for each point. On research facilities, see Peking Radio (Aug. 18, 1977), *in* FBIS, Aug. 24, 1977, at E5-6; *Chairman Hua Calls on Us to Advance Toward Modernization of Science and Technology — On the Work Meeting of the Chinese Academy of Sciences*, RMRB, July 7, 1977; and Liaoning Rado (Sep. 26, 1977), *in* FBIS, Sep. 30, 1977, at L4.

151. Mass Criticism Group of the Ministry of Education, *The Political Struggle Around the Question of Basic Theory in the Natural Sciences*, GMRB, Jan. 16, 1977; and Yu Wen, *Vigorously Strengthen Basic Scientific Research*, RMRB, Oct. 26, 1977.

152. Editorial, *Build up a Contingent of Scientists and Technicians of the World's First Rank*, GMRB, Sep. 25, 1977.

153. Liaoning Radio (Sep. 26, 1977), *in* FBIS, Sep. 30, 1977, at L3; and Anhui Radio (Sep. 24, 1977), *in* FBIS, Sep. 26, 1977, at G3.

154. Peking Radio (Apr. 19, 1977), *in* FBIS, Apr. 25, 1977, at E23-25; and Peking Radio (Dec. 22, 1977), *in* FBIS, Dec. 22, 1977, at E12.

155. Peking Radio (Jan. 23, 1978), *in* FBIS, Jan. 27, 1978, at E13-14.

156. *Do We Need to Import Advanced Technology?* Peking Radio (Oct. 29, 1977), *in* FBIS, Nov. 3, 1977, at E3-5; and NCNA (May 27, 1978), *in* FBIS, June 1, 1978, at A4-5.

157. Editorial, *supra* note 152.

158. The principal published speeches at the conference are those of Deng Xiaoping, *supra* note 143; and Liu Xiyao, *supra* note 144.

159. *See, e.g.*, Theoretical Group of the Ministry of Education, *It is Imperative to Run a Group of Key Schools Well*, GMRB, Jan. 13, 1978; and Commentator, *Restore Order from Disorder, Conduct Education Work Well*, HQ, No. 6, 1978, at 11-15.

160. Peking Radio (Oct. 20, 1977), *in* FBIS, Oct. 21, 1977, at E1-7; Peking

Radio (June 13, 1978), *in* FBIS, June 19, 1978, at E16-19.

161. Commentator, *It is Essential to Create the Social Atmosphere of Respecting the People's Teachers,* Sha'anxi Radio (Oct. 9, 1977), *in* FBIS, Oct. 14, 1977, at M4-5; and Lin Pinglan, *supra* note 128.

162. Yuan Ting, *Explode Jiang Qing's Plot of Criticizing the "Absolute Authority of a Teacher,"* Peking Radio (Feb. 28, 1977), *in* FBIS, Mar. 7, 1977, at E14-17; and He Xiaoxiao, *Criticize the Fallacy of Making Revolution Without Teachers,* Peking Radio (Feb. 28, 1977), *in* FBIS, Mar. 11, 1977, at K9-10.

163. NCNA (May 15, 1978), *in* FBIS, May 15, 1978, at E21; and Liu Xiyao, *supra* note 144.

164. Shanxi Provincial Education Bureau, *supra* note 115; and Theoretical Group of the Ministry of Education, *supra* note 115.

165. Peking Radio (Oct. 19, 1977), *in* FBIS, Oct. 25, 1977, at E19-20; and NCNA (Jan. 21, 1978), *in* FBIS, Jan. 23, 1978, at E8-9.

166. *Earnestly Grasp Well the Running of Different Types of Schools,* GMRB, Dec. 18, 1977. Briefly, July 21 Universities are to be full-time 2-3 year programs funded and staffed by industrial enterprises. Students will be drawn from the pool of workers in the sponsoring enterprise; graduates will be eligible for posts requiring specialized technical training. May 7 Colleges are the analogue in rural areas. Locally funded, these schools will provide instruction in agricultural subjects on a full- or part-time basis.

167. Liu Xiyao, *supra* note 144.

168. Policies in the aggregate appear to have evolved more or less as indicated by the following curve:

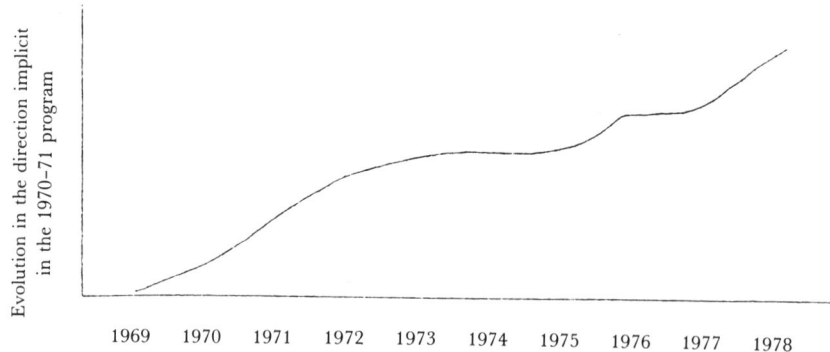

169. The importance of rules and "style" of political behavior were illustrated by publication of Mao's 1962 *Talk at an Enlarged Working Conference Convened by the Central Committee of the CCP.* This document and related commentary spell out the importance of democratic centralism and observance of Party discipline. Mao's address was first published in RMRB, July 1, 1978. Typical commentaries include Editorial, *Powerful Ideological Weapon for Fulfilling the General Task of the New Period,* HQ, No. 7, 1978, at 38-42; and Editorial, *Conscientiously Implement Democratic Centralism,* RMRB, July 2, 1978.

# 2
# The Domestic Politics of China's Global Posture, 1973-78

*Harry Harding*

## Introduction

The transformation of Chinese foreign policy in the post-Cultural Revolution decade (1968-78) ranks among the most important developments in world politics in the post-war era, comparable to the onset of the Cold War in the 1940s, or the emergence of the Sino-Soviet dispute in the 1960s. At the height of the Cultural Revolution, Chinese foreign policy was characterized by intense hostility toward both the Soviet Union and the United States, relative isolation from economic and cultural contacts with foreign countries, suspicion of virtually all established governments in the Third World, and friendship toward only a handful of sympathetic governments and political movements. In the early 1970s, however, Chinese foreign policy underwent a sweeping reorientation. The Soviet Union was identified, first implicitly, and then explicitly, as China's principal enemy. To counter the Soviet threat, Peking began the gradual modernization of its armed forces, engaged in rapprochement with the United States, improved its relations with Japan and Western Europe, and encouraged all Third World governments, regardless of their domestic political orientations, to join in opposition to Moscow's alleged drive for global hegemony. Increasingly, too, China came to regard the expansion of

---

Support for this research project was provided by the United States Department of State (Contract No. 1722-620241), and by the Stanford University Arms Control and Disarmament Program. Some of the initial research was conducted while the author was a National Fellow at the Hoover Institution on War, Revolution and Peace. Frank Hawke provided valuable research assistance.

Harry Harding is associate professor of political science at Stanford University. He earned his A.B. at Princeton University in 1967, his M.A. at Stanford University in 1969, and his Ph.D. at Stanford University in 1974.

scientific and economic contacts with the West as a useful instrument for promoting its own economic development.

In little more than ten years, in short, China's "global posture"—defined here as its general diagnosis of the international situation, its relationship with the two superpowers, and its military and strategic policy—experienced fundamental change. Gone was Peking's earlier emphasis on world revolution. Instead, China had become increasingly concerned with maintaining the international status quo against a perceived Soviet threat.

Not surprisingly, this reorientation aroused considerable debate and controversy within the highest levels of China's leadership. Sweeping change is always difficult to understand and accept, particularly when, as in this instance, it runs counter to long-standing policies and deeply-held ideological beliefs. Furthermore, preparations for the succession to Mao Zedong had generated intense conflict within the Chinese elite during the late 1960s and early 1970s, so that it was only logical that the changes in Chinese foreign policy would become closely intertwined with this struggle for power. China's post–Cultural Revolution global posture thus encountered substantial opposition—not only from those who sincerely disagreed with its basic premises, but also from those who feared that it would threaten their own personal or organizational interests, and from those who hoped that criticism of China's new foreign policy would further their quest for political power.[1]

This chapter attempts to provide a history and interpretation of an important segment of this debate: the five years between the Tenth Party Congress in August 1973 and the Fifth National People's Congress in February 1978. These two national meetings served as important turning points in the evolution of China's post–Cultural Revolution foreign policy. It was at the Tenth Party Congress that radical elements in the Chinese leadership, later known as the "gang of four," began actively to criticize the course of Chinese foreign policy since the Sino-Soviet border clashes of 1969. And it was at the Fifth National People's Congress that Chinese leaders concluded, at least temporarily, an intense discussion of the proper pace of military modernization, and accelerated their efforts to secure diplomatic recognition from the United States.

Debate over China's global posture between these two meetings occurred in a series of interconnected and overlapping rounds, during which the issues at stake became ever more narrowly defined. In Round One, between 1973 and 1975, Chinese leaders considered the suitability of the "theory of the three worlds," proposed by Mao Zedong and elaborated by Deng Xiaoping, as the conceptual basis of China's overall foreign policy. In Round Two, conducted almost simultaneously, Peking attempted to define the nature of the Soviet threat, and to identify a suitable coping strategy. In Round Three, between 1974 and 1977, the principal issue concerned the desirability of the modernization and professionalization of the People's Liberation Army (PLA). Round Four, which ended with the approval of the Fifth Five-Year Plan at the Fifth National People's Congress in early 1978, dealt more specifically with the pace at which military modernization should proceed.

Some of these rounds have already been the subject of Western scholarly research. Merle Goldman and Kenneth Lieberthal have analyzed the debates over policy toward the Soviet Union and the necessity for military modernization that were reflected in allegorical articles in the Chinese press between 1973 and 1976.[2] Jonathan Pollack, Paul Godwin, Ellis Joffe, and Gerald Segal have discussed the debates over military modernization since the death of Mao and the purge of the "gang of four."[3]

While all these studies have made important contributions to our understanding of China's current global posture, many questions remain unanswered and there is still much to learn from another look at the domestic politics of Chinese foreign policy in the mid-1970s. The work of Goldman and Lieberthal relied almost exclusively on the articles about Chinese history published during the campaign to criticize Lin Biao and Confucius (the *Pi Lin Pi Kong* campaign) in 1973 and 1974—articles that ostensibly dealt with the struggle between "Confucianists" and "Legalists" in China's past, but which also spoke allegorically on such contemporary issues as national defense and military strategy. Crucial as they are, these materials must be supplemented with other types of information, including the criticisms of Lin Biao's military strategy in 1974-75, the attacks on Deng Xiaoping's views on military modernization in 1976, and the criticisms of the "gang of four" in 1977 and 1978. These additional sources of evidence, particularly the criticisms of the "gang of four," call into question some of Goldman's and Lieberthal's conclusions.[4]

Similarly, the research on Chinese strategic policy and military modernization since the death of Mao needs to be placed in a broader context. Recent articles have concentrated on the evolution of China's military strategy and doctrine since the purge of the "gang of four," and have devoted insufficient attention to the controversy that strategic issues have generated. Furthermore, they have not fully examined the relationship between the discussions of military modernization in 1977-78 and the earlier debates over military policy between 1973 and 1976.

This chapter, then, offers a general overview of the domestic politics of China's global posture between 1973 and early 1978. It will deal with each of the four policymaking rounds in turn, attempting to show the complex interrelations among them. It concludes by considering the implications of the events of the mid-1970s for a more general understanding of the Chinese foreign policymaking process.

## I. Round One (1973–75):
## General Conceptions of Foreign Policy

*"Countries Want Independence, Nations Want Liberation, People Want Revolution"*

The Tenth Party Congress, held in August 1973, marked an important turning point in public discussions of China's global posture. In his political report to the Congress, Premier Zhou Enlai advocated a foreign policy that combined, somewhat uncomfortably, two principal themes. First, Zhou depicted an emerging struggle between the poor and developing countries of the Third World and the American and Soviet superpowers as the main feature of international politics. In Zhou's words, the "awakening and growth of the Third World" was "a major event in contemporary international relations." The Third World, Zhou declared, "has strengthened its unity in the struggle against hegemonism and power politics of the superpowers and is playing an ever more significant role in international affairs." Zhou placed particular emphasis on the efforts of Third World countries to "win and defend national independence and safeguard state sovereignty and national resources" against threats from the United States and the Soviet Union.[5]

In keeping with this analysis, Zhou endorsed a broad united front against the two superpowers that would include virtually all Third World countries, regardless of their social system or political structure. He proposed that the people of China "strengthen our unity with the proletariat and the oppressed people and *nations* of the whole world and with all *countries* subject to imperialist aggression, subversion, interference, control, or bullying" (emphasis added). This international united front would be directed entirely against international forces—"imperialism, colonialism, and neocolonialism"—rather than against nonprogressive governments or leaders within Third World countries. This first theme of Zhou's report on foreign policy was summed up in the slogan, "Countries want independence, nations want liberation, and the people want revolution." The order in which these three items appeared strongly suggests an emphasis on the Third World's common struggle for independence and sovereignty, rather than on revolutionary movements within Third World countries.

The second theme of Zhou's report concerned China's policy of gradual rapprochement with the United States. The U.S. withdrawal from Vietnam, and even more importantly, President Nixon's visit to China in February 1972, had demonstrated to many Chinese leaders that the United States could serve as a useful counterweight to the Soviet Union. As a result, although Zhou still described the hegemonism of both superpowers as the major "cause of world intranquility," he emphasized the tensions between Moscow and Washington produced by their "contention for hegemony." In Zhou's analysis, the United States was a power "on the decline," while the USSR was expanding its influence in Asia, Africa, and the Middle East. This made it possible for China to engage in "necessary compromises" with the United States—manipulating the tensions between the United States and the Soviet Union in ways that could increase China's security against the USSR.

Turning from a global to a regional analysis, Zhou acknowledged that the United States now posed a lesser military threat to China than did the Soviet Union. While calling on China to be "fully prepared against any war of aggression that [U.S.] imperialism may launch," he placed particular emphasis on preparations against "surprise attack on our country by Soviet revisionist social-imperialism." Zhou's scathing criticism of Moscow's policy toward China stood in sharp contrast to his admission that, as a result of the Nixon visit, "Sino-U.S. relations have been improved to some extent." These factors, too, made it possible to include the United States in an informal united front against the Soviet Union.

Significantly, Zhou Enlai's report did not receive the unanimous support of all delegates to the Tenth Party Congress. The Congress also heard a report on the revision of the Party Constitution, delivered by Wang Hongwen, the newly elected Party vice-chairman who would later be identified as a member of the "gang of four."[6] Wang's address contained only two paragraphs on foreign affairs, compared to the eleven paragraphs in Zhou Enlai's broader discussion of Party policy. Nonetheless, Wang was still able, in just those few sentences, to express clear reservations about China's emerging relationship with the United States and its policy toward the Third World.

Unlike Zhou, Wang Hongwen made no reference, either implicit or explicit, to the recent improvement in Sino-American relations. Indeed, Wang seemed to reject any suggestion that the United States presented a lesser threat to China than the Soviet Union. He described the threats posed by the two superpowers in identical terms, declaring that "we must, without fail, prepare well against any war of aggression and guard against surprise attack by *imperialism and social-imperialism*" (emphasis added). In so doing, Wang appeared to deny an essential premise behind China's policy of rapprochement with the United States.

At the same time, Wang also offered a substantially different interpretation of the international united front against the two superpowers than did Zhou Enlai. Wang called on China to "stand together with the proletariat and revolutionary people of the world," but did not propose unity with any "nations" or "countries," as Zhou had done. Furthermore, Wang described the targets of this united front as "imperialism, modern revisionism and all *reaction*" (emphasis added), with "reaction" very likely referring to conservative governments in the Third World. Wang's report did not contain Zhou's formula, "countries want independence, nations want liberation, and the people want revolution," which may have assigned a lower priority to revolutionary movements than Wang desired.

Other evidence of controversy and dissent was provided in two passages in Zhou's report that implicitly defended Chinese foreign policy against unnamed critics. One insisted that Lenin's theses on imperialism and proletarian revolution "remain the theoretical basis guiding our thinking today." The other defended the new Sino-American relationship by drawing a distinction between "necessary compromises between revolutionary countries and imperialist countries" and the "collusion and compromise between Soviet revisionism and U.S. imperialism." These passages suggested that Chinese post–Cultural Revolution foreign policy had been criticized for departing from Leninist principles, and for engaging in unprincipled compromises with the United States. But who might these critics have been?

One possibility, of course, was that Zhou was responding to criticisms levied against Peking by the Albanians. As early as November 1972, Albanian Defense Minister Balluku had cautioned the Chinese against drawing any distinctions between "imperialism" and "revisionism," reasserting Albania's belief that "one is as dangerous as the other."[7] In mid-1977, nearly four years after the Tenth Party Congress, the Albanian newspaper *Zeri i Popullit* attacked Chinese foreign policy as incompatible with the basic theses of Leninism because it failed to distinguish between progressive and reactionary governments in the Third World.[8] It is highly likely that similar criticisms had been issued privately to the Chinese well before 1977 and that Zhou's report was an attempt to refute them.

It is also possible, although by no means certain, that some of China's more radical leaders may have echoed Albanian doubts about the ideological pedigree of Peking's global posture. Foreign Minister Huang Hua charged in 1977 that "there seemed to be a tacit agreement between the 'gang of four' and the Albanians to simultaneously attack Chairman Mao's line in foreign affairs and Premier Zhou, who carried out this line, inside and outside China."[9] If such an agreement had been reached by the time of the Tenth Party Congress, then it is possible that the radicals' objections to Chinese foreign policy went far beyond those expressed publicly in

Wang Hongwen's report, and questioned the very doctrinal underpinnings of China's new global posture.

## The "Theory of the Three Worlds"

These objections did not, however, prevent a further, and even more controversial, restatement of China's foreign policy in April 1974. At a special session of the United Nations General Assembly, Deng Xiaoping presented an analysis of the international situation which, it was later said, had first been suggested by Mao Zedong in a conversation with a foreign head of state two months before.[10]

According to Deng, "all the political forces in the world have undergone drastic division and realignment" since the 1950s and early 1960s. The Soviet Union had degenerated into "social-imperialism," and, as a result, the socialist camp was "no longer in existence." The global influence of the United States had peaked, and the "Western imperialist bloc" had begun to disintegrate. Moreover, decolonization had produced a large number of new nations in Asia, Africa, and Latin America, which were "playing an ever greater role in international affairs." This process of division and realignment had produced a world divided into three parts: a "First World," consisting of the United States and the Soviet Union; a "Second World," comprising Japan, Australia, New Zealand, and the developed countries of Eastern and Western Europe; and a "Third World," including all the developing countries, among them China itself. The resistance of both the Third and Second Worlds against the "hegemonism" of the two superpowers had become, in this analysis, the major feature of contemporary world politics.

This "theory of the three worlds," as it would later come to be known, was quite similar to the world view presented by Zhou Enlai at the Tenth Party Congress the previous summer. But it contained several features that, from the radicals' point of view, made it even more objectionable than Zhou's earlier formulation. For one thing, the theory of the three worlds explicitly denied the continued existence of a socialist camp, and strongly suggested that the principal contradiction in international politics was no longer that between socialism and imperialism. Second, the theory proposed an alignment of the remaining socialist states not simply with the Third World, but also with the developed Western capitalist nations, in opposition to the United States and the Soviet Union. Moreover, the theory described a world in which the principal actors were established nations and governments, and assigned virtually no role to revolutionary forces and national liberation movements.

Resistance to the theory of the three worlds was evident on two occasions in 1975: at the Fourth National People's Congress in January, and at a high-level meeting of foreign affairs officials the following March. Zhou Enlai's report to the Congress once again contained a long passage on foreign policy that restated and defended China's post–Cultural Revolution global posture. While Zhou did not explicitly mention the theory of the three worlds, he did provide implicit endorsement by describing China as a "developing socialist country belonging to the Third World" and by praising the "countries and people of the Second World" for their struggle against the superpowers. He reiterated his call for a broad international united front by stating that the Chinese people "must ally ourselves with all the forces in the world that can be allied with," presumably including nonprogressive Third World governments and Western capitalist regimes, in opposition to "colonialism, imperialism, and hegemonism." And Zhou repeated the formula that "countries want independence, nations want liberation, and the people want revolution."[11]

In contrast, neither the new State Constitution adopted at the Congress nor Zhang Chunqiao's report on the document, can be considered a strong endorsement of China's post–Cultural Revolutionary foreign policy. The preamble of the new constitution did declare China's opposition to the hegemonism of the two superpowers, and expressed support for "all oppressed people and oppressed nations" in their struggle against the "imperialist and social-imperialist policies of aggression and war." But it did not mention the theory of the three worlds, as would the constitution adopted in February 1978, nor did it include Zhou's formula about independence, liberation, and revolution.[12]

Zhang Chunqiao's report on the new constitution offered even less support for Chinese foreign policy. Zhang ignored most of the provisions on foreign policy in the preamble of the constitution, referring only to the pledge that China would "never be a superpower." He then went on to add merely that China would always unite with the people of all countries in the "common struggle to abolish the system of exploitation of man by man over the face of the globe." Compared to Wang Hongwen's statement at the Tenth Party Congress, Zhang's remarks did not express open opposition to Zhou's presentation of China's global posture, but neither did they provide the slightest endorsement.[13]

A second instance of dissent over China's official world view appears to have occurred in March 1975, at a meeting concerning the implementation of the *Pi Lin Pi Kong* campaign within the Ministry of Foreign Affairs. According to documents released by the Taiwan government, Jiang Qing made a speech to the meeting criticizing both the policy of forming a united front of established Third World governments and the policy of improving relations with the Second World and the United States. Jiang cited Zhou's formula that "countries want independence, nations want liberation, and the people want revolution," but asserted that the "people's revolution," rather than liberation or independence, should be the "focal point of the argument." She went on to warn against rapprochment with the West at the expense of relations with the Third World. "We do not have any 'white friends,' 'big friends,' or 'rich friends,'" Jiang declared. Instead, she insisted, China should place the "emphasis in our diplomacy on our 'black friends,' 'little friends,' and 'poor friends.'"[14]

Important as these two instances of open disagreement are, the most persuasive evidence of debate over China's post–Cultural Revolution global posture stems from acts of omission rather than acts of commission. Zhang Chunqiao's refusal to support Zhou Enlai's policy at the Fourth National People's Congress suggests such a strategy. Another remarkable example concerns the failure of the Chinese press between 1974 and 1976 to endorse the theory of the three worlds announced by Deng Xiaoping in 1974. A policy announcement of this importance would ordinarily have been followed by a long series of exegeses in the Chinese press, yet in the three and a half years between Deng's speech to the United Nations in April 1974 and the full exegesis published in November 1977, only one major explanation of this view of the world appeared: an article by Ren Guping in *Renmin Ribao*, in October 1974.[15] Other than this, the theory of the three worlds, which would be described in 1977 as one of Mao's most important contributions to Marxism-Leninism, received no further elaboration.

In summary, then, the evidence outlined above suggests that China's general global posture aroused substantial opposition, particularly from the radical leaders later known as the "gang of four," and that they used their influence over the Chinese news media and in the Politburo to keep explanations of the theory of the three worlds out of the press and constitution. Like the Albanians, the radicals probably objected to three implications of China's new global posture: (1) that the United States presented less of a threat than the Soviet Union and that compromises could be made to gain Washington's participation in a united front against Moscow; (2) that all Third World countries, regardless of social system, could be a part of the same united front and that China would be more interested in mobilizing their opposition to hegemonism than in promoting domestic revolution; and (3) that the Second World, despite its remaining economic and political contradictions with the Third World, and despite the capitalist economies of Western Europe and Japan, could also be an important ally of China in opposing the Soviet Union. As an article on the theory of the three worlds put it in November 1977, the "gang of four":

opposed China's support to the third world, opposed China's effort to unite with all forces that can be united, and opposed our dealing blows at the most dangerous enemy. They vainly tried to sabotage the building of an international united front against hegemonism and disrupt China's antihegemonist struggle, doing Soviet social-imperialism a good turn. To a certain extent, their disruptive activities had a deleterious effect, but our Party and government have unswervingly adhered to the revolutionary line in foreign affairs formulated by Chairman Mao.[16]

While the radicals' objections to the theory of the three worlds are fairly easy to understand, identifying their counterproposal presents a more difficult problem. If Albanian views on the international situation provide any guide, it seems likely that the radicals sought to maintain the Chinese world view articulated by Lin Biao, first in 1965 and again in 1969,[17] that both superpowers should be considered China's enemies, and that the united front against them should be based on national liberation movements, Maoist political parties, and progressive governments in the Third World—not on an unprincipled assemblage of Second and Third World governments.

## II. Round Two (1973-75): China's Response to the Soviet Threat

*Controversy over Sino-Soviet Relations*

From Peking's point of view, Sino-Soviet relations in late 1973 presented a combination of threat and opportunity. On the one hand, the Soviet Union continued to improve, if not expand, its military forces along the Sino-Soviet border, while the Chinese were still constrained by a freeze on military procurement imposed after the purge of Lin Biao in 1971. On the other hand, in June 1973, the Soviets made an important diplomatic overture to the Chinese, designed to coincide with the opening of the Tenth Party Congress. Moscow proposed that the two countries agree to base their relations on the principle of "peaceful coexistence," that they sign a nonaggression treaty to prohibit the use or threat of any kind of force, and that their leaders hold a summit conference to discuss further improvement of relations. This proposal supplemented earlier Soviet suggestions that the two countries expand scientific, cultural, and economic relations, and Soviet acceptance, in principle, of the Chinese demand that the riverine boundary between the two countries run along the middle of the navigable channel, rather than along the Chinese bank.[18]

The combination of threat and opportunity produced strong pressures in China for a reassessment of Peking's policy toward the Soviet Union.

Moscow's proposal apparently stirred up some controversy among Chinese leaders, for Zhou Enlai's report to the Tenth Party Congress failed to mention, let alone respond to, the overture. Instead, Zhou said vaguely that the "Sino-Soviet boundary question should be settled peacefully through negotiations free from any threat," and went on to suggest that Moscow, as a sign of "good faith," might "withdraw [its] armed forces from Czechoslovakia or the People's Republic of Mongolia and return the four northern islands to Japan."[19] Since Zhou made these proposals while discussing the Soviet Union's global policy, they were not necessarily preconditions for settlement of the Sino-Soviet border dispute. Nonetheless, Zhou's reply did not seem encouraging, leading Brezhnev to complain in September that the Chinese did "not even deign to respond" to Moscow's offers.[20]

It was only in late October 1973, in an interview with C. L. Sulzberger of *The New York Times*, that Zhou Enlai finally replied publicly to the Soviet offer. Zhou claimed that, at their meeting at the Peking airport in September 1969, he and Prime Minister Kosygin had agreed to negotiate a new border treaty, relying upon existing treaties as a basis. According to Zhou the two leaders had also reached an understanding that, in the meantime, the two countries would accept the existing lines of control, avoid armed clashes, and, most significantly, withdraw their forces from all the disputed areas along the border. Zhou said that the Soviet Union had not lived up to this agreement in the intervening four years and implied that the June 1973 Soviet package would not be acceptable until the Soviets honored the earlier understanding.[21]

Zhou's interview not only revealed China's belated response to the Soviet offer but also provided, for the first time, China's version of the September 1969 meeting between Zhou and Kosygin. In October 1969, the Chinese had publically presented their proposal that, "pending an overall settlement of the Sino-Soviet boundary question through peaceful negotiations, [the two sides] maintain the status quo of the border, avert armed conflicts and disengage the armed forces of the Chinese and Soviet sides by withdrawing them from, or refraining from sending them into, all the disputed areas along the Sino-Soviet border."[22] The Chinese, however, had never previously claimed that Kosygin had *accepted* the Chinese proposal at the Peking airport meeting. Significantly, the official Chinese media did not report Zhou's revelation for another year.

Both Zhou's delay in responding to the Soviet overture and the Chinese media's failure to publicize his claim that the Soviet Union had already agreed on the conditions for negotiating a permanent border settlement, strongly suggest that Chinese leaders could not agree over the best way to deal with Moscow. These differences broke into the open in 1974, during the *Pi Lin Pi Kong* campaign. Public statements, private interviews, and allegorical articles about China's historical relations with "northern barbarians" all suggest that there were two contending positions on Sino-Soviet relations. One, associated with the Ministry of Foreign Affairs, argued for a more flexible and conciliatory position toward the Soviet Union. The other, associated with China's radical leaders and, more speculatively, with the PLA, called for a rigid position on the border question and for more extensive defense preparations against a possible Soviet attack.

*Calls for Flexibility*

Advocates of the first position proposed that China demonstrate its flexibility toward the Soviet Union by restating Peking's negotiating position in ways that might prove attractive to Moscow, and by initiating limited but symbolic unilateral gestures of good will. Such a strategy, its proponents believed, was desirable for two reasons. First, Moscow remained an important and powerful adversary that, in line with Mao's instructions on the proper ways to deal with opponents, should be "despised strategically" but "respected tactically."[23] An effective way of deterring the Soviet Union from military action against China, according to this analysis, would be to hold out the prospect of a limited Sino-Soviet détente.

Second, the hint of possible improvements in relations between Peking and Moscow would have advantages for Sino-American relations as well. It would warn the United States that Sino-Soviet hostility was not necessarily permanent, that a Chinese "tilt" toward the United States could not be taken for granted, and that Washington would have to take Chinese concerns into account when formulating its own policy toward the Soviet Union.

This first approach to Sino-Soviet relations was embodied in three overtures to the Soviet Union in 1974 and 1975. Each of these moves, in its content and timing, reflected the desire to both manage tensions with the Soviet Union and keep the U.S. government guessing about Sino-Soviet relations. But these moves also aroused opposition and dissent inside China from those who believed that they represented little more than appeasement of Moscow.

The first of these initiatives was contained in a message sent to the Soviet Union by the Standing Committee of the National People's Congress in 1974, on the anniversary of the October Revolution.[24] This message formally presented Zhou Enlai's version of the understanding allegedly reached by Zhou and Kosygin in September 1969, and stated that China still considered implementation of this understanding to be the precondition for successful negotiation of the border issue. But the message did not repeat earlier Chinese demands that the Russians acknowledge the inequality of the nineteenth century border treaties, or that the treaties, rather than the line of actual control, should form the basis for a permanent border settlement.[25] Most important of all, the message also stated that a nonaggression treaty, included in the Russian proposal of June 1973, could be made an integral part of the implementation of the 1969 Zhou-Kosygin understanding. In its willingness to respond relatively favorably to the 1973 Russian offer, the National People's Congress message remained flexible in substance and conciliatory in tone.[26]

The second and least official initiative, an article published in the journal *Lishi Yanjiu* (*Historical Studies*) at the end of 1974, suggested a variety of ways the Russians could show enough "good faith" to enable the Chinese to begin serious border negotiations.[27] Some of these alternatives—proposals that the Russians withdraw their forces from Outer Mongolia, or reduce their forces along the Sino-Soviet frontier to pre-1964 levels—required more of the Soviets than the terms of the agreement allegedly reached in 1969.[28] But two other suggestions represented a softening of Peking's previous terms. One was that the Russians cease all military exercises and "provocations" along the border; the other, that Moscow stop sending "spies" into China. The article did not explicitly promise that Russian acceptance of these proposals could be a substitute for implementation of the 1969 understanding, but neither did it describe implementation of that understanding as a necessary precondition for settlement of the border issue.

The third, and most significant, Chinese initiative occurred in December 1975, when Peking announced the release of three crew members of a Soviet helicopter that had penetrated Chinese airspace in March 1974. Moscow had always contended that the helicopter was on a medical mission and had strayed over Chinese territory accidentally. Initially, the Chinese had responded that the helicopter carried no medical supplies, that it must therefore have been on an espionage mission, and that the crew would be tried accordingly before a Chinese court. But on December 27, 1975, Vice Foreign Minister Yu Zhan informed Soviet ambassador Tolstikov that the Chinese public security organs, after investigation, had accepted the crew's claims that they had entered China accidentally, despite continued Chinese insistence on the nonmedical nature of the "armed reconnaissance helicopter." As a result, the Chinese returned the crew as well as "the helicopter with all equipment and documents aboard."[29] In 1977, Yu Zhan would describe this unilateral Chinese action as a "gesture of good will toward the Soviet people."[30]

These three initiatives exemplified the "flexible" strategy. While none consituted a major concession, each exhibited some sign of flexibility, indicating a willingness to reach an accommodation on the border issue.

Moreover, each gesture was timed so as to warn the United States to take Chinese concerns into account if it wanted to prevent an improvement of relations between Peking and Moscow. The 1974 message on the anniversary of the October Revolution occurred shortly after the Vladivostok summit meeting between President Gerald Ford and Leonid Brezhnev, and on the eve of Henry Kissinger's relatively unsuccessful visit to China. Similarly, the release of the helicopter crew in December 1975 occurred immediately after Ford's visit to China, during which the Chinese had expressed their dissatisfaction with alleged American appeasement of the Soviet Union.

*Demands for a More Rigid Approach*

None of these three initiatives had a measurable effect on the Soviet Union. Moscow rejected the 1974 gestures out of hand and simply ignored the release of the helicopter crew in 1975. But each of these initiatives aroused substantial controversy inside China. Only the international service of Radio Peking broadcast the November 1974 message, thus limiting its dissemination to foreign ears. A few weeks later, unidentified sources in China informed Neville Maxwell, a British correspondent, that the message did not represent any change in the Chinese position and that the Soviet helicopter crew would soon be tried for espionage.[31] Furthermore, an intensification of anti-Soviet propaganda in early 1976 accompanied the December 1975 release of the Soviet helicopter crew, which effectively negated any good will generated by the crew's release. Allegorical articles published during this period criticized historical figures for returning prisoners of war and captured "war booty," and an essay by the radical writing group Liang Xiao denounced those who, like Lin Biao, advocated "secret negotiations" with the Soviet Union.[32] All these statements and articles represented, implicitly or explicitly, a repudiation of one or more of the diplomatic overtures taken toward the Soviet Union in 1974 and 1975.

Besides denouncing the three specific initiatives outlined above, radical writing groups also offered a more comprehensive criticism of the strategy of diplomatic flexibility toward the Soviet Union. The radicals presented their views in a series of allegorical articles published during the *Pi Lin Pi Kong* campaign in 1974—articles that ostensibly dealt with China's historical relations with foreign enemies, but that had clear implications for contemporary Sino-Soviet relations.[33]

The first premise of the radicals' critique was that the proponents of flexibility toward the Soviet Union had "failed to perceive the true features" of the USSR, had overestimated Moscow's strength, and had therefore adopted a strategy of "national betrayal" toward the enemy to the north. According to the radicals, the advocates of flexibility had vastly overrated the superiority of the Soviet forces in Asia, and had painted an unrealistically dire portrait of the "horrors of war" with the Soviet Union. As a result, the radicals charged, the moderates insisted that the Chinese would have to "wait until we obtain the atom"—presumably a reference to a more credible Chinese nuclear deterrent—before they could "get tough" with the Kremlin. In the meantime the moderates allegedly tried to prevent a Soviet attack by appeasing Moscow through offers of negotiation.

Second, the radical writing groups also sought to draw a connection between the "national betrayal" that they accused the moderates of advocating abroad and the "revisionism" and "restoration" they practiced at home. This connection, the radicals argued, was not accidental. Revisionists always fear the progressive social reforms and mass mobilization necessary to build a strong and powerful state able to resist external aggression. As a result, they can only rely upon concessions and appeasement in their attempt to deal with foreign invaders. As one article published during the *Pi Lin Pi Kong* campaign explained, "If one cannot in home affairs enforce a political line that stands fast for progress and opposes regression, that adheres to reform and opposes sticking to the old, it is virtually impossible to uphold the patriotic stand of opposing aggression."[34] An article written in September 1975 similarly stated: "Those who practice revisionism are bound to be capitulationists."[35]

What, then, was the radicals' policy toward the Soviet Union? The radicals began with a somewhat inconsistent and paradoxical assessment of Soviet power and intentions. On the one hand, the radical writers insisted that the Russians "have not given up their wild ambition to subjugate China," either through subversion, direct military pressure, or even a "surprise attack."[36] On the other hand, the radicals also described the Soviet Union as being much weaker than more moderate leaders had suggested. While proponents of flexibility toward Moscow had, as we have seen, cautioned that the Soviet Union's tactical strength was worthy of respect, an article in mid-1974 by the radical Shanghai writing group Fang Hai pointed to the "fragile and vulnerable nature" of the Soviet Union, and criticized those who "overestimate the strength of imperialism and the reactionaries and underestimate the strength of the people."[37]

In contrast to the relatively flexible and accommodating policy proposed by the moderates, then, the radicals believed that China should adopt a more intransigent line, and should undertake a substantial improvement of its own defense posture. In two important allegorical articles, both dealing with China's policy toward "aggression from the north" in ancient times, the radicals described the Chinese people as traditionally "resolute in calling for resistance" to aggression, and proposed that China devote ample financial resources to national defense, increase weapons manufacture, and strengthen defense preparations along the northern border. China, they argued, should be "building fortresses for defense and setting up plants to produce arms." This would enable China not only to resist future aggression, but also to recover some of the territory lost to the Russians in the past.

The radicals appeared to believe that a firm, unyielding stand toward the Soviet Union could best be exemplified by a series of harassments against Soviet personnel inside China. Circumstantial evidence strongly suggests, for example, that it was the radicals who were most adamant in demanding that the Soviet helicopter crew captured in 1974 be tried for espionage. In February 1974, Chinese militia and public security forces arrested five Soviet embassy officials, allegedly while receiving secret information from one of their Chinese agents, charged them with espionage, and expelled them from the country. As Kenneth Lieberthal suggests, Chinese counterintelligence agencies may have carefully set up the incident to demonstrate that China was willing to take firm and direct countermeasures against Soviet provocations.[38] And a third, more mysterious incident occurred in April 1976, shortly after the riots in Tienanmen Square, when a bomb exploded outside the Soviet Embassy in Peking. This, too, may have been an attempt by radical sympathizers to dramatize resistance to the Soviet Union, even at a time of domestic disorder inside China.

To the moderates, this combination of defense preparations and deliberate provocations must have appeared both dangerous and unnecessary. The radicals' harassment of Soviet officials in China ran the risk of increasing tensions with Moscow and even of eliciting some form of Soviet retaliation. Furthermore, many moderates also denied the need for an escalated program of military preparedness, such as the radicals were demanding. Moderate spokesmen consistently downplayed the Soviet threat, arguing that Moscow's global strategy was not directed against China but rather against the United States and Western Europe. In his report to the Tenth Party Congress, for example, Zhou Enlai declared that the "key point" of contention between the Soviet Union and the United States lay in Europe, and that Moscow, while appearing to be preoccupied with China, was actually "making a feint in the east while attacking in the west."[39] Similarly, in an interview given to foreign visitors in October 1974, a ranking official of the Ministry of Foreign Affairs stated that a war between China and the Soviet Union now appeared unlikely, and that Soviet forces in Asia were principally directed against the United States and Japan, rather than against China.[40]

## Competing Policy Packages

The debate over Sino-Soviet relations in 1974 and 1975 centered around two competing policy packages.[41] The first, premised simultaneously on the improbability of a major Soviet attack, and yet also on the need to take Soviet military power seriously, favored a policy of limited concessions to the Soviet Union. This flexible package probably originated in the Ministry of Foreign Affairs, with Vice Foreign Minister Yu Zhan, the ministry official directly responsible for relations with the Soviet Union, probably playing the key role. The strategy was designed to appeal to civilian leaders interested in promoting China's economic development, for it argued that the Soviet threat could be deflected by diplomatic means, without requiring an increase in expenditures for national defense. It also appealed to those who were concerned with the risk of a Sino-Soviet conflict.

This first strategy appears to have won the support of a number of prominent civilian leaders. It is unlikely, for example, that so dramatic (and contentious) a gesture as the release of the Soviet helicopter crew could have been undertaken without the consent of Mao Zedong or without the approval of Deng Xiaoping — the man in charge of day-to-day Party and government affairs in late 1975. Hua Guofeng, then minister of public security, probably supported this approach as well, for the announcement of the release of the helicopter crew pointedly revealed that it had been the Ministry of Public Security that had concluded that the crewmen had not been on a deliberate espionage mission.

The second strategy, in contrast, was based on the belief that the Soviet Union was likely to attack China, but that Moscow could be defeated if China undertook a program of accelerated military preparations. It envisioned, as we have seen, an uncompromising and inflexible position toward Soviet provocations and diplomatic initiatives alike.

This second strategy, designed primarily by radicals on the Politburo, was intended to win its proponents two important bases of political support. First, the radicals sought to demonstrate that the moderates were betraying Chinese interests to the Kremlin, and that this national betrayal was directly linked to the moderates' socioeconomic programs. Patriotic Chinese could, in the radicals' analysis, best defend China's national interests by defending the progressive policies of the Cultural Revolution. Second, and perhaps more important, the radicals were also appealing to the military. Military procurement had remained essentially static since 1971, and the PLA's regional commanders underwent a rotation of duty that effectively demoted them in late 1973. The PLA could thus be described as an aggrieved, yet powerful, interest group. The radicals' call for stronger defense preparations, more arms production, and a tougher line toward the

Soviet Union—as well as their effusive praise of the military units involved in the Paracel Island operation—can therefore be explained as an appeal for army support in the emerging succession struggle.

Interestingly, Zhou Enlai appears to have taken a position that lay somewhere between these two extremes. It is true that Zhou was a prominent spokesman for the thesis that the Soviet Union was only "feinting to the East" and no longer posed an immediate military threat to China, and that he consistently advocated the "normalization of relations" between the two countries—an idea that radical writing groups described as impossible short of a fundamental change in the Soviet social and economic system. Yet Zhou also imposed relatively tough preconditions for negotiations with the Kremlin. At the Tenth Party Congress, by demanding that the Soviet Union withdraw all its forces from Outer Mongolia as a sign of good faith, Zhou seemed to discourage, rather than encourage, serious border negotiations. Moreover, at the Fourth National People's Congress (NPC) he reintroduced China's demand that Moscow would have to implement the Kosygin-Zhou understanding of 1969 before a meaningful dialogue could begin. In so doing, Zhou effectively withdrew the overtures contained in the November 1974 message from the NPC and the inititatives embodied in the December 1974 article in *Lishi Yanjiu*.

On each occasion, Zhou may have been speaking on behalf of the entire Politburo, rather than simply for himself, but a posthumous account of his position on Sino-Soviet relations implied that the premier consistently maintained that the implementation of the 1969 understanding would be the key to serious negotiations between Peking and Moscow.[42] On balance, then, the available evidence suggests that Zhou Enlai favored a flexible approach toward the Soviet Union, but that he also insisted on a tougher negotiating stand than some of his colleagues in the Foreign Ministry.

## III. Round Three (1974-77):
## The Desirability of Military Modernization

In China, as elsewhere, successful politicians readily perceive that political issues may be seized from the groups that originally raised them. Recognizing that their rivals on the Politburo tried to gain military support through promotion of more active defense preparations, moderate leaders decided, in effect, to steal the issue from the opposition. In late 1974, therefore, they began advocating the modernization of the PLA in a way that linked modernization with moderate social and economic programs. This placed the radicals in an awkward position. While they continued to charge the moderates with "national betrayal" and "capitulationism" because of their advocacy of a flexible policy toward the Soviet Union, the radicals could no longer accuse them of ignoring national defense. They could only criticize the moderates' program for military modernization on the grounds that it represented an unacceptable departure from Mao Zedong's doctrine of people's war.

Unlike similar debates in the 1950s and 1960s, no specific external event sparked this controversy over military modernization. To be sure, it was partially stimulated by Sino-Soviet border clashes in the summer of 1974, by the emerging opportunity for China to purchase advanced weaponry from the West, and by the October 1973 war in the Middle East, which led military staffs around the world to consider the implications of precision-guided munitions. But the debate was primarily aroused by internal political forces. By late 1974, Chinese leaders had begun preparations for the Fourth National People's Congress and must have begun discussing the desirability of setting forth as major national goals the "four modernizations"—modernization of agriculture, industry, national defense, and science and technology. Moreover, by questioning the adequacy of China's military preparedness in the *Pi Lin Pi Kong* campaign earlier in the year, the radicals had already placed the issue of national defense on the Chinese political agenda.

The debate over military modernization occurred in three sub-rounds, between 1974 and 1976, with the issue posed in different terms during each stage. In the first sub-round, the desirability of military modernization was debated in the press through allegorical articles critical of former Defense Minister Lin Biao. In the second sub-round, in mid-1975, the controversy focused more specifically on the PLA's weapons procurement and military training programs, which were discussed in a series of important meetings of the Military Affairs Commission (MAC) of the Central Committee. Finally, in 1976, the disagreement concerned implementation of the decisions taken by the MAC in 1975, which the radicals attempted to block by manipulating the emerging campaign to criticize Deng Xiaoping.

*Establishing the Need for Modernization*

The *Pi Lin Pi Kong* campaign, formally launched in early 1974, began as an attempt by radical leaders to defend the socioeconomic programs of the Cultural Revolution, and to criticize the moderates' rehabilitation of veteran officials overthrown by the Red Guards. After the campaign disrupted industrial production and after wall posters appeared in major Chinese cities attacking central and provincial leaders, the Politburo decided to redefine the purpose of the movement. In a directive issued on July 1, 1974, the Politburo ordered that work stoppages cease, industrial production return to normal, and controversial issues concerning wages and management practices be shelved for future discussion.[43]

This central directive did not, however, signal the end of *Pi Lin Pi Kong*.

Instead, the movement was transformed, to a large degree, into a debate over military strategy. Until this point, only Lin Biao's domestic policies and political philosophy had been criticized, with little reference to foreign policy. Now, Lin's military career began to receive attention, and critics denounced it for its departure from Mao's theories of military strategy.[44] Of course, an accurate assessment of Lin Biao's prowess as a military commander was not their goal. Instead, they hoped to provide, through analogy, recommendations for Chinese military policy in the mid-1970s.

Interestingly, two different assessments of Lin Biao's military career appeared in the Chinese press during this period. One group of articles urged more attention to military preparedness, implicitly rejected reliance on people's war to defend China, and called for the study and adoption of more modern military doctrine and weaponry. One essay, for example, in criticizing Lin Biao's performance in the Beiping-Tianjin campaign during the Chinese Civil War, charged that he had been unwilling to shift from small-scale guerrilla tactics to large-scale positional warfare and thus could not meet the new tasks of fighting "big battles" and attacking "big cities."[45] Other authors accused Lin of mechanically relying on outdated doctrinal principles, even after they had clearly lost their utility. As one article stated, "wars of different historical periods, different states and nations, and different natures are governed by different laws guiding war and [by] different strategic and tactical principles."[46] Although the same author acknowledged in another article that "future wars against aggression" would still, in some sense, be "people's wars," he strongly suggested that they would be fought with different strategies and different weapons than those of the 1930s and 1940s.[47]

In this same vein, the military training exercises conducted in 1964 underwent a reexamination in 1974. During the Cultural Revolution, these military "tournaments" had been described as examples of the "bourgeois military line" imposed on the army by Luo Ruiqing, chief of staff at the time, over Lin Biao's objections. In September 1974, however, the military tournaments were "rehabilitated" and Lin's opposition to them condemned. One article described as a "fallacy" Lin's belief that "accuracy in marksmanship is a matter of secondary importance." "Under modern war conditions where there have been new changes in the technical equipment and operational characteristics on the part of both the enemy and ourselves, particularly, it is all the more necessary for us to strengthen our training so that we shall master new techniques." But Lin Biao had "criminally aimed at terminating our military training program, so that we would not be able to shoot accurately, to move our tanks, and to make contacts in telecommunication operations, thus reducing the PLA to an army good only in cultural but not in military affairs and an army with no fighting power whatsoever." In so doing, Lin placed China in a position where it would have no alternative other than being placed "under the protection of the Soviet 'nuclear umbrella'"—no alternative, in other words, to capitulation to Soviet demands.[48]

Still other articles called for greater attention to military preparedness and to military professionalization. One critique, written by officers in the Canton military region in August 1974, invoked the danger of a surprise attack from the Soviet Union to support its demand for the renewal of military training exercises in the PLA. While acknowledging that the army must still be able to "fight with the pen as well as with guns," and that the Party's "basic line" of continuing class struggle must still command military affairs, the article nonetheless called for an adjustment of the balance between ideological work and military training.[49]

A second group of articles, in contrast, defended the principles of people's war and denied the need for extensive military modernization. These articles dealt with the strategy Lin advocated during the Jiangxi Soviet War (early 1930s) and the Anti-Japanese War (1937–45), rather than with his activities during the Civil War (1945–49). They charged that, in defiance of Mao's instructions, Lin had favored fighting "regular and large-scale battles" against the Nationalists and the Japanese, rather than a "people's war." Accordingly, Lin had considered the strategy of luring an invader deep into friendly territory, the basic principle of people's war, to be outdated, and had underestimated the role of the masses in helping a numerically and technologically inferior army to achieve victory. Lin's advocacy of regular war led him to favor "positional warfare" and "passive defense," which resulted inevitably in battles of attrition and unacceptable losses. These criticisms of modern warfare were often coupled with the charge that Lin had favored fighting the Japanese "in coordination with the Guomindang"—a thinly disguised criticism of those Chinese leaders who, in the mid-1970s, sought to deter the Russians through rapprochement with the United States.[50]

In short, these discussions of Lin Biao's military career presented two very different portraits of the former defense minister: one, the man who in the 1940s could not move on from outmoded guerrilla strategies to large-scale positional warfare and had blocked necessary military training programs in 1964; the other, a man who had insisted on positional warfare in the 1930s and thereby violated Mao's principles of people's war. The first version of Lin's career justified the position of those who, in 1974, wanted to promote the modernization of the PLA, while the second version supported those who sought to block such a course.

Despite the debate, the proponents of military modernization had won some important preliminary victories by early 1975. In accord with their pleas for development of new and improved weapons, the 1975 New Year's Day editorial, for the first time in many years, mentioned the expansion of "national defense construction" as one of the year's principal tasks.[51] The Second Plenum of the Central Committee, meeting in 1975, appointed Deng Xiaoping as the PLA chief of staff, and very likely also approved the reorganization of the General Staff Department, an increase in military procurement, and the military training exercises that occurred in 1975.[52] Moreover, in his report to the Fourth NPC later that month, Zhou Enlai announced that the modernization of national defense, one of the "four modernizations," would be achieved by the year 2000.

*Drawing Up a Program*

Despite these preliminary decisions, the problem of *how* to modernize the PLA still remained. The Military Affairs Commission fully discussed this complex issue in meetings in May and July of 1975, and possibly at other planning meetings over the course of the year. Armed with instructions from Mao, probably written in May, that the PLA should "prepare itself for fighting" and that "the army needs to be rectified," Defense Minister Ye Jianying and Chief of Staff Deng Xiaoping both gave speeches to the MAC presenting a program for military modernization.[53]

Deng's summary of the MAC's discussions, presented at the MAC meeting on July 14, focused on four principal themes. First, Deng emphasized the PLA's need for advanced weapons. "Our army talks in terms of fighting hard battles," Deng said, which would require more than high morale and revolutionary zeal. "Fighting hard battles, in the real sense, means fighting battles of steel." To win a war, therefore, would require more weapons. More weapons would require the production of more steel, and the production of more steel would, in turn, require the rapid modernization of the industrial sector of the Chinese economy.

A second element of Deng's program was a reduction in the overall force levels of the PLA. According to United States government sources, Deng proposed that the Chinese armed forces, then numbering approximately four million men and women, be reduced by 25 percent. While Deng never provided a full rationale for this proposal, he appears to have hoped that manpower reductions could provide financial savings that would be channeled into weapons production and procurement. In addition, Deng probably believed that many of China's military units, particularly the local and regional forces, could be eliminated without significantly affecting the PLA's military capability.[54]

Third, Deng went on to complain that because of its neglect of military training since the beginning of the Cultural Revolution the PLA was unprepared to use even the weapons it already had. Arguing that military training should be considered one of the "key links" in the PLA's work, Deng promised that, "if soldiers shed more sweat in peacetime, they will shed less blood during wartime." To give the army additional time to devote to military training, Deng proposed that its participation in civilian activities be reduced. Deng made two specific suggestions that were anathema to the radical leadership: that the training of urban militia forces by the PLA be severely curtailed; and that the military units sent to manage schools, factories, colleges, and hospitals during the Cultural Revolution be recalled.

Finally, Deng harshly criticized the tendencies toward factionalism and disunity within the army, which, he claimed, had produced serious problems of insubordination. According to one account, Deng proposed the restoration of formal military ranks, abolished in 1965 on the eve of the Cultural Revolution, as a way of reestablishing proper military discipline.[55] More importantly, Deng argued for a full-scale rectification of the PLA as a prerequisite for improving combat readiness and military discipline. Under Deng's proposal, work teams would be dispatched to reorganize the army's leadership at various levels in an effort to weed out both inefficient and incompetent officers as well as those aligned with the radicals. These men would then be replaced with more experienced officers, who would be better able to reestablish a secure chain of command and promote military training. Deng described the rectification of the PLA as a "key link" in the army's work.

Although not stressed in Deng's speech, the MAC meetings apparently also considered a fifth matter, the modernization of the navy. In response to the expansion of Soviet naval forces in the Pacific in the early 1970s, the navy had drawn up a long-term modernization program, which was discussed at the MAC meeting in May 1975. On May 3, Mao expressed his support for naval modernization by issuing an instruction to build a powerful naval force. Shortly thereafter, Mao approved the specific proposal adopted by the MAC, adding that, in his opinion, it could be accomplished within ten years.[56]

Altogether, the MAC appears to have reached several important decisions in its meetings in mid-1975. In addition to the long-range naval development program just mentioned, it also adopted a decision on overall military modernization and a program for the rectification of the armed forces. It also made several more specific decisions: to rehabilitate Luo Ruiqing, the former chief of staff, by providing him with an important role in supervising the modernization of the PLA; to call a national conference on political work in the army; to reopen academies for training the PLA's officer corps; to revise the army regulations on discipline; and to complete arrangements for the purchase of Rolls Royce Spey jet engines from Britain to power the fighters and fighter-bombers the air force planned to produce.

Significantly, however, while all of these decisions were promulgated through internal Party and army channels, none received publicity in the Chinese press. Instead, the policies adopted by the MAC were communicated to the Chinese people through a series of allegorical articles published in 1975 that summarized the most important elements of the military modernization program.

The first of these articles, written by a group of industrial workers and historians, praised the proposals for resisting Western aggression advanced by the Qing official Wei Yuan in the nineteenth century. Like the radicals in 1974, the writers of this essay stated that, because "powerful weapons are not as important as a united people,"[57] China's military and technological inferiority would not necessarily prevent the PLA from defending the country successfully. Indeed, the authors continued, it would be wrong to overestimate the power of the enemy and particularly wrong to engage in appeasement of the aggressor. The remainder of the article, however, contained a strong indictment of the PLA's lack of military preparedness and an impassioned call to learn the advanced military technology of the West. Always presenting their case in allegorical terms, the writers warned that even China's "crack troops" were dangerously ill-prepared. It would be necessary, therefore, to enlist troops "on a highly selective basis,"[58] train them strictly and regularly, and maintain them "rationally."[59] It would also be necessary to learn Western industrial techniques, develop Chinese industry rapidly, expand China's weapons production, and even import weapons (the article mentioned "guns" and "warships") from abroad. In a direct rebuke of the radicals, the writing group denounced those who used charges of "appeasement" and "capitulation" to strangle the study of foreign experience. On the contrary, they claimed, one could learn from the advanced techniques of foreign countries in a spirit of self-respect and self-reliance, as Wei Yuan had done. "Although Wei Yuan advocated learning from the West, nowhere was there a sense of national inferiority; on the contrary, he carried with him a strong sense of national dignity and a firm feeling of self-confidence." Indeed, the article concluded, those who described importing foreign technology as "capitulation" were, by obstructing the modernization of China, creating a situation in which capitulation to foreign threats would be inevitable. "Wei Yuan pointed out: those who branded the people as traitors were traitors themselves."[60]

A second article, ostensibly dealing with the Long March, was in fact a defense of the rectification and reorganization of the PLA.[61] It criticized those "'Left' opportunist leaders," who, during the Long March, "practiced flightism in retreat, were only on the defensive without attacking, merely parried the blows of others without striking back, and most erroneously called for retreating to the destination 'to put away their baggage before hitting back at the enemy.'" All this could be read as a criticism of the "luring deep" strategy characteristic of people's war and a call for a more active modern defense. More importantly, the essay defended calls by Deng Xiaoping and Ye Jianying for a reorganization and rectification of the PLA by pointing out that, after the Cunyi Conference in 1935, the Red Army had been "reorganized" and "streamlined." It complained that, at that time, Lin Biao had opposed these policies because he did not understand the "changes in the situation."[62]

The third article, by Hong Cheng, an author or writing group active in discussions of military affairs in the mid-1970s, ostensibly presented an historical analysis of the Ming Dynasty general Qi Jiguang and his strategy of resistance to Japanese pirate raids and invasions in Zhejiang in the mid-sixteenth century. But the article's description of Qi's military doctrine corresponded closely to that presented to the MAC by Deng Xiaoping. First, since he believed that the merit of an army lay in its efficiency, and not in its numbers, Qi advocated reducing its noncombat manpower, just as Deng had apparently called for a decrease in the PLA's civilian activities and a reduction in its force levels. Second, Qi demanded that his army have sound organization and tight discipline, just as Deng had complained about the tendencies toward factionalism and insubordination within the PLA. Third, while paying due attention to the political quality of the troops and the political training of officers, Qi Jiguang supposedly placed particular emphasis on military training and had developed military tournaments based on current combat requirements. Qi purportedly commented, "If you do not learn military skills, you are idiots and do not cherish your lives[63] — a striking parallel to Deng's argument that soldiers who shed more sweat in peacetime will shed less blood in time of war. Finally, the essay described Qi's advocacy of weapons' modernization, the study of foreign technology, and the development of the Chinese navy. Interestingly, however, the article concluded with a denunciation of those who tried to appease the enemy through gifts — perhaps an indication that, like the authors of the article on Wei Yuan, Hong Cheng opposed the overtures to the Soviet Union that had been undertaken in 1974 and 1975.

*Radical Response to the MAC Program*

Developments in 1976, and criticisms of the "gang of four" that appeared in 1977 and 1978, indicated that the radical Politburo members strongly opposed the MAC's proposed modernization of the PLA. First, they feared such a program would substantially weaken whatever influence they had within the PLA, especially when coupled with a rectification of military command positions. Second, and more generally, the modernization of the PLA was integrally linked with a broader set of domestic social and economic programs opposed by radicals. As Deng Xiaoping had pointed out, to create an "army of steel" required more rapid economic development; thus, those who favored military modernization should, in Deng's argument, also support his plans for abandoning the socioeconomic programs of the Cultural Revolution.

But how could the radicals express their opposition? One critical problem faced by the "gang of four" was its inability to control decisions within the MAC. Of the four principal radical leaders, according to information compiled by the Central Intelligence Agency, only Wang Hongwen and Zhang Chunqiao belonged to the MAC in mid-1975.[64] Neither Jiang Qing nor Yao Wenyuan is reported to have ever attended the meetings that year even as observers. While the radicals may conceivably have received some support from regional military commanders and regional political commissars, their power base in the MAC was clearly limited.

As a result, Wang Hongwen and Zhang Chunqiao made no objections to the modernization program when it was presented to the MAC. Instead, according to later accounts, they praised Deng's speech for its candor, lauded Ye's address, and expressed no opposition to presenting the documents of the meeting to Mao Zedong for review.[65] If they did anything at the MAC meetings, they attempted to soften the PLA's rules on discipline, most likely as a way to blunt the force of the rectification campaign, and to leave some leeway for their supporters within the PLA to resist implementation of the modernization program.[66]

Once the MAC referred the program to the Politburo, however, the radicals had a stronger base and a better chance to express opposition. Even there, however, they apparently failed to protest distribution of the MAC conference documents in the name of the Central Committee. But they apparently did raise important objections about the plan for naval development. According to articles written in 1977, after the purge of the "gang of four," Zhang Chunqiao countered the naval development program with a defense program for the ground forces. "We advocate land forces," Zhang reportedly stated. "Rockets and guided missiles have been developed to such an extent that, launched by ground forces, they can reach any place. It is no longer necessary for an all-out effort to build a navy."[67] Zhang allegedly called for reductions in naval expenditures (described later by his critics as a "theory of abolishing the navy") on grounds that the navy "wastes money and manpower," and Jiang Qing advocated transforming the navy into a "convoy fleet" or "reserve force."[68]

But the radicals' principal strategy was not to prevent adoption of the military modernization program, but rather to try to sabotage its implementation. In 1975, they pursued this goal through a variety of mechanisms. As director of the General Political Department of the PLA, Zhang Chunqiao continued efforts, begun earlier, to establish a framework for the rectification of the PLA that would permit rapid promotion of younger officers who presumably would owe a debt of gratitude to the radicals. The radicals also described the rehabilitation of veteran military commanders as political favoritism, accused these commanders of relying on past personal experience at the expense of political theory, and thus demanded a "house-cleaning of the army,"[69] that would eliminate the "old fellows."[70] To try to ensure that his definition of rectification, rather than that proposed by Deng Xiaoping, would remain the official one, Zhang Chunqiao ignored the MAC's decision to convene a conference on political work in the PLA.

The radicals also tried to obstruct implementation of other parts of the 1975 defense modernization program. According to charges made in 1977 and 1978, military and civilian officials opposed to the program diverted material and equipment intended for national defense industries, transferring them to the urban militia; delayed or blocked naval construction projects that were part of the naval development program approved by the MAC; and undermined the PLA's new military training program by insisting that the troops practice exercises found in traditional Chinese opera and that they train with broadswords as well as modern weapons.

As a result of their continuing influence over the mass media, the radicals not only successfully denied extensive coverage of the decisions reached by the MAC, but they also published articles that allegorically criticized those decisions. One such article appeared in *Renmin Ribao* on July 4, 1975. It presented an extremely unusual description of Lin Biao, accusing him of having placed military affairs in command of the army during the periods 1959-64 and 1969-71 — the bulk of his tenure as minister of defense. The article seemed to warn that other military leaders were trying to repeat the same error in 1975. Another article, appearing in *Renmin Ribao* the following month, ostensibly summarized the historical debates between Confucianists and Legalists over military affairs. It concluded, in line with the traditional justification of people's war, that human will could overpower natural forces and that a country's ability to win a war depended less on the equipment available to its military forces than on the strength of the people. While appearing to praise the desirability of military modernization, the article actually concluded that modernization should not be regarded as a major priority. It described Lin Biao as a "fetishist of weapons," particularly of nuclear weapons, the air force, and strategic missles. Lin erred, of course; the correct line was that, while weapons are "important in war, . . . only the people are the makers of history." Despite their technological inferiority, the troops of the Red Army had "defeated Chiang Kai-shek's planes and tanks with millet plus rifles."[71]

Similar writings apparently circulated within the PLA. According to charges published in 1977 and 1978, opponents of the military modernization program repeated the arguments, first made in 1974, that the Soviet Union was a weak adversary. They "devised all ways and means to undermine the education constantly conducted by our army on the situation of preparedness against war. They negated the dual nature of imperialism and social-imperialism and talked only about their being paper tigers without saying that they also are real man-eating tigers."[72] Following the MAC conference, the radicals argued that China needed few additional military preparations against as weak a threat as the Soviets, and that the MAC's modernization program would be a waste of money. Opponents of the program circulated materials on the development of the armaments industry within the Soviet Union, arguing that it consumed too large a part of the national budget, and warned against the same phenomenon occurring in China. In short, opponents of the decisions reached by the MAC in 1975 "totally negated the meeting," described it as "full of problems," and "spared no efforts to interfere with and undermine efforts to relay and implement the spirit of the meeting."[73]

The growing criticism of Deng's domestic programs in late 1975, though centered around his educational policies, also permitted the radicals to escalate their campaign against the military modernization program. It was at this point that they sought to foster active debate within the PLA itself over the need for rapid modernization. On December 29, 1975, apparently with the direct encouragement of radical leaders in Shanghai, the "Good Eighth Company of Nanjing Road," a model unit during the Cultural Revolution, began to criticize Deng Xiaoping and his military program, without, however, mentioning Deng by name. The Good Eighth Company promptly received praise in the national press for its resistance to the "deviationist trend of trying to reverse correct verdicts" and for its defense of Mao Zedong's policies in military affairs. Descriptions of the company's activities noted that it stressed political and ideological work and devoted relatively less attention to military training. These political activities included "unfold[ing] criticism of revisionism and the bourgeoisie from time to time," participating in "class struggle in society at large," and conducting "social investigations in factories, schools, and shops at regular intervals"[74] — precisely the kind of involvement in civilian affairs that Deng had hoped to limit. As a *Jiefangjun Bao* editorial on the company concluded, "an army company can develop the power of a thunderbolt militarily only if it places politics in first place."[75]

With the Good Eighth Company as a model, radical representatives began visiting other basic-level military units, bypassing the region and district commanders in the process. They encouraged soldiers to rebel against the "bourgeoisie in the Party,"[76] and to criticize the MAC modernization program. They promoted the use of techniques usually restricted to the civilian sector—wall posters, "great debates," and the like—as a way of illustrating rank and file opposition to the military modernization program. All these actions directly defied a directive issued jointly by the Central Committee and the MAC in the spring of 1976 that "the army should be kept stable."[77]

Once Deng Xiaoping had been dismissed from office in April 1976, in the aftermath of the riots in Tiananmen Square triggered by memorial activities for the late Premier Zhou Enlai, the radicals could begin direct and open criticism of Deng's military policies and the modernization program adopted in 1975. Articles in the Chinese press in the summer of 1976 accused Deng of promoting a program that was both unnecessary and undesirable. Modernization was unnecessary because the PLA, as the Zhenbao and Paracel Island incidents demonstrated, was already well prepared to fight.[78] Furthermore, it was unnecessary because it overestimated the importance of weapons and technology in warfare. In speaking of the need for an "army of steel," Deng had allegedly ignored the fact that "the things that are really hard are not iron and steel, nor one or two new weapons, but the revolutionary fighters and the masses of people guided by the correct line."[79]

At the same time, these articles warned, the modernization program actively contributed to the emergence of revisionism in China. By focusing exclusively upon "the overt armed enemies" outside China, Deng's program prevented the PLA from struggling against the "covert enemies without guns" inside the Party. This constituted, one article declared, an attempt to "distort our army's basic tasks and negate the necessity for it to wage struggle against the capitalist-roaders within the Party." If successful, it would "make the broad masses of cadres and fighters forget class struggle and become political philistines."[80] The program further contributed to revisionism because of its close link to a broader package of domestic economic programs, all of which emphasized efficiency and productivity at the expense of political and social values. Deng had forged this linkage deliberately, in order to make abandonment of the programs of the Cultural Revolution appear as a matter of national survival. As Deng's critics put it, he had "wildly advocate[d] fighting 'battles of steel' as though he were very concerned with preparedness against war. Actually, he [made] use of the question of war to peddle the reactionary theory of productive forces."[81]

*Competing Policy Packages*

Thus, the debate over military modernization between 1974 and 1976 involved two competing policy packages. One proposed, in some detail, increased weapons production, higher levels of military procurement, more rigorous military training, adoption of new strategic and tactical principles, reductions in overall troop strength, and the import of foreign military technologies. This first package was based on the assumption that the Soviet Union posed a serious military threat to China and might even launch a surprise attack across the Sino-Soviet frontier, with the PLA woefully unprepared to meet the invader. This package, adopted formally by the MAC in mid-1975, most likely received support from many professional military commanders, particularly in the central PLA headquarters, and received the endorsement of such members of the Politburo as Ye Jianying, Deng Xiaoping, and Zhou Enlai.

The second package represented, in effect, a defense of the status quo. Proponents of this package denied that the Soviet Union presented the principal threat to China, arguing that "revisionist" elements within the Chinese Communist Party posed a more immediate danger. The PLA, if if continued to rely primarily on a people's war strategy, could deal adequately with any likely Soviet threat. To adopt the modernization program presented to the MAC, therefore, would be to take expensive measures to meet a secondary threat, while sharply limiting the PLA's ability to combat domestic revisionism. Proponents of this second package probably included not only the radical leaders on the Politburo, but also political commissars within the PLA, who would have resisted any reduction in the army's civilian activities, and possibly some regional commanders, whose forces would have been the first to be streamlined, but the last to be modernized.[82]

Interestingly, these two packages do not correspond to the two competing proposals for managing Sino-Soviet relations, outlined in the discussion of Round Two earlier in this essay. Compare, for example, the program presented by the radical Politburo leaders in 1974 to that presented in 1974–76 debate. In 1974, the radicals had warned that the PLA was not prepared to meet the threat of the Soviet Union and demanded greater attention to military preparedness. In the later debate, however, the radicals downplayed the Soviet threat and described existing levels of military preparedness as fully adequate. Even more striking are the differences between the flexible policy toward the Soviet Union in 1974–75 and the military modernization program adopted in 1975. The advocates of flexibility toward Moscow had assumed a relatively remote Soviet threat, but proponents of military modernization warned of the possibility of a surprise

Russian attack and criticized "capitulation" to and "appeasement" of Moscow.

These differences should alert us to the complexity of Chinese politics during the mid-1970s. They demonstrate how such moderate civilian leaders as Deng Xiaoping had been able to steal the issue of military preparedness from their radical opponents. But they also reveal the tensions between these civilian moderates and the military. The modernization program reflected, above all, the interests of the PLA. Moderate civilian leaders such as Deng were willing to promote military modernization in order to obtain the PLA's support in the succession struggle but disagreed with the military's criticism of their diplomatic initiatives toward the Soviet Union. Further, as we will see below, the civilians and the military would soon differ over the pace at which modernization should proceed.

The purge of the "gang of four" did not totally resolve the debate over the MAC program. Although military representatives, particularly from the national defense industries, resumed public advocacy of the plan early in 1977, significant signs of opposition and dissent still existed in the first six months of the year.[83] One article not only argued that the Soviet Union had been forced to abandon its plans for attacking China, thus alleviating the need for significant increases in defense expenditures, but also repeated the radicals' assertion that "weapons are an important factor in war, but not the decisive factor. It is people, not things, that are decisive."[84] In the same vein, an article by one Chi Chuan, identified only as belonging to the Peking PLA units, declared that "men are more powerful than weapons, including the atomic bomb. . . . Of course, . . . we are not negating the role of weapons. . . . Today, we also have aircraft, tanks, and atomic bombs. We will continue to work hard to modernize our national defense. *However,* we should *still* criticize the theory that weapons decide everything, *even though* we are in a new historical condition" (emphasis added).[85] The article, entitled "Long Live the Spirit of Millet Plus Rifles," implied that, as in the war against the Japanese and the Guomindang, the PLA could defeat a militarily superior enemy without possessing comparably sophisticated weapons. Finally, a third article, in reviewing Mao's discussion of nuclear weapons in the early 1950s, insisted that the "outcome of a war is still determined by its nature and the will of the people" and described people's war as the "most effective magic weapon" for dealing with the atomic weapons of the superpowers. It concluded by denouncing the "gang of four" not only for denying the "important role of weapons [in war]," but also for negating the "decisive role of man."[86] Few other articles voiced the latter criticism.

All three articles acknowledged the general need for military modernization. At the same time, however, they refuted both the key premises and the principal conclusion of the moderates' program. They denied that the Soviet Union posed a serious and immediate threat to China, that China suffered from any serious military disadvantage vis-à-vis the Soviet Union, or that new historical conditions existed that made people's war obsolete. They therefore denied that China seriously needed an extensive and rapid program of military modernization. Instead, they reached a significantly different conclusion: that China could not compete effectively in an expensive arms race with the superpowers and that people's war, together with China's existing conventional and nuclear capability, would sufficiently deter the Soviet Union.

## IV. Round Four (1977-78): The Pace of Military Modernization

Despite the rearguard criticisms of the 1975 MAC program, it soon became apparent that the post-Mao leadership had committed itself, at least in principle, to the modernization of the armed forces. Commentaries on Mao Zedong's 1956 speech, *On the Ten Major Relationships,* published officially for the first time in December 1976, stressed the late Chairman's interest in the modernization of the PLA and called for the development of "the most advanced national defense technology."[87] In February 1977, four major conferences on military affairs — on air defense, aircraft production, defense planning, and military research and production — most likely reaffirmed the basic conclusions of the 1975 MAC meetings. To remove any doubts that modernization of the armed forces had the support of the highest leadership of the Party, both Hua Guofeng and Ye Jianying wrote inscriptions, published on June 5, 1977, calling for the modernization of the PLA.[88]

To ensure their support, important reassurances were given to those in the PLA who feared the impact of military modernization on the structure, size, and traditions of the armed forces, and who may therefore have shared the radicals' opposition to the MAC program in 1975-76. First, the militia and regional forces would still be given an important role in Chinese strategic policy and would not be neglected in favor of the more modernized main force units. People's war, albeit in modernized form, would continue to be China's principal strategic doctrine.[89] Second, modernization would not mean an end to political training but would be coupled with a campaign to "revolutionalize" the PLA so as to preserve its traditions of Party control, ideological study, criticism and self-criticism, and close relations between officers and men.[90]

Despite this new consensus, a vitally important issue remained: How quickly should modernization proceed? The Chinese leadership discussed two aspects of this issue. First, they reconsidered the nature of the Soviet threat, to determine the amount China *needed to spend* to ensure its security. Second, they debated the relationship of military spending to the civilian economy, to determine the amount China *could afford to spend* on national defense. In general, those who wished to spend more on defense emphasized the threat posed by the Soviet Union, while those who wanted to spend less stressed the competing demands of the civilian economy. But each side also attempted to rebut the other's premises. Those who wanted to spend less on defense sought to downplay the severity of the threat from the north, and, less frequently, those who advocated higher defense expenditures sought to demonstrate that the modernization of the PLA would not constitute a drain on the civilian economy.

## The Nature of the Soviet Threat

Three identifiable positions existed with regard to the nature and magnitude of the threat to China posed by the Soviet Union. First, there were those who sought to minimize, if not deny altogether, the menace of the "polar bear." In an interview with William Safire in March 1977, a high Chinese official argued that the Soviet Union could not attack China until it had first subordinated both the United States and Western Europe. In his words, "until the Soviet Union defeats the United States, the Soviet Union will not launch an attack against China."[91] Two months later, in an interview with the German newspaper *Die Welt,* Vice Foreign Minister Yu Zhan repeated the same argument in even stronger terms: "The Soviet Union must first occupy Europe and the Mideast and defeat the United States before it can solve 'the Chinese problem' the way it wants to solve it [presumably by force]. Before that, Moscow will not unleash an aggressive war against China."[92]

Why, then, did the Soviet Union maintain such a large force along the Sino-Soviet border and in Mongolia if the main focus of its global strategy lay in Europe? To answer this, proponents of this first position pointed out that the bulk of the Soviet armed forces were in fact stationed in the European theater and that the number of Soviet troops along the Sino-Soviet frontier had not increased significantly in recent years.[93] They also repeated the claim, first made in 1974, that Soviet forces in Asia were directed less against China than against the United States and Japan. They first stated this theory formally in an article on the Soviet Union written by the Institute of World Economy of the Academy of Social Science in July 1977: "Massing a million troops along the Chinese border, [the Soviet Union] has as its *primary targets* the United States and Japan, while posing a serious threat to China's security as well."[94] The authoritative exegesis of the theory of the three worlds, published by the editorial department of *Renmin Ribao* in November 1977, offered a similar analysis: "In the Far East, Japan is also faced with a serious threat. The massive Soviet military buildup in the Far East, aimed at China as it is, is directed *primarily* against the United States and Japan."[95]

As a final argument, those who downplayed the Soviet threat to China pointed to evidence of the political and economic weaknesses of the Soviet Union, which would seriously constrain Moscow's ability to undertake military action against China. The article by the Institute of World Economy, while still acknowledging "the danger of Soviet social-imperialism unleashing a world war," nonetheless insisted that the Chinese should "perceive its feeble nature as a paper tiger." Excessive military spending had seriously weakened the Soviet economy: "[A]s a result of the one-sided emphasis on development of the munitions industry which is adversely affecting agriculture and light industry as well as undermining the normal proportionate economic development, the national economy [of the Soviet Union] has become more and more lopsided. . . . Its munitions industry continues to develop at an 'excessive speed,' but the growth rate of its national economy falls steadily."[96] As a result, the deteriorating economic situation in the Soviet Union had produced serious "political problems," including "confrontations between the rulers and the working class" and an "unprecedented sharpening of [the] national contradictions" between the Russians and the nation's ethnic minorities.[97]

As Jonathan Pollack has pointed out, such denigrations of the Soviet threat were vitally important to those who sought to limit defense spending.[98] In his 1956 speech, *On the Ten Major Relationships* — which was being used as a basic guide for Chinese economic planning in early 1977 — Mao had called for reductions in defense expenditures but had premised his analysis on the assessment that China would live in peace. As Mao put it at the time, "it seems unlikely that there will be a new war of aggression against China or another world war in the near future, and there will probably be a period of peace for a decade or more."[99] It was vital that proponents of this first position demonstrate that there would not be a "new war of aggression against China . . . in the near future"; otherwise, the limitations Mao imposed on defense spending could no longer be said to apply.

A second position expressed frequently in 1977 was that the Soviet Union posed a very serious threat to China and might even launch a surprise attack. A Peking Radio broadcast on June 20 warned that all imperialist powers necessarily relied on "deceptive methods" and "surprise attacks" in dealing with other countries and gave as examples the German attack on Poland in World War II, the Japanese attack on Pearl Harbor, and the Soviet invasion of Czechoslovakia in 1968.[100] Similarly, a commentary on war preparations published by *Jiefangjun Bao* in July, warned that, as in World War II, a "surprise attack launched by imperialism is entirely possible."[101] Su Yu, the vice minister of defense, also mentioned the possibility of a surprise Soviet attack in an article he wrote to commemorate Army Day in 1977.[102]

While there were some references to the dangers of surprise attack, advocates of this second position generally made only vague references to the possibility that the Soviet Union might launch an "early war" against China—the kind of war that Yu Zhan thought could not possibly occur. A *Jiefangjun Bao* editorial on June 5 called on the PLA to be "prepared for a war breaking out at an early date and be prepared for a big war."[103] Liu Guangtao, a professional political commissar before the Cultural Revolution, and then first secretary of the Heilongjiang provincial Party committee, also called for a "race against time" to prepare against a "major, early war."[104] Finally, an article by the Academy of Military Sciences published in August stated that "we must be prepared to fight an early and large scale war" against the Soviet Union.[105]

Proponents of this second position also based their conclusions on the need for "worst case analysis" in military planning. As the *Jiefangjun Bao* editorial of June 5 put it, "we must step up the work of army building in a still better way . . . so that we will be fully prepared for *any possible contingency.*"[106] In the words of the same paper's commentary on war preparations, published in July, "we must base our work and arrangements on the *possibility* that imperialism and social-imperialism may launch a surprise attack on us sooner than we think."[107] Furthermore, the article by the Academy of Military Sciences cited above stated that "we must plan and arrange our work in terms of the *worst possibilities.*"[108] Making the same point indirectly, other editorials criticized the "gang of four" for denying the danger of war and called on the Party to "overcome the false sense of peace and tranquility which holds that war is a remote affair."[109] Carrying this argument one step further, some writers suggested that China could ensure its security only if it achieved military superiority, as opposed to mere parity, in relation to its adversaries, such that the PLA would "not only have what the enemy has but also what he lacks."[110]

A third point of view on the Soviet threat represented a careful compromise between the two extremes. This group of leaders agreed that the Soviet Union "never gives up its hope of subjugating us"[111] but did not believe that China needed to prepare for a surprise attack, or an early war, on the basis of worst case planning. Most of the central leadership accepted this position in 1977. It appeared, for example, in the Central Committee's January circular on learning from Daqing, in Li Xiannian's opening speech to the Daqing Conference in April, in Yu Qiuli's report to the same conference, and in Hua's report to the Eleventh Party Congress in August.[112] In his report on the revision of the Party Constitution, Ye Jianying appeared to support this third position by acknowledging the possibility that imperialism or social-imperialism might "start an armed aggression against our country," but by refraining from referring to a surprise attack or an early war.[113] In short, Hua and most of China's principal civilian leaders willingly endorsed the gradual modernization of the PLA but did not lend support to an extreme view of the Soviet threat that would justify an excessively high level of defense expenditures.

### The Implications of Military Spending for the Civilian Economy

The second dimension of the debate over the pace of military modernization concerned the effect of defense expenditures on China's civilian economy. Passages in Mao's speech *On the Ten Major Relationships* strongly influenced this discussion. As indicated above, this 1956 speech had endorsed "improvements in armaments," describing the modernization of national defense as an "indispensable" policy goal. Significantly, however, Mao's conclusion called for a reduction in defense spending from the high levels of the Korean War period in order to devote more resources to economic modernization. In the long run, the Chairman argued, this would be the only way to promote military modernization. "If we are not to be bullied in the present-day world, we cannot do without the [atomic] bomb. Then what is to be done about it? One reliable way is to cut military and administrative expenditures down to appropriate proportions and increase expenditures on economic construction. Only with the faster growth of economic construction can there be greater progress in defense construction."[114] More specifically, Mao proposed that military and administrative expenditures, constituting 30 percent of the total state budget during the First Five-Year Plan, be reduced to 20 percent during the Second Five-Year Plan.

The publication of this document—a decision almost certainly reached by Hua Guofeng, as chairman of the Central Committee's subcommittee on the publication of Mao Zedong's writings—placed the proponents of large defense expenditures and rapid military modernization on the defensive. No one could reject Mao's statements and it would be extremely difficult to ignore this particular passage from such an important speech. Nonetheless, as discussion of the issue in the spring of 1977 demonstrated, different interpretations of Mao's statement were possible.

One issue involved the theoretical relationship between civilian economy and military spending, or, in Chinese terms, that between "economic construction" and "national defense." Most writers addressing this question followed Mao's analysis in his speech, *On the Ten Major Relationships*. They argued that, in the short run, high levels of military spending would conflict with civilian development projects and could not be tolerated; while, in the longer run, the growth of the civilian economic base would permit steady but gradual expansion of the national defense industry. An article prepared by the National Defense Industry Office of the State Council, however, took a significantly different point of view. It argued that military spending could stimulate the civilian economy and should therefore be seen as complementary to, not competitive with, economic construction. In the article's words, the national defense industry has a degree of "independence and initiative" that can "*motivate* the development of the entire national economy." While the first position argued for placing limitations on the defense budget with gradual future expansion, the second position supported a substantially higher level of military spending, on grounds that it would simply be an alternative method for promoting economic development.[115]

A second issue concerned the specific limits to be placed on the military budget. Mao's speech had imposed the stringent requirement that only 20 percent of the state budget be allocated to military spending and the concomitant civilian administrative cost. Using Mao's speech as a guideline for policymaking in 1977 raised the question of whether such a limit was still in effect. One of the few articles to address this question directly responded in the negative, assuring military leaders that defense expenditures could never be reduced "without limit," but only "as appropriate." Indeed, the article argued, the implication of Mao's speech was not that military expenditures should necessarily be *reduced,* but rather that a ceiling should be placed on the proportion of the state budget allocated to national defense. Such a ceiling, the article went on, would still allow for gradual increases in military spending as government revenues increased. As the article put it, "it should be pointed out that military expenditures in the state budget are to be cut to an appropriate proportion, but the absolute amount of such expenditures may still increase as a result of the development of economic construction." The article did not specify, however, what proportion of the state budget should be allocated to military spending.[116]

The available evidence suggests that the Fifth National People's Congress, held in February 1978, reached a compromise on this issue.[117] The Congress probably rejected some of the most sweeping proposals for limiting the military budget (e.g., the conversion of national defense industry to civilian uses in peacetime, the restriction of defense expenditures to 20 percent of the total state budget, a substantial reduction in the size of the PLA). On the other hand, those who argued that the Soviet threat to

China warranted a costly and rapid program of military modernization were also overruled. Instead, Chinese leaders have apparently decided on a more gradual program. Most authoritative statements on military spending have asserted that the needs of the civilian economy must be given priority over military requirements and have acknowledged that, as a result, the PLA will be using its presently available equipment for some time to come.[118]

In fact, both the military and economic arguments for such a compromise position were compelling. Obviously, a crash program of modernization, particularly one that required extensive purchases of military technology from abroad, would have greatly strained the civilian economy and China's foreign exchange accounts. Equally important, the PLA was simply not prepared for a massive infusion of modern technology. China's military commanders appeared convinced that their troops would need much more advanced technical training and their officers more experience in conducting large-scale, multi-service exercises, before the PLA would be ready to absorb large numbers of modern weapons.[119]

Nonetheless, this more gradual program still carries the promise that the PLA will transform itself into a modern military force by the turn of the century. In this sense, it is particularly apt that China's civilian leaders have described economic modernization and scientific development as a "race against time." It will be a challenge, indeed, to expand the nation's economic and scientific base rapidly enough to fulfill the pledge of military modernization by the year 2000.

## V. Conclusions

This analysis of the debate over China's global posture between 1973 and 1978 can not only increase our knowledge of an important and dramatic historical episode in contemporary Chinese history, but can also contribute to our broader understanding of the process by which foreign policy is debated, formulated, and implemented in China. More specifically, this case study provides insights into three aspects of the Chinese foreign policymaking process: (1) the criteria by which foreign policy options are evaluated, (2) the process by which foreign policy is formulated, and (3) the strategies by which different groups and individuals pursue their personal and organizational interests in the Chinese foreign policy arena.

### Evolution of the Terms of Debate

One of the most basic conclusions of this study is that in the post-Cultural Revolution decade, the major elements of China's global posture—its view of the world, the major outlines of its foreign policy, its policy toward the two major powers, and its military doctrine and force posture — have all been highly controversial issues among the Chinese elite. They joined a series of recurring debates over foreign and military policy. Debates over military policy in 1955-56 and 1958-59, disagreements over China's response to the Great Leap Forward and the emerging Sino-Soviet split in the early 1960s, controversies over the escalation of American involvement in Vietnam in 1964-65, and a protracted debate over policy toward the Soviet Union and the United States between 1966 and 1972 provide a few examples.

As the evidence collected in this study suggests, the Chinese debated the question of China's global posture between 1973 and 1978 in terms similar to those that provided the framework for earlier controversies.[120] Foreign military policy became controversial under three principal circumstances, the first two illustrated by portions of the foregoing analysis of the rounds of debate, and the third involving a process described throughout the period examined in this study.

*Opposing Responses to Difficult International Problems.* Policymakers offer different opinions on the most effective response to complex and often intractable international problems. China's foreign policymakers, for example, at times cannot agree on defining the international situation, on assessing the principal military threats facing their country, on determining which strategy to adopt in confronting those threats, and on determining which tactics would be most effective in particular diplomatic and military circumstances. These differences arise not only because of the inherent difficulty in answering these questions, but also because policymakers differ over the ideological acceptability of a particular world view or strategy or, alternatively, because they differ over the degree to which ideological constraints should be loosened for the sake of specific diplomatic or military advantage.

During the period under discussion in this study, controversies arose over each of the issues alluded to above. The question of defining *the international environment* constituted a major source of disagreement throughout the period, particularly during Round One, between 1973 and 1975. Both the Albanians and the more radical leaders inside China expressed concern that the theory of the three worlds, developed by Mao and presented by Zhou Enlai and Deng Xiaoping in 1974, was both empirically and ideologically incorrect. Critics maintained that it negated the role of revolutionary movements in the modern world and ran counter to Leninist teachings on the nature of international politics in the era of imperialism. In this sense, the 1973-75 round seemed similar to earlier disagreements over the relative rapaciousness of the United States and the Soviet Union and the degree of collusion and contention between them.[121]

Chinese leaders also offered different *assessments of the Soviet threat* throughout the period discussed in this essay, especially in Round Two, between 1973 and 1975. Policymakers disagreed over the likelihood of a Soviet attack against China and the military balance between Peking and Moscow. Some saw a Soviet Union too preoccupied with the United States and Western Europe to launch a major attack against China. Others claimed that a surprise attack, a frequent tactic of imperialist countries, could not be ruled out. Some warned that, because of China's economic and technological backwardness, the Soviet Union posed a serious threat to Chinese security. Others argued, primarily on ideological grounds, that the "internal contradictions" within the Soviet Union, the crucial role played by "human factors" in war, and the popular support enjoyed by the Chinese government, would enable the Chinese to defeat the Russians despite China's technological inferiority. In this sense, these more recent debates resembled those of 1955-56 and 1964-65, in which Chinese leaders also differed significantly over the degree to which the United States posed an immediate military threat to Chinese security.[122]

On the issue of global *strategy,* Chinese leaders differed over several questions between 1973 and 1975. What kind of united front should be constructed to deal with the current international environment? What should be its principal targets? Would it be ideologically justifiable for China, in order to defend against the Soviet threat, to compromise with the United States, improve its relations with the capitalist countries of Western Europe and Japan, and form a broad united front with all established Third World governments, some of which could not possibly be considered progressive? Or should China restrict membership in the united front to governments and movements with "purer" revolutionary credentials and direct the front equally against both the United States and the Soviet Union? In this sense, the debates of 1973-75 recalled the controversy over the so-called *sanhe yishao* (three conciliations and one reduction) program of the early 1960s. Under that plan China would have reduced its assistance to revolutionary movements and attempted an improvement in relations with "imperialism, revisionism and [Third World] reaction"—all in an attempt to bolster its security in the aftermath of the Great Leap Forward.[123]

Finally, Chinese leaders had serious differences in the mid-1970s over the proper *tactics* to be applied in their relations with the Soviet Union. Some argued for a flexible diplomatic approach; others argued for intransigence, and seemed even to condone the use of military force. This supports the proposition, first suggested by Allen Whiting, that Chinese leaders have often differed over the proper response to an external threat, with some advocating the use of "deterrence and diplomacy," and others favoring "direct confrontation and the controlled use of force."[124] The

Round Two debate over policy toward the Soviet Union in 1973-75 indicated that this question involves both pragmatic and ideological considerations. Chinese leaders ask which strategy will work best in a particular circumstance, but those who favor direct confrontation often argue that, by the very nature of imperialism, those who try to deal with it through concession and compromise will fail.

*Conflicting Concerns over Related Domestic Issues.* Foreign policy is linked, often through trade policy and military policy, to important domestic social and economic issues. Controversy may thus arise over the effects on domestic policy resulting from a particular foreign policy stance. For example, during Round Three (1974-77), China's leaders knew that even a program of gradual military modernization would place greater demands on scarce economic resources and would therefore tend to make economic efficiency an even more important goal in economic planning. This, in turn (as suggested in Thomas Fingar's chapter in this volume) would have important policy implications in the areas of education, science and technology, industrial management, and agriculture. For this reason, the Military Affairs Commission's modernization program became controversial in 1975. Both moderate and radical leaders saw it as part of a broader package of socioeconomic programs, emphasizing productivity and efficiency over egalitarianism and populism. For the moderates, military modernization provided a strong justification for abandoning most of the "new born things" of the Cultural Revolution. From the radicals' perspective, the program would have been incompatible with their interest in "continuing the revolution" and combating internal revisionism, not only because of its interconnected socioeconomic policies but also because of the resulting reduction in PLA participation in civilian political and ideological activities.

On a more pragmatic level, civilian planners and managers apparently tried to prevent military spending from interfering significantly with economic development projects. In the course of Round Four, from 1977 to 1978, proponents of higher defense spending reacted to such opposition by invoking the spectre of a Soviet surprise attack to justify a crash program of military modernization and even argued that military spending would indirectly stimulate, rather than restrain, the civilian economy. As in the 1955-56 controversy, the proponents of high-speed military modernization were, at least until 1978, unable to persuade their opponents that the external risks justified the domestic costs and a more gradual program of modernization was ultimately adopted.

*Political Power Plays.* Finally, foreign policy can become a controversial issue as it is manipulated in the quest for political power. Chinese foreign policymaking has been examined as if it were a selfless and rational process, by which decision makers develop programs they consider best suited to achieving China's domestic and international goals. But less high-minded, more selfish, goals also play an important part in the policymaking process. Leaders may pursue their corporate interests by attempting to maximize the opportunities (duties and responsibilities) and resources (status, influence, manpower, or budgets) assigned to the organizations for which they are responsible, and by preventing encroachments by other agencies. They may also pursue their own personal interests by attempting to acquire status, influence, promotions, wealth, or security, either for themselves or friends. As Vernon Aspaturian described this phenomenon in the Soviet Union: "Differences and conflicts over foreign policy in the party may result from . . . personality differences at the very highest levels, involving personal ambitions for power, prestige, and status."[125]

In this study, for example, it was observed that regional military commanders most likely opposed the 1975 military modernization package because it threatened their corporate and personal interests. It would have reduced the size of the regional forces, stripped them of many domestic political and economic responsibilities, increased the relative prestige and budgets of the main forces, and might even have caused a decrease in the number of military regions, costing commanders their jobs.

More importantly, the radical leaders on the Politburo attempted to manipulate foreign policy issues in their struggle for power. Placed on the defensive by the moderates on domestic issues in the early 1970s, radicals accused their opponents of adopting foreign policies that amounted to "capitulationism" and "national betrayal." Once these charges attracted attention, the radicals advanced to the next step in their strategy: to link the "capitulationist" foreign policies with moderate domestic programs.

*Policy Process*

This study suggests that the Chinese government formulates foreign policy in a process similar to that identified by Thomas Fingar concerning China's domestic policy. Policymaking proceeds through a series of rounds, with the specific issues under consideration changing from one round to the next. Debate in each round is constrained by decisions made in previous rounds, the outcome of each round raising further issues to be considered in subsequent rounds. For these reasons, debates over China's global posture between 1973 and 1978 dealt with ever more specific issues over time. Discussions of a general world view in 1973–75 gave way to debate over strategies and tactics for dealing with the Soviet Union. Once the Chinese resolved the debate over the desirability of military modernization, policymakers proceeded to address a more specific issue: the speed with which such modernization should be pursued.

Some qualifications and amendments to this general model of policymaking are necessary, however. First, the *rounds in the process may overlap*. New issues may be taken up before old issues are completely resolved, and old issues that had presumably been settled may be raised again in later rounds. Thus, the discussion of the theory of the three worlds occurred simultaneously with the debate over what policy to apply in relations with the Soviet Union. The issue of the desirability of military modernization was revived, albeit in a very limited way, in early 1977 — long after that issue had presumably been "resolved."

Second, in most rounds, leaders must choose between *competing policy packages*. These packages differ widely — some are thoughtful and thorough; others are sketchy and simplistic. Some packages contain detailed proposals for action yet others simply criticize established policies. However, the differences between competing packages should probably not be overstated. Usually, they differ not over the goals to be pursued, but over the priorities to be established in the event that goals conflict. The radicals, for example, never repudiated the *concept* of military modernization in 1975, nor denied the importance of technology in warfare. Instead, they objected to the emphasis that the Military Affairs Commission placed on these aspects of military policy. As one article put it, "We have never denied the need to have iron and steel to wage war, nor have we ever denied the necessity of improving weapons and equipment, intensifying military training, and raising the level of military technology. The question is to put these things in proper perspective."[126]

Third, debate over global posture displayed much more *fluidity* than the debate over domestic politics during the same period, as described by Fingar. As the foreign policy debate proceeded, two types of change were evident:

- Policy packages changed significantly from one round to the next. It would be wrong to speak of a single "radical" position throughout this period, for example. The emphasis on war preparations, so important in the 1974 package, was totally absent from that which the radicals promoted in 1975–76. Conversely, while civilian moderates seemed to deny the need for military preparations in 1974, they incorporated military modernization into their policy package in 1975–76.
- Coalitional alignments changed from one round to the next, as the issues under debate changed. Thus, central military leaders were wooed actively by the radicals in 1974, joined with civilian

moderates in 1975 and 1976, but then appeared to split with many of the moderates over the pace of military modernization and the nature of the Soviet threat in 1977–78.

These dynamic elements in the policymaking process produced considerable uncertainty in Chinese foreign policy between 1973 and 1978. The formal adoption and promulgation of the theory of the three worlds was effectively blocked between 1974 and 1977, even though this may have had relatively little effect on actual policy. Conversely, although military modernization was formally adopted as national policy in 1975, implementation was obstructed until 1977.

*Strategies*

Based on their distinctive strategies of political maneuver, we can identify four types of participants in this policymaking process.

First, there are those who constitute the *establishment*. These are the leaders who, during a particular period or round, dominate the formal policymaking arena, and whose policy package therefore prevails. Because they constitute, in effect, the "government," they must define their policy package with a high degree of specificity. In so doing, they obviously try to maintain the support of the members of their coalition, and to strengthen that coalition if they possibly can. At the same time, because they are the "government," they can try to tighten organization discipline, even to the extent of launching rectification campaigns against potential opponents, in order to force compliance with their policy package.

*Advocates* are a second type of leader. These are officials who wish to challenge prevailing policy, but do not seek higher political office themselves. Advocates may present their alternative policy packages at central work conferences in the press, hoping to convince the hitherto undecided or to woo support away from the governing coalition. In the period covered by this essay, the proponents of high military spending in 1977–78 are perhaps the most prominent examples of political advocates, although the "gang of four" may have acted as advocates in earlier rounds of the post–Cultural Revolution debates.

In contrast to advocates, *contenders* are those who manipulate policy debates to gain office for themselves and their followers. Contenders attempt to discredit the establishment's policy package by isolating and criticizing its most vulnerable components. In so doing, they may describe the policy package in vastly exaggerated terms—they may, for instance, describe a flexible diplomatic policy toward the Soviet Union as an instance of "capitulationism," or a program of military modernization as abandonment of "people's war." In addition, they may opportunistically jump from one issue to another, abandoning earlier positions once the political advantage has been lost. Contenders also try to assemble an alternative policy package that will gain the support of disgruntled groups, but their package is usually much less specific than that of the establishment. Indeed, it is often a negativistic package; that is, long on criticism of prevailing policy, but short on detailed alternatives.

Finally, a fourth category of leaders may be described as *disrupters:* those who, having lost the debate in a given round, seek to sabotage the implementation of policy, perhaps in an attempt to discredit it. Their tactics, as illustrated by the "gang of four's" attempt to sabotage implementation of the 1975 military modernization program, can include denying favorable publicity to the prevailing policy, writing articles that directly or indirectly criticize it, stimulating debate at local levels over the wisdom of the policy, and insisting that local levels should have the authority to ignore policy directives they deem to be incorrect.

Obviously, disrupters must, if they are to sabotage policy implementation, have some way of communicating doubt and dissent to lower levels, and of assuring potential supporters that criticism and insubordination is permissible. The influence of the "gang of four" over the news media provided the first of these prerequisites; while the legacy of the Cultural Revolution, and particularly the radicals' ability to insert the principle of "going against the tide" into the 1973 Party Constitution, provided the second. Whether members of future Chinese elites will be able to satisfy these same two conditions is difficult to say. But there is little doubt that, since the purge of the "gang of four," Chinese leaders have attempted to ensure that disruption will not be a political strategy available in future struggles for power.

## Notes

1. The relative weight of foreign policy questions and issues of domestic policy in the succession struggle is beyond the scope of this essay. In general, I agree with Jonathan Pollack that domestic issues were more important than foreign policy, and that questions of China's economic relations with the West, as discussed in Ann Fenwick's chapter in this volume, were more controversial than geopolitical and military issues. *See* Jonathan D. Pollack, *Political Succession and Foreign Policy in China,* JOURNAL OF INTERNATIONAL AFFAIRS 275–89 (No. 2, 1978).

2. Merle Goldman, *China's Anti-Confucian Campaign, 1973–76,* CHINA QUARTERLY, Sep. 1975, at 435; Kenneth Lieberthal, *The Foreign Policy Debate in Peking as Seen Through Allegorical Articles, 1973–76,* CHINA QUARTERLY, Sep. 1977, at 528. *See also* KENNETH LIEBERTHAL, SINO-SOVIET CONFLICT IN THE 1970s (1978) [hereafter SINO-SOVIET CONFLICT].

3. *See* John W. Lewis' chapter in this volume. *See also* Jonathan Pollack, China's Changing Polity (Jan. 2-7, 1978) (presented to the Workshop on Security and Arms Control in the Pacific, Aspen Institute for Humanistic Studies, Punalu'u, Hawaii); and Paul H. B. Godwin, *China's Defense Dilemma: The Modernization Crisis of 1976 and 1977,* CONTEMPORARY CHINA, Fall 1978, at 63-85.

4. I plan to publish separately a detailed account of my disagreements with Goldman and Lieberthal over the foreign policy debates during the *Pi Lin Pi Kong* campaign.

5. Chou En-lai [Zhou Enlai], *Report to the Tenth National Congress of the Communist Party of China* (Aug. 24, 1973) *in* THE TENTH NATIONAL CONGRESS OF THE COMMUNIST PARTY OF CHINA 1-37 (1973) [hereafter TENTH NATIONAL CONGRESS].

6. Wang Hongwen, *Report on the Revision of the Party Constitution* (Aug. 24, 1973), TENTH NATIONAL CONGRESS, *supra* note 5, at 39-57.

7. Compare the speeches by Ye Jianying [Yeh Chien-ying] and Bequir Balluku at the November 6, 1972, banquet to welcome an Albanian military delegation to China. New China News Agency (Peking) [hereafter NCNA], Nov. 6, 1972, *in* FOREIGN BROADCAST INFORMATION SERVICE, DAILY REPORT: PEOPLE'S REPUBLIC OF CHINA [hereafter FBIS], Nov. 7, 1972, at A2.

8. *The Theory and Practice of Revolution,* Zeri i Popullit (editorial, July 7, 1977), *in* FOREIGN BROADCAST INFORMATION SERVICE, DAILY REPORT: EASTERN EUROPE, July 8, 1977, at B1-14.

9. *Huang Hua's Report on the World Situation* (July 30, 1977), ISSUES AND STUDIES, Dec. 1977, at 76, 93. *See also Huang Hua's Report on the World Situation,* ISSUES AND STUDIES, Nov. 1977, at 78; *Huang Hua's Report on the World Situation,* ISSUES AND STUDIES, Jan. 1978, at 94. The quotation is drawn from the passage in the December 1977 issue at 93. Here, Huang was referring specifically to events in late 1975.

10. *Speech by Teng Hsiao-p'ing* [Deng Xiaoping], *Chairman of Delegation of People's Republic of China, in* PEKING REVIEW [hereafter PR], Apr. 12, 1974 (Supp.).

11. Zhou Enlai, *Report on the Work of the Government* (Jan. 13, 1975), *in* DOCUMENTS OF THE FIRST SESSION OF THE FOURTH NATIONAL PEOPLE'S CONGRESS OF THE PEOPLE'S REPUBLIC OF CHINA 45 (1975) [hereafter FOURTH NATIONAL PEOPLE'S CONGRESS].

12. *Compare* THE CONSTITUTION OF THE PEOPLE'S REPUBLIC OF CHINA (1975), in FOURTH NATIONAL PEOPLE'S CONGRESS, *supra* note 11, at 3, *with* THE CONSTITUTION OF THE PEOPLE'S REPUBLIC OF CHINA (1978), *in* PR, Mar. 17, 1978, at 5.

13. Zhang Chunqiao, *Report on the Revision of the Constitution* (Jan. 13, 1975), *in* FOURTH NATIONAL PEOPLE'S CONGRESS, *supra* note 11.

14. *Chiang Ch'ing's [Jiang Qing's] Speech to Foreign Affairs Cadres* (Mar. 1975) *in* CHINESE LAW AND GOVERNMENT, Spring-Summer 1976, at 49-61. Deng Xiaoping's speech to the Third Plenum in July 1977, again according to Taiwanese sources, directly refuted Jiang Qing's formulation: "Any foreign policy which aims only at befriending the blacks, the poor, and the small countries, while opposing indiscriminately the whites, the rich, and the powerful is an erroneous line which completely disregards the international class struggle, and is seemingly leftist but actually rightist." *See Notes of Deng Xiaoping's Speech at the 1977 CCP Central Committee Plenum,* BACKGROUND ON CHINA, May 17, 1978.

15. Ren Guping, *The Third World Countries Are a Great Motive Force that Pushes Forward History,* Renmin Ribao [People's Daily, hereafter RMRB], Oct. 14, 1974, *in* SURVEY OF THE PEOPLE'S REPUBLIC OF CHINA PRESS [hereafter SPRCP], No. 74–45, at 52.

16. Editorial Department of Renmin Ribao, *Chairman Mao's Theory of the Differentiation of the Three Worlds Is a Major Contribution to Marxism-Leninism,* PR, Nov. 4, 1977, at 18.

17. Lin Biao, *Long Live the Victory of People's War,* RMRB, Sep. 3, 1965, and Lin Biao, *Report to the Ninth National Congress of the Communist Party of China* (delivered on Apr. 1, adopted on Apr. 14, 1969), *in* PR, Apr. 30, 1969, at 16–35.

18. The principal exception to this last Russian offer was that the Soviet Union wished to retain jurisdiction over Heixiazi Island, on the Chinese side of the Thalweg. See SINO-SOVIET CONFLICT, *supra* note 2, at 8–22, for a summary of Soviet diplomatic initiatives between 1969 and 1973.

19. Zhou Enlai, TENTH NATIONAL CONGRESS, *supra* note 5, at 27.

20. Pravda, Sep. 25, 1973, *cited in* CURRENT DIGEST OF THE SOVIET PRESS, Oct. 24, 1973, at 4–5, *quoted in* SINO-SOVIET CONFLICT, *supra* note 2, at 14.

21. C. L. Sulzberger, *Chou Attacks Russians for Delaying Border Pact,* New York Times, Oct. 29, 1973, at 1, col. 5.

22. *Document of the Ministry of Foreign Affairs of the People's Republic of China,* PR, Oct. 10, 1969, at 8, 15. *See also Statement of the Government of the People's Republic of China, id.* at 3.

23. Yan Feng, *Strategically Despise the Enemy, Tactically Take Him Seriously,* HONG QI [RED FLAG, hereafter HQ], No. 11, 1974, *in* PR, Dec. 13, 1974, at 6.

24. English Version of Greetings Message to USSR, Peking Radio (Nov. 7, 1974), *in* FBIS, Nov. 11, 1974, at A3.

25. *Compare* the 1974 NPC message *with* the Chinese government statements of October 7 and October 8, 1969, *supra* note 22.

26. This interpretation contrasts with that of Kenneth Lieberthal. Lieberthal points out that the proposal made publicly in November 1974 had been made to the Russians privately in 1971, and concludes that the NPC message did not represent a significant Chinese initiative. SINO-SOVIET CONFLICT, *supra* note 2, at 56. But one important feature of the "flexible" program was to make *public* overtures to the Soviet Union, even if they merely repeated private proposals made earlier. Moreover, Lieberthal ignores the failure of the November 1974 message to demand that the Soviet Union acknowledge the inequity of the nineteenth century border treaties or to insist that those treaties be taken as the basis of a border settlement.

27. Shi Yuxin, *Refute the Fabricators of Lies,* LISHI YANJIU [HISTORICAL RESEARCH], No. 1, 1974, *in* SELECTIONS FROM PEOPLE'S REPUBLIC OF CHINA MAGAZINES [hereafter SPRCM], No. 75–1, at 1.

28. The first proposal had appeared in Zhou Enlai's report to the Tenth Party Congress; the second was new, but would reappear in Hua Guofeng's report to the Fifth National People's Congress in February 1978.

29. *Soviet Armed Reconnaissance Helicopter Crew Released,* PR, Jan. 2, 1976, at 7.

30. William Safire, *To Catch a Flea,* New York Times, Mar. 31, 1977, at A25, col. 2.

31. Neville Maxwell, *U.S. Said to Warn China on Soviets,* Washington Post, Nov.

25, 1974, at C1, C17, cols. 4–5. [hereafter Maxwell].

32. One Renmin Ribao article in October seems to have been part of an ongoing debate over the fate of the Soviet helicopter. It concerned a horse "captured by the Liangshan peasant army" in the novel WATER MARGIN, but then returned to the "emperor" by Song Jiang, "who had usurped the seat of second in command in the insurgent army." Song Jiang "apologized time and time again" to the officer who had ridden the horse into battle, and said that, "if he did not return the horse to the emperor, he would be guilty of resisting the mandate of heaven." RMRB, Oct. 7, 1975. For another, later, article criticizing the return of prisoners of war, see Liu Xianzhao and Wei Shiming, *From Class Capitulationists to National Capitulationists*, RMRB, June 3, 1976.

For a criticism of Lin Biao's desire to have "secret negotiations" with the Soviet Union, see Liang Xiao, *Critique of Lin Biao's Capitulationism*, RMRB, Jan. 28, 1976.

33. This paragraph is based principally on the following articles: Theoretical Group of "389" Warship of PLA Navy, *A Just War Will Surely Win*, HQ, No. 12, 1974, in SPRCM, No. 74-24, at 46–51; Liang Xiao, *Study "On Salt and Iron"— Big Polemic between the Confucian and Legalist Schools in the Middle Western Han Dynasty* [hereafter *On Salt and Iron*], HQ, No. 5, 1974, in FBIS, May 21, 1974, at E1; Luo Siding, *On the Struggle Between Patriotism and National Betrayal During the Northern Sung Period* [hereafter Luo Siding], HQ, No. 11, 1974, in FBIS, Nov. 20, 1974, at E1. Unlike Kenneth Lieberthal, I see no difference between the arguments presented by Liang Xiao and Luo Siding in these two articles.

34. Luo Siding, *supra* note 33, at E2.

35. RMRB, Sep. 7, 1975. For other articles attempting to demonstrate a necessary connection between revisionist (or retrogressive) policies at home and appeasement abroad, see: *On Salt and Iron, supra* note 33; Shi Feng, *The Struggle Between the Honor-Confucius and Oppose-Confucius Lines During the War of Resistance Against Japan*, XUEXI YU PIPAN [STUDY AND CRITICISM, hereafter XXYPP], No. 6, 1974, in SPRCM, No. 74-13, at 6; Hua Tian and Zhi Guang, *Revisionists Inevitably Are Capitulationists*, Guangming Ribao [Guangming Daily, hereafter GMRB], Oct. 9, 1975, in SPRCP, No. 75-43, at 200; and *Unfold Criticism of "Water Margin,"* RMRB, Sep. 4, 1975, in SPRCP, No. 75-38, at 16–18.

36. See *Dead Soul of Confucius, Fond Dreams of New Tsars*, RMRB, Jan. 24, 1974, in PR, Feb. 8, 1974, at 12.

37. Fang Hai, *Be Good at Seeing the Essence Through the Appearance*, XXYPP, No. 6, 1974, in SPRCM, No. 74-13, at 15, 18.

38. SINO-SOVIET CONFLICT, *supra* note 2, at 109.

39. Zhou Enlai, TENTH NATIONAL CONGRESS, *supra* note 5, at 24.

40. John Burns, *Chinese Leaders in Policy Change Play Down Moscow as a Threat*, New York Times, Oct. 5, 1974, at 10, col. 4.

41. At least one article, published in the radical journal XXYPP, tried to forge a middle-of-the-road position that combined elements of both packages. In allegorical terms, it began by agreeing with the "radicals" that the Soviet Union could be defeated, even though it had a "mighty army of one million strong," because there was "disunity within its ranks and instability in society." But the article went on to

criticize the factional activities of the radical leaders in the Politburo by warning that China could defeat the Soviet Union only if Chinese society was unified and stable, and if there was "harmony among generals and ministers." It concluded by warning that it would be wrong to "overestimate" one's own strength, and underestimate that of the enemy. Little wonder that the article was criticized in a later issue of the same journal for "factual errors." For the article, see Li Xingbin, *On the Battle of Feishui*, XXYPP, No. 12, 1974, *in* SPRCM, No. 75-03, at 12; and the criticism, *Several Opinions About "On the Battle of Feishui,"* XXYPP, No. 2, 1975, *in* SPRCM, No 75-11, at 44.

42. Theoretical Study Group of the Ministry of Foreign Affairs, *Premier Chou [Zhou] Creatively Carried Out Chairman Mao's Revolutionary Line in Foreign Affairs*, PR, Jan. 28, 1977, at 13.

43. *The Central Committee Notice Concerning Grasping Revolution and Promoting Production*, Zhongfa No. 21, 1974, *in* ISSUES AND STUDIES, Jan. 1975, at 101, 103.

44. On the redefinition of the focus of the *Pi Lin Pi Kong* Campaign, see *Conscientiously Study Chairman Mao's Military Writings*, HQ, No. 9, 1974, *in* PR, Sep. 20, 1974, at 9; and the joint editorial of Renmin Ribao, HONG QI and Jiefangjun Bao [Liberation Army News, hereafter JFJB], Oct. 1, 1974, *in* PR, Oct. 4, 1974, at 14.

45. Hong Cheng, *Brilliant Ideas, A Great Victory*, RMRB, Oct. 9, 1974, translated as *A Splendid Strategic Plan* in PR, Sep. 27, 1974, at 30.

46. Shen Si, *Dissecting the Reactionary Nature of Lin Biao's "Six Tactical Principles,"* LISHI YANJIU, No. 1, 1975, *in* SPRCM, No. 75-11, at 1, 7.

47. Shen Si, *Penetratingly Criticize Lin Biao's "Six Tactical Principles,"* HQ, No. 8, 1974, *in* SPRCM, No. 74-14, at 57.

48. *What is Behind his Trumpeting About "A Matter of Secondary Importance"?* GMRB, Sep. 12, 1974, *in* FBIS, Sep. 25, 1974, at E2.

49. *Heighten Vigilance, Defend the Motherland*, HQ, No. 8, 1974, *in* SPRCM, No. 74-14, at 78.

50. See Yu Zidao, *Lin Biao's Right Military Line as Seen from the Strategic Shift in the Early Period of the War of Resistance Against Japan*, XXYPP, No. 8, 1974, *in* SPRCM, No. 74-15, at 4; Yu Xuejun, *The Struggle Between Two Military Lines During the War to Liberate the Northeast*, XXYPP, No. 9, 1974, *in* SPRCM, No. 74-18, at 1; and Zhan Libo, *A Critique of Lin Biao's "On Short Swift Thrusts,"* HQ, No. 1, 1975, *in* SPRCM, No. 75-04, at 45.

51. Editorial Departments of Renmin Ribao, HONG QI and Jiefangjun Bao; *New Year Message*, RMRB, Jan. 1, 1975, *in* PR, Jan. 3, 1975, at 6.

52. On the reorganization of the General Staff Department, see *Two Provincial Party Chiefs Identified Six Posts Still Vacant*, China News Summary, No. 549, January 2, 1975; and *A Low Key May Day*, China News Summary, No. 565, May 7, 1975. On the increase in military procurement in 1975, see JOINT ECONOMIC COMM., SUBCOMM. ON PRIORITIES AND ECONOMY IN GOVERNMENT, 94TH CONG., 2ND SESS., ALLOCATION OF RESOURCES IN THE SOVIET UNION AND CHINA — 1976 (Comm. Print 1976). On the 1975 military exercises, see Pollack, *supra* note 3, at 37.

53. For a radical critique of Deng's speech, see *Forever Adhere to Chairman Mao's Line on Army Building*, HQ, No. 8, 1976, *in* SPRCM, No. 76-26, at 66. For a defense

of Deng's speech, see *Speed up the Revolutionization and Modernization of Our Army, Build a Powerful National Defense Army,* HQ, No. 8, 1977, *in* SPRCM, No. 77-29, at 1; and *Fifty Years of Glorious Fighting by the Chinese PLA,* JFJB, July 28, 1977, *in* FBIS, Aug. 2, 1977, at E9. An attempt to reconstruct the events of the 1975 MAC meetings appears in Ding Runru, *The Struggle Between Critics and Defenders of Deng Within the Bandit Army,* FEIJING YUEBAO [BANDIT AFFAIRS MONTHLY], Sep. 5, 1976, at 18.

54. On the force reduction proposals presented in 1975, see Victor Zorza, *China's Scrutable Struggle,* Washington Post, April 11, 1976, at C1, C5, cols. 5-6; and MORTON ABRAMOWITZ, CHINESE MILITARY CAPACITIES, *in* HOUSE COMM. ON INTERNATIONAL RELATIONS, 94TH CONG., 1ST SESS., UNITED STATES-SOVIET UNION-CHINA: THE GREAT POWER TRIANGLE (1976).

55. *Army Day 1976 and the Army in the Past Year,* China News Summary, No. 625, Aug. 5, 1976.

56. On the naval development program and Mao's reaction, see *Chairman Mao's Revolutionary Line Guides Chinese Navy Forward,* NCNA, Sep. 15, 1977, *in* SPRCP, No. 77-39, at 15. A previous article justified naval development by referring to the Soviet naval buildup in the Pacific and argued that a powerful navy was needed if China was to liberate Taiwan and defend its islands in the South China Sea. The Theoretical Study Group of the Navy, *Hold High the Banner of Chairman Mao, Build a Powerful Navy,* RMRB, June 24, 1977, *in* SPRCP, No. 77-27, at 53.

57. Workers' Theoretical Group of the Peking Equipment Installation Company and the Editing and Writing Group of *Manuscripts on the Modern History of China, Wei Yuan's Thought Against Aggression,* WENWU [CULTURAL RELICS], May 1975, *in* SPRCM, No. 75-27, at 1, 3.

58. *Id.* at 5.

59. *Id.*

60. *Id.* at 7-8.

61. Jun Da, *The Campaign of Four Crossings of the Chi River is a Brilliant Example Embodying Chairman Mao's Strategic Thought,* RMRB, Oct. 17, 1975, *in* SPRCP, No. 75-45, at 60, 63.

62. *Id.*

63. Hong Cheng, *Qi Jiguang's Thought of Running the Army,* LISHI YANJIU, No. 6, 1975, *in* SPRCM, No. 76-4, at 36, 40.

64. CENTRAL INTELLIGENCE AGENCY, CHINESE COMMUNIST PARTY ORGANIZATION, Reference Aid A(CR) 75-34 (1975).

65. The Criticism Group of the Academy of Military Science, *The Fierce Struggle with Lin Biao and the Gang of Four for Control of the Army over a Period of 10 Years,* Peking Radio (Apr. 16, 1978), *in* FBIS, Apr. 18, 1978, at E1, E3.

66. *See* The Criticism Group of the Military Science Academy, *Our Army Discipline Brooks No Undermining,* RMRB, Feb. 4, 1977, *in* FBIS, Feb. 7, 1977, at E14; On a matter less directly related to military modernization, the MAC also discussed retirement provisions for military officers and adopted a plan that would have transferred retired officers to civilian posts and guaranteed them salaries equivalent to those they received in military service. Zhang Chunqiao allegedly opposed these provisions on the grounds that they gave "special privileges" to military officers, but

no one else supported his objections. After the meeting, Zhang allegedly commissioned two articles, published in a Shanghai newspaper and in XXYPP, which, by insinuation, charged the PLA with seeking special favors. *See* Xiang Jun, *Tiao Xiaosan's Logic and Bourgeois Rights — Criticizing Two Sinister Articles Against the Army Concocted on Chang Chun-chiao's [Zhang Chunqiao's] Instructions,* JFJB, Mar. 10, 1977, *in* FBIS, Mar. 23, 1977, at E15.

67. Theoretical Group of the PLA Navy, *Hold Chairman Mao's Banner High, Build a Powerful Navy — Some Insights Acquired After Reading "The Chinese People Have Stood Up!",* RMRB, June 24, 1977, *in* FBIS, June 30, 1977, at E4; and *Gang of Four's Crime In Sabotaging China's Navy Building Exposed,* NCNA, Mar. 19, 1977, *in* SPRCP, No. 77-12, at 171.

68. Theoretical Group of the PLA Navy, *supra* note 67, at E4-5.

69. Hsieh Cheng, *A Sinister Programme for Usurping Party and State Power,* PR, Dec. 10, 1976, at 13; and Hsieh Cheng, *Ferreting Out the Bourgeoisie in the Army — Another "Gang of Four" Scheme,* PR, Mar. 4, 1977, at 9.

70. *Id.*

71. An Miao, *Confucianist Capitulationism and the Traitor Lin Biao,* RMRB, Aug. 12, 1975, *in* SPRCP, No. 75-34, at 171, 178, 179.

72. The theoretical unit of the Military Training Department of the Grand General Staff, *Cut Off the Sinister Tentacles,* RMRB, Dec. 4, 1976, *in* SPRCP, No. 76-50, at 134, 141.

73. The Criticism Group of the Academy of Military Science, *The Fierce Struggle with Lin Biao and the Gang of Four for Control of the Army over a Period of 10 Years, supra* note 65, at E3.

74. *Heroic Army Company Daring to Fight Bourgeoisie Inside and Outside the Party,* RMRB, Aug. 11, 1976, *in* SPRCP, No. 76-33, at 163, 166.

75. *Id.* at 166; *see also* The Party Branch of the "Good Eighth Company" on Nanjing Road, *Actively Participate in Struggle to Hit Back at the Right Deviationist Wind to Reverse Verdicts,* HQ, No. 4, 1976, *in* SPRCM, No. 76-11, at 38. The experience of the Good Eighth Company stood in direct contrast to that of the "Hard Boned Sixth Company." This, the model unit of those who supported the military modernization program, was described as giving due attention to "line education" and political training but clearly placed greater emphasis on military preparedness. The Hard Boned Sixth Company reappeared as the PLA's principal basic level model in 1977. *See generally* Party Branch of "Tough Bone Sixth Company" of a Certain Unit of PLA Nanjing Units, *Grasp the Line Education, Promote the Work of Preparations Against War,* HQ, No. 1, 1976, *in* SPRCM, No. 76-3, at 102.

76. Hsieh Cheng, *Ferreting Out the Bourgeoisie in the Army — Another Gang of Four Scheme, supra* note 69, at 9.

77. *Id.* at 11; *See* The Criticism Group of the Academy of Military Science, *The Fierce Struggle with Lin Biao and the Gang of Four for Control of the Army over a Period of 10 Years, supra* note 65, at E1.

78. Hong Cheng, *What is Required to be Reorganized?,* RMRB, Aug. 3, 1976, *in* SPRCP, No. 76-32, at 191.

79. "International First Class Meritorious Service Company" of a certain unit of

the Wuhan units, *Victory or Defeat in War is Determined by People Not Things,* RMRB, Aug. 5, 1976, *in* SPRCP, No. 76-33, at 141, 142.

80. Liu Zhongnan, *Deng Xiaoping is not Allowed to Distort the Basic Tasks of Our Army,* RMRB, Aug. 5, 1975, *in* SPRCP, No. 76-34, at 107.

81. "International First Class Meritorious Service Company" of a certain unit of the Wuhan units, *Victory or Defeat in War is Determined by People Not Things, supra* note 79, at 142.

82. Victor Zorza, *The Peking Struggle over the Military,* Washington Post, May 21, 1976, at A25, col. 5.

83. *See generally* The Theoretical Group of the National Defense Industry Office, *The Strategic Policy on Strengthening Defense Construction—On Studying Chairman Mao's Dissertation on the Relationship Between Economic Construction and Defense Construction,* GMRB, Jan. 20, 1977, *in* FBIS, Jan. 31, 1977, at E1 (this article is one of the first and most important articles advocating military modernization after the purge of the "gang of four").

84. Hu Xue, *Get Rid of the Blind Belief in Nuclear Weapons,* RMRB, May 13, 1977, *in* FBIS, May 18, 1977, at E1, E2.

85. Chi Chuan, *Long Live the Spirit of Millet Plus Rifles,* Peking Radio (June 3, 1977), *in* FBIS, June 6, 1977, E10-11.

86. Xie Zhan, *The Atom Bomb is a Paper Tiger,* RMRB, June 21, 1977, *in* SPRCP, No. 77-29, at 9, 11, 13.

87. *On the Ten Major Relationships: It is Necessary to Strengthen Defense Construction on the Basis of Developing Economic Construction,* Peking Radio (Feb. 5, 1977), *in* FBIS, Feb. 7, 1977, at E5, E6; *See On the Ten Major Relationships: Strengthen National Defense Building on the Basis of Developing the Economy,* Shanghai Radio, (Feb. 15, 1977), *in* FBIS, Feb. 17, 1977, at E1.

88. *Chairman Hua and Vice-Chairman Ye Issue Call to Learn from "Hard-Boned 6th Company,"* JFJB, June 5, 1977, *in* PR, June 17, 1977, at 18.

89. *See* Su Yu, *Great Victory for Chairman Mao's Guideline on War,* RMRB, Aug. 6, 1977, *in* PR, Aug. 19, 1977, at 6; *Vice Chairman Yeh Chien-ying's [Ye Jianying's] Speech at the Grand Rally Celebrating the 50th Anniversary of the Chinese People's Liberation Army,* PR, Aug. 5, 1977, at 8. An earlier article acknowledging the continued need for a militia that could perform economic, political, and military tasks is *Give Full Play to the Great Role of the Militiamen in Their Hundreds of Millions,* JFJB, June 19, 1977, *in* FBIS, June 20, 1977, at E1.

90. *See Vice Chairman Ye Jianying's Speech at The Grand Rally Celebrating the 50th Anniversary of the Founding of the Chinese People's Liberation Army, supra* note 89, at 8; Xu Xiangqian, *Always Uphold the Principle that the Party Commands the Gun,* RMRB, Sep. 19, 1977, *in* FBIS, Sep. 20, 1977, at E1; Academy of Military Science, *Hold High Chairman Mao's Great Banner, Build a Mighty Proletarian Army,* RMRB, Aug. 5, 1977, *in* FBIS, Aug. 10, 1977, at E7.

91. William Safire, *Chinese Say Purging of "Gang of 4" Will Not Better Ties with Soviets,* New York Times, Mar. 25, 1977, at A9.

92. Die Welt [The World], May 15, 1977, *in* FBIS, May 17, 1977, at A3, A4; and Agence France Press, Nov. 1, 1976, *in* FBIS, Nov. 2, 1976, at A3.

93. Safire, *supra* note 91.

94. Institute of World Economy of the Chinese Academy of Social Science, *Soviet Social-Imperialism—Most Dangerous Source of War,* PR, July 15, 1977, at 5.
95. Editorial Department of Renmin Ribao, *Chairman Mao's Theory of the Differentiation of the Three Worlds is a Major Contribution to Marxism-Leninism,* PR, Nov. 4, 1977, at 10, 30.
96. Institute of World Economy, *supra* note 94, at 9.
97. *Id.* at 10.
98. Pollack, *supra* note 3, at 7.
99. Mao Zedong, *On the Ten Major Relationships* (Apr. 25, 1956), *in* PR, Jan. 1, 1977, at 12.
100. Li Qiulong, *It Is Imperative To Be Prepared Against Sudden Attacks by Aggressors,* Peking Radio (June 20, 1977), *in* FBIS, June 22, 1977, at E7, E8.
101. *Should or Should We Not Be Ready for War?,* JFJB, Peking Radio (July 10, 1977), *in* FBIS, July 12, 1977, at E6, E8.
102. Su Yu, *supra* note 89.
103. *Chairman Hua and Vice-Chairman Ye Issue Call to Learn from the "Hard-Boned 6th Company," supra* note 88, at 19.
104. *Liu Guangtao Stresses Eventuality of "Early, Major War,"* Harbin Radio (June 17, 1977), *in* FBIS, June 20, 1977, at L1, L2.
105. Theory Group of the Academy of Military Science, *Speed Up the Revolutionization and Modernization of Our Army, Build a Powerful National Defense Army,* HQ, No. 8, 1977, *in* SPRCM, No. 77-29, at 1. *See also Grasp the Key Link and Run the Army Well,* JFJB, Jan. 26, 1977, Peking Radio (January 26, 1977), *in* FBIS, Jan. 27, 1977, at E2-E7.
106. *Chairman Hua and Vice-Chairman Ye Issue Call to Learn from the "Hard-Boned 6th Company," supra* note 88, at 19 (emphasis added).
107. *Should or Should We Not Be Ready for War?, supra* note 101, at E11 (emphasis added).
108. Theory Group of the Academy of Military Science, *supra* note 105, at 2 (emphasis added).
109. *Persist in the Party Taking Charge of the Armed Forces and Strengthen Militia-Building,* Sha'anxi Ribao [Sha'anxi Daily], June 18, 1977, Xi'an Radio (June 10, 1977), *in* FBIS, June 20, 1977, at M7.
110. Su Yu, *supra* note 89, at E16. *See also Hold High Chairman Mao's Great Banner, Build a Mighty Proletarian Army,* RMRB, Aug. 5, 1977, *in* FBIS, Aug. 10, 1977, at E7-E9.
111. *Party Central Committee Calls for Upsurge in Learning from Tach'ing [Daqing],* PR, Feb. 4, 1977, at 3-4.
112. Li Xiannian, *Opening Speech at the National Conference on Learning from Daqing in Industry,* PR, Apr. 29, 1977, at 17; Yu Qiuli, *Mobilize the Whole Party and the Nation's Working Class and Strive to Build Daqing-Type Enterprises Throughout the Country,* PR, May 27, 1977, at 17; and Hua Guofeng, *Political Report to the 11th National Congress of the Communist Party of China* (Aug. 12, 1977), PR, Aug. 26, 1977, at 23-57.
113. Ye Jianying, *Report on the Revision of the Party Constitution* (Aug. 13, 1977), *in* PR, Sep. 2, 1977, at 25.
114. Mao Zedong, *supra* note 99, at 13-14.

115. National Defense Industry Office, *The Strategic Policy of Strengthening Defense Construction,* GMRB, Jan. 20, 1977, *in* FBIS, Jan. 31, 1977, at E2.

116. *It Is Necessary to Strengthen Defense Construction on the Basis of Developing Economic Construction,* Peking Radio (Feb. 5, 1977), *in* FBIS, Feb. 7, 1977, at E5, E9.

117. Ellis Joffe and Gerald Segal, *The Chinese Army and Professionalism,* PROBLEMS OF COMMUNISM, Nov.-Dec. 1978, at 1, 19.

118. *Grasp the Key Link and Run the Army Well, supra* note 105, at E6.

119. Russell Spurr, *The Biped Cavalry Regroups for Sophisticated Warfare,* FAR EASTERN ECONOMIC REVIEW, Oct. 6, 1978, at 42-43.

120. The conceptual framework used here draws heavily on one I developed in an earlier paper. See Harry Harding, Linkages Between Chinese Domestic Politics and Foreign Policy (August, 1976) (paper presented to the Workshop on Chinese Foreign Policy, sponsored by the Joint Committee on Contemporary China, Ann Arbor, Michigan).

121. THOMAS M. GOTTLIEB, CHINESE FOREIGN POLICY FACTIONALISM AND THE ORIGINS OF THE STRATEGIC TRIANGLE (1977).

122. ALICE LANGLEY HSIEH, COMMUNIST CHINA'S STRATEGY IN THE NUCLEAR ERA (1962); and HARRY HARDING & MELVIN GURTOV, THE PURGE OF LO JUI-CH'ING: THE POLITICS OF CHINESE STRATEGIC PLANNING (1971).

123. ALLEN S. WHITING, THE CHINESE CALCULUS OF DETERRENCE 37-40 (1975).

124. *Id.* at 157.

125. Vernon Aspaturian, *Internal Politics and Foreign Policy in the Soviet Union, in* R. BARRY FARRELL, *ed.,* APPROACHES TO COMPARATIVE AND INTERNATIONAL POLITICS 212 (1966).

126. Shen Ping, *Forever Adhere to Chairman Mao's Line on Army Building,* HQ, No. 8, 1976, *in* SPRCM, No. 76-26, at 66.

# 3
# China's Military Doctrines and Force Posture

*John Wilson Lewis*

Western and Soviet military policies, defense budgets, and national priorities are shaped, in part, by theoretical constructs on the use of force, the requirements and consequences of modern warfare, and the role of specific weapons systems. These theories, or military doctrines,[1] are subject to continuing change and debate, especially in the United States. For historical reasons, doctrines may be more explicit in respect to, say, strategic nuclear weapons than to tactical nuclear or conventional weapons, and bureaucratic or other biases may affect the formulation or the impact of specific doctrines. Although authorities everywhere differ on precisely what doctrines are or should be, most agree that such doctrines do exist, sometimes implicitly, in all military establishments and have great importance. In addition to shaping the procurement and deployment of forces, the development of new weapons, and the guidelines issued to military commanders, doctrines influence agendas and help structure debates on the full range of defense issues. China is no exception. Yet, despite a preoccupation with military doctrines in Peking and their use in decision making, we have had only the most superficial and somewhat dated understanding about the doctrinal underpinnings of Chinese military policy.

This study seeks to deepen our understanding of China's military doctrine and its relationship to perceptions of the international situation, domestic priorities, and the organization, training, and equipment of the People's Liberation Army (PLA).

John Wilson Lewis is William Haas Professor of Chinese Politics and director of the Arms Control and Disarmament Program at Stanford University. He received his A.B. (1953), M.A. (1958), and Ph.D. (1962) at UCLA.

## I. Chinese Views on the Use of Force

The way a country regards the use of force derives from its goals and perceived threats to its security and other interests. Peking's determined aim to end superpower dominance, for example, shapes China's analyses of external threats and policies for countering those threats. Memories of revolution and fear of encirclement by hostile powers have imbued the Chinese assessment with both a strong military bias and a sober realism. Thus, when weighing alternative military policies, China's leaders take into account the country's military vulnerability, its lack of credible allies, and its heavy dependence on domestic resources.

Peking regards the use of military force as a norm in international relations.[2] PRC armed actions involving Korea, Taiwan, Tibet, India, Vietnam, Laos, Burma, and the Paracel Islands all suggest that the Chinese are willing to assume the risks of warfare. They believe that the external use of military force can be consistent with their interests and see the use of force by other nations as expected international behavior. As internal documents noted in 1973, "The alleged nonuse of force in international relations is an even bigger lie. . . . 'War is the continuation of politics.' In order to oppose the use of force in international relations, one must oppose the policy of aggression and wars of imperialism and social-imperialism. One must oppose unjust wars and support just wars."[3]

The Chinese evaluate conditions in international politics according to the prevailing balance or "correlation" of forces in the world. Relative military strength is only one of many elements considered in making an assessment. This leads them to argue that even though general or global war is "inevitable," it can be postponed "indefinitely" through adequate preparations, unfailing efforts to thwart aggression, and uncompromising opposition to appeasement. Selective use of force, under certain circumstances, can prevent aggression (or escalation) that might lead to general war. It follows that settling a dispute by military action can be as legitimate as a resolution produced by negotiations at a time when the perceived military balance is unfavorable.[4] For example, the Chinese took no diplomatic action to resolve the Paracel Islands controversy prior to the successful 1974 attack. They proclaimed their sovereignty over these South China Sea islands and then, when the military balance shifted in their favor because of the U.S. withdrawal from Vietnam, ordered an assault against South Vietnam's naval units defending the islands. One Chinese author, shortly after the 1974 naval victory, said: "It is impossible to 'settle disputes' by the application of 'benevolence and righteousness.'"[5] Chinese actions in Vietnam in February and March 1979 followed the principle of settling disputes by the application of force.

The major premises underlying PRC views on the use of military power have been debated in Peking since the 1950s and continue to undergo fundamental reappraisal as China's capabilities and the international situation change. In general, however, the Chinese evaluate power in the overall global context. Superpower dominance resting on the American and Soviet monopoly of intercontinental weapons is viewed as the major source of injustice and instability in the world, but the main arenas of superpower contention, Europe and the West's sea-lanes, lie beyond the effective range of Chinese military forces. Thus China's ability to counter the superpowers and to influence developments in distant regions is limited, and the PRC must rely primarily on economic and political means. Closer to home, the capacity to employ military force assures Peking of greater leverage against Soviet influence in Vietnam and other Asian states, adds to China's salience in Japanese political calculations and, above all, forces the Soviet Union to consider Chinese reactions before acting in Asia.

Peking continues to treat the USSR as its principal global adversary, despite persistent parallel references to "U.S. imperialism." The Chinese consider the Soviet military buildup a sword raised against China and a part of Moscow's larger strategy of intimidation and nuclear blackmail. Although the Chinese often exaggerate the number and bellicosity of the Soviet forces arrayed against them, the scope of China's national defense efforts suggests that the threat from the "polar bear" is taken very seriously. One of the accusations leveled against the "gang of four" (Wang Hongwen, Zhang Chunqiao, Jiang Qing, and Yao Wenyuan, who were purged by Hua Guofeng after the death of Mao in 1976) is that they slighted war preparedness and downgraded the possibility of a Soviet surprise attack.[6] A typical criticism was, "They negated the dual nature of imperialism and [Soviet] social-imperialism, and talked only about their being paper tigers without saying they are also real man-eating tigers."[7]

Peking has alleged, "Soviet revisionism never gives up its hope of destroying us. It has stationed a million-man army in areas bordering on China, thus severely threatening China's safety."[8] To protect against this menace, the PRC uses its defense capabilities to project an image of defiance and readiness for waging total combat for national survival. Accordingly, the PRC has posted roughly two-thirds of its 121 main force infantry divisions in the northern and northeastern sectors of the country.[9]

China's leaders regard the country's capacity to display, deploy, or commit its armed forces as an essential ingredient of national sovereignty. The unimpaired ability to utilize military power is seen as distinguishing the new China from its semicolonial past, and as enabling the PRC to respond to provocations by the superpowers and to the emergence of new adversaries and conflict situations. The PRC's uncompromising repudiation of U.S.

calls for Peking to declare its peaceful intent toward Taiwan has several roots, but one is surely China's strong aversion to any compromise of its sovereign right to employ force as it alone sees fit.[10] Peking's rejection of the limited nuclear test ban and nuclear nonproliferation treaties is also, in part, a result of its determination to maintain sovereign control of its forces. As early as 1963, the Chinese government declared:

> Nuclear weapons in the possession of a socialist country [a category that now excludes the USSR] are always a means of defense against nuclear blackmail and nuclear war. . . . It is absolutely impermissible for two or three countries to brandish their nuclear weapons at will, issue orders and commands, and lord it over in the world as self-ordained nuclear overlords, while the overwhelming majority of countries are expected to kneel and obey orders meekly, as if they were nuclear slaves. The time of power politics has gone forever, and major questions of the world can no longer be decided by a few big powers.[11]

It was in this mood that on the occasion of exploding its first atomic bomb in 1964, the PRC proclaimed, "[I]n developing nuclear weapons, China's aim is to break the nuclear monopoly of the nuclear powers."[12]

Thus, the fundamental premise underlying China's current view of the use of military force is an updated version of Mao's maxim, "political power grows out of the barrel of a gun."[13] The Chinese are convinced that only a globally effective military force can guarantee their lasting sovereignty and international political influence. The year 2000 is the target date set by Mao, Zhou Enlai, and Hua Guofeng for attaining such power.[14] Until then China must steer a treacherous and variable course between nuclear war and irreversible compromise. Its emphasis now is on acquiring the potent means for the future, but few Chinese would claim to know to what ends these means might be directed in the years ahead.

*Weapons and Technology*

Most Chinese leaders have maintained that the outcomes of military conflict are decided by more than net capabilities, and that weapons alone cannot prevent war or determine its outcome. China's consistent line is that "war has its own laws [and] whether war breaks out or not is independent of man's will."[15] Until 1976, the official position was that once a war had started, man became the decisive factor. Mao again provided the authoritative line, "Weapons are an important factor in war, but not the decisive factor; it is people, not things, that are decisive. The contest of strength is not only a contest of military and economic power, but also a contest of human power and morale."[16] Victory, according to Mao, could be gained by achieving numerical and "moral" superiority and by not overstepping material limitations.[17]

In 1977, however, Peking's press appeared to give somewhat greater weight to the relative importance of weapons in warfare. One typical article noted that "[A]n army with revolutionized troops and modernized weapons and equipment is like a tiger with wings." It added, however, "We should never place blind faith in nuclear weapons. . . . In the future we will continue to rely on the people to fight a people's war in case of invasion by imperialism or social-imperialism."[18] Another article, "A Handgun Surely Defeats a Sharp Arrow," recounted the tale of Robinson Crusoe and his "enslaved" man Friday, and concluded, "[T]he decisive factor for victory in war is man—man with weapon in hand."[19] Yet another article hailed this statement by Engels: "The victory of brute force is based on the production of weapons." The article also derided the "gang of four" for sabotaging "the material base of the fighting power of our army in a vain attempt to keep our army poorly equipped and supplied and in the passive position of having to receive blows in the future war against aggression."[20] This emphasis on weapons has grown since 1977 and leads to a principal conclusion of this study: *technology has begun to displace politics and ideology as the force motivating Chinese military policies.* This does not mean that Chinese and U.S. security theories will necessarily converge, but it does challenge some common assumptions and estimates about Chinese military behavior.

*Nuclear Deterrence: Some Preliminary Comparisons*

China's positions on nuclear arms and nuclear deterrence are both shaped by its enduring principles on the use of military force. According to the Defense Intelligence Agency, these principles stress tactical offensiveness and strategic defensiveness.[21] To clarify the meaning of these terms in the nuclear context and to increase our understanding of underlying doctrines, it is useful to begin with interpretations of American defense officials. In 1974, former U.S. Secretary of Defense James Schlesinger stated, "We do not yet have much insight into the strategic and political objectives that the PRC is seeking to achieve with these deployments. But certain interesting features about them are already evident. The Chinese are clearly sensitive to the importance of second-strike nuclear capabilities and are making a considerable effort to minimize the vulnerability of their strategic offensive forces."[22] In the FY 1978 military posture statement, General George Brown elaborated:

> The People's Republic of China . . . can be expected to attempt to strengthen its military capability to counter perceived Soviet threats. While it is anticipated that the PRC will be on the offensive in political, economic, and

> psychological spheres, its military strategy will likely continue to be defensive in outlook with deterrence of an attack its primary objective. . . . This increasingly important nation complicates calculations in Moscow and Washington. . . . Shortcomings, while significant, will not prevent them from developing a formidable nuclear arsenal. An effective deterrence, however, does not always require the highest level of sophistication.[23]

These assessments suggest that China seeks to build a credible nuclear deterrent and is sensitive to the concern underlying American and Soviet strategic doctrines.

The Chinese, however, do not normally use the term "nuclear deterrence" except to describe the doctrines of, or the effects of certain actions on, other states.[24] They have frequently disparaged the concept's Western bias and rejected its direct application to China. In Chinese, "deterrence" in the general sense has long been translated *hezu liliang* (literally: the power to force inaction by frightening), while "deterrence" applied to strategic problems is *weishe* (literally: to force into a state of fear), and "nuclear deterrence is rendered somewhat awkwardly as *heweishe lilang*. Until recently, the Chinese could not realistically conceive of doctrines principally in terms of bipolar conflicts fought by weapons of mass destruction. Lacking the necessary warheads and delivery vehicles, they found no point in fashioning a theory based on assured nuclear retaliation. Thus most Western formulations of nuclear deterrence were inconsistent with both Chinese experience and capabilities. Theirs had been a complex, changing world of revolution and large conventional engagements, where deterrence had constituted only one policy objective, and often a minor one at that. In the process of prolonged combat, China's post-1949 leaders amassed a far more versatile arsenal to influence and control potential conflicts.

Beyond semantics and general perceptions, one notes a sharp contrast between the U.S. and Chinese versions of deterrence in respect to the level of violence threatened. In the U.S., the degree of theoretical development varies directly with the level of violence under consideration.[25] The opposite is very nearly the case in China. The Chinese theory of intimidation, born more out of historical reality than abstract prescription, becomes more precise and formal at lower levels of violence, especially in regard to limited conventional war. It is precisely in the realm of limited conventional war, however, that U.S. deterrence theory seems least successful or even relevant. According to one study, U.S. "attempts to examine the workings of deterrence at the level of limited war and below have discovered deterrence to be less sharply visible."[26] It thus appears that Chinese and U.S. deterrence policies have been developed from very different images of what constitutes the most likely conflicts or threats.[27]

The Chinese reject the theory, exemplified by the views of Andre Beaufre,[28] that weaker nuclear powers can deter nuclear attack by the threat of a suicidal counterattack. However, recent statements and behavior suggest that the PRC may be moving toward qualified acceptance of what Beaufre calls "defensive deterrence," even though Chinese leaders do not accept his view of either the risks of ultimate destruction or the "coercive persuasion" of their ability to retaliate. As noted earlier, they appear to believe that the fundamental reason one country would or would not mount an all-out attack on another has little to do with the way China (or any other victim state) deploys its weapons and forces. Rather, in most Chinese analyses, a first strike initiated by foreign leaders would result from conditions that Peking could not control.[29] They belittle as "sheer illusion" any theory that "asserts the balance of nuclear power can avert war."[30]

As of 1976, one could find little in the Chinese view of strategic war and its origins that corresponded to crucial elements of prevailing Western or Soviet theories of deterrence. Chinese doctrine differed from these theories in reaching the following conclusions:

1. Nuclear weapons, though highly destructive and universally "condemned by the people," are not essentially different from other weapons.[31] No need exists for a deliberately contrived nuclear firebreak; the likelihood of escalation from conventional to nuclear war is reduced by the nonutility of nuclear weapons in most situations.[32]
2. Nuclear weapons are not the main determinants of a crisis or conflict. The maintenance of stability in a crisis is not a central goal; any effort to do so through the threat of nuclear attack would constitute unacceptable nuclear blackmail.
3. Nuclear weapons have no special power to prevent an enemy attack or to dominate the battlefield. They do not constitute the ultimate risk.
4. Special doctrines need not be devised for nuclear weapons. In the end their use will be dictated by the total situation which, in China's case, gives decisive advantages to the defender and ensures an invader's ultimate defeat or frustration.

Despite these differences, China's position does have some similarities with current Western theories. With the changes wrought since the death of Mao Zedong, the Chinese have seemed to move closer to prevailing views of deterrence. This shift is illustrated by the following excerpts from articles typical of many that appeared in 1977.

> Everybody knows that when both sides have nuclear weapons, the threat is much greater to imperialist and social-imperialist countries where industries and populations are highly concentrated. . . . [N]o modern weapons can destroy our economy or crush it by bombing.[33]
>
> One may have nuclear weapons, others may have them too. If one wants to drop atom bombs on others, one has to consider that others are also capable of using the same things against you.[34]

Such statements illustrate China's acknowledgement, muted for more than a decade, that nuclear weapons in the hands of an opponent affect, though not determine, any decision to launch nuclear war.[35]

Chinese doctrine evinces elements of deterrence theories that are important to any military planner, namely, the need to have adequate forces to make a potential adversary think twice about launching an attack. This is the meaning of *hezu liliang,* a term the Chinese do *not* use for nuclear deterrence. This view of military force has been relevant throughout the history of warfare. Any sensible commander seeks a position in which his units cannot be devastated by the initial assault of an opponent, and this position, when attained by several states, can lead to mutual restraint. Chinese commanders are no exception, and see nuclear war in this light.

A key point to keep in mind when comparing Chinese and Western doctrines is that the nuclear policies of all countries must continually respond to changes: in technology, in the weaponry of potential adversaries, in each leadership's projection of national power, and in the perception of other states' intentions. For example, U.S. strategies, driven by developing technological capabilities and force requirements, have altered the operational meaning of deterrence almost continuously. It would not be surprising, therefore, if technological and political factors also caused further evolution of China's nuclear policies, or if *some* elements of Chinese strategic thinking began to echo Western nuclear deterrence theories. Mao Zedong long ago argued for a flexible, realistic approach to strategy that, he said, "develops in accordance with the development of history and of wars."[36]

*Deterrence and Chinese Doctrine*

Having examined certain differences between Western and Chinese nuclear doctrines and noted that China seems to be accepting some of the tenets of prevailing theories, the next step is to inquire toward which "type" of deterrence doctrine the Chinese might be moving. The simple answer is "their own type," and the use of the term deterrence with all its Western overtones can be misleading. Nevertheless, for the purpose of examining Chinese nuclear doctrines it is useful to distinguish between the "mutual assured destruction" (MAD) and the "limited response" (Schlesinger doctrine) schools of U.S. deterrence theory.[37] While both theories embrace deterrence (and such elements as survivability of retaliatory forces and agreed measures of confidence), they sharply diverge concerning whether nuclear weapons should be used only to threaten unacceptable damage so as to prevent the outbreak of war, or also to keep the level of conflict low, with varying levels of nuclear war fighting possible if nuclear deterrence fails. Should the Chinese begin to accept deterrence doctrines as such, it is quite clear that they would side with the "limited response" school that favors a policy combining both goals.

Chinese doctrine, like Western deterrence theory, also has begun to call for rough parity of forces. Even now some PRC writings echo James Schlesinger's view that "[W]e should be prepared to match the Soviet Union, more or less, given the whole set of criteria, on the basis of general equivalence in force."[38] For example, two PRC soldiers affirmed that "While the enemies are sharpening their knives, we, too, have to sharpen ours." Elaborating further, they called for a one-for-one matched buildup of forces and weapons.[39] It should be noted, however, that balance does not imply stability for the Chinese. On the contrary, they assert, "It is impossible to achieve a 'stable balance.'"[40]

Recent articles advocate that China build a full range of conventional and nuclear weapons and delivery systems. Many spokesmen for the PLA seem to appreciate the importance of the flexibility that a diverse arsenal will provide; or at least they oppose acquiring only a few types of highly specialized weapons. Their logic may be equated, in part, with the U.S. "limited response" school advocating a deterrent that derives its credibility from the fact that American forces would be prepared to meet the full range of high probability threats. The Chinese also seem to reject the totalism inherent in the doctrine of "massive retaliation" and to be convinced that their troops should be equipped to counter a variety of different threats. To cover this new insight, recent articles have stretched Mao's dicta on despising the enemy strategically but taking him seriously in tactical matters and on concentrating a superior force to destroy the enemy forces one by one.[41]

Finally, one should note that most Chinese leaders would accept deterrence theory only to the extent that it accommodates their preexisting notions of war and politics. Classically, Chinese military strategists have stressed *bu jan er churen zhibing* or *bu jan er sheng* (to win victory without fighting a war).[42] In this sense they seek to attain a position of force that will paralyze or deter their adversaries. As the following section suggests, they believe that preparations for war can deter an adversary by demonstrating one's ability to survive in case war breaks out. Hua Guofeng explained this point in 1978: "[T]he outbreak of war can be put off, but then the people of all countries must close ranks, sharpen their vigilance, prepare against all eventualities, oppose appeasement, [and] resolutely struggle against the [superpowers'] war machinations."[43] Such a strategy seeks to render an adversary passive; but, unlike the superpowers, the Chinese would not willingly put *themselves* in a position of being deterred.[44] Deterrence is thus not to be reciprocated; the goal is not *mutual* deterrence.[45]

As noted earlier, although the Chinese view of nuclear deterrence is changing, the PRC approaches questions of China's vulnerability far differently than do U.S. advocates of "mutual assured destruction." One perhaps could apply the same caveat in analyzing Soviet deterrence doctrines.[46] Indeed, China's current interest in air and civil defense suggests possible similarities between Chinese and Soviet military postures. If correct, the emphasis on defense contrasts sharply with the U.S. offense-dominated or "mutual hostage" approach.

When the United States and the Soviet Union signed the ABM Treaty in 1972, it was hailed as a step toward firmer, more general acceptance of an offense-dominated deterrence relationship. Such a relationship was considered more stable than defense-dominated deterrence because, by being vulnerable, neither side would be tempted to launch a first strike and neither would launch an arms race to overcome an adversary's defenses. The "limited response" school challenges the offense-dominated posture of the U.S., but its adherents disagree on the importance and cost effectiveness of defending civilians. The Chinese, it is clear, stand squarely on the side of a strong civil defense.

The Chinese have acted inconsistently with the doctrinal assumptions that underlay the 1972 ABM Treaty because they consider themselves only a potential victim of nuclear aggression, not its initiator. Thus, they have attempted to render their urban populations less vulnerable to annihilation, but since the late 1960s they have taken only modest additional steps to protect their offensive missiles. Mao's slogan for war preparedness was: "Dig tunnels deep, store grain everywhere, and never seek hegemony." PRC leaders have taken this dictum quite literally in an effort to protect civilians. China's press noted in 1977 that in many cities air raid shelters with underground tunnel networks could accommodate "at the sound of the siren, several hundred thousand to one million people."[47] One eye-witness description of China's defense works is as follows:

> The sub-area served by the shelters [air raid shelter in the Daxialan dichu, Peking] houses 70,000 people and 45 shops. There are 90 entrances to this system, divided more or less evenly between the shopping zone and the residential area. The system has three purposes: 1) defense against a surprise attack in which all people will temporarily be sheltered underground; 2) in a

long war, dispersal of the old, young, and the sick with the shelters then to be used for production, sheltering young fighters, and hospitals; and 3) defense against invasion with provisions for actual fighting underground. The facility was largely a maze of tunnels that have been completed since February 1969, when work began. The tunnels, 7-10 meters underground, are small, generally between 1.2 and 1.5 meters wide. Some of the latest tunnels are up to six feet (1.8 meters) wide, and all are about 7 feet high. A one kilometer system took one year to complete. It was said that in the suburban areas the tunnels are large enough for trucks to drive through.... The facility is clearly intended for conventional, not nuclear war, although there is discussion about upgrading the tunnels to withstand nuclear blasts. There now are intermittent concrete doors about two inches thick which are hung on rather weak metal hinges; they would obviously blow out quite easily.[48]

The Chinese stressed the protection of civilian targets at the 1977 conference on PRC air defenses.[49] The defensive emphasis of Chinese nuclear doctrine is also evident in this mid-1977 pronouncement: "Anti-atom bomb education for the masses, digging deep tunnels for cover, and other similar measures offer defenses against an atomic attack. To drop atom bombs you need airplanes or guided missiles, or other types of vehicles. But, airplanes can be dealt with by guided missiles, and guided missiles can be surpassed by antimissile missiles."[50]

If the foregoing sounds equivocal, one reason may be the ambiguous nature of the evidence on Chinese deterrence policy. Another is that during 1977 the Hua Guofeng government appeared to be redefining the next round of China's military development. To date, no single Chinese view on this subject has emerged publicly, and, as of this writing, a debate appears to be in progress.[51]

*Chinese Military Doctrine: Summary*

PRC military doctrines derive from divergent origins—China's history of conventional and revolutionary war, its culturally and ideologically biased views of enemies and threats, and its growing arsenal of modern weapons. The orientation of its doctrines is strategically defensive, globally variable, and still evolving. They differ sharply from nuclear deterrence theories that emphasize the unique risks of nuclear weapons, the special problems of stabilizing nuclear-related crises, and the need to devise special doctrines for nuclear weapons. However, Peking is selectively adapting its doctrines to cover nuclear weapons in ways that resemble the doctrine of "limited response." At present, even the Chinese leadership might not agree on the specifics of their nuclear doctrine or how it relates to their overall military policy. The Chinese leadership faces the dilemmas of controlling a highly differentiated country and of having both to modernize and to exert greater international influence in an era of increasingly complex problems. For the present they might see advantages in compartmentalized and partially disaggregated systems of command, control, and communication. Words other than "deterrence" probably should be used to label Chinese doctrines and to characterize their behavior; if needed, "deterrence" should at least be used with special caution.

## II. Operational Elements in Chinese Military Policies: A First Approximation

In spite of limited information, it is possible to develop tentative conclusions about operational emphases in Chinese military policies.[52]

*Weapons Acquisition: China Seeks to Cover the Full Spectrum of Defense Contingencies*

China's acquisition policy takes into account enemy weaknesses and threats, technology, deployment requirements, and potential weapon uses. This has led the PRC to acquire a variety of weapons and to maintain "a relatively small, but carefully conceived, strategic program."[53] Chinese leaders have disagreed on which parts of a comprehensive military program should receive priority and what balances should exist among the various defense capabilities, but they now appear to be closing ranks on the question of what values should guide their acquisition program.

While preparing for contingencies across a broad spectrum of conventional and nuclear conflicts, China has tended to concentrate on preparations for border and theater warfare, and somewhat less for strategic war. As shown in Table 3.1, these preparations have created important strengths in all weapon categories relevant to such conflicts. The PLA seeks to acquire a heavy conventional capability close to, but not right at, the Soviet border in order to have some time to meet any attackers. The PRC's commanders apparently have instructed some units to engage an adversary as soon as the border is breached by an invader, as at Zhenbao Island in 1969.[54] They do not, however, want the stationing of their forces to provoke an assault.[55] Given superior Soviet armament, Peking is attempting to procure weapons, perhaps even tactical nuclear weapons, that will complement and strengthen their conventional weapons shield against a Soviet invasion.

It should be noted that the PRC has acquired a small strategic bomber force and land-based strategic nuclear missiles that are deployed against the Soviet Union. The Chinese also are working on submarine-launched ballistic missile forces and on air and civil defenses. In addition, China has orbited eight satellites, is modernizing substantial general purpose forces,

TABLE 3.1
China's Force Levels[a]

1. Conventional

| | |
|---|---|
| ARMY<br>3.6 Million | Organized in about 40 armies (comparable to U.S. corps) with 210+ (178 main force) divisions as follows: 121+ infantry, 11 armored, 3 airborne, 40 artillery (2nd Artillery Corps controls strategic missiles), 15 railway and construction engineer, 3 cavalry plus signal, motor transport units with other combat support. PRC has about 8-9,000 tanks (including T-59 which is copy of Soviet T-54A), 15-18,000 artillery pieces, 5-6,000 heavy mortars, and 2-3,000 APC and fighting vehicles (esp. M-1967 tracked APCs).[b] PLA assigns 3-4 dozen tanks per infantry division. |
| NAVY<br>300,000 (including 30,000 in naval air with 600-1,000 shore-based aircraft and including 28,000 Marines) | Navy has an inventory of 23 principal surface combatants. 1 Golf (ballistic missile) and 1 Han (nuclear powered) class subs; 91 Romeo, Whiskey, and Ming (diesel powered) class medium-range (2,400 n.m.) subs; 7 Lu-ta class 3,700 ton DDG; 16 other DD and DE; 16 patrol escorts; 39 subchasers; 140 Osa and Hoku-type FPBG with Styx SSM; 30 minesweeps; 54 landing ships; plus 1,100 small naval craft under 100 tons each. Organized into North Sea, East Sea, and South Sea Fleets. New shipyards at Huludao and Guangji. Naval air arm has a version of the F6 called Fantan-A.[c] |
| AIR FORCE<br>400,000 (including 10,000 pilots) | More than 5,000 aircraft as follows: 80+ TU-16 (Badger) and 12 TU-4 (Bull) medium bombers; 400+ IL-28 (Beagle) and 100 TU-2 (Bat) light bombers; 1,700 MiG-15 (Fagot) and 17 (Fresco); 2,000 MiG-19 (F6 or Farmer); 80 MiG-21 (Fishbed);[d] and 200+ F9 (Fantan); 400 other military transport aircraft and 300-400 helicopters (including 13 French Super Frelon helicopters). 120,000 men in air defense; many air defense sites have SAMs (CSA-1 which is variant of Soviet SA-2). 4,000+ aircraft are assigned to strategic air defense. China does not appear to be developing an intercontinental bomber. Planes operate from about 400 airfields. |
| PARAMILITARY | 300,000 security and border troops; 7+ million in civilian armed militia organized into about 75 divisions. |

TABLE 3.1 (cont.)

2. Nuclear

| | |
|---|---|
| Warhead arsenal | An estimated 225–300 fusion (most in 3–4 MT range) and fission (most in 20–40 KT range) warheads. Specialists disagree on whether China intends to develop battlefield (tactical) nuclear weapons. It will be noted in Table 3.2 that many of China's nuclear tests are in the low KT range. Also the China-designed F9 aircraft and the IL-28 could deliver these weapons in battlefield support operations against invading troops. |
| Medium to intermediate range bombers | Most probably would use the 80+ TU-16s (carries 6,600 lbs., 1,650/3,200 n.m.) and 12 TU-4s (10,000 lbs. with range of 1,550/3,050 n.m.); and 400+ IL-28s (2,200 lbs., 550/1,000 n.m.) |
| MRBM (CSS-1) (600 nautical mile range) | About 35 single-stage transportable missiles are now deployed in soft sites or caves. Under operational command of Second Artillery Corps. Many in the northeast; has 20 kiloton warhead. Missiles are liquid fueled and are developed from Soviet SS-2. Described as "obsolescent and cumbersome."[f] |
| IRBM (CSS-2) (most 1,500 to 2,500 mile range) | 35 single-stage liquid-fueled missiles with 2–3 megaton warhead being deployed; some in caves or steel-concrete silos; testing multistage IRBM with solid fuel (solid propellant rocket motor facilities are being expanded). |
| ICBM (CSS-3 and CSS-X-4) | Limited-range ICBM (CSS-3) capable of 3,000 n.m. range (flight tested in 1976). Developing CSS-X-4 multistage missile with 7,000/8,000 mile range and MT range warhead. Will be longer than Soviet SS-9; silos believed under construction but only a small number could be deployed before late 1980s. |
| Missile subs | 1 Golf-class diesel-powered ballistic missile sub built in 1964; 3 missile tubes but no missiles aboard yet. Estimates are of two-stage solid fuel system and a nuclear-powered ballistic missile sub. |
| Satellites | China launched 8 satellites between 1970 and 1978. The dates of China's satellite launches are: April 24, 1970; March 3, 1971; July 26, 1975; November 26, 1975; December 16, 1975; August 30, 1976; December 7, |

TABLE 3.1 (cont.)

1976; and January 26, 1978. The one launched on November 26, 1975, weighed 6,000-10,000 lbs. and was returned to earth on December 2, 1975, and two others launched on December 7, 1976, and January 26, 1978, returned a few days later.

| Abbreviations: | | |
|---|---|---|
| | APC | armored personnel carrier |
| | DD | destroyer |
| | DE | destroyer escort |
| | FPBG | fast guided-missile patrol boat |
| | ICBM | intercontinental ballistic missile |
| | IRBM | intermediate range ballistic missile |
| | KT | kiloton |
| | MT | megaton |
| | MRBM | medium range ballistic missile |
| | n.m. | nautical mile |
| | SAM | surface-to-air missile |
| | SSM | surface-to-surface missile |

[a] The figures (up to date as of March 1979) in these and other tables are from unclassified sources and meant to be as authoritative as possible. Since even official United States sources often disagree, I have given precedence to the most recent United States military posture and Secretary of Defense statements and to DEFENSE INTELLIGENCE AGENCY, HANDBOOK ON THE CHINESE ARMED FORCES (1976), thence to CIA, DIA, and DOD Congressional testimony in the most recent appropriations hearings; and finally to INTERNATIONAL INSTITUTE OF STRATEGIC STUDIES, THE MILITARY BALANCE 1978-1979 (1978). Some figures are extrapolations. For example, IISS gives the number of MiG-15s as 200 and the DIA *supra*, at 7-8, states that the PRC has more than 400 MiG-15 and F9 aircraft. Hence the figure 200 F9s.

[b] The comparative figures for major weapons and equipment-ground forces are: Tanks—U.S./10,000, USSR/45-50,000, and the PRC/8-9,000; APC and Fighting Vehicles—U.S./22,000, USSR/45-55,000, and the PRC/2-3,000; Artillery—U.S./5,000, USSR/19,000, and the PRC/15-18,000; Heavy Mortars—U.S./3,000, USSR/7,000, and the PRC/5-6,000. These figures are taken from GEORGE BROWN, UNITED STATES MILITARY POSTURE FOR FY 1979 at 70 (1978).

[c] For rundown on 1,215 ships, see DIA, *supra* note a at 6-6.

[d] At the start of the attack on Vietnam the New York Times, Feb. 18, 1979, put the figure at 80. The earlier figure was 75.

[e] According to G. BROWN, *supra* note b, at 87, the Chinese have 70 MRBMs and IRBMs "deployed in a strategic role." The warhead and aircraft capability figures are from DIA, *supra* note a. Pictures of the CSS-1 and CSS-X-4 are in AV. WEEK AND SPACE TECH., Feb. 5, 1979, at 19.

[f] GEORGE BROWN, UNITED STATES MILITARY POSTURE FOR FY 1977, at 46 (1976).

and has given high priority to improving command-and-control systems and logistical support capabilities.

On balance, PRC military planners appear to have taken the long view. "They have patience. They establish an adequate defense posture, stretch out procurement . . . and apparently allocate more resources to internal development, accepting no alien influences except when absolutely necessary. The burden of armaments appears not to be so oppressive."[56] This judgment, reached in 1975, seems even more valid in the era of Hua Guofeng.

*Deployment: The Chinese Have Deployed Their Weapons to Attain a Range of National Purposes*

China has been and remains willing to consider conventional armed conflict, both as initiator and defender. As tactics change, so do deployments.[57] The PLA assigns and exercises its armies to maintain a high state of readiness in light of changing circumstances. It does not anticipate or plan for a long-term military standoff in the event of impending hostilities, but deploys its units for maximum advantage.

Peking's weapons deployment decisions in the past have been guided almost entirely by strategic defensive considerations and a deep commitment to offsetting the country's vulnerabilities. China's over-all military outlook is shaped by the PLA's revolutionary history and, since 1949, by hostile U.S. and Soviet policies which at times have included attempts at nuclear blackmail. China has shifted to a tactically offensive posture when it has regarded the territory involved as its own. Such has been the case with the various border conflicts and the Paracels, and could become the case with Taiwan. Relations with Burma provide a minor exception to this pattern.

Although the general situation could change as China approaches major power status, the fear of invasion brought about by military inferiority plays the critical role in Peking's military calculus. Moreover, China must consider more than just the Soviet Union and the United States in its war plans. Vietnam, Taiwan, and even Korea must also be considered as potential security threats. Defensive deployments in so many quarters inevitably place a predominantly military stamp on all Chinese policies.

China's military deployments affect its perceived overall security and flexibility. Zhou Enlai stated in March 1973: "We must not be ensnared by [the Soviets]. It seems likely that, for a comparatively long period, the Soviet revisionists would not dare to make a big fight with us except provoking some skirmishes along the frontier. We all have the numbers in our mind, as they understand that we are prepared for fighting a big battle."[58] By "numbers in our mind" (probably *xinzhong you shu*) Zhou was making a classical allusion to keeping the entire situation in mind. Possibly he also was suggesting that since most Soviet divisions are deployed in the West, those on the Chinese border are roughly matched by the PLA. These "numbers," according to Zhou, would induce caution among Soviet planners. Apparently some Chinese leaders believe that Zhou's prediction was validated during the 1979 Vietnam crisis since the Soviet Union did not respond. When PRC writers assert that Chinese preparations have blunted Soviet ambitions, they increasingly sound themes reminiscent of Western deterrence theory. As one Chinese historian wrote during the anti-Confucius campaign, "There is no danger when there is preparedness; without preparations, there is bound to be danger."[59]

*Employment of Nuclear Weapons: The Chinese Assume
That in the Event of a Large-scale Soviet Attack
Both Sides Will Probably Resort to Nuclear Weapons*

China's leaders argue that nuclear weapons, like all weapons, can have both political and military uses. Political use means blackmail, and the Chinese expect such use by the superpowers. "Whenever any new weapon appears in history, the exploiting class will invent some kind of myth to scare people in a vain attempt to attain the objectives of aggression and expansion."[60] Nuclear arms can have a real blackmail potential against China only if it flinches in the use of lesser force under crisis conditions. Such fear would not keep the Soviet Union from employing nuclear arms first, and thus China should not alter its military or political behavior in a mistaken attempt to avoid a nuclear attack. On the contrary, nuclear blackmail and other efforts at national intimidation are tests of strength that can be met by a fearless but weaker power. The 1979 attack on Vietnam after threats by Moscow is regarded by Peking as a case of China having met that test successfully. According to a *Renmin Ribao* article in May 1977, fear of nuclear war amounts to superstition. The article concludes: "[W]e are constantly strengthening our defense and are making preparations for war—for a big war that may break out at an early date. If Soviet social-imperialism launches aggression against China—even if it drops hydrogen bombs in China—it is not China that will be destroyed but the nuclear overlord itself, which is courting its own ultimate destruction."[61]

An underlying premise of this "paper tiger" thesis is that "against a struggle waged by the people, atom bombs by themselves will be of no avail." This premise was stated by Mao in 1955 when he argued that "the Chinese people are not to be cowed by U.S. atomic blackmail. . . . The United States cannot annihilate the Chinese nation with its small stack of atom bombs."[62]

Although Mao's statement implies that the use of nuclear weapons against the PRC would not prove decisive, its present operational consequences are unclear. For example, a recent official Chinese visitor to the United States interpreted the statement, when applied to the USSR, to mean that the Soviets would grasp the futility of launching a nuclear strike against his country: "If there is another war, it is likely to be a conventional war because the destruction of a nuclear war is too great. If one were to unleash a war and obliterate everything, what is the use of war? What is the use of entering a city which has been completely destroyed?" Despite many such statements, other evidence suggests that China expects a Soviet nuclear strike "out of the blue" and may even contemplate a limited nuclear response as part of the conventional defense of its own soil.[63] Such a response need not signal Armageddon, in this Chinese view, since Peking holds that limited use of nuclear weapons need not escalate into general nuclear war.[64]

To my knowledge, the Chinese have issued no publications that discuss their policies on the use of specific weapons. Nevertheless, Peking routinely cites Mao's dictum on the conduct of an active, protracted defense.

> All previous revolutionary wars in our country started with large-scale attacks against us by enemies superior in both numbers and equipment, and these wars were fought for fairly long periods of time when the enemies were strong and we were weak. For this reason, "The primary problem, and a serious one, too, is how to conserve our strength and await an opportunity to defeat the enemy. Therefore, the strategic defense is the most complicated and most important problem facing the Red Army in its operations." Chairman Mao formulated the strategic principle of "active defense," a defense that calls for counter-attacks and offensives.[65]

A Chinese foreign affairs official told a Stanford group in July 1978, "We have our own ways of fighting even if we do not have advanced weapons. . . .[W]e will not invade [the Soviet Union], so the fighting will be on Chinese soil." In an attack by the Soviets, the Chinese clearly expect to reverse any Soviet advance with its main force units, without assistance from the civilian militia. While it seems likely that the militia would be engaged as a last resort,[66] it remains uncertain when the Chinese might use nuclear weapons in actual combat.

Since the Chinese expect any Soviet invasion to involve nuclear weapons, one might ask: Is there a contradiction between China's deployment of nuclear weapons as a putative part of its "conventional" shield against a Soviet attack and its "no-first-use" pledge? It is possible that the Chinese have made their no-first-use pledge for purposes of enhancing their international position and staking out a defensible stand on disarmament, or that it applies only to the use of such weapons beyond China's borders.

Since Soviet armies across the border possess a massive nuclear capability, the pledge puts the Russians at a political disadvantage should Moscow threaten to use these weapons against China.

This pledge does not ensure that the PRC would not use its nuclear weapons, particularly if the situation involved Soviet troops on Chinese territory. One sign of their limited commitment to the no-first-use idea is that China has yet to press for an agreement on it in the UN even though they could have gained politically from such a stand because of the substantial sentiment for the concept in the General Assembly. Questioning China's interest in no-first-use pledges, however, does not imply that PRC leaders fail to appreciate the risks of nuclear war. Moreover, I disagree with the thesis, widely circulated in the late 1960s, that China's security predicament had caused the PLA to place its nuclear missile units on a "launch-on-warning" alert. The 1967 and 1969 antiballistic missile (ABM) hearings in the U.S. Congress raised the spectre of Peking having to launch its nuclear weapons on warning simply because they were so vulnerable. The testimony also contained the accusation by Department of Defense officials that the PRC exhibited both unusual irrationality and a willingness to engage in nuclear blackmail.[67] Some of these officials linked the alleged launch-on-warning status of PRC nuclear forces and Peking's purported reckless behavior to China's basic military weakness.

> The Chinese first generation ICBM capability will undoubtedly be small in numbers and thereby vulnerable to attack. A small and vulnerable nuclear delivery system presents a problem to its possessor. In time of crisis, it must be launched first in a surprise attack or it runs the risk of total elimination. This characteristic of a small vulnerable system could create pressures toward reckless behavior, even in a people not by nature reckless. An area ABM defense for the United States . . . by denying a threat by Communist China of destruction of U.S. cities should provide an additional indication to Asians that we intend to deter China from nuclear blackmail against them.[68]

Although China does possess a small and still vulnerable nuclear delivery system, I can find no evidence that it ever adopted a launch-on-warning policy, or exhibited recklessness in respect to nuclear war.

### III. China's Nuclear Development

China's interest in acquiring "the bomb" began in the early days of the People's Republic. Immediately after concluding the 1950 Valentine's Day treaty of friendship with the Soviet Union, the PRC entered into an agreement with Moscow to jointly explore for "nonferrous and rare metals" in

Xinjiang. Years later, the Chinese were to allege that under this and other arrangements, "China furnished the Soviet Union with more than 1,400 million new roubles' worth of mineral products and metals. Among the most important items were: 100,000 tons of lithium concentrates, 34,000 tons of beryllium concentrates. . . . Many of these mineral products are raw materials which are indispensable for the development of the most advanced branches of science and for the manufacture of rockets and nuclear weapons."[69] Presumably, however, the Chinese also found these strategic resources important for their own missile and nuclear programs. Between early 1953 and mid-1955, there followed a number of Sino-Soviet agreements for scientific cooperation in atomic research and in March 1956, the Chinese became partners in the Joint Institute of Nuclear Research at Dubna, USSR, eventually contributing 20 percent of its funds.[70] In 1955, "a chemical separation plant, vital to the production of weapons grade uranium-235 and plutonium, was established with Soviet aid in Xinjiang."[71] The same year, Ye Jianying called for the PRC to acquire "a sufficient quantity of the most modern material to arm the Chinese People's Liberation Army."[72]

On April 25, 1956, Mao Zedong advocated obtaining A-bombs in his speech entitled *On the Ten Major Relationships*.[73] The resultant nuclear weapons program is one of the most highly valued achievements of China's last twenty years. Zhou Enlai is now said to have guided the formulation of the twelve-year plan for scientific development (1956–67), and to have emphasized "the rapid development of atomic and rocket technique" and to have opposed pressures for cutbacks in the plan during the crisis of the sixties.[74] In 1957, Moscow agreed to provide China prototype nuclear weapons; but in the following year, Mao apparently decided to pursue a parallel, self-reliant course in acquiring such an arsenal.[75] At this time, the PLA promulgated a draft program stating that one object of military training was "to learn the co-ordination of the various branches of the army in combat under the modern conditions of atomic bombs, chemical warfare and guided missiles."[76] In June 1958, Mao said, "Let us work on atom bombs and nuclear bombs. Ten years, I think, should be quite enough."[77] This pronouncement was preceded by a debate concerning the "mechanical application of foreign experience."[78] Mao's own position on this related issue seems to have been clarified in June: "It is not practical to execute orders in accordance with the Soviet army ordinances in wartime. We should rather develop our own ordinances. . . . At present, the things worked out by the Soviet military advisers (such as operational plans and thinking) are all of an offensive nature, based on victory; no provision is made for the defensive and for defeat. . . . As regards the problem of superstructure and the problems of military science and tactics, we have a system of our own."[79] That settled, the PRC was launched on its own path of nuclear development.

Although this discussion will only emphasize organizational decisions, a full review of China's nuclear development would include the polemics over agreements reached with the Russians in 1957-58 and the charge that Moscow unilaterally negated these agreements in 1959. In the late fifties and early sixties, the PLA reorganized its divisions to accommodate modern advanced weapon units.[80] Although the Second Artillery Corps later assumed operational control of the first-generation MRBM missiles (CSS-1), at least in northeast China, the PLA did not set up a strategic rocket forces command based on the Russian model. (See Figure 3.1 for organization of Chinese forces.)

As far as is known, China's nuclear units are integrated into regular divisional structures under command of regular army officers. Moreover, China does not appear to have formed a joint service command-and-control arrangement similar to the U.S. Joint Strategic Targeting Staff. The decision not to make organizational changes comparable to those that took place in the Soviet Union when the Kremlin created the Strategic Rocket Forces probably enabled the PLA to avoid the kind of divisions and political struggle that occurred in the Soviet military.[81] The new Soviet strategic missile command created a somewhat independent base for promotions and bureaucratic maneuver, which added yet another dimension for political in-fighting within the Soviet military establishment. By avoiding such an organizational arrangement, the Chinese ensured (perhaps unintentionally) a broadly supported nuclear program and more secure institutional mechanisms. This was especially true in the case of the Party Central Committee's Military Commission and the National Defense Scientific and Technological Commission, both of which survived the Cultural Revolution (1966-69) reasonably intact.[82]

Beginning in October 1964, the Chinese began a nuclear testing program, as summarized in Table 3.2.[83] As of late 1979, China had conducted 24 nuclear tests that can be roughly grouped as follows: 14 in the 20-50 KT range, 3 in the 200-500 KT range, and 7 in the 1-4 MT range. Though modest compared to the U.S. or Soviet programs, this test series does suggest the ambitious scope of China's nuclear plans. As Mao said in January 1965: "No matter what country it is, what bombs they are, atomic bombs or hydrogen bombs, we must overtake [the superpowers]."[84] In the course of this development, Zhou Enlai reportedly presided over nearly 100 related meetings in a period of more than ten years, and became deeply committed to the nuclear-test program.[85] One article expressed the PRC leadership's reaction to a successful test as follows: "In 1964, while viewing the film recording of the first nuclear test, Premier Zhou clapped his hands

## FIGURE 3.1
## Military Organization of the PRC[a]

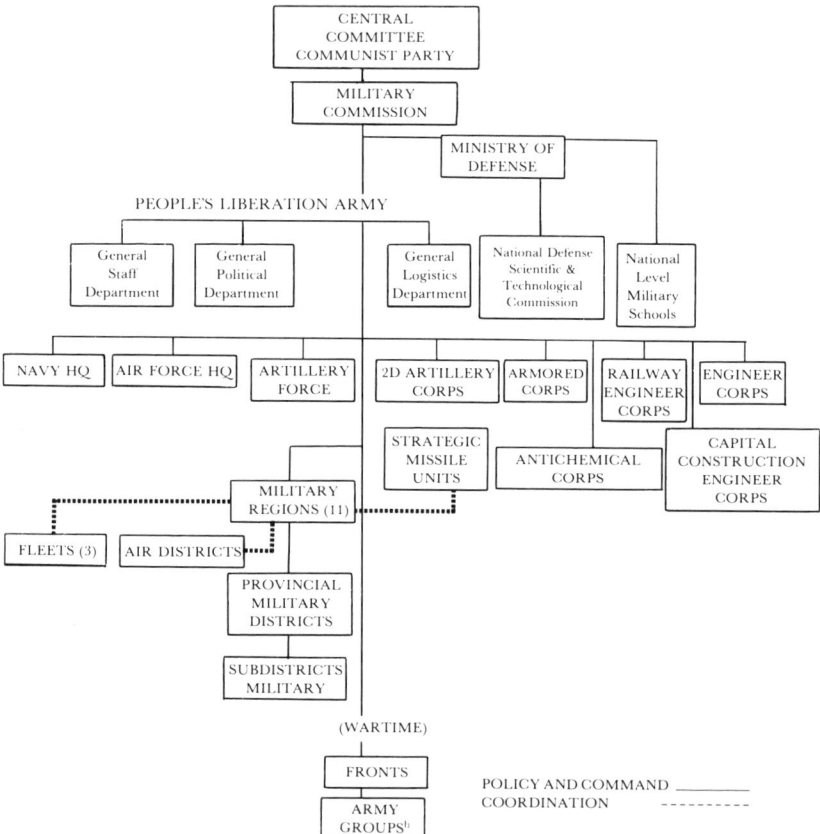

Source: Defense Intelligence Agency, Handbook on the Chinese Armed Forces A-1 (1976).
[a]As modified by CIA chart CR78-11398 (Mar. 1978).
[b]Chinese Term = U.S. Field Army.

TABLE 3.2
China's Nuclear Tests

| Test | Date | Yield | Delivery System | Location | Other Information |
|---|---|---|---|---|---|
| 1 | 10/16/64 | 20 KT | Ground (tower-mounted) | Lop Nor | Implosion device, U-235 |
| 2 | 5/14/65 | 20–50 KT | Air (TU-4 medium bomber) | Lop Nor | Fission, U-235 |
| 3 | 5/9/66 | 200–300 KT | Air (TU-16 medium bomber) | Lop Nor | Fission, U-235 and some thermonuclear material (lithium 6) |
| 4 | 10/27/66 | 20–30 KT | Missile (Soviet-type SS-4 over 500 miles) | Shuangchengzi/Lop Nor | Fission, U-235 |
| 5 | 12/28/66 | 300–500 KT | Ground (tower-mounted) | Lop Nor | Fission, U-235 and some thermonuclear material (lithium 6) |
| 6 | 6/17/67 | 3 MT | Air (TU-16); air explosion | Lop Nor | Thermonuclear warhead, fission-fusion-fission type using U-235 |
| 7 | 12/24/67 | 20–25 KT | Air (TU-16) | Lop Nor | Not announced by government. U-235 and thermonuclear material (lithium 6). (Apparently a partial failure with, possibly, only a fission cycle completed.) |
| 8 | 12/27/68 | 3 MT | Air (TU-16); air explosion | Lop Nor | Thermonuclear warhead using U-235 and containing some plutonium. |
| 9 | 9/22/69 | 20–25 KT | Underground explosion | Lop Nor | Fission device |
| 10 | 9/29/69 | 3 MT | Air (TU-16); air explosion | Lop Nor | Thermonuclear warhead suitable for ICBM |
| 11 | 10/14/70 | 3 MT | Air (TU-16); air explosion | Lop Nor | Not announced by government. Thermonuclear warhead. |

TABLE 3.2 (Cont.)

| Test | Date | Yield | Delivery System | Location | Other Information |
|---|---|---|---|---|---|
| 12 | 11/18/71 | 20 KT | Ground (tower-mounted) | Lop Nor | Possibly containing plutonium |
| 13 | 1/7/72 | Under 20 KT | Air explosion | Lop Nor | Possibly containing plutonium. Apparently a partial failure. |
| 14 | 3/18/72 | 20–200 KT | Air explosion | Lop Nor | Possibly a trigger device, containing plutonium, for a thermonuclear warhead. Apparently a partial failure. |
| 15 | 6/27/73 | Over 2 MT | Air delivery; air explosion | Lop Nor | Thermonuclear warhead |
| 16 | 6/17/74 | 200 KT–1 MT (probably close to 1 MT) | Air explosion | Lop Nor | Thermonuclear warhead |
| 17 | 10/27/75 | 20 KT | Underground explosion | Lop Nor | Fission device |
| 18 | 1/23/76 | Under 20 KT | Air explosion | Lop Nor | Fission device |
| 19 | 9/26/76 | 200 KT | Air explosion | Lop Nor | Fission device; probable partial failure of fusion |
| 20 | 10/17/76 | Under 50 KT | Underground explosion | Lop Nor | Fission device |
| 21 | 11/17/76 | 4 MT | Air explosion | Lop Nor | Thermonuclear device |
| 22 | 9/17/77 | 20 KT | Air explosion | Lop Nor | Fission device |
| 23 | 3/15/78 | Under 20 KT | Air explosion | Lop Nor | Fission device |
| 24 | 12/14/78 | Under 20 KT | Air explosion | Lop Nor | Fission device |

*Source:* The information in this table is taken from published reports in the Chinese and Western press.
Abbreviations: KT—kiloton or equivalent to 1,000 tons of TNT; MT—megaton or equivalent to 1,000,000 tons of TNT.

happily when he saw the rise of the mushroom cloud. He said: 'We have won! Chairman Mao said that he wanted to present Khrushchev a 1-ton medal to thank him for spurring us on to success in making an atom bomb.'"[86]

## IV. Major Issues Facing the Chinese in Developing Their Military Forces

China's leaders have faced—and continue to face—several major dilemmas in the development of PRC military forces. Some of the consequences of those dilemmas and the way they have been resolved are evident in the history of China's nuclear program and in comparisons of nuclear weapons and other PLA weapons systems. The pages that follow examine seven continuing dilemmas and their implications.

### Development of a Second-Stage Nuclear Posture

The PLA has discovered the difficulty of advancing beyond the initial stage of nuclear deployment. However, despite its primitive nature, this first stage has doubtless enhanced China's international political standing. In addition, if there is something like a "minimum deterrent," even without an explicit doctrine, China has achieved it. Potential adversaries know that an attack on China would be much more costly than if the PLA lacked nuclear weapons. Nevertheless, the Chinese now must decide how to move beyond this primitive level. This will require difficult doctrinal and developmental choices.

For technical, political, and economic reasons, the PRC has been delayed in moving much, if at all, beyond the net military capabilities they attained years ago. Technical problems have included moving from nonstorable liquid to storable rocket fuels, perfecting missile guidance systems, developing fixed-site launch protection, obtaining remote command-and-control communications with reliable advanced warning systems, reducing warhead size through better yield-to-weight ratios, and building a workable nuclear submarine. The Chinese did attempt to maximize the utility of their first-stage nuclear forces through mobility and the use of terrain for concealment and protection, but Soviet and U.S. targeting advances could steadily erode the utility and survivability of those forces.

The Chinese experienced a number of failures in their nuclear weapons programs and also came to realize, along with Moscow and Washington, how vulnerable fixed land-based missile sites might soon become. Questions asked by PRC military attachés in various capitals indicate that China's leaders have barely begun to grasp the complex technical, economic, and other difficulties involved in shifting from their current fixed-position missile programs to reliance on more secure systems. If they are to make such a change, the Chinese must make decisions in areas of military science for which their industrial, educational, and technical base is still inadequate, and for which their existing doctrines provide little direct guidance.[87]

Events since 1972 have added other, principally political, complexities to the upgrading of China's strategic posture. China still has comparatively few nuclear weapons but is strengthening its relations with the United States. Does this mean that China enjoys something akin to an American nuclear umbrella? This is a sensitive matter in the PRC; a major accusation against Lin Biao was that he wanted to place China under the Soviet nuclear umbrella.[88] His sin was not so much that he turned to the Soviets as that he allegedly proposed placing China's security in the hands of a foreign power. The issue is sensitive, but ex-CIA Director William Colby has stated that "détente with the United States" was one reason, among many, for the decline in Chinese defense spending in 1971.[89] Such a statement, if accurate, contradicts the common perception of China's defense strategy and also indicates that PRC leaders may be responsive to the U.S.'s role in influencing China's security.

Yet, the extent to which U.S. war plans actually bolster China's defenses against Moscow or complicate Soviet calculations remains unclear. We might consider this briefly by comparing China's situation to that of Japan.[90] Japan has a formal security treaty with the U.S., but the treaty is quite vague in terms of what actually will happen militarily. The treaty does not refer to nuclear weapons, but the U.S. nuclear umbrella is regarded by the Japanese as an effective guarantee against the unlikely, but by no means impossible, threat of attack. Japan's dependence on the U.S. nuclear deterrent is made explicit in the series of Japanese defense buildup plans dating from 1958. The term "umbrella" symbolizes the conviction that American power helps Japan and keeps that country from having to adopt costly defense measures.

In contrast to Japan, China does not have a specific defense commitment from the United States. The Chinese must operate according to the "strategic equation" of the moment, often from limited and even misleading information. This fact, which the U.S. attempted to change somewhat in 1978 by passing high-level security information to Peking, helps to account for Peking's sometimes excessive reaction to minor shifts in U.S.-Soviet relations. Even a slight improvement in U.S.-Soviet relations weakens any tacit protection by American power and undercuts policies and politicians that assume such protection.

*Technological Considerations in the Development of a
Modern Military Force*

China's selection of appropriate defense technologies poses ideological, technical, bureaucratic, and political problems. In a recent discussion, a leading U.S. energy specialist said:

> The reason I want to go to China is the Chinese have a petroleum economy like the U.S. had in the 1890's. We know how we went through a learning process to develop our oil fields, and apparently the Chinese are now repeating our history. But that's idiotic, because they now have the technologies available that would let them start doing things according to a 1980's technological level. We can't get the 1980's technology into our fields because we've already got the old drilling and pumping rigs in place. Why do they do it? Do they want to re-invent every "wheel" that we invented?[91]

Some Chinese leaders seem to have a mind-set that requires repeating the West's developmental experience, if only to assure mastery of basic skills. But periodic debates over importing Western scientific knowledge reveal that others disagree sharply with such an approach. In contrast, they stress the importance of reaching "advanced world standards" and working at the frontiers of science and technology. To do so requires specific organizational, educational, and other policies. Some writings on military-related scientific priorities in the early sixties, for example, insisted on the need for advanced specialization, scientific standards in determining the relevance of research, and giving all necessary authority to experts.[92] The following excerpt from an article by Qian Xuesen is typical of this viewpoint.

> If there are urgent social needs, forces are organized at once to proceed with the work in totality. For example, when there were only a few micrograms of a compound of plutonium 239, once its physical and chemical properties were ascertained, and its usefulness proven, a factory capable of producing several kilograms of plutonium 239 was designed, and the output was increased at one stroke by 1,000 million times. . . . Today, in what is called pioneering technology, in the utilization of atomic energy and in interstellar navigation, a composite force comprising thousands of scientists, engineers, designers, and technicians is working in each field. . . . Judging by the concrete situation in China, scientific and technical specialization and division of labor are even more important.[93]

While views such as Qian's were submerged by the political line imposed with the onset of the Cultural Revolution in 1966, the more recent emphasis on defense modernization makes those views acceptable once again.

Even so, Chinese leaders have not yet agreed on whether it is possible to impose a "stage two" science and technology on a "stage one" society, and the PRC has struggled to find a middle ground on technological modernization. It has emphasized the importance of making foreign technologies serve China and the need to make far-reaching internal changes to realize that objective.[94] This would, in turn, accelerate the modernization of science and technology for national defense.[95] The goal of using foreign technology to achieve rapid development of industry, agriculture, and the military was formally endorsed at the First National Science Conference in March 1978.[96] However, China's leaders also continue to advocate the indigenous development of "professional scientific research programs [and] . . . research on such new technologies as electronics, infrared, microwaves, lasers, and atomic energy."[97]

U.S. evaluations of Chinese military programs stress their strong technological focus and their advanced research and development (R&D) methodologies. In 1976, General George Brown reported:

> Emphasis is clearly on programs with long-range implications such as the construction of one of the world's most modern shipyards at [Huludao]; impressive new facilities for producing large quantities of nuclear material, solid propellant missiles; and R&D initiatives addressing advanced airframes and sophisticated engines. The temptation to yield to programs which would provide a more immediate strategic posture and perception of growing strength apparently has been resisted. . . . The PRC has the capability to perform R&D in support of advanced weapons programs. Advanced systems continue to receive the greatest emphasis in resource allocations. . . . Developments at the major Chinese aircraft missile research and development facilities between 1972 and 1975 firmly indicate that a determined effort is underway to modernize the weapons available to China's strategic and tactical forces.[98]

A year later, Brown reaffirmed these conclusions and added that the Chinese "seem to be following two approaches in obtaining more advanced systems. First, they are pushing their domestic research programs; and second, they are attempting to acquire foreign technology, equipment and weapon systems."[99] There is no doubt that Peking systematically seeks to ascertain which advanced technologies are essential in its defense-related needs and to acquire at least some of them. The major problems for China's leaders have been to select the specific technologies to be acquired and to decide how to introduce them. The acquisition of advanced technologies per se has not been a critical problem.

Preparing for the long run, the PRC has labored since the mid-1960s to build the R&D and production base needed for its strategic programs. For example:

The Chinese have dedicated millions of square feet of floor-space to current and future missile production. . . . The PRC may also have elected to emphasize research and development as they move from the production of Soviet-supplied systems to their own indigenous missile force. Modern facilities and a technical base are being established to support future and more advanced missile hardware. . . . In contrast with the decline in output [of older fighter aircraft] there has been a modest increase in airframe and engine plants and aviation institutes in the last five years and a significant increase in the size of R&D centers.[100]

The Chinese are also credited with having established the necessary industrial systems for "production of all types of ground forces matériel" and for advanced shipbuilding and repair.[101] The expansion and improvement of their R&D test facilities, U.S. sources estimate, "will permit test support of more than one new aircraft or missile system at a time and the improvement will permit testing of increasingly complex systems."[102]

A question related to the level of technology is: How and when should China enter the advanced electronics revolution? The Middle East October War in 1973 appears to have taught the Chinese that the steady military development upon which they were embarked might prove fruitless. With electronic, precision-guided munitions (PGMs), warfare had gone through a major revolution, and China must face the fact that gradual improvements in tank turrets, the purchase of better aircraft engines, and similar conventional advances will not fundamentally improve the PRC's capacity to deal with Soviet or American forces.

Adoption of advanced technologies has been debated in terms of preserving China's revolutionary roots and its hard-won independence. Modernization that entails dependence on external sources is viewed as dangerously costly. Moreover, there is considerable "conservatism" or inertia in the PLA that impedes consideration and adoption of new technologies.[103] For the PLA, true understanding of highly advanced weapons might mean concluding that its soldiers and the bulk of its equipment would prove quite ineffective in a showdown.

There are signs that such traditional thinking is beginning to change. One such indicator is the fact that Chinese articles on military modernization up to 1977 dealt almost exclusively with the navy, artillery, air force, air defense, nuclear weapons, and missile forces. However, technical journals thereafter began to consider the needs of the common foot soldier and the value of shoulder-held air defense weapons and other advanced infantry equipment.[104] Although most 1977 articles mentioning the infantry talked in terms of force readiness, by early 1978 greater emphasis was being placed on advanced armament, mobility, and technical projects such as the new laser range finders in antitank weapons.[105] Such steps toward technological sophistication apparently signal a policy change "to reduce the fixed number of troops, reduce military and administrative expenditures, and spend more money on building more factories, manufacturing more machinery, and starting more economic projects."[106]

It thus appears that the PLA is reassessing China's needs with respect to advanced technologies that could be introduced in all services. The Chinese have instructed at least some of their military attachés abroad to find out everything possible about advanced weapons. Their mission, openly stated to some foreign contacts, is to purchase selected items, to investigate the status of advanced weapons systems, and to inquire into weapon use doctrines as well as hardware details. Upgrading China's infantry forces by acquiring precision-guided munitions and other "next generation" weapons is a logical next step in weapons development. Such weapons add greater military capability for the same cost than do alternative conventional weapon technologies. Although the Chinese do not now have conventional or nuclear firepower on the northern border equivalent to that of the opposing Soviet units, they could, in time, begin to match the Red Army by introducing the most advanced generation of weapons.

However, significant upgrading of ground forces through introduction of advanced weapons is not likely to happen soon—at least not without considerable political conflict. Senior military and political leaders appreciate the advantages and technological necessity of moving to advanced weapons, but, besides the expense involved, upgrading the military will require substantial educational and attitudinal change. For example, the PLA will have to retrain its soldiers to accept and use sophisticated systems, making them highly "weapon conscious."[107] Light, portable, advanced electronic gear would replace a large number of infantrymen and would move the military men further from the traditional PLA stress on man over weapons. In 1979, the need to make such moves received added impetus following evaluations by Peking of the PLA's poor mobility and logistics in Vietnam.

Articles published since mid-1977 strongly suggest that technological modernization will take precedence over revolutionary values should the two conflict. A series in *Jiefangjun Bao* argued for the "integration of revolutionized people with sophisticated weapons," for the purpose of attaining two main goals: "(1) We must obtain sophisticated weapons and equipment, including constantly improved and renovated weapons, guided missiles and nuclear weapons; (2) we must have men who can handle these sophisticated weapons and who possess modern military knowledge, technology and tactics necessary for utilizing them."[108] Similarly, Fang Yi told a national meeting on science and technology in 1978 that the PLA must be equipped "with the latest achievements in science and technology."[109] He specifically mentioned computers, lasers, and space technology among other areas capable of making direct contributions to defense. Yet, one must wonder how far the trend toward ever higher priority for scientific and technological standards can go without threatening cherished "revolutionary" values. The contest between revolution and technological modernization in China's national defense remains unsettled.

*Cost of the Defense Sector*

The Chinese have begun to recognize the tremendous economic costs of military modernization and that any lesser investments might make little relative difference in their military capability. For the next several years, substantial expenditures appear likely in aircraft and offensive missile production, and in the development and procurement of tanks, ships, and other conventional weapons. According to one source, "In China the [economic] burden [of military programs] has varied over the course of the decade from a level roughly comparable to that of the United States and Soviet Union in the early years, rising to a peak in 1971 higher than either of the others, and returning in recent years to around the initial level."[110] Table 3.3 gives figures on estimated Chinese defense expenditures.

The director of the Defense Intelligence Agency has assessed recent and future trends in PRC military spending as follows: "Chinese military procurement costs decreased in 1976 compared to 1975 but were higher than the previous 3 years. Annual procurement remained relatively constant . . . during the 1972–74 period. . . . It appears likely that procurement costs can be expected to grow."[111]

Whatever the actual financial impact of new military programs, by mid-1977 Chinese officials were telling foreign delegations that they were prepared to pay the necessary price. In 1977, direct military expenditures were estimated to represent approximately 8 to 10 percent of China's GNP.[112] The impact of this expenditure was suggested by Vice Premier Li Xiannian's comments to a Japanese youth delegation. "China would keep developing nuclear weapons of its own if the United States and the Soviet Union did not cease to develop theirs. . . . [It does] not have much money left over for other things because of the heavy cost of its preparedness for a possible war."[113]

In mid-1979, the Chinese published the state accounts for 1978. Out of a total state expenditure of 111,093 million yuan, approximately 18 percent (20,230 million yuan) was spent on national defense and "preparations against war." The Minister of Finance explained that this percentage was expected to rise in 1979 because of added costs associated with the conflict in Vietnam and other border defense needs. Since the figure of 20,230 million yuan would convert to about $12.9 billion at 1978 exchange rates,

Table 3.3

ESTIMATE FOR PRC MILITARY EXPENDITURES AND GNP

| Year | MILITARY EXPENDITURES (MILEX) Millions of Dollars | | GROSS NATIONAL PRODUCT (GNP) Millions of Dollars | | MILEX/GNP |
|------|---------|----------|---------|----------|------|
|      | Current | Constant | Current | Constant | %    |
| 1967 | 15700 | 24900 | 106751 | 169100 | 14.7 |
| 1968 | 17100 | 26000 | 112110 | 170050 | 15.3 |
| 1969 | 19600 | 28400 | 130770 | 189050 | 15.0 |
| 1970 | 22400 | 30800 | 159661 | 219450 | 14.0 |
| 1971 | 24700 | 32300 | 179057 | 234555 | 13.8 |
| 1972 | 24700 | 31100 | 194802 | 245480 | 12.7 |
| 1973 | 26200 | 31200 | 232448 | 277020 | 11.3 |
| 1974 | 29300 | 31700 | 265294 | 287375 | 11.0 |
| 1975 | 32700 | 32700 | 307040 | 307040 | 10.7 |
| 1976 | 34400 | 32800 | 322793 | 307315 | 10.7 |

*Source:* U.S. Arms Control and Disarmament Agency, *World Military Expenditures and Arms Transfers 1967-1976* 39 (1978).

the official PRC figures for defense outlays fall far below those given in Table 3.3. Presumably, either Chinese calculations exclude certain items that U.S. analysts might include or American estimates—as has been the case with Soviet estimates—have exaggerated Chinese defense spending.[114] All agree that PRC defense budgets are rising.

*Setting National Priorities in China*

As reflected in the series of commentaries that followed the 1977 publication of Mao's *On the Ten Major Relationships,* the Chinese became engaged in yet another round of setting national priorities.[115] Similar debates during the sixties unfolded as follows. The 1958-64 expenditures associated with the nuclear weapons program caused a commensurate reduction in funds for the PLA's conventional forces and for infrastructural investments. According to some analysts, this led a group of army and political officials to compensate by embracing "people's war" (in 1965-67) in an attempt to increase expenditures on the ground forces. With the onset of the Sino-Soviet break and the example of the U.S. intervention in Vietnam, these leaders believed that China's readiness to fight such a war would force the Russians to contemplate "many Vietnams" if they attacked China. But most Chinese military officers reportedly opposed this emphasis on either people's war or nuclear weapons alone. They felt that Mao's nuclear program was too provocative and that the priority given people's war had left China too vulnerable in the conventional field.

The legacy of that earlier debate entered into 1977-78 deliberations on national priorities. In a major speech to the May 1977 National Conference on Learning from Daqing in Industry, Ye Jianying (vice chairman of the Chinese Communist Party Central Committee and minister of defense) quoted Mao's addendum to the "ten major relations" concerning national defense priorities: "Chairman Mao said in 1964: 'We have had two fists and one rump. One fist is agriculture, the other the defense industries. If we want the fist to pack a wallop, our rump must be firm, the rump being the basic industries.'"[116] Other senior leaders have echoed the call to emphasize "economic construction" at the expense of military procurement, but there is apparently some disagreement over just how long this emphasis should continue. For example, whereas Ye stressed the need for speed so that military construction could begin in a few years, Vice Premier Yu Qiuli's speech at the same conference pointed out that it would take many years to build the country's infrastructure.[117]

China's enduring political debates indicate that the criteria for determining national priorities remain in dispute. Removal of the "gang of four" and formation of the post-Mao leadership have already reshaped military doctrines and policies, but coalitions form around many issues and few questions are decided in isolation. Since military policies affect possibilities in several other policy areas (e.g., industrial investment, science, treatment of intellectuals), all decisions are likely to spark debate and political maneuver.[118] Political struggle could cause the Chinese to delay in accepting resource, credit, or technical help from abroad, and to miss opportunities for bettering their relations with Moscow or Hanoi in order to reduce their border force requirements. If the conclusion discussed above is correct and doctrine follows China's technical capabilities, then it is likely that short-run constraints on capability will cause high-level defense debates to focus on resource allocation rather than on military doctrine.

An article describing a major army meeting in 1975 indicates that Vice Premier Deng Xiaoping attempted with only temporary success to settle the dispute over where the military should rank in the list of national priorities.[119] The directives from that meeting, though quickly lost in the political struggle that temporarily cost Deng his job, are illustrated by the use of such slogans as "The army must be consolidated" and "Be prepared for war." Priorities were to be set forth in "a whole set of concrete guidelines, general policies and measures suitable for different conditions in industry, agriculture, trade, education, military affairs, administrative affairs and party affairs."[120] Military policy would continue to give "serious attention to revolutionizing people's ideology," but higher priority was to be accorded to studying "modern national defenses," to having "not only more airplanes and artillery pieces but also atomic bombs," and to training "in the defense of the country and becoming a modern army."[121] While the emphasis on modern technology was clear enough, it left unanswered the question of defining and operationalizing "people's war."

*The Role of People's War*

Chinese authors regularly discuss people's war and mass military training,[122] but the PLA has not deployed the country's military power as a people's army or guerrilla force since the late 1940s nor has the citizenry been adequately trained for sustained combat.[123] Commenting on the Yan'an Campaign of 1947, a March 18, 1977, *Renmin Ribao* article applauded Mao's military use of "luring in deep," but this was defined as luring opponents deep into the country in order to smash them with main force units. The point of the article was to explain how to use the main force units most advantageously against temporarily superior armies. Deployment and timely engagement were described as crucial to success; popular resistance was all but ignored in this description of "people's war."

It is widely believed that during the mid-1960s, and perhaps as early as 1958, a serious difference of opinion about people's war existed within the PRC leadership. According to this assessment, in 1965-67, the PLA began to organize its forces as if China were moving toward greater reliance on guerrilla or popularly-based warfare. Discussion and actual military policies in this period are thought to have been shaped by Mao's (and Lin Biao's) doctrine of people's war. Implementation of this line proved to be short-lived, however, and reality and dogma again diverged as modernization returned as a priority. Policies of the early 1970s placed increased emphasis on regular forces and improved weaponry. Advocates of traditional people's war responded with arguments typified by the following excerpt: "The application of modern science and technology on the battlefield is bound to bring about some new changes in future wars. But one must realize that future wars against aggression will still be people's wars in character."[124] In effect, this article urged that the people continue to be emphasized on the theory that the civilian militia is "the solid basis for waging a modern people's war. The more modernized the war is . . . the more we should emphasize the militia's role."[125] On balance, the tension that has long existed between the heritage of people's war and "the new changes in the technical equipment and operational characteristics between the enemy and us" appears to favor the "new changes."[126]

Currently, the rhetorical and ideological aspects of the people's war concept probably continue to make a difference in military training, in bolstering morale, in trying to involve the populace in national defense projects, and in civil defense programs. For these purposes, people's war themes have a solid rationale. But they do not appear to be central to current war plans. While Article 19 of the 1978 State Constitution stresses the integration of all armed forces, requiring them to be "a combination of the field armies, the regional forces, and the militia," relevant commentaries have made no mention of people's war. Many post-1976 articles dealing with the militia, army unity, discipline, and readiness have been linked to doctrines of people's war, though the reasons for this linkage have been left unclear. Given that China's military programs were moving away from complete reliance upon manpower and placing renewed emphasis on weapons modernization, it appears these articles were intended to deal principally with the morale, discipline, and training problems anticipated as the PLA becomes a more modern, weapons-conscious force. "People's war" was becoming a slogan for making the transition to modernity, not a prescription for popular resistance. One senior Chinese military leader, Su Yu, writing in 1977, seemed to agree, "The future war against aggression will be a people's war under modern conditions. If we strengthen our modernized construction, we will be able to strengthen greatly the power of the people's war."[127] Some months later, he added that some of Mao's principles "no longer fit the actual conditions of future wars and should be abandoned."[128]

*Military Cooperation with Other Nations*

Peking speaks approvingly of people's wars of national liberation almost solely in terms of struggles by Third World peoples against the oppression of advanced industrial societies, especially the two superpowers. While Chinese military power, political-economic assistance, and propaganda backing can help thwart the "aggressive designs" of the powerful against the weak, the Chinese argue that the peoples of each country must wage their own struggles for national independence. Therefore, with the special exception of North Korea, direct military cooperation does not constitute an important part of Chinese foreign policy.

Peking in the past decade has maintained close contact only with Vietnamese and Korean military officials, and only in the case of North Korea does this contact now appear to involve operational military ties of any significance. Indeed, the relations between Hanoi and Peking deteriorated rapidly in 1978 as China not only disputed Hanoi's links to Moscow and the ownership of islands in the South China Sea but also denounced Vietnam's border violations and alleged mistreatment of its Chinese residents. China moved additional troops to its borders with Vietnam and ended all aid to Hanoi. In early 1979, after Vietnam had nearly crushed China's Cambodian allies, the PLA attacked Vietnam to "punish" Hanoi, to discredit the Moscow-Hanoi tie, and to ease Vietnam's pressure on Cambodia. After about three weeks of intense fighting, the Chinese halted and withdrew. The stage was thus set for a long period of tension and later hostilities.

The Korean case is also complex. Should war break out on the peninsula, China's nuclear and conventional power would affect U.S. decisions concerning the use of tactical nuclear weapons and any actions that might extend the war to China. Short of actual hostilities, China tends to inhibit Kim Il-sung's military flexibility, while acclaiming Kim's political ends. China also has tacitly joined the superpowers in limiting the availability of the most advanced weapons on the Korean peninsula. It thus appears that China uses the Korean connection to control the dangers of conflict while at the same time countering Soviet influence.

The greatest possibility for modification of China's opposition to foreign military ties exists in relation to countries of the Second World. The doctrinal underpinnings for the "first-second-third world" distinction are traceable to the Chinese theory of the "intermediate zone."[129] The most recent formulation of the theory is "Chairman Mao's thesis differentiating the three worlds" that was set forth in 1974. Deng Xiaoping propounded this thesis before the United Nations the same year, and Hua Guofeng reaffirmed its correctness at the Party's Eleventh National Congress in August 1977.[130] In speaking of the Second World (Japan, France, and other "middle level" capitalist states), Hua noted, "The second world countries have a dual character; on the one hand they oppress, exploit and control the third world countries, and on the other they are controlled, threatened and bullied by both hegemonic powers in varying degrees."[131]

In December 1971, Zhou Enlai attempted to come to grips with Japan's place in these "worlds" or "zones."[132] Zhou explored the possibility of treating Japan's economic and military potential in "third world" terms while also realizing that country's "second world" aspects. He said: "The Japanese people belong to the sphere of the Asian, African, and Latin American revolutionary strength while the Japanese rulers belong to the category of the second intermediate zone." Japan thus belongs to two "zones" at the same time (one "good" and one "bad"), and as a "third world" target of the superpowers it could be considered a potential ally of the world's revolutionaries. This use of Mao's "theory" predictably provoked fears in Moscow that Tokyo and Peking might form a military partnership. One Soviet article in 1977 charged that Japanese defense officials had secretly visited the PRC to discuss military strategy and that visits by ships of the Japanese Self-Defense Forces to Chinese ports had taken place.[133] Another article stated that former Japanese military personnel were giving guidance to the Chinese air force and other elements of the PLA.[134] My own discussions with Japanese defense specialists indicate that a number of Japanese military planners did visit China during 1977 and that their discussions were indeed quite far-ranging.

Peking's pronouncements about Europe and NATO merit special consideration when examining Chinese policies toward the "second world." Some Pentagon officials reportedly dismiss China's pro-NATO statements as pure rhetoric. It is true that Chinese harangues about Moscow's "making a feint to the East while attacking the West" were designed initially to influence the number of Soviet forces arrayed against China rather than to describe the actual vulnerability of NATO. Peking presumably hoped that the U.S., by bolstering military defenses in Europe, would divert Soviet divisions westward. As a history of their actions toward Europe shows, the Chinese did not believe that Moscow was simply "feinting to the East" from 1969 to 1971. Only in late 1972 did China really come to focus on the defense of Europe as a means of reducing pressures on itself. By the spring of 1973, when Peking officials first used the "feint to the East" slogan to criticize U.S. policies of accommodating the Russians, they already were beginning to assign a higher priority to Europe in their overall strategies.[135]

By early 1973, the Chinese seem to have concluded that their earlier emphasis on the danger of a Soviet surprise attack against China was allowing the U.S. to take Peking for granted. This concern heightened during Nixon's Watergate debacle as China's leaders came to believe that the U.S.

might negotiate further agreements allowing Moscow to relax in the West (as at Vladivostok in 1974 and Helsinki in 1975). The real weaknesses of NATO also became more apparent after the 1973 October War in the Middle East and with the rising fortunes of European Communist parties. Thus, by 1974–75 the Chinese had genuine reasons to believe their earlier and somewhat contrived slogans on Soviet ambitions vis-à-vis China and Western Europe, and over time, the Chinese gave greater substance to their pro-NATO line. For example, the PRC established relations with the European Economic Community in May 1975, expanded contacts with European leaders, and sent Deng Xiaoping and other PRC officials (including the PLA deputy chief of staff) to Europe. Thus did the gap between propaganda and reality begin to close.

Finally, there is the much debated range of possible Chinese cooperation with the "first world" superpowers. Possibilities range all the way from military cooperation with the U.S. to a Sino-Soviet rapprochement.[136] From the viewpoint of a minority of Chinese military planners, the case for improving Sino-Soviet relations apparently has had some appeal ever since the initial rupture in the late fifties, but Hua's government seems to have ruled out any real moves in this direction for the foreseeable future. Nonetheless, the determinants of ties among nations are changing, and it is impossible to foresee what international circumstances might trigger a reversal of Sino-Soviet animosity.

In 1978–79, normalization of U.S.-China relations occurred against the backdrop of intensified anti-Soviet rhetoric from PRC leaders and raised the possibility of an anti-Soviet partnership. Yet even though full diplomatic relations have been established, the basis for any future military cooperation remains extremely tenuous. American caution in this regard has been influenced not only by continuing ties to Taiwan, but also by Soviet reactions, especially since China's attack on Vietnam in early 1979. China's commitment to self-reliance and to transforming the country into a powerful, independent state does not preclude selective purchase of U.S. military technologies or the creation of tacit military understandings between Washington and Peking. But ideology and conflicting interests impose severe limits on Sino-American ties despite Soviet accusations to the contrary.[137]

In the final analysis, the extent of Chinese military cooperation with the United States will be governed more by political considerations than by technological requirements. The Chinese can purchase virtually all the equipment and even production facilities they need from Western Europe and Japan.[138] An examination of potential cooperation should focus on which internationally visible ties could enhance the PRC's security, even temporarily, and what costs the Chinese would tolerate in return. Thus far, beyond the political effects of normalization, such "ties" with the U.S. have been predominantly symbolic: the highly publicized visits of an anti-Soviet U.S. senator, a former U.S. secretary of defense and other current cabinet and National Security Council staff members, a prominent military affairs columnist, and a former chief of naval operations. Vice Premier Deng Xiaoping's visit to the U.S. in 1979 dramatized the element of reciprocity and mutuality in the new relationship. U.S. officials for their part have used these and other recent contacts with China for purposes of their own[139] and have leaked documents on debates or otherwise hinted about Washington's high-level consideration of military sales, either by the U.S. or its allies, to the PRC.[140] To date neither side has been willing to go much further than symbolic (but by no means unimportant) acts, although advocates for a stronger military relationship continue to press their case.

Chinese leaders seem to recognize that the relationship with Washington affects their freedom of action. The recognition that their attack on Vietnam could antagonize the United States apparently was a factor, albeit a minor one, in their decision to stop the conflict. Their weapon programs and the form of their support to Hanoi during the Vietnam War and more recently to North Korea long ago signalled respect for American power and a strong aversion to direct confrontation with the U.S. So long as the Soviet Union is considered the chief enemy, the Chinese will maintain their enthusiasm for actions by the U.S. and its allies that preserve and enhance Western military might. Such "support" for the West appears to be the major focus of China's international military cooperation in the near future.

*China's Stand on Arms Control*

Given the realistic possibility that China may begin to accept some aspects of traditional deterrence thinking and the logical connection between deterrence and arms control (as distinguished from disarmament), Peking could move toward a more active and positive interest in arms control measures, particularly those related to nuclear nonproliferation. To date, Peking has argued that the superpowers must begin their own total nuclear disarmament or watch the inevitable moves of others to acquire nuclear weapons. Any middle stance on arms control, Chinese officials insist, merely serves the interest of the superpowers against the weaker, non-nuclear weapons states and constitutes "collusion." As a result of this perspective China has denounced every arms control initiative and agreement advanced by the Soviet Union or the United States since the 1963 Limited Nuclear Test Ban Treaty.

The Chinese have relented in their opposition to arms control only where Third World countries have called for nuclear-free zones to constrain the

Soviet Union and the United States. In 1974, Peking ratified Protocol II of the Treaty for the Prohibition of Nuclear Weapons in Latin America.[141] China does not promote nuclear proliferation; but then neither does it condemn proliferation where it happens. Deng Xiaoping told a U.S. congressional delegation in 1975 that China does not engage in nuclear proliferation, "but if others do proliferate we can do nothing. As for India, it would rather starve and have nothing to eat in order to develop nuclear weapons. That is its right. Taiwan can decide for itself if it wants nuclear weapons. That is its right."[142]

While sometimes flexible in private, the public stance of Chinese officials on arms control has remained virtually unyielding for more than a decade. Their annual remarks at the United Nations were essentially the same from 1971 to 1977, but at the 1978 special General Assembly session on disarmament the Chinese position did contain minor modifications from earlier years. The PRC's basic position is clearly set forth in Foreign Minister Huang Hua's 1977 UN address:

> We are for genuine disarmament and against sham disarmament. We have consistently stood for the complete prohibition and thorough destruction of nuclear weapons. As the first step, all nuclear countries, and particularly the two nuclear superpowers, the Soviet Union and the United States, must first of all undertake the unequivocal obligation that they will not be the first to use nuclear weapons at any time and in any circumstances, and in particular will not use nuclear weapons against non-nuclear countries and nuclear-free zones, and that they must dismantle *all their nuclear bases* on the territories of other countries and withdraw from abroad *all their nuclear armed forces and nuclear weapons*. We support the demands of the countries and people in the regions of the Indian Ocean, the Mediterranean and the Red Sea and in Southeast Asia, South Asia and Latin America for the establishment of peace zones, security zones and nuclear-free zones. We are strongly opposed to the superpowers' policies of nuclear blackmail and nuclear monopoly and to their disarmament fraud.[143]

Huang's statement apparently precludes any overt Chinese interest in strategic arms control agreements and is consistent with their longstanding repudiation of "so-called nuclear disarmament talks between the nuclear powers behind the backs of the non-nuclear countries."[144] However, China's nuclear power does influence the arms calculations of the superpowers, a fact that Peking's leaders clearly understand and privately welcome. After visits to China and the Soviet Union in 1973, I concluded that the PRC even then was

> becoming a silent partner at the Strategic Arms Limitation Talks. By agree-

ing to the antiballistic missile treaty in 1972, the Soviet Union—and the United States—increased the "value" of each Chinese offensive missile. The greater probability of China's warheads hitting undefended targets added measurably to their deterrent effect.... [A]s early as SALT I China was beginning to affect the future of the strategic arms negotiations ... [and] SALT III will inevitably be more finely tuned to the Chinese nuclear program.[145]

Moreover, if China closes the military gap between itself and the superpowers, the growing complexity of the PLA strategic systems could impel its military commanders to incorporate arms control considerations into their procurement and deployment decisions. For example, if naval arms control discussions materialize, the PRC would have the choice of playing the spoiler by significantly augmenting its sea-based nuclear forces or of becoming the passive beneficiary should any substantial agreement be reached for the Pacific. How the SALT negotiations finally rule on U.S. cruise missiles or Soviet mobile ICBMs will bear directly on the viability of China's own programs and the need to consider alternatives.

However, Chinese leaders will begin to reformulate their policies on arms control only insofar as they can equate the potential results with China's national interest. Foreign Minister Huang Hua stressed the following in his 1978 speech to the Special Session of the United Nations General Assembly on Disarmament:

> The Chinese delegation is ready to join the representatives of other countries in discussing disarmament. . . . Since the hegemonist powers, the Soviet Union and the United States, claim that their security can be assured only through a military equilibrium between themselves, the small and medium-sized countries are all the more justified to demand that these powers be the first to reduce their super-arsenals, for they are threatened by the superpowers' superior military strength. . . . Their armaments should certainly be cut drastically. . . . Disarmament must start with the two superpowers. . . . The Chinese people badly need an enduring peaceful international environment for the great task of developing China into a modern and powerful socialist country by the end of the century. . . . Questions of disarmament and international security, which concern the interests of all countries, should be deliberated by an international organ with the participation of all countries under the auspices of the United Nations. The items and procedures of disarmament negotiations should be decided on by this organ, while machinery responsible for disarmament negotiations should be truly free of superpower control and should be set up through consultations by the above-mentioned deliberative organ.[146]

In 1979, the PRC began participating in the work of the UN Disarmament

Commission and, in May, laid before it a formal proposal. Thereafter, Peking's officials began more active discussions on specific arms control measures.[147] By contrast, Chinese spokesmen denigrate SALT because in their view its outcomes have spurred, not slowed, the arms race. Nevertheless, PRC leaders appear to understand that their military programs do weigh in the SALT calculus, and their actions thus far have not been designed to jeopardize further strategic arms agreements.[148]

The critical obstacle to involving China in arms control measures stems from the inability of PRC leaders to make a connection between arms control and the country's defense needs. As currently perceived by the Chinese, arms control still holds little promise of improving China's security. The emergence of arms control thinking as a corollary of Western deterrence theories strengthened its acceptance in Washington but vitiated it in China, where nuclear deterrence itself has seemed inadequate or unattainable. Arms control will probably become a salient issue for Peking's military planners only when China's own security is on a par with the superpowers' or when arms control itself clearly fosters that security.

## V. Policy Implications for the United States

The seven issues summarized above will challenge the political ingenuity not only of the Chinese but also of Western leaders. Assuming satisfactory advances in the coming period of U.S.-China relations (and this is by no means certain), U.S. officials will continue to take into account — and debate — the long-range security needs of the PRC as China moves toward major power status. This is a matter that goes beyond the narrow debate over military technology sales and defense contracts that, as noted, has received close scrutiny for the past several years.[149] The key question is: Can the United States constructively affect the direction of China's military programs and its attitude toward arms control by enhancing the peace and well-being of the Pacific region?

The question for the U.S. is not *whether* to have a security relationship with Peking, but of *what type* it will be. The Chinese view of U.S. and Soviet deployments has been dramatically reversed over the past two decades, and China now advocates increasing American strength. Indeed China's anti-Soviet stand and support for maintenance of continued U.S. troops in Europe has led Chinese officials to drop their long-standing demand that the U.S. withdraw from all overseas bases as a condition for participating in disarmament meetings. For the same reason, Peking no longer sees Europe as a suitable ground for a "no-first-use" nuclear policy.[150] Peking perceives Soviet influence to be on the advance everywhere and regularly adjusts its policies to check that influence, particularly in Asia. How the

United States meets the Soviet challenge, therefore, will be a major determinant of the future course of Chinese military programs.

In the Shanghai Communiqué of February 1972, China and the United States agreed to base their future relations on the principles of peaceful coexistence. They agreed that "international disputes should be settled . . . without resorting to the use or threat of force."[151] That commitment could be the basis for further bilateral exploration of a wide range of modalities for reducing "the danger of international conflict."[152] In short, the basis for strengthening U.S.-China cooperation on security matters already exists. The emerging scientific and technical cooperation between the two countries promises to promote the process.

These opportunities for cooperation come at a pivotal moment when several key changes intersect. This chapter has attempted to show that China's military doctrines are now being driven by technological considerations but that technology itself presents China with a variety of dilemmas. Moreover, China must decide which course its military programs will take, which doctrinal emphases to embrace, and which strategies of military-political action to pursue just as other major countries are confronting similar military-political paradoxes. A central task of world leaders in the coming decade will be to devise an effective international framework for a world in which many nations will have or can quickly acquire nuclear weapons. Present control programs, such as SALT, simply are inadequate because of the absence of key nations, in particular, China. Although the need for rethinking international approaches to security and arms control transcends the China dimension, the importance of involving the Chinese increases in accordance with the evolving sophistication of their military might. It is a rare occasion in the life cycle of any major international problem when opportunity and need coincide. That moment may be at hand.

## Notes

1. As used in this paper, doctrine refers to theories and assumptions on the use of conventional and nuclear weapons, and on the nature of warfare. This is the usage found in the strategic literature and in writings on arms control and disarmament. This paper gives much less attention to the ideological underpinnings of PRC foreign policy in general.

2. *See* Richard Garthoff ed., *Sino-Soviet Military Relations 1945–66,* SINO-SOVIET MILITARY RELATIONS (1966); Harold P. Ford, *Modern Weapons and the Sino-Soviet Estrangement,* CHINA QUARTERLY, Apr.–June 1964, at 160–73 (Apr.–June 1964); and Allen S. Whiting, *The Use of Force in Foreign Policy by the People's Republic of China,* 402 ANNALS OF THE AMERICAN ACADEMY OF POLITICAL AND SOCIAL SCIENCE 55–66 (July 1972).

3. *The Kunming Documents, reprinted in* 8 CHINESE LAW AND GOVERNMENT 44 (No. 1, 1975).
4. MAO ZEDONG, 4 SELECTED WORKS OF MAO TSE-TUNG 87-88 (1965).
5. WENWU [CULTURAL RELICS] 42 (Mar. 1974).
6. This theme continued to be stressed through 1977. *See, e.g.,* Jiefangjun Bao, *Should We or Should We Not Be Ready for War?, in* FOREIGN BROADCAST INFORMATION SERVICE, DAILY REPORT: PEOPLE'S REPUBLIC OF CHINA [hereafter FBIS], July 12, 1977, at E6-11.
7. Renmin Ribao [People's Daily, hereafter RMRB], Dec. 4, 1976.
8. Guangming Ribao [Guangming Daily, hereafter GMRB], Jan. 20, 1977.
9. *United States-Soviet Union-China: The Great Power Triangle: Hearings Before the Subcomm. on Future Foreign Policy Research and Development of the House Comm. on International Relations,* 94th Cong., 1st & 2d Sess., 184 (1975-76).
10. Li Xiannian's statement to an American visitor in July 1977 is typical: "As to when and in what way the Chinese people will liberate their sacred territory Taiwan . . . that is entirely China's internal affair which brooks no interference from other countries." *Vice-Premier Li Xiannian on Sino-American Relations,* PEKING REVIEW, July 15, 1977, at 3. A similar statement was made by Hua Guofeng at the Eleventh Party Congress in August 1977. PEKING REVIEW [hereafter PR], Aug. 26, 1977, at 42.
11. PEOPLE'S REPUBLIC OF CHINA, PEOPLE OF THE WORLD, UNITE, FOR THE COMPLETE, THOROUGH, TOTAL AND RESOLUTE PROHIBITION AND DESTRUCTION OF NUCLEAR WEAPONS! 22, 85 (1971).
12. PEOPLE'S REPUBLIC OF CHINA, BREAK THE NUCLEAR MONOPOLY, ELIMINATE NUCLEAR WEAPONS 3 (1965).
13. MAO ZEDONG, 2 SELECTED WORKS OF MAO TSE-TUNG 224 (1965).
14. Zhou Enlai, *Report on the Work of the Government,* PR, Jan. 24, 1975, at 23 and Hua Guofeng, *The Situation and Our Tasks,* PR, Aug. 26, 1977, at 53-54. At the Eleventh National Congress of the Communist Party of China (Aug. 12-18, 1977), Hua Guofeng said, "To make China a great, powerful and modern socialist country in the last quarter of the 20th century, we urgently need to educate and train a great many people who are both red and expert." *Id.* at 48-51. The goal of a "powerful socialist country" is now enshrined in the Party's new constitution (adopted Aug. 18, 1977).
15. The official wording of this line is: "The continued fierce rivalry between the two superpowers is bound to lead to war some day. This is independent of man's will." Qiao Guanhua, *The Chinese Government Will Continue to Carry Out Resolutely Chairman Mao's Revolutionary Line and Policies in Foreign Affairs,* PR, Oct. 15, 1976, at 13.
16. See HONG QI [RED FLAG, hereafter HQ] No. 12, 1974, at 38-42 for discussion.
17. *Id.* at 15-19.
18. FBIS, June 6, 1977, at E11.
19. FBIS, Apr. 13, 1977, at E4-6.
20. RMRB, May 26, 1977.
21. DEFENSE INTELLIGENCE AGENCY, HANDBOOK ON THE CHINESE ARMED FORCES

(1976) at 1-7, 3-6 to 3-7, and 4-1.

22. JAMES R. SCHLESINGER, REPORT OF THE SECRETARY OF DEFENSE TO THE CONGRESS ON THE FY 1975 DEFENSE BUDGET AND FY 1975-1979 DEFENSE PROGRAM 31 (1974).

23. GEORGE BROWN, UNITED STATES MILITARY POSTURE FOR FY 1978, at 5, 106.

24. Thus, for example, the Chinese reported that prior to the adoption of a new military strategy in 1977, French strategy had been "based on the idea of nuclear deterrence." Significantly, they also noted that, in accordance with its new strategic concept, France would further develop its conventional forces while strengthening its nuclear power. *See, France's New Strategic Concept,* PR, Feb. 25, 1977, at 25-26.

25. ALEXANDER GEORGE & RICHARD SMOKE, DETERRENCE IN AMERICAN FOREIGN POLICY: THEORY AND PRACTICE 45 (1974).

26. *Id.* at 46.

27. *Id.* at 47.

28. ANDRE BEAUFRE, DETERRENCE AND STRATEGY (1965).

29. PEOPLE'S REPUBLIC OF CHINA, *supra* note 11, at 41-45; *Two Different Lines on the Question of War and Peace, reproduced in* PEOPLE'S REPUBLIC OF CHINA, THE POLEMIC OF THE GENERAL LINE OF THE INTERNATIONAL COMMUNIST MOVEMENT 235-42 (1965); MAO TSE-TUNG [MAO ZEDONG], MISCELLANY OF MAO TSE-TUNG THOUGHT 108 (Joint Publications Research Service, No. 61269-1 and 2, 1974).

30. FBIS, Apr. 12, 1978, at A1.

31. PEOPLE'S REPUBLIC OF CHINA, THE DIFFERENCES BETWEEN COMRADE TOGLIATTI AND US 13 (1963).

32. In 1958, Mao recalled a discussion in which he compared nuclear weapons and historical weapons: "I maintained that modern weapons were not as powerful as the big sword of China's Guan Yunchang. . . . Not very many people were killed in the two World Wars, 10 million in the first and 20 million in the second, but he had 40 million killed in one war. So how destructive were the big swords! We have no experience in atomic war. So how many will be killed cannot be known." Mao Zedong, *supra* note 29, at 109. Later in the same year he added: "I don't see the reason for the atomic bomb. Conventional weapons are still the thing." *Id.* at 137.

33. RMRB, Aug. 6, 1977.

34. FBIS, July 28, 1977, at E14.

35. PEOPLE'S REPUBLIC OF CHINA, *supra* note 11, at 70.

36. RMRB, Mar. 17, 1975.

37. *See* JAMES R. SCHLESINGER, ANNUAL DEFENSE DEPARTMENT REPORT FY 1976 AND FY 197T (1975); SUBCOMM. ON ARMS CONTROL, INTERNATIONAL ORGANIZATIONS, AND SECURITY AGREEMENTS OF THE SENATE FOREIGN RELATIONS COMM., 94TH CONG., 1ST SESS., ANALYSES OF EFFECTS OF LIMITED NUCLEAR WARFARE (Comm. Print 1975). As Henry Rowen shows, U.S. government statements have frequently incorporated contradictory elements of the MAD and limited response schools as declared policy and flip-flopped on operational policy. *See* Henry Rowen, *Formulating Strategic Doctrine, in* COMMISSION ON THE ORGANIZATION OF THE GOVERNMENT FOR THE CONDUCT OF FOREIGN POLICY, 4 Appendix 217 (1975).

38. *Soviet Compliance with Certain Provisions of the 1972 Salt I Agreements: Hearings Before Subcomm. on Arms Control of the Senate Armed Services Comm.*, 94th Cong., 1st Sess., 11 (1975).
39. FBIS, Apr. 14, 1977, at H2.
40. FBIS, Apr. 12, 1978, at A1.
41. HQ No. 11, 1974, at 34–39, and RMRB, Nov. 8, 1974.
42. The classical quote, from SUN TZU, THE ART OF WAR 77 (S. D. Griffith trans. 1963), is: "For to win one hundred victories in one hundred battles is not the acme of skill. To subdue the enemy without fighting is the acme of skill."
43. Hua Guofeng, *Unite and Strive to Build a Modern, Powerful Socialist Country!*, PR, Mar. 10, 1978, at 36.
44. "Traitors" such as Peng Dehuai and Lin Biao are blamed for "carrying out a strategic policy of passive defense." RMRB, Aug. 6, 1977.
45. Mutual deterrence is described as "one of the theoretical foundations of the trend toward appeasement." FBIS, Apr. 12, 1978, at A1.
46. For discussion of this debate, see SENATE SELECT COMM. ON INTELLIGENCE, SUBCOMM. ON COLLECTION, PRODUCTION, AND QUALITY, 95TH CONG., 2D SESS., THE NATIONAL INTELLIGENCE ESTIMATES A-B TEAM EPISODE CONCERNING SOVIET STRATEGIC CAPABILITY AND OBJECTIVITY (Comm. Print 1978).
47. FBIS, Aug. 19, 1977, at E5.
48. Stanford University United States–China Relations Program, Report of a Visit to the People's Republic of China by the Stanford International Security and Arms Control Group, at 30 (1978). *See also,* SENATE FOREIGN RELATIONS COMM., 94TH CONG., 2D SESS., THE UNITED STATES AND CHINA 26 (Comm. Print 1976).
49. *Chairman Hua and Vice-Chairman Ye Receive Representatives to National Conference on People's Air Defence Work and Other Meetings,* PR, Feb. 11, 1977, at 3–4.
50. FBIS, July 28, 1977, at E14.
51. *See* Jonathan Pollack, *China's Changing Polity: New Direction in Peking's Military and Foreign Policy,* THE BULLETIN OF ATOMIC SCIENTISTS, Jan–Feb. 1979.
52. Compare ALLEN WHITING, THE CHINESE CALCULUS OF DETERRENCE (1975), chap. 7.
53. GEORGE BROWN, UNITED STATES MILITARY POSTURE FOR FY 1976, at 47 (1975).
54. Neville Maxwell, *The Chinese Account of the 1969 Fighting at Chenpao,* CHINA QUARTERLY Oct.–Dec. 1973, at 730–39.
55. *See* J. CHESTER CHENG, ed., THE POLITICS OF THE CHINESE RED ARMY 191 (1966).
56. SENATE FOREIGN RELATIONS COMM. AND HOUSE INTERNATIONAL RELATIONS COMM. SEVENTH CONGRESSIONAL DELEGATION TO THE PEOPLE'S REPUBLIC OF CHINA, 94TH CONG., 1ST SESS., THE UNITED STATES AND CHINA 25 (Comm. Print 1975).
57. FBIS, Apr. 14, 1977, at H1-2.
58. CHOU EN-LAI [Zhou Enlai], *Reports on the International Situation,* ISSUES AND STUDIES, Jan. 1977, at 120–21.
59. RMRB, Aug. 1, 1974.
60. FBIS, June 15, 1976, at L5.
61. RMRB, May 13, 1977.

62. *The Atom Bomb is a Paper Tiger: Notes on Studying Volume 5 of the "Selected Works of Mao Tse-Tung,"* PR, July 22, 1977, at 16.

63. *See generally* DEFENSE INTELLIGENCE AGENCY, HANDBOOK ON THE CHINESE ARMED FORCES 8-2, 8-3 (1976).

64. PEOPLE'S REPUBLIC OF CHINA, POLEMIC, *supra* note 29, at 242-48.

65. RMRB, Aug. 6, 1977 (emphasis in original deleted).

66. The militia would serve under the command of PLA officers, not as an independent force. *See* FBIS, Aug. 9, 1978, at E1-10.

67. *See Scope, Magnitude and Implications of the United States Antiballistic Missile Program: Hearings Before the Subcomm. on Military Applications of the Joint Comm. on Atomic Energy of the Congress of the United States,* 90th Cong., 1st Sess. (1967); *The Strategic and Foreign Policy Implications of Antiballistic Missile Systems: Hearings Before the Subcomm. on International Organization and Disarmament Affairs of the Comm. on Foreign Relations of the United States Senate,* 91st Cong., 1st Sess. (1969).

68. *Hearings Before the Subcomm. on Military Applications of the Joint Comm. on Atomic Energy of Congress of the United States, supra* note 67, at 8 (statement of Paul H. Nitze).

69. PEOPLE'S REPUBLIC OF CHINA, SEVEN LETTERS EXCHANGED BETWEEN THE CENTRAL COMMITTEE OF THE COMMUNIST PARTY OF CHINA AND THE COMMUNIST PARTY OF THE SOVIET UNION 25 (1964).

70. DONALD P. WHITAKER, RENN-SUP SHINN, HELEN A. BARTH, JUDITH M. HEIMANN, AND JOHN E. MACDONALD, AREA HANDBOOK FOR THE PEOPLE'S REPUBLIC OF CHINA 488 (1972); GEORGE MODELSKI, ATOMIC ENERGY IN THE COMMUNIST BLOC 134-38 (1959). For Chinese attitudes on Dubna, see Wolfgang Panofsky, *Observations on High Energy Physics in China* 31-32 (Stanford University United States-China Relations Program 1977).

71. D. WHITAKER, *supra* note 70, at 488.

72. *See* ALICE HSIEH, COMMUNIST CHINA'S STRATEGY IN THE NUCLEAR ERA, chap. 2 (1962).

73. Mao Zedong, *On the Ten Major Relationships,* Apr. 25, 1956, PR, Jan. 1, 1977, at 13. In 1977, a leading Chinese nuclear physicist traced the development of China's A-bomb to early 1955, when Mao had chaired a meeting that decided to expand research in atomic energy. He noted: "You can scarcely imagine what difficulties we had. . . . The imperialist blockade prevented us from obtaining any equipment." FBIS, Sept. 26, 1977, at E10.

74. *See* FBIS, Sept. 12, 1977, at E34.

75. John Gittings, *New Light on Mao,* CHINA QUARTERLY, Oct.-Dec. 1974, at 758. Gittings says the decision was made at a meeting of the Military Commission in June 1958.

76. Jiefangjun Bao, *in* SURVEY OF CHINA MAINLAND PRESS, No. 1786, June 6, 1958, at 6.

77. JOHN GITTINGS, THE WORLD AND CHINA, 1922-72, at 231 (1974).

78. H. Ford, *supra* note 2, at 164.

79. Mao Zedong, *Speech at the Group Leaders Forum of the Enlarged Conference of the Military Affairs Commission,* 1 CHINESE LAW AND GOVERNMENT 16, 19, 20 (No. 4, 1968-69).

80. H. Ford, *supra* note 2, at 161–62; Cheng, *supra* note 55, at 250, 253, 260–62; and Jiefangjun Bao, *supra* note 76.

81. The Soviet "case" was, of course, more complex than this suggests; *see* Roman Kolkowicz, The Soviet Military and the Communist Party chap. 5 (1967); and Thomas Wolfe, Soviet Strategy at the Crossroads chaps. 12–13 (1964).

82. The National Defense Scientific and Technical Commission is said to be in charge of satellites and missile test firings. *See* FBIS, Nov. 16, 1978, at N1 and Jan. 4, 1979, at E11–13.

83. An article by the Institute of Atomic Energy written in March 1978 summarizes some aspects of the PRC's nuclear weapons programs in the 1960s and 1970s. Such programs, it is said, were the main activity of the Institute in the 1960s and its personnel thus "had no time to develop the use of nuclear energy for peaceful purposes." FBIS, Mar. 31, 1978, at E12.

84. J. Gittings, *supra* note 77, at 232.

85. FBIS, Jan. 21, 1977, at E2.

86. *Id.* A photographer who witnessed the work at the nuclear weapons test site was moved to paint a picture he described as follows: "Rolling mushroom clouds are rising upward in the clear blue sky; the workers are busily calculating the preliminary experimental results; and the excited site director is reporting the news of success to the Party Central Committee and awaiting instructions. A worker comrade is placing his fist on the table, indicating the determination of the Chinese working class to . . . exceed the technological standards of the developed nations." Hangkong Zhishi, Mar. 1975, at 32.

87. As one Chinese source acknowledged in 1978: "The rapid development of modern science and technology and its wide military application pose new problems for research in military theory." FBIS, June 7, 1978, at E3.

88. HQ, No. 8, 1974, at 62.

89. *Allocation of Resources in the Soviet Union and China—1975: Hearings Before the Subcomm. on Priorities and Economy in Government of the Joint Economic Comm. of the Congress of the United States,* 94th Cong., 1st Sess., 46 (1975).

90. *See* articles by Takuya Kubo and Morton Halperin in Franklin Weinstein, ed., United States–Japan Relations and the Security of Asia: The Next Decade (1978).

91. Private communication to the author.

92. *See* Qian Xuesen in HQ, No. 22, 1963, at 19–27; RMRB, May 29, 1964; and HQ, No. 7–8, 1964, at 45–49.

93. Qian Xuesen, *supra* note 92, at 20.

94. *E.g.,* RMRB, Apr. 22, 1977 and May 19, 1977.

95. HQ, No. 7, 1977, at 3–5.

96. For key speeches by Deng Xiaoping, Hua Guofeng, and Fang Yi, see PR, Mar. 24, 1978, Mar. 31, 1978, and Apr. 7, 1978.

97. FBIS, June 28, 1977, at G5.

98. George Brown, United States Military Posture for FY 1977, at 46 (1976).

99. G. Brown, *supra* note 23, at 102. A disagreement in Washington concerning the appropriate U.S. policy on the second approach was revealed in a leak to the New York Times, June 24, 1977, §A, at 1, col. 5, of a Policy Review Memorandum

that reportedly had recommended against the U.S. sale of military technology to China. Some weeks later, however, Secretary of Defense Harold Brown issued what was called a "key decision that may spur the sale of American material with a military capacity to China." *Id.*, Sep. 11, 1977, at 1, col. 1. This issue continued into 1979. *See id.,* Jan. 4, 1978, §A, at 7, col. 1, June 9, 1978, §A, at 1, col. 1, and March 1, 1979.

100. G. BROWN, *supra* note 23, at 101-2.

101. *Id.* at 102.

102. *Id.* at 106.

103. The 1977 article by PLA officers discussing efforts to reduce the weight on saddles for mules, horses, and camels illustrates the strength of inertia in traditional Chinese military thinking and biases against any radical upgrading of China's military forces. *See* FBIS, Apr. 15, 1977, at E24.

104. HANGKONG ZHISHI, May 1977, at 10-11.

105. FBIS, Mar. 31, 1978, at E11 and Apr. 6, 1978, at E16.

106. FBIS, Feb. 17, 1977, at E2. This approach was set forth by Mao in 1956 in his address entitled *On the Ten Major Relationships.* Official publication of this address in December 1976 appears designed to buttress the arguments of those who seek to limit military spending in order to strengthen the economy to insure greater military strength in the future. *See* Mao, *supra* note 73, at 13.

107. *See* FBIS, Jan. 26, 1978, at E12.

108. FBIS, Sep. 26, 1977, at E12.

109. FBIS, Mar. 29, 1978, at E6.

110. U.S. ARMS CONTROL AND DISARMAMENT AGENCY, WORLD MILITARY EXPENDITURES AND ARMS TRANSFERS, 1966-1975, at 5 (1976). *See also Allocation of Resources in the Soviet Union and China — 1976: Hearings Before the Subcomm. on Priorities and Economy in Government of the Joint Economic Comm.,* 94th Cong., 2d Sess., 31 (1976) (discussion of PRC military expenditures by George Bush, then director of the CIA).

111. *Allocation of Resources in the Soviet Union and China — 1977: Hearings Before the Subcomm. on Priorities and Economy in Government of the Joint Economic Comm. of the Congress of the United States,* 95th Cong., 1st Sess., 86 (1977).

112. *Allocation of Resources, supra* note 110, at 45.

113. FBIS, July 28, 1977, at A3 (the quotation is a paraphrase by a Japanese source).

114. See report by Zhang Jingfu in FBIS, July 3, 1979, at L7 and 13. For a Soviet estimate, see FOREIGN BROADCAST INFORMATION SERVICE, DAILY REPORT: SOVIET UNION [hereafter FBIS:SOV], Aug. 4, 1977, at C3-4.

115. Two series of articles on the "ten major relationships," (Mao, *supra* note 73) were issued, one from Peking (16 articles) and one from Shanghai (11 articles). The 16 items (in parentheses) of the Peking series can be found in FBIS, Feb. 7 (6), 9 (1), 10 (2,3), 11 (4), 14 (5), 17 (7), 23 (8), and 24 (9), 1977, and Mar. 1 (10), 2 (11, 12), 3 (13, 14), 8 (15), 9 (16), 1977; the Shanghai series in Feb. 11 (1), 17 (4), and 25 (2), 1977, and Mar. 2 (3), 4 (5), 9 (6, 10), 11 (7-9), and 14 (11), 1977. Numbers 6 in the Peking series and 4 in the Shanghai series deal with defense issues.

116. FBIS, May 13, 1977, at E3.

117. Yu's speech can be found in FBIS, May 9, 1977, at E5-26. Yu's implied timetable was endorsed by a senior provincial leader in June 1977. He said, "We must prepare for the eventuality of an early, major war. We must race against time and against the enemy and work as quickly as possible, making one year count as two." FBIS, June 20, 1977, at L2.

118. *See* Thomas Fingar, Politics and Policy Making in the People's Republic of China, 1954-1955 (unpublished Ph.D. dissertation, Stanford University 1977).

119. FBIS, Feb. 22, 1978, at E9-20.

120. *Id.* at E12.

121. *Id.* at E15 (emphasis in original is deleted).

122. *E.g.*, FBIS, Mar. 1, 1978, at E2-6.

123. THE UNITED STATES AND CHINA, *supra* note 56, at 36-38.

124. HQ, No. 8, 1974, at 55.

125. FBIS, Aug. 7, 1978, at E1-2.

126. Quotation is from GMRB, Sept. 12, 1974.

127. FBIS, Aug. 8, 1977, at E16.

128. FBIS, Jan. 22, 1979, at E9.

129. Seiichiro Takagi, An Analysis of Chinese Behavior Toward Japan, 1950-1965: An Examination of Three Models of International Behavior 2 (unpublished Ph.D. dissertation, Stanford University, 1977).

130. *Chairman of Chinese Delegation Teng Hsiao-p'ing's [Deng Xiaoping's] Speech at Special Session of U.N. General Assembly,* PR, Apr. 19, 1974, at 6-7. Harry Harding's chapter in this volume examines this point in detail.

131. The "first" world now comprises the two superpowers. "The two hegemonic powers . . . are the biggest international exploiters and oppressors of today and the common enemies of the people of the world. The Third World countries suffer the worst oppression and hence put up the strongest resistance; they are the main force combating imperialism, colonialism, and hegemonism." Hua Guofeng, *Political Report to the Eleventh National Congress of the Communist Party of China,* PR, Aug. 26, 1977, at 41.

132. Zhou Enlai, *supra* note 58, at 118.

133. Literaturnaya Gazeta, May 18, 1977, *in* FBIS:SOV, May 24, 1977, at C3; *see also* FBIS:SOV, May 2, 1977, at C6.

134. FBIS:SOV, May 3, 1977, at C4; *see also id.,* June 13, 1977, at C3.

135. The slogan apparently was first used publicly by Zhou Enlai at the Tenth Party Congress in August 1973. *See Report to the Tenth National Congress of the Communist Party of China* (Aug. 24, 1973), *reprinted in* PR, Sep. 7, 1973, at 17-22.

136. *See* A. DOAK BARNETT, CHINA POLICY—OLD PROBLEMS AND NEW CHALLENGES, 51-63 (1977).

137. Michael Pillsbury, *U.S.-Chinese Military Ties?* FOREIGN POLICY, Fall 1975, at 52-56.

138. A summary of China's 1978 purchases is provided in TIME, July 3, 1978, at 29, and AV. WEEK AND SPACE TECH., Dec. 4, 1978, at 21.

139. *See Ford Approves Computer Sale to China,* AV. WEEK AND SPACE TECH., Oct.

25, 1976, at 18; *U.S. Agrees to Sell China a Computer with Defense Uses,* New York Times, Oct. 29, 1976, at 1, col. 6; *U.S. in Reversal, Will Sell China Equipment Withheld from Soviet,* New York Times, June 9, 1978, at 1, col. 1; *U.S. Reported Acting to Strengthen Ties with Peking Regime,* New York Times, June 25, 1978, at 1, col. 6; *Sale of Computers is Sought for China,* Washington Post, Oct. 29, 1976, at 13, col. 1; *U.S. in Reversal, Supports Chinese Bid for Equipment,* Washington Post, June 10, 1978, at 10, col. 4.

140. Pollack, *Peking's Nuclear Restraint,* New York Times, Apr. 12, 1976, at 29, col. 2; Middleton, *What the Chinese Forces Lack: Most Types of Modern Weapons,* New York Times, June 24, 1977, at 3, col. 2; *Brown Sets New Technology Policy Expected to Favor China's Needs,* New York Times, Sep. 11, 1977, at 1, col. 1; and *China Showing Interest in Buying U.S. Warplanes,* New York Times, Mar. 1, 1979.

141. In the early 1950s, the PRC ratified the 1929 Geneva Protocol prohibiting chemical and bacteriological weapons. This was the only other arms control agreement accepted by Peking.

142. THE UNITED STATES AND CHINA, *supra* note 56, at 17; *see also Utilization of Nuclear Energy and the Struggle Against Hegemony,* PR, Apr. 14, 1978, at 10-12.

143. PR, Oct. 7, 1977, at 39 (emphasis added). This speech puts more emphasis on nuclear forces than do most recent statements. Huang's wording closely approximates Qiao Guanhua's in 1971, PEOPLE'S REPUBLIC OF CHINA, *supra* note 11, at 12, but diverges from Qiao's 1972-75 calls for the superpowers to "withdraw from abroad all their armed forces, including nuclear-missile forces, and dismantle all their military bases, including nuclear bases, on the territories of other countries." The Chinese indicated to a Stanford group in July 1978 that China does not oppose foreign bases in countries that oppose the Soviet Union and are not "artificially divided" (as are the cases of South Korea and Taiwan), and whose governments are supportive.

144. PEOPLE'S REPUBLIC OF CHINA, *supra* note 11, at 3.

145. Lewis, *China as Silent Partner,* New York Times, Nov. 19, 1973, at 35, col. 2.

146. FBIS, May 30, 1978, at A3-13.

147. FBIS, Jan. 25, 1979, at A1-2; and FBIS, May 16, 1979, at A1-7.

148. Lewis, *supra* note 145.

149. The U.S.'s approach to this issue has depended on the state of play within the Soviet-China-American power game as well as some of the interrelated contests regarding technology, energy, and opportunities for intervention in third-party conflicts. In his recent study, CHINA POLICY, A. Doak Barnett has reviewed the pros and cons of steps toward closer U.S.-China military cooperation and has concluded, "All in all, the issues in this field are so complex and sensitive that they demand continuing study. All the potential ramifications, both political and military, of any moves the United States might make must be carefully considered, and in the meantime precipitous steps should be avoided." A. DOAK BARNETT, *supra* note 136, at 63.

150. THE UNITED STATES AND CHINA, *supra* note 56, at 17.

151. *Text of U.S.-Chinese Communiqué,* New York Times, Feb. 28, 1972, at 16, col. 3.

152. *Id.*

# 4
# Chinese Foreign Trade Policy and the Campaign Against Deng Xiaoping

*Ann Fenwick*

The Cultural Revolution decisively shattered the image of a monolithic leadership and elite policy consensus in the People's Republic of China (PRC). Nevertheless, it still remains frustratingly difficult to discern details and alignments in all but the most explosive of policy debates and factional conflicts in the PRC. Western understanding of China's policy process is necessarily superficial and speculative, especially in the analysis of linkages between domestic and foreign policy. With but few detailed studies of policy linkages involving foreign trade, we know very little about how, when, and why foreign trade has become a controversial issue in the PRC.[1]

Yet at times the door does open a crack, affording a tantalizing glimpse into the generally secret realm of Chinese policy debates. For example, criticisms leveled during campaigns of denunciation and rejection can provide much information, but they must be approached with caution. Exaggeration and post hoc distortion are integral to the process by which a target of criticism is transformed, during the course of a campaign, into a negative example. Despite these caveats, campaign criticisms can be a valuable and frequently unequaled source of information on policy conflicts in the PRC. They indirectly reveal issues of controversy, suggest personnel divisions over such issues, and afford often unintended insights into the dynamics of the Chinese policy process.

The 1975-76 campaign against Vice Premier Deng Xiaoping identified a number of divisive issues and demonstrated the importance and derivative

---

Ann Fenwick is a doctoral candidate in political science at Stanford University. She earned her B.A. at the University of British Columbia in 1973 and her M.A. at the University of Michigan in 1975.

character of foreign trade policy. Contemporaneous media criticisms, texts of criticized 1975 policy planning documents associated with Deng, and post–"gang of four" refutations of the campaign provide a wide range of original data. This information reveals policy debates covering a broad spectrum of issues. Although the Chinese media concentrated on domestic issues, both during the campaign and in reinterpretations issued after the fall of the "gang of four" in October 1976, foreign trade also played an important supporting role. In fact, foreign trade was by far the most openly denounced aspect of nondomestic policy in the campaign, known in China as *Pi Deng* (criticize Deng).

The campaign against Deng discussed trade as it related to self-reliance, an approach that suggests a framework for foreign-domestic policy linkage. The doctrine of self-reliance evolved in response to conditions confronting the Chinese Communist Party during the early years of revolution. In the 1930s and 1940s, the Party's weak and isolated guerrilla bases were faced with the dilemma of survival in a hostile environment. In the 1950s and 1960s, international ostracism and isolation resulting from the Western trade embargo and the Sino-Soviet split shaped the thinking of Party leaders charged with fostering development and security. One result was the evolution of "self-reliance" as a flexible approach to policy questions. Close interconnection of foreign and domestic policy is an important part of that approach.

This paper will examine the role of foreign trade in the campaign against Deng Xiaoping by focusing on four major topics: (1) historical background that influenced, shaped, and complicated trade policy during the campaign; (2) specific foreign trade issues illuminated during *Pi Deng* and their linkage to domestic policy; (3) the different roles played by various domestic groups; and (4) the impact of the campaign on contemporaneous implementation of PRC trade policy. By focusing on these topics, this paper will attempt to enhance our understanding of the campaign itself, and to shed additional light on the development of China's foreign trade policy in the 1970s.

## I. Background to Trade Policy Development

### Self-Reliance

Any examination of Chinese foreign trade policy should begin with the concept of self-reliance. Two characteristics of this concept are particularly important to the background to *Pi Deng*: the historical roots and flexibility of self-reliance. The concept of self-reliance evolved through decades of painful Chinese experience beginning in the mid-nineteenth century and aggravated by the split with Moscow in the late 1950s. Self-reliance can be seen as the Chinese response to a long legacy of political and economic humiliations suffered at the hands of foreign powers. Supporters of *Pi Deng* attempted to capitalize on the legacy and sanctity of self-reliance to enflame passions and undermine policies with which they disagreed.

Probably the most widely quoted and authoritative formulation of self-reliance was—and still is—Mao Zedong's injunction to "rely mainly on our own efforts while making external assistance subsidiary, break down blind faith, go in for industry, agriculture and technical and cultural revolution independently, do away with slavishness, bury dogmatism, learn from the good experience of other countries conscientiously and be sure to study their bad experience too, so as to draw lessons from it. This is our line."[2] This explanation embodies potentially contradictory ideas and thus, as in so many Chinese policy concepts, allows for considerable flexibility in application. The ambiguity inherent in Mao's formulation also enhances the potential for leadership disagreements and political maneuver on policy issues such as foreign trade that involved the task of concretely interpreting self-reliance.

Deng Xiaoping presented a considerably more detailed definition of self-reliance in his 1974 speech at the United Nations. In that address, he touched upon several points that were subsequently debated in *Pi Deng* articles on foreign trade.

> By self-reliance we mean that a country should mainly rely on the strength and wisdom of its own people, control its own economic lifelines, make full use of its own resources, strive hard to increase food production and develop its national economy step by step in a planned way. The policy of independence and self-reliance in no way means that it should be divorced from the actual conditions of a country; instead, it requires that distinction must be made between different circumstances, and that each country should work out its own way of practicing self-reliance in the light of its own conditions. At the present stage, a developing country that wants to develop its national economy must first of all keep its natural resources in its own hands and gradually shake off the control of foreign capital. . . . Self-reliance in no way means "self-seclusion" and rejection of foreign aid. We have always considered it beneficial and necessary for the development of the national economy that countries should carry on economic and technical exchanges on the basis of respect for state sovereignty, equality and mutual benefit, and the exchange of needed goods to make up for each other's deficiencies.[3]

Deng's formulation reflects the second characteristic of self-reliance—flexibility. As the passages quoted above indicate, self-reliance as a framework for Chinese foreign trade aimed at neither autarky nor xenophobia. Self-reliance was sufficiently broad to permit large-scale

Chinese imports of Soviet plants, equipment and technology throughout the 1950s.[4] Nevertheless, the sharp decline and prolonged stagnation of China's foreign trade throughout the 1960s (see Table 4.1) was attributable not only to the PRC's international ostracism but also to a characteristic that lay at the core of self-reliance — a conscious effort to avoid dependency. More specifically, the tenets of self-reliance require formulation of policies that minimize "strategic and financial dependence on foreign countries"[5] and maximize utilization of domestic resources. This approach seeks to limit and make efficient use of budgetary outlays and to conserve scarce foreign exchange for use in carefully planned, qualitatively significant imports of plants and technologies. Even during the more isolationist formulation of self-reliance that dominated the 1960s, foreign trade and technology purchases were assigned an important role in Chinese domestic development. However, despite its flexibility, self-reliance dictated that trade and imports supplement rather than substitute for indigenous development.

*The 1970s: A New Approach to Trade Policy*

The campaign against Deng Xiaoping was launched formally in the spring of 1976 and was directed primarily at policies spelled out in documents prepared in the summer of 1975. To fully understand the critiques of 1975–76, however, it is necessary to go back at least as far as 1972 when trade policies were reformulated in accordance with a bold reinterpretation of self-reliance. PRC foreign trade had been minimal and nearly stagnant for more than a decade (see Table 4.1) when key decisions were made to accelerate the pace of development through stepped-up purchases from abroad.[6] The increased pace and volume of equipment and technology imports were to facilitate more rapid development of the domestic economy. "Key" sectors such as heavy industry, petrochemicals, and electronics were assigned high priority in the evolving strategy of using trade to overcome technological obstacles to growth and security. Export industries were to be stimulated in order to pay for increased imports. The revamped strategy was reminiscent of the 1950s when the pace of China's economic development was accelerated by large-scale imports from the Soviet Union. Two developments in the early 1970s probably shaped the decision to rely more heavily on foreign trade. One was the greater availability of funds for domestic investment resulting from cuts made in the defense budget after the fall of Lin Biao in 1971.[7] The other was that sizable foreign exchange earnings from petroleum exports began to appear feasible at about this time.

The impact of the change in foreign trade policy was extensive. By the end of 1974, China had purchased over $2 billion in turnkey plants from

TABLE 4.1
China's Foreign Trade (in millions of U.S. $)

| Year | Total Trade | | | |
|---|---|---|---|---|
| | Total[a] | Exports | Imports | Balance |
| 1950 | 1,210 | 620 | 590 | 30 |
| 1951 | 1,900 | 780 | 1,120 | −340 |
| 1952 | 1,890 | 875 | 1,015 | −140 |
| 1953 | 2,295 | 1,040 | 1,255 | −215 |
| 1954 | 2,350 | 1,060 | 1,290 | −230 |
| 1955 | 3,035 | 1,375 | 1,660 | −285 |
| 1956 | 3,120 | 1,635 | 1,485 | 150 |
| 1957 | 3,055 | 1,615 | 1,440 | 175 |
| 1958 | 3,765 | 1,940 | 1,825 | 115 |
| 1959 | 4,290 | 2,230 | 2,060 | 170 |
| 1960 | 3,990 | 1,960 | 2,030 | −70 |
| 1961 | 3,015 | 1,525 | 1,490 | 35 |
| 1962 | 2,670 | 1,520 | 1,150 | 370 |
| 1963 | 2,775 | 1,575 | 1,200 | 375 |
| 1964 | 3,220 | 1,750 | 1,470 | 280 |
| 1965 | 3,880 | 2,035 | 1,845 | 190 |
| 1966 | 4,245 | 2,210 | 2,035 | 175 |
| 1967 | 3,915 | 1,960 | 1,955 | 5 |
| 1968 | 3,785 | 1,960 | 1,825 | 135 |
| 1969 | 3,895 | 2,060 | 1,835 | 225 |
| 1970 | 4,325 | 2,080 | 2,245 | −165 |
| 1971 | 4,765 | 2,455 | 2,310 | 145 |
| 1972 | 6,000 | 3,150 | 2,850 | 300 |
| 1973 | 10,300 | 5,075 | 5,225 | −150 |
| 1974 | 14,080 | 6,660 | 7,420 | −760 |
| 1975 | 14,575 | 7,180 | 7,395 | −215 |
| 1976 | 13,255 | 7,250 | 6,005 | 1,245 |

*Source:* Central Intelligence Agency, National Foreign Assessment Center, *China: International Trade, 1976-77* (ER 77-100674, November 1977), p. 9.

[a]Data are rounded to the nearest $5 million. Because of rounding, components may not add to totals shown.

Japan and the West. These were financed primarily through deferred installment payments, usually with 6 percent interest, that were really loans with a bit of window dressing. This marked a significant break from the pay-as-you-go policies of the previous decade. In addition, despite traditional suspicion of foreign presence in any form, China permitted 2,000–3,000 foreign technicians to supervise the construction and initial operation of the turnkey plants. Trade-related construction involved lengthy stays by foreigners in numerous parts of the country, a phenomenon almost unknown since the withdrawal of Soviet technical advisers more than a decade earlier. Furthermore, the importing of plants and technologies led to the travel or training abroad of approximately 1,000 Chinese technicians.[8]

China's exports also reflected the new trade policy. Long an importer of petroleum products, China began to talk about exporting oil in 1964. However, concrete steps to become a major supplier were not begun until 1973. This effort benefitted from the favorable world market created by the Arab oil embargo. Sales to the PRC's biggest customer, Japan, increased substantially each year: 1.3 million metric tons in 1973, 4 million in 1974, and 8 million in 1975 — 10 percent of Chinese production.[9]

By the end of 1974, however, China found that its reformulated trade policy was embroiling it in the problems of an extremely uncertain world economy. Recession and double-digit inflation contributed to a $760 million trade deficit in 1974, the largest since 1949 (see Table 4.1).[10] PRC leaders disagreed on how to deal with these problems and the resulting controversy was reflected in *Pi Deng*.

One further point should be made in considering those aspects of the trade policy reformulation which were to figure prominently in the anti-Deng campaign. Groups existed within the Chinese leadership, generally identified in the West as the ideological "left" or the "radicals," who disapproved of the way self-reliance had been redefined to justify increased foreign trade. Their opposition found intermittent expression in PRC media during the 1974 campaign to criticize Confucius (*Pi Kung*), and in more focused articles published in 1975.[11]

Unquestionably, those later purged as members or supporters of the "gang of four" were responsible for many of the critical articles published during this period. Opponents of the new trade policy controlled much of the media and were able to publicize their objections. Perhaps more significant is the fact that articles and information from the "gang's" regional powerbase of Shanghai figured prominently in the public denunciations of "worshipping and fawning on foreign things." Several of the most repeated themes in the *Pi Deng* critique of foreign trade policy, such as its negative effects on Shanghai's shipbuilding industry,[12] could be interpreted as efforts by political leaders to defend the interests of their constituents. However, they could also reflect an effort to exploit available evidence and discontent for broader political purposes. All this suggests that *Pi Deng,* at least in regard to foreign trade, was not a sudden attempt to topple one man. At the level of policy debate, it suggests that *Pi Deng* was more than an attempt to question the policy proposals drafted in the summer and fall of 1975. Instead, the campaign should be viewed as the climax of a long debate that began before the formal rehabilitation of Deng Xiaoping in 1973 and involved a number of issues and specific measures stemming from the late 1972 policy shift on foreign trade.

One of these issues centered on the balance of payments deficit. The speed with which imports were reduced and exports promoted in reaction to the large deficit in 1974 demonstrated the leadership's unwillingness to continue running substantial deficits. Quick and drastic actions cut China's deficit in half within a year.[13] Yet to those who were uneasy with or who opposed the activist trade strategy of 1972-74, this renewed stringency was of little comfort. Although the percentage of the gross national product contributed by foreign trade declined in 1975, the drop was minimal. Also the total value of trade continued to climb, remaining well above the low levels of the previous decade (see Tables 4.1 and 4.2). In fact, trade policy was among the targets in *Pi Deng* precisely because it was apparent that the activist trade stance had not been repudiated or discarded. Continued adherence to an activist trade policy was evident throughout 1975 both in terms of formal and actual implementation.[14]

Zhou Enlai's speech at the Fourth National People's Congress in January 1975 is typical of pronouncements endorsing an activist trade policy. In that address, the late Premier announced China's commitment to an ambitious program of national development. The short-term goal was to create "an independent and relatively comprehensive industrial and economic system . . . before 1980."[15] The long-range objective was to attain comprehensive agricultural, industrial, military and scientific modernization by the year 2000. The magnitude and timetable for these goals implicitly but unmistakably eliminated the possibility of a return to the near autarkic stance of the Cultural Revolution.

Exports of natural resources in 1975 provide further evidence of consistent adherence to an activist policy. Rhetoric and criticisms notwithstanding, exports of natural resources continued during this period. More significantly, negotiations with Japan for a long-term oil purchase agreement reveal a commitment by key leaders to put foreign trade on a more permanent footing by linking PRC policy and development plans to binding bilateral agreements. Such agreements would limit China's freedom of action, but they would also remove some of the unpredictability of par-

TABLE 4.2
Value of China's Foreign Trade

| Year | Gross National Product (Bil 1976 US $) | Foreign Trade as Percentage of GNP |
|---|---|---|
| 1950 | 63 | 1.92 |
| 1951 | 74 | 2.57 |
| 1952 | 87 | 2.17 |
| 1953 | 93 | 2.47 |
| 1954 | 97 | 2.42 |
| 1955 | 106 | 2.86 |
| 1956 | 115 | 2.71 |
| 1957 | 122 | 2.50 |
| 1958 | 145 | 2.60 |
| 1959 | 138 | 3.11 |
| 1960 | 134 | 2.98 |
| 1961 | 106 | 2.84 |
| 1962 | 118 | 2.26 |
| 1963 | 132 | 2.10 |
| 1964 | 149 | 2.16 |
| 1965 | 165 | 2.35 |
| 1966 | 185 | 2.29 |
| 1967 | 178 | 2.20 |
| 1968 | 179 | 2.11 |
| 1969 | 199 | 1.96 |
| 1970 | 231 | 1.87 |
| 1971 | 247 | 1.93 |
| 1972 | 258 | 2.33 |
| 1973 | 292 | 3.53 |
| 1974 | 302 | 4.66 |
| 1975 | 323 | 4.51 |
| 1976 | 324 | 4.09 |

*Source:* GNP figures from Central Intelligence Agency, National Foreign Assessment Center, *China: Economic Indicators* (ER 77-10508, October 1977), p. 3. Figures in last column based on total foreign trade as given in Table 4.1.

ticipation in the world market. Agreement was reached on long-term export of Chinese fuel coal to Japan in November 1975; an oil agreement was achieved in 1978.[16]

Despite cutbacks in 1975 to reduce the 1974 trade deficit, large-scale imports of foreign plant, equipment, and technology remained an important element in the new strategy of development. For example, continued Chinese interest in making major foreign purchases to accelerate domestic development was revealed by a Japanese oil executive who reported in the spring of 1975 that Peking was prepared to utilize foreign technology in the development of its petroleum resources.[17] By the end of that year discussions were underway with Japan, France, and West Germany concerning massive imports of plant and equipment to speed development of China's reserves of natural gas and to facilitate exports of liquified natural gas.[18]

Public confirmation of the continuation of an activist trade policy was made by Vice Minister of Foreign Trade Chai Shufan in a rare interview with a German journalist in the fall of 1975. Chai told the reporter that China planned to purchase complete plants and heavy equipment for petrochemical and various mineral industries and that it "could" import German patents and pure technology. He also said that installment financing arrangements for imports were acceptable, and that the PRC "could" discuss barter agreements in which, for example, German mining equipment or special purpose pipe would be exchanged for Chinese coal or oil. Appropriately enough, the vice minister is reported to have commented, "within China's principle of self-reliance, the Chinese foreign trade policy is 'very flexible'."[19]

Thus, on the eve of the campaign against Deng Xiaoping, Peking was clearly prepared to enact foreign trade policies designed to further realization of an ambitious domestic program. Despite negative experience with the fiscal uncertainties of increased participation in the world market in 1974, China seemed committed to continuation and even regularization of an activist trade policy. This policy envisioned sizable exports of natural resources and selective but potentially large-scale imports of foreign equipment, complete plants, and advanced technologies. Given its recent emergence from a decade of minimal trade governed by a more autarkic interpretation of self-reliance, the PRC's new policy was significant and highly controversial. In a particularly prescient passage on Chinese foreign trade written in 1974, A. Doak Barnett said:

> China is moving cautiously to increase its involvement in the international economy.
> The question is how far [the Chinese] may be willing to go in this direction. Today China still remains highly autarkic in basic respects. To go much fur-

ther (which would require greater emphasis than in the past on the development of the country's export capacity, or the acceptance of larger credits or loans from abroad, or both) would necessitate significant compromise of values that China's top leadership has rated very highly in recent years. This issue could be a major subject of debate in China in the period ahead, and how it is decided will have a major impact on the pace and direction of Chinese development.[20]

Barnett's prediction came true in 1976, when opponents of the activist approach to trade intensified their criticisms and directed their attack at Deng Xiaoping as the source and embodiment of unpalatable policies.

## II. The Campaign

*Political Factors*

Before analyzing the role of trade policy in *Pi Deng*, it is necessary to consider the background of struggle and succession politics against which the campaign unfolded. By early 1976, Zhou Enlai had died and Mao was obviously dying. Cleavages in the leadership, whether originally based on personal rivalries, policy differences, or organizational antagonisms, were exacerbated by the loss of these two crucial balancers and unifiers. Efforts to shape the distribution of power in the post-Mao era were already underway in 1975. These efforts included the rehabilitation of veteran cadres purged during the Cultural Revolution and a scheduled comprehensive Party rectification drive to be led by Deng Xiaoping.[21]

It appears that political and policy rivalry combined with the underlying question of succession sparked the outbreak of *Pi Deng*. This campaign should be viewed, at least in part, as the creation of members of the leadership who felt increasingly threatened by the trend of events that had begun in the early 1970s. Evolving policies and the imminent rectification campaign threatened to undermine their position in the succession contest. This raises the question of whether policy criticisms made during *Pi Deng* were evidence of actual policy conflict or merely opportunistically raised polemical weapons in a power struggle. A conclusive answer to this question is beyond the scope of this paper. Nevertheless it is important to bear in mind that *Pi Deng* involved a power struggle of unprecedented urgency and magnitude that almost certainly contributed to the politicization of policy decisions in all areas, including foreign trade.

*The Emergence of the Foreign Trade Issue in* Pi Deng

Foreign trade was clearly of less importance than were domestic issues in the campaign to criticize Deng Xiaoping. Foreign policy as a whole was criticized little during the campaign, whereas all types of domestic policies were subjected to sustained abuse. Foreign trade was drawn into the discussion through linkages to various domestic issues.[22] During the early stages of *Pi Deng*, the trade-related issue of foreign technology acquisition was occasionally linked to the then central question of scientific and technological research policy. In this context, reliance on foreign technology was criticized on a general, superficial level as antithetical to reliance on mass movements to promote scientific and technical progress.[23] Usually, however, foreign trade was linked with the domestic policy concerns put forward by Deng in his 1975 policy paper, *On Certain Problems in Speeding Up Industrial Development* (also known as *The Twenty Points*). These concerns included questions of industrial centralization, factory management, and the role of technology and technicians in industrial development. This framework for linkage was logical because Chinese trade policy was becoming increasingly oriented toward rapid advancement of domestic industrial modernization.

The emergence of trade-related criticisms generally mirrored the dynamics of the campaign as a whole. Ignored during the educational debate in autumn 1975—the prelude to *Pi Deng*—trade initially was mentioned only indirectly and superficially in connection with scientific and technological research in late January 1976. Trade policy *per se* first became a target in a March 1976 article in the *People's Daily*.[24] In the article, the vice chairman of Qinghua University's political department stated that under the guise of concern for modernization, national and international capitulation had been practiced to such a degree that China was being led back towards its old semicolonial status as little more than a supplier of raw materials.

After a short period of relatively obscure references, trade policy suddenly and dramatically emerged as a central campaign target around the time of Deng's public fall from power on April 7, 1976. As a consequence of the decision to publically attack the three major policy documents associated with Deng, detailed and authoritative critiques of trade policy were published in *People's Daily*, *Red Flag*, and *Study and Criticism*.[25] Criticism centered upon two proposals contained in *The Twenty Points* document. One proposal recommended further imports of advanced foreign technologies to promote national economic development. This recommendation was accompanied by an uncharacteristically explicit warning that, although development was to remain within the guiding framework of self-reliance, "under no circumstances must we become cocky, close our door and refuse to learn from the good things of other countries." A second proposal called for a "major policy" of accelerated resource development in which foreign loans—in the form of deferred and installment payments—and long-term contracts for coal and petroleum exports would be used to finance imports of complete plants.[26] These two points envisaged regularization and expansion of the activist foreign trade policy first evidenced in late 1972.

Themes from the programmatic critiques of early April were repeated and expanded with increasing frequency toward the end of May. These critiques paved the way for a veritable high tide of trade-related media criticisms during June, July, and August when the campaign was at its most virulent. Although somewhat abated by autumn, criticism of "worshipping things foreign" and "the doctrine of trailing behind at a snail's pace," shorthand epithets for the activist trade policy, received continued publicity until the day before the detention of the "gang of four" on October 6, 1976.[27]

*Substance of the* Pi Deng *Critique of Foreign Trade Policy*

The substantive content of the trade policy critique articulated during the campaign reveals dissatisfaction and disagreement over an activist trade policy at both a general and a specific level. Lest this paper be judged guilty of one of the principal sins attributed to the "gang of four"—creating false dichotomies and finding contradictions where none exist—it should be emphasized that, despite the rhetorical virulence of the campaign, disagreement was usually a matter of emphasis and degree. All parties agreed upon the basic framework of self-reliance; only their interpretations differed. Furthermore, no one advocated complete isolation. Even the most inflammatory articles of *Pi Deng* characteristically included passages affirming the need to continue selective imports of advanced foreign equipment and technology.

Broadly speaking, the *Pi Deng* critique argued against a trade policy that would increase Chinese entanglement in the economic uncertainties of the world market. A typical argument was, "'Under no circumstances must we tie the fate of our socialist construction to the belt of others.' These words sharply draw our attention to the danger of our necks being held by others."[28] On a general level, activist policies were attacked not only for reducing economic independence, but also for making the formerly insulated domestic economy vulnerable to external international economic crisis. "The phenomenon of . . . economic interdependence is determined by the capitalist system and the world capitalist economic system. Precisely because of this, once an economic crisis occurs in one country, like a plague it quickly spreads. . . . Those countries which depend on others . . . once a storm blows they will be beset with this and that crisis and practically cannot master their own destinies."[29] The critique reflected concern about the trade deficit and disapproval of recent policies that endorsed tying export prices to world market fluctuations.[30] Critics argued that commodities needed for domestic development and to improve living standards were being exported wantonly. They argued further that long-term mineral and fuel resource contracts would not lead to accelerated economic development, but rather to disastrous loss of control over sovereign rights.[31]

Activist policies were also denounced for excessive reliance on imports. This practice, the critics argued, stemmed from an unquestioning and groundless belief in the inherent superiority of foreign products. While conceding the need for selective imports of foreign technology, the *Pi Deng* critique insisted that import strategies had actually stunted the development of certain domestic industries such as shipbuilding.[32] In this way, it was argued, import policies were weakening self-reliance. Such policies, according to the critique, could only lead to one of three alternatives: failure to modernize, rapid but temporary economic growth that would soon collapse due to lack of a supportive domestic infrastucture, or modernization along ideologically unacceptable Soviet or Western lines.[33]

Such criticism and arguments challenged the basic economic premise of the activist trade policy, namely that expanded trade would lead to sustained domestic development. The *Pi Deng* critique also attacked trade policy for betraying or downgrading the ideological premise of self-reliance — that self-generated economic transformation was a necessary safeguard for revolutionary purity. Concern over a shift toward economic growth at the expense of revolutionary values was a central theme of the campaign as a whole. In terms of foreign trade, this was reflected in complaints that an activist trade policy would retard the "revolutionary struggle" to promote the self-confident and independent economic and technological creativity of the masses. As one critic wrote, "If foreign dogmas and foreign idols are not swept away, it will be impossible to generate the dynamic revolutionary spirit."[34]

*Foreign Trade: Criticism by Historical Analogy*

During the peak of the campaign, criticisms of foreign trade policy often took the form of fascinating and detailed historical analogies. Articles in this vein drew on China's numerous humiliating experiences with past policies that allowed foreigners and things foreign to play an important role in Chinese economic development. Examined carefully, these historical critiques reveal an attack not only on the policies specifically connected with *The Twenty Points,* but, more importantly, a comprehensive critique of the full set of measures and procedures that had emerged in China's post-1972 approach to foreign trade.

A good example of criticism by historical analogy can be found in the carefully crafted article published in *Guangming Daily* on June 17, 1976.[35]

This article was one of many that drew an explicit and scathing analogy between Deng and the hapless "westernizers" of the late Qing dynasty: Li Hongzhang, Zeng Guofan, and Zhang Zhidong. It described how they tried to promote national regeneration through massive imports of advanced foreign machinery and weapons. Li Hongzhang was castigated for his belief that the way to enrichment and self-improvement lay in the purchase of expensive foreign ships to build a navy. He was mocked for foolishly importing seventeen foreign naval ships, all of which turned out to be either antiquated or of shoddy quality. Such derogatory comments on the purchase of worthless ships and their presumed benefits to China were designed to discredit contemporary practices and political leaders. The PRC recently had purchased a low-priced scrap ship from the West to rebuild for domestic use near Shanghai.[36] More generally, the article decried the fact that Li's "fetish for foreign munitions" was financed by squandering the national wealth and by taking out large foreign loans. He purchased weapons derided as "all kinds of fantastic and crazy inventions of the era . . . 'bullets that could not be loaded into rifles and shells that could not be fired by guns.'" This criticism can be interpreted as one of the many attacks on contemporary trade policy as it related to shipping and the shipbuilding industry. More significantly, the critique can be viewed as a snide swipe at Peking's brief interest, exhibited in 1975, in imports of foreign military technology. During 1975, China purchased $200 million in military jet engines from Rolls Royce and showed noticeable interest in importing Western radar, sonar, and antitank missiles.[37] The entire approach of reliance on foreign equipment and loans is scornfully noted to have helped triple the value of imports in the years 1860–90. It is not difficult to discern the intended contemporary parallel when the article concludes that "the unfavorable balance of trade amounted to over 50 million taels of silver each year. This was the result of the 'search for enrichment' by the faction for foreignization."

Another *Guangming Daily* article that appeared a month later was clearly designed to discredit the recent importation of complete plants.[38] This article examined Zhang Zhidong, the nineteenth-century "westernizer," and his ill-fated scheme to enrich China by establishing foreign-equipped factories and mines. Zhang's venture was said to have involved poor quality, endlessly troublesome yet exorbitantly priced foreign imports, Chinese recourse to usurious loans and installment payments, and increasing foreign debts leading to political and economic emasculation. Specific mention is made of an ironworks project where all machinery and equipment were imported. Since all building materials were foreign, construction had to be interrupted frequently to await the arrival of new supplies. This point could be interpreted as an indirect reference to problems encountered in the construction of foreign designed and supplied plants.³⁹ A further parallel between Zhang Zhidong's ironworks and present-day China's complete plant imports was the former's reliance not only on foreign equipment but also on an army of highly paid foreign experts who, the article asserted, completely monopolized technical power.

The general issues of concern and disagreement over foreign trade policy were clearly set forth in these and many other articles appearing during the campaign to criticize Deng Xiaoping. On the export side, the most frequently denounced practices involved the sale of petroleum, coal, and mineral resources. The criticism in these areas centered on "which sectors of the Chinese economy, and what proportion of different sectors, should be used to pay for imports."⁴⁰ Turbogenerators, ships, and the general category of complete plants seemed to be the only specifically mentioned import controversies.⁴¹ It is plain, however, that a critical over-arching issue was the ideological and financial feasibility of increased reliance on imports to accelerate economic growth.

*Shipbuilding as a Mini Case Study*

A further interesting characteristic of the *Pi Deng* foreign trade critique was its focus on shipbuilding and related merchant shipping industries. Not only were these industries repeatedly mentioned for purposes of general illustration but, in addition, they were often discussed in an uncharacteristically detailed manner. There are several potentially interrelated explanations for this focus.

Beginning in the early 1970s, the PRC commenced an overt drive for maritime expansion. This was reflected in numerous purchases of new and secondhand foreign vessels and in the placing of sizable ship construction orders with shipyards abroad. The new emphasis on maritime capacity paralleled and was apparently linked to the development of Chinese oil exports. Between 1974 and 1976, the Chinese oil tanker fleet increased dramatically from virtually zero to an estimated thirty vessels totaling 1,346,232 deadweight tons. In 1975 alone, China acquired seventeen foreign tankers. Ship purchases, totaling approximately $400 million, accounted for almost 20 percent of China's 1975 capital goods expenditures.⁴² As "one of the most important elements in China's recent equipment acquisition program,"⁴³ ship imports provided a logical and visible target for those in the leadership unhappy with post-1972 trade policies.

A second probable explanation for the *Pi Deng* focus on shipping also derives from the salience of ship purchases. Despite sizable expansions in domestic shipbuilding since the 1960s, only one-sixth of the PRC's total merchant marine fleet in 1976 came from native shipyards. Of the four major strategies employed by China to expand its shipping capacity—domestic shipbuilding, contracting with foreign shipyards, purchasing cheap secondhand foreign vessels, and chartering foreign ships—emphasis was clearly being placed on purchasing and contracting abroad. Chinese output of larger vessels had increased during the 1970s. However, the PRC still exhibited a noticeable tendency to concentrate domestic efforts on "basic" ships and to contract abroad for more technically demanding, specialized vessels.[44] This practice was criticized on the grounds that trade policy was overemphasizing things foreign and, in so doing, slowing the growth of domestic industry.

The geographical structure of the shipbuilding industry points to a third likely reason for the importance of shipping as an issue. Some of China's largest shipyards are located in Shanghai, the powerbase of several central leaders associated with the campaign against Deng. Personal links to Shanghai and protests from their "constituency" may well have increased the salience of shipbuilding as a foreign trade issue in the campaign. Presumably, these links could increase the Shanghai-based leaders' degree of access to detailed relevant information, as well as their ability to mobilize the Shanghai shipbuilding sector in support of the *Pi Deng* trade critique. This information and mobilization hypothesis seems to be supported by the numerous and often detailed critiques of trade policy authored by those connected with Shanghai shipbuilding. No other groups supported the trade criticisms as consistently or as outspokenly as did Shanghai's Jiangnan and Hudong Shipyards, and Shanghai's Municipal Shipbuilding Company.

Shipping and shipbuilding-related criticisms reflected resentment over what was clearly interpreted as an unjustly high central budgetary allocation for procurement of foreign-built vessels. Furthermore, critics argued that this allocation was made at the expense of a promising domestic industry. As a surprisingly candid passage in one of the Jiangnan Shipyard articles complains, "We are certainly not opposed to all import of ships, it is alright to import a few, according to national needs. But at the same time, millions of yuan of the national capital are being drawn upon to buy several hundred thousands of tons of old foreign ships. Would it not be possible to import a few less boats, and to save a bit of capital to give to our shipbuilding industry to build it up . . . ? Their answer was they wouldn't give a penny."[45]

In calling attention to the wide range of specialized vessels already successfully built in domestic shipyards since the Cultural Revolution, the articles implicitly reflect dissatisfaction with the central leaders' persistent preference for contracting abroad for all but "basic" ships. Further campaign criticisms were aimed at merchant shipping. Only one-third of China's foreign trade was carried on PRC flagships, and reliance on foreign charters remained common.⁴⁶ These factors reinforced the critique's implied demand for expansion of the domestic shipbuilding sector.

*Domestic Reaction to the* Pi Deng *Critique*

Apart from the domestic shipbuilding sector, support for the *Pi Deng* trade critique, as reflected in authorship of media articles, was remarkably narrow. Even perfunctory support by central government agencies and the People's Liberation Army was conspicuously absent. The trade critique, paralleling the campaign as a whole, was advanced largely through articles emanating from either collective writing groups, individuals using pen names, or bastions of "gang of four" support such as Peking and Qinghua Universities.

The most interesting example of the lack of bureaucratic support for the *Pi Deng* trade critique was the Ministry of Foreign Trade. In fact, from the beginning of the campaign the Ministry of Foreign Trade adamantly opposed the *Pi Deng* critique. A barrage of trade-related campaign criticisms began in April 1976, about the time of Deng's fall. Yet, simultaneously, Vice Minister Chai Shufan publicly confirmed the continuation of the import and export policies that were then under attack. He affirmed the continued relevance of plans to increase exports of raw materials to Germany and to maintain the current level of German imports despite a deficit trade balance. Three months later, at the height of the campaign, Chinese officials meeting with representatives of the National Council for U.S.-China Trade declared that the PRC's foreign trade would continue to develop in tandem with China's domestic economic growth, and that policy was not "subject to change with the death or removal of individuals."⁴⁷ Indeed, during the campaign officials at all levels of the Ministry of Foreign Trade, from Canton [Guangzhou] Trade Fair personnel to Minister Li Qiang, consistently and openly assured foreign statesmen and foreign trade groups that campaign rhetoric would not influence the actual implementation of PRC trade policy. Vice Premier Gu Mu and officials of the Ministry of Foreign Affairs issued similar statements.⁴⁸ Officials who favored the activist trade policy communicated their views through unorthodox channels such as conversations with foreign businessmen. This strategy was probably the result of two factors. First, post–"gang of four" exposés indicated that intense top-level confrontation on the foreign trade issue occurred in various leadership forums from March to July 1976.⁴⁹ Second, the mass media were under the control of and articulated the critical views of campaign proponents. Bureaucratic supporters of the activist trade stance were denied access to the domestic media while trade policy was becoming increasingly salient as a campaign target. Under these circumstances, it is

*The Campaign's Effect on Policy Implementation*

Bureaucratic efforts to insulate foreign trade policy from the *Pi Deng* onslaught met with varying success in 1976. After the fall of the "gang of four," Chinese officials claimed that the campaign had produced deleterious consequences for foreign trade. Attacks on trade policy were said to have created serious internal disruption and to have weakened China's position in the international market. However, assessment of the consequences of the campaign is complicated by a host of intervening factors on which available data are less than explicit. Trade estimates for 1976 suggested an overall picture largely congruent with the aims and trends of pre-campaign policy. A one percent rise in PRC exports, combined with a sharp reduction in imports—an estimated 19 percent drop over 1975—produced a much desired trade surplus (see Table 4.1). In light of the campaign's emphasis on shipping, it is significant that China completely halted the purchase of foreign vessels after Deng's purge in April. Expenditures for ships plummeted by $350 million in 1976, a decline accounting for virtually the entire drop in Chinese capital goods imports.

The campaign also affected other aspects of foreign trade. For example, several complete plants were purchased in early 1976, but buying declined when the campaign turned against trade policy.[50] *Pi Deng* may have contributed to the reduction in plant purchases and to the substantial overall decrease in imports, especially if the campaign thwarted implementation of the Fifth Five-Year Plan and its concomitant foreign trade budgetary allocations. Another possible explanation, however, is based upon more prosaic economic factors. One is the continuing determination, first evidenced in 1975, to balance the trade budget. Another is the earmarking of scarce currency reserves for installment payments due on the foreign plants.

One other possible indicator of fluctuations in trade policy, the spring 1976 Canton Trade Fair, provides only imperfect and inconclusive evidence on the impact of the campaign. A Foreign Trade Corporation official was quoted as having remarked privately that the campaign had brought about a 10–15 percent drop in the output of producer units supplying commodities to the corporation. Yet although there were serious Chinese supply shortages, they were at least partially attributable to economic factors unconnected with *Pi Deng*. Sales to Japan did plummet, but otherwise there were no major changes. Business negotiations reportedly took place in an atmosphere of cordiality, amid assurances by Chinese officials that the campaign would not affect trade policy.[51]

However, the most significant potential test of campaign influence on the implementation of trade policy is the deterioration in trade relations with Japan, the PRC's major trading partner. Japanese sales to China experienced a 19.8 percent drop in 1976.[52] In February of that year, Peking suddenly and without explanation cut oil exports to Japan by 50 percent. Further cuts of 40 and then 50 percent followed in March and April. Despite an upturn at the end of the year, Japan received only about 6.8 million tons of Chinese crude oil in 1976. This was less than in 1975 and well below the 10-million-ton figure anticipated by the Japanese. Concomitantly, China broke off negotiations for a long-term crude oil export agreement. Similarly abrupt, unexplained suspensions occurred in several other ongoing Sino-Japanese trade negotiations at approximately the time of the Tiananmen riots and the fall of Deng. These breakdowns in trade talks, some of which did not resume until well after the fall of the "gang of four," were probably byproducts of the campaign.[53] The role of *Pi Deng* in the critical matter of decreased oil exports, however, is far from clear.

Chinese commentators offered an intriguing explanation explicitly linking decreased oil exports with *Pi Deng*. Oil intended for export was claimed to have been hurriedly diverted for domestic use by supporters of the "gang" who created artificial shortages in 1976 by exceeding regional fuel quotas and by arbitrarily converting numerous industrial enterprises from coal to oil.[54] The possible influence of unexpected domestic shortages, induced in part or wholly by campaign dislocations, cannot be discounted. However, other equally plausible explanations exist. Emergency oil shipments to North Korea and Romania were reported, as was a rumored explosion at the huge Daqing oilfield. Even pique on the part of the Chinese might have contributed to the decrease in oil exports. PRC officials were known to be upset not only over high Japanese steel and chemical fertilizer prices but also, and more importantly, over Japan's unexpected reneging on earlier promises to purchase larger and long-term quantities of Chinese crude oil.[55]

In sum, the evidence suggests that the campaign indirectly disrupted the implementation of trade policy through domestic squabbling and dislocations. Furthermore, the campaign is a strong contender among several possible explanations for the generally less activist trade stance evidenced in 1976. The almost immediate post–"gang of four" reaffirmation of the activist policy lends further support to the possibility that *Pi Deng* did, in fact, impede further development of the trade policies adopted around 1972.

## III. Conclusion

The focus of this paper has been on foreign trade policy in the campaign against Deng Xiaoping. The historical roots and actual policy targets of the campaign appear to antedate and extend beyond the 1975 policy proposals associated with Deng himself. In the early 1970s, the PRC adopted a less autarkic formulation of self-reliance. This formulation posited a closer linkage of trade policy to Chinese domestic development goals. The outcome was a shift to a more activist trade program in late 1972. Thereafter, China's media carried intermittent articles evincing discontent with this change of policy. Political maneuver related to Mao's imminent death and succession caused this dissatisfaction to erupt into a full-scale onslaught on trade and other policies during *Pi Deng*.

This study suggests that the campaign, in its trade policy dimension, was waged by a small group with few identifiable bases of support. In addition, this group apparently had only minimal influence in the trade bureaucracy responsible for implementation of official guidelines. It is apparent that the foreign trade bureaucracy and the trade policy area were well insulated and lost relatively little ground in the fracas. Nevertheless, *Pi Deng* delayed implementation of activist trade policies adopted in 1972, and it was not until the fall of the "gang of four" that China was able to launch major new trade initiatives.

How typical of Chinese policy and of *Pi Deng* in general are these conclusions about foreign trade? A more than speculative answer to this question would require a detailed study of domestic policy issues in the campaign. It should be noted that evidence from another study suggests that the more central domestic policy component of *Pi Deng*, like the trade issue, also had its roots in policy decisions made in the early 1970s.[56] Another broad analysis of *Pi Deng* also implies that supporters of the campaign lacked strength in many segments of the bureaucracy, not merely that dealing with foreign trade.[57] On the other hand, the impact of the campaign on contemporaneous policy implementation in general was often more severe than was the case in the trade area. *Pi Deng* appears to have had widely varying effects depending on the policy in question, the stage of the campaign, and the geographic region in which it was to be applied.[58] These observations suggest that this paper's findings on policy development in the 1970s and *Pi Deng*, while hardly prototypical, are nonetheless far from unique to foreign trade.

## IV. Postscript: The Shape of Things to Come

The elimination of what was presumably the core of domestic opposition to expanded trade and the current emphasis placed on rapid economic development strongly suggest that PRC trade policy will continue to develop along its present activist lines. The current leadership is unabashedly outspoken in

*Foreign Trade Policy and Deng Xiaoping*

its support for increased foreign trade and there is no doubt that the exhortation to "use foreign things to serve China" has replaced the xenophobic and isolationist cries of 1976 and earlier years about "worshipping and fawning on things foreign." Post-campaign trade policy has exhibited a strong trend toward increased flexibility and further expansion of the activist stance. This has resulted in unprecedentedly high levels of foreign trade in the two years since *Pi Deng*.[59]

The current Chinese stance on imports is clearly articulated in the following quotation from an April 1978 article in *Guangming Daily*:

> Science and technology are essentially the common wealth of mankind.... learning from and importing a foreign country's advanced technology is a very normal phenomenon ... [and] should not be regarded as following this country's road of capitalist development.... If we do not adopt as much advanced technology as possible and build our country into a modern and socialist state, we will be unable to effectively prevent capitalist restoration and to cope with aggression and subversion by social imperialism and imperialism.[60]

The implications of this heightened receptivity to technology transfer have been discussed by Deng Xiaoping himself. During his American tour in early 1979, Deng spoke of Peking's "vast import plans." He stated that China "would need billions of dollars in foreign exchange, possibly scores of billions, over the next few years for its modernization plans."[61]

The 1977 Daqing Conference clearly reflected renewed and strengthened commitment to the development of petroleum exports. A recently concluded long-term trade agreement with Japan centers on Chinese oil and guarantees the PRC a growing export market. Oil will doubtless continue in its current role as the key to an expanding drive for foreign currency to finance imports needed for rapid development.

However, even with these factors supporting the current activist trade policies, there are several equally strong constraints on future Chinese involvement in the international economy. First, China's immediate export expansion capacity is limited, especially in the crucial petroleum sector. Chinese crude oil has already proven to be expensive and difficult to refine and transport. Peking's largely unsuccessful search for markets outside Japan, coupled with predictions of steadily rising Chinese domestic demand, suggest that the export increase required to sustain a continued activist policy may prove to be a significant stumbling block.[62] The problem of financing is a related constraint. Estimates of future import bills for China's modernization drive range from $40 billion to $250 billion.[63] Payment will demand modification of China's conservative preference for balanced trade budgets. Recent Chinese policy has already shown increasing flexibility here. The PRC is now willing to utilize a range of finance options including government-to-government loans, joint ventures, barter agreements, and countertrade. However, factors complicating the payment problem remain. They include the domestic constraints on export earning capacity, sluggish Chinese agricultural output which creates a need for expensive grain imports, and the commitment of sizable foreign currency reserves to progress or installment payments on past import purchases.[64]

There is also the very real problem of China's absorptive capacity. The PRC has already identified its lack of an adequate domestic infrastructure of trained scientific and technological personnel, the result of a decade of turmoil and disarray on the education front, as a major constraint on foreign trade. Finally, the ideological principles of the Chinese Communist Party function as an underlying constraint. The Chinese approach to development and to foreign trade continues to be governed by the flexible concept of self-reliance. Flexibility, however, does not imply that self-reliance is meaningless. This concept cannot help but have a continuing, cautionary impact on future trade policy, especially since its injunctions against overinvolvement in the world economy dovetail so well with the powerful voice of long, consistently negative Chinese experience.

## Notes

1. Harry Harding, Jr., Linkages Between Chinese Domestic Politics and Foreign Policy 25-27 (August, 1976) (unpublished paper presented at the Workshop on Chinese Foreign Policy, Ann Arbor). For one of the few efforts to examine trade policy linkages, see Kent Morrison, *Domestic Politics and Industrialization in China: The Foreign Trade Factor,* 18 ASIAN SURVEY 687-705 (No. 7, 1978).

2. Quoted in Fang Hai, *Criticize the Slavish Comprador Philosophy,* HONG QI [RED FLAG, hereafter HQ], No. 4, 1976, at 21-26, *translated in* SELECTIONS FROM PEOPLE'S REPUBLIC OF CHINA MAGAZINES [hereafter SPRCM], No. 76-11, at 20-26.

3. *Chairman of the Chinese Delegation Teng Hsiao-p'ing's [Deng Xiaoping's] Speech,* PEKING REVIEW [hereafter PR], Apr. 19, 1974, at 6-11.

4. For example, the PRC explicitly acknowledged that massive imports of complete plants from the Soviet Union served as the core of the first Chinese Five-Year Plan (1953-57). *See* Robert F. Dernberger, *Economic Development and Modernization in Contemporary China: The Attempt to Limit Dependence on the Transfer of Modern Industrial Technology from Abroad and to Control its Corruption of the Maoist Social Revolution, in* FREDERIC J. FLERON, JR. *ed.,* TECHNOLOGY AND COMMUNIST CULTURE 231, 233, 240-241 (1977).

5. Hans Heymann, Jr., *Acquisition and Diffusion of Technology in China,* JOINT ECONOMIC COMM., 94th Cong., 1st Sess., CHINA: A REASSESSMENT OF THE ECONOMY, 678 (1975).

6. The reformulated trade policy was first reflected in the PRC's increased plant

purchases of late 1972. However, the date of the policy decisions governing this shift remains a subject of controversy. In this volume, Thomas Fingar argues for 1970-71. Alexander Eckstein speaks of a series of decisions between 1970 and 1972. ALEXANDER ECKSTEIN, CHINA'S ECONOMIC REVOLUTION 239 (1977). Victor Li opts for late 1971 or early 1972. See *Trade with China: An Introduction, in* VICTOR LI, ed., LAW AND POLITICS IN CHINA'S FOREIGN TRADE 7 (1977).

7. Although never formally announced by the PRC, recent analyses posit that, since 1972, "Chinese military expenditures may have declined by as much as 25 percent, measured in constant dollars." A. ECKSTEIN, *supra* note 6. On the relationship of defense cuts to changing perceptions of the international situation, see John Lewis's contribution to this volume.

8. *See* U.S.-CHINA BUSINESS REVIEW, Sep.-Oct. 1976, at 33-39; *Id.*, Nov.-Dec. 1976, at 28-32; *Id.*, Jan.-Feb. 1977, at 24-35.

9. Toshio Obi, *Trade Between China and Japan,* CONTEMPORARY CHINA, Feb. 1977, at 9-10.

10. U.S. CENTRAL INTELLIGENCE AGENCY: NATIONAL FOREIGN ASSESSMENT CENTER, CHINA: INTERNATIONAL TRADE 1976-77 9 (1977); *see also* A. ECKSTEIN, *supra* note 6, at 276; Nicholas Lardy, *Foreign Economic Issues Facing the New Chinese Leadership,* CONTEMPORARY CHINA, Jan. 1977, at 35-36.

11. *See generally* Wei Pingkui, *Persist in the Principle of Maintaining Independence and Keeping the Initiative in Our Own Hands and Relying on Our Own Efforts in Achieving Regeneration,* HQ, No. 1, 1974, *translated in* SPRCM, No. 74-1, at 92-96; Tian Zhisong, *Adhere to the Policy of Independence and Self-Reliance,* Renmin Ribao [People's Daily, hereafter RMRB], Mar. 22, 1974, *translated in* SURVEY OF PEOPLE'S REPUBLIC OF CHINA PRESS [hereafter SPRCP], Apr. 1974, at 2-6; Li Xin, *Self-Reliance is a Question of Line,* PR, Aug. 8, 1975, at 14-15, 23. *See also* A. ECKSTEIN, *supra* note 6, at 241-42; FAR EASTERN ECONOMIC REVIEW, ASIA 1975 YEARBOOK 156 (1975).

12. FAR EASTERN ECONOMIC REVIEW, ASIA 1975 YEARBOOK 156 (1975).

13. N. Lardy, *supra* note 10, at 35.

14. *See* Thomas Fingar's discussion of formal, rhetorical, and actual policies in Chapter 1 of this volume.

15. Chou En-lai [Zhou Enlai], *Report on the Work of the Government, in* PEOPLE'S REPUBLIC OF CHINA, DOCUMENTS OF THE FIRST SESSION OF THE FOURTH NATIONAL PEOPLE'S CONGRESS OF THE PEOPLE'S REPUBLIC OF CHINA 55 (1975).

16. U.S.-CHINA BUSINESS REVIEW, Jan.-Feb. 1976, at 53. On conclusion of a multi-year trade agreement with Japan, see Tracey Dahlby, *Peking Opens the Door to Japan,* FAR EASTERN ECONOMIC REVIEW, Mar. 3, 1978, at 40-41.

17. U.S.-CHINA BUSINESS REVIEW, Mar.-Apr. 1975, at 53.

18. Henri Hymans, *Japan Eyes Peking's Liquid Gas,* FAR EASTERN ECONOMIC REVIEW, Feb. 20, 1976, at 37-39.

19. U.S.-CHINA BUSINESS REVIEW, Nov.-Dec. 1975, at 12-13.

20. A. DOAK BARNETT, UNCERTAIN PASSAGE: CHINA'S TRANSITION TO THE POST-MAO ERA 165 (1974).

21. *See On the General Program of Work for the Whole Party and the Whole Nation* and *Some Problems in Accelerating Industrial Development, reprinted in* CHI HSIN, THE CASE OF THE GANG OF FOUR 208, 209, 216, 233-234, 241-244 (1977).

22. Harry Harding makes the same point at a more general level in his contribution to this volume.

23. *See* Mass Criticism Group of Beijing and Qinghua Universities, *Hit Back at the Right-Deviating Wind of Reversing Verdicts in Science and Technology Circles,* HQ, No. 2, 1976, *translated in* SPRCM, No. 76-5, at 8-9.

24. Vice Chairman of the Qinghua University Political Department, *The Capitalist Roaders are Still Capitalist Roaders and the Revolutionaries are Still Struggling,* RMRB, Mar. 5, 1976.

25. The three documents drafted under Deng's aegis in the summer and fall of 1975 were: *On the General Program of Work for the Whole Party and the Whole Nation, The Twenty Points,* and *Outline Report of Work in the Academy of Sciences (Outline of Summary Report).* Pi Deng articles quoting from and discussing these documents include Zhai Qing, *Read An Unpublished Manuscript,* XUEXI YU PIPAN [STUDY AND CRITICISM, hereafter XXYPP], Apr. 14, 1976, at 11-19; *Criticism of Selected Passages of 'Certain Questions on Accelerating the Development of Industry', Id., translated in* SPRCM, No. 76-15, [hereafter *Criticism of Selected Passages*], at 1-12 and Kang Li and Yen Feng, *The Circumstances Surrounding the Appearance of 'Outline of Summary Report', Id., translated in* SPRCM, No. 76-23, at 16-28. The three documents have never been published in their entirety by the PRC although comprehensive and mutually consistent versions are now available in very different sources. *See* Chi Hsin, *supra* note 21, at 203-272, 277-286; ISSUES AND STUDIES, July 1977, at 90-113; *Id.* Aug. 1977, at 77-99; *Id.* Sep. 1977, at 63-70.

26. *Criticism of Selected Passages, supra* note 25, at 3.

27. *See, e.g.,* Feng E, *Is it "Bringing it Here-ism" or Admitting and Being Infatuated by Everything Foreign?* and *Concentrate Firepower on Condemning the "Regulations" Deng Xiaoping Cooked Up,* RMRB, Oct. 5, 1976.

28. Fang Hai, *supra* note 2, at 22.

29. *Id.* at 24.

30. *Id.* at 24; *Criticism of Selected Passages, supra* note 25, at 4; Criticism Group of the Chinese Committee for the Promotion of International Trade, *Redress the Crimes of the "Gang of Four," Develop Socialist Foreign Trade,* RMRB, Jan. 2, 1977, *reprinted in* PIPAN "SI RENBANG" POHUAI CAIMAO GONGZUODE ZUIXING [CONDEMN THE "GANG OF FOUR'S" CRIME OF SABOTAGING FINANCE AND TRADE WORK] 16 (1977).

31. *Criticism of Selected Passages, supra* note 25, at 3-4.

32. Fang Hai, *supra* note 2, at 22; *Criticism of Selected Passages, supra* note 25, at 3; Report Dictated by a Retired Elderly Worker at the Jiangnan Shipbuilding Factory, *At All Times Criticize the Foreign Slaves,* XXYPP, May 1, 1976, at 41.

33. *See* Liang Xiao and Ren Ming, *Criticize "Taking the Three Directives as the Key Link,"* RMRB, Feb. 29, 1976; *The Great Proletarian Revolution Continues and Deepens,* March 19, 1976, at 9, 10.

34. Fang Hai, *supra* note 2, at 25.

35. Workers' Historical Research Group of Turbine Workshop of Wuchang Shipyard and the Deartment of History of Central China Normal College, *The Traitorous Behavior of Worshippers of Things Foreign as Viewed from Li Hung-chang's [Li Hongzhang's] Navy Building,* Guangming Ribao [Guangming Daily, hereafter

GMRB], June 17, 1976, translated in SPRCP, June 28–July 2, 1976, at 148–52.
  36. *See The "Yacht" Incident,* PR, Mar. 4, 1977, at 19.
  37. *See* U.S. CENTRAL INTELLIGENCE AGENCY, PRC: INTERNATIONAL TRADE HANDBOOK 5 (1976); FAR EASTERN ECONOMIC REVIEW, ASIA 1977 YEARBOOK 46 (1976); Leo Goodstadt, *Setting the Stage for a Showdown,* FAR EASTERN ECONOMIC REVIEW, Jan. 9, 1976, at 9, 10. For military procurement, see the chapter by John Lewis in this volume.
  38. Qing Shi, *Bankruptcy of Slavish Comprador Philosophy as Viewed from Zhang Zhidong's Running of Factories,* GMRB, July 22, 1976, *translated in* SPRCP, August 2–6, 1976, at 116–19.
  39. Paul Strauss, *Chinese Steel Expansion Lags,* FAR EASTERN ECONOMIC REVIEW, June 11, 1976, at 111.
  40. Stephen Andors, *Issues of China's Industrial Political Economy in 1976,* CONTEMPORARY CHINA, Jan. 1977, at 28, 29.
  41. Turbogenerators are discussed in *Criticism of Selected Passages, supra* note 25, at 3; *Bankruptcy of Deng Xiaoping's Slavish Comprador Philosophy,* RMRB, June 17, 1976, *translated in* SPRCP, July 6–9, 1976, at 98, 99–104; *Another Victory for the Principle of Self-Reliance,* PR, Aug. 9, 1976, at 22–23. *See also* Central Study Group of CCP Comm. for Hutong Shipyard, *Telling Exposure of Deng Xiaoping's Slavish Comprador Philosophy,* RMRB, May 13, 1976.
  42. *Shipping Notes,* U.S.-CHINA BUSINESS REVIEW, Nov.–Dec. 1976, at 54, 55; FAR EASTERN ECONOMIC REVIEW, ASIA 1977 YEARBOOK 104; U.S. CENTRAL INTELLIGENCE AGENCY, *supra* note 37.
  43. Peter Weintraub, *China: Sounding a Warning,* FAR EASTERN ECONOMIC REVIEW, Oct. 15, 1976, at 56.
  44. Irwin Millard Heine, *China's Merchant Marine,* U.S.-CHINA BUSINESS REVIEW, Mar.–Apr. 1976, at 6, 11–12; U.S. CENTRAL INTELLIGENCE AGENCY, CHINESE MERCHANT SHIP PRODUCTION 1, 3 (1976).
  45. Jiangnan Shipbuilding Factory, *supra* note 32.
  46. I. M. Heine, *supra* note 44, at 9–12; Jin Bainian, *Li Hongzhang and the China Merchant Steamship Navigation Company,* XXYPP, July 14, 1976, *translated in* SPRCM, No. 74-14, at 1–5.
  47. *Broadcast by Hamburg, D.P.A., on Apr. 8, 1976, printed in* FOREIGN BROADCAST INFORMATION SERVICE, DAILY REPORT: PEOPLE'S REPUBLIC OF CHINA, [hereafter FBIS], Apr. 9, 1976, at A13, A14; *Council Activities,* U.S.-CHINA BUSINESS REVIEW, Sep.–Oct. 1976, at 19, 20–21.
  48. A. ECKSTEIN, *supra* note 6, at 243; FAR EASTERN ECONOMIC REVIEW, ASIA 1977 YEARBOOK 160 (1976); Paul Strauss, *Trade Prospects Remain Fair,* FAR EASTERN ECONOMIC REVIEW, Apr. 30, 1976, at 56–57; Susumu Awanahara, *Peking's Pledges to Tokyo, Id.,* May 28, 1976, at 112. *See also* Peking, New China News Agency [hereafter NCNA] (Mar. 16, 1976), *in* FBIS, Mar. 19, 1976, at A20–21; FBIS, Mar. 23, 1976, at A18.
  49. *See, e.g.,* [Guo Ji], *Foreign Trade: Why the "Gang of Four" Created Confusion,* PR, Feb. 25, 1977, at 17–18.
  50. U.S. CENTRAL INTELLIGENCE AGENCY, *supra* note 10, at 1, 4, 18.

51. *Notes From the Fair—Canton 39: Why Do They Keep Coming?* U.S.-CHINA BUSINESS REVIEW, May–June 1976, at 47–48; P. Strauss, *supra* note 48, at 57–58.

52. CONTEMPORARY CHINA, Feb. 1977, at 50.

53. Susumu Awanahara, *Japan Wary of Peking Power Play,* FAR EASTERN ECONOMIC REVIEW, Apr. 23, 1976, at 128; *International China Notes,* U.S.-CHINA BUSINESS REVIEW, May–June, 1976, at 56; FAR EASTERN ECONOMIC REVIEW, ASIA 1977 YEARBOOK 160 (1976); U.S. CENTRAL INTELLIGENCE AGENCY, CHINA: REAL TRENDS IN TRADE WITH NON-COMMUNIST COUNTRIES SINCE 1970 21 (1977).

54. NCNA, *A Serious Step Towards Sabotaging the Party and Usurping Power,* RMRB, Jan. 14, 1977.

55. Alistair Wrightman, *Japan and China's Oil—Proceeding with Caution,* U.S.-CHINA BUSINESS REVIEW, Mar.–Apr. 1976, at 31; *International China Notes, Id.* May–June 1976, at 57–58; Peter Weintraub, *China: Ideology, Then Oil,* FAR EASTERN ECONOMIC REVIEW, June 18, 1976, at 37; FAR EASTERN ECONOMIC REVIEW, ASIA 1977 YEARBOOK 102, 150 (1976); Toshio Obi, *Trade Between China and Japan,* CONTEMPORARY CHINA, Feb. 1977, at 10.

56. *See* Thomas Fingar's paper on domestic policy in this volume.

57. Kenneth Lieberthal, *Strategies of Conflict in China During 1975–1976,* CONTEMPORARY CHINA, Nov. 1976, at 7, 8–9.

58. *See* Fingar, *supra* note 56.

59. U.S. CENTRAL INTELLIGENCE AGENCY, CHINA: INTERNATIONAL TRADE 1, 5 (1978).

60. *"Sinister" Article Against Foreign Technology Denounced,* GMRB, Apr. 23, 1978, *translated in* FBIS, May 5, 1978, at E12–13.

61. Fox Butterfield, *In Texas Deng Talks of Vast Import Plans,* New York Times, Feb. 4, 1979, at 1.

62. *Exporter's Notes,* U.S.-CHINA BUSINESS REVIEW, Jan.–Feb. 1976, at 41; N. Lardy, *supra* note 10, at 36; U.S. CENTRAL INTELLIGENCE AGENCY, *supra* note 59, at 6.

63. *See, e.g., China Faces Reality,* TIME, Mar. 12, 1979, at 89, and *Cutting a Deal with China,* NEWSWEEK, Mar. 12, 1979, at 75.

64. U.S. CENTRAL INTELLIGENCE AGENCY, *supra* note 59, at 6; *China to Consider U.S. Trade Accord, Peking Officer Says,* New York Times, Dec. 19, 1978, at A1; Nai-Ruenn Chen, *Economic Modernization in Post-Mao China: Policies, Problems, and Prospects,* CHINESE ECONOMY POST-MAO, A COMPENDIUM OF PAPERS SUBMITTED TO THE JOINT ECONOMIC COMM., 95th Cong., 2d Sess. 196–97 (1978); David L. Denny, *Recent Developments in the International Financial Policies of the PRC,* 10 STANFORD JOURNAL OF INTERNATIONAL STUDIES 178 (Spring, 1975).

# 5
# Sovereignty at Sea: China and the Law of the Sea Conference

*Victor H. Li*

The People's Republic of China (PRC) entered the United Nations as that body was attempting to rewrite the law of the sea. For the past six years China has been an active participant in this process, first in the United Nations Committee on the Peaceful Uses of the Seabed and the Ocean Floor Beyond the Limits of National Jurisdiction, and later at the Third Conference on the Law of the Sea (UNCLOS).

China's active interest in UNCLOS is readily understandable since it has long argued that "the old international law" reflected the desires of "imperialist" countries. Accordingly, Peking has urged that new rules of international law be formulated, preferably in a multilateral treaty that would take a fair approach by considering the wishes and needs of the developing countries. UNCLOS presents an excellent opportunity to reduce the advantages in exploiting the ocean enjoyed by the developed countries and to protect the resources of developing countries.[1] Moreover, the fact that U.S. and Soviet interests concerning many law of the sea issues coincide (e.g., on freedom of navigation) lends credence to China's contention that the two superpowers are "colluding" in ocean exploitation.

PRC positions at UNCLOS illustrate the underlying considerations that shape Peking's view of international relations: the Chinese concept of sovereignty. In what ways are concerns with sovereign rights reflected in

---

Support for this research project was provided by the U.S. Department of State (Contract no. 1722-620241). The views and conclusions contained in this study should not be interpreted as representing the official opinions or policy of the Department of State.

Victor H. Li is Shelton Professor of International Legal Studies, Stanford Law School. He earned his B.A. at Columbia University in 1961, his J.D. at Columbia Law School in 1964, his L.L.M. at Harvard Law School in 1965, and his S.J.D. at Harvard Law School in 1971.

China's views of law of the sea issues? Does China's willingness to limit its right of unilateral action, by agreeing to follow internationally decided norms and by vesting the power to exploit the seabed in an International Seabed Authority (ISA), indicate a change in its stress on national sovereignty? This paper will argue that the law of the sea does not involve problems that would force China to reconsider its attitude on sovereignty.

Law of the sea issues provide an interesting starting point for analyzing the roots of PRC policy since China's substantive positions have changed very little during the six years it has participated in law of the sea discussions. The legal language used by China has become more detailed and deliberate, but the level and style of political rhetoric have remained about the same. The lack of change is striking simply because it contrasts so sharply with the general picture of PRC policy in the 1970s. The attempted coup by Lin Biao, the deaths of Zhou Enlai and Mao Zedong, the falls and rises of Deng Xiaoping, and the purge of the "gang of four" had virtually no effect on PRC policies concerning the law of the sea. Several facts peculiar to the law of the sea help explain the lack of linkage between this foreign policy area and domestic political developments. First, there is a broad consensus concerning the importance of preserving territorial sovereignty and limiting the ability of the superpowers to act. This consensus transcends political cleavages and other policy differences. Second, few law of the sea issues have domestic components. Policies in this area simply do not impinge on important domestic interests. In addition, China gains much but gives up little by supporting a new law of the sea that stresses the sovereign rights of coastal states. Thus, the law of the sea is quite different from other foreign policy problems (e.g., security, trade, joint ventures, tourism, and scientific exchanges) that often lack a broad consensus precisely because they impinge on major domestic concerns.

## I. The Concept of Territorial Sovereignty[2]

In international law, territorial sovereignty refers to the power of a state to exercise jurisdiction over persons and things within its own territory, usually to the exclusion of all other authorities.[3] Western attitudes toward the law of the sea are shaped by and expressed in terms of this concept. There has been considerable debate about which political entities are to be considered sovereign, the extent to which international law could or should limit sovereign rights, and the amount of water and air that could be claimed as territory.

Although the idea of sovereignty originated in the West, China has fervently embraced the concept. Its reasons for doing so, however, differ from those underlying Western development of the concept.

In the West, Bodin first used the term "sovereignty" in 1577 to describe the absolute power of a monarch within his own state, subject only to the law of God.[4] This concept was quickly accepted and adapted to the international system. The 1643 Treaty of Westphalia helped to specify which political entities were sovereign and therefore free from outside interference in their internal affairs. Under this concept of sovereignty, medium size states were protected from invasion by more powerful actors, but were permitted to exercise control over smaller "nonsovereign" feudalities.

A corollary of this principle of territorial sovereignty was the principle of sovereign equality.[5] Since a sovereign was all-powerful within his own territory, it was possible to regard all sovereigns as essentially the same type of being, and, in some theoretical sense, equal. The relative equality of the European states in the seventeenth and eighteenth centuries supported this point of view. In due course, the European states developed international legal rules concerning recognition, jurisdiction, immunity, acts of state, etc., that prescribed the manner in which sovereign equals were to deal with each other.

As the European powers began to colonize other areas of the world, the role of sovereignty in regulating international relations began to change. Most of the colonies or "new" states were not considered fully sovereign; therefore, they were not entitled to all the rights of sovereignty.[6] Only by meeting a number of criteria, which reflected Western political and cultural interests, could a new state become a full-fledged sovereign member of the "family of nations." One important criterion was willingness to adhere to the existing rules of international law developed by the imperialist countries. In addition, the ability of powerful states to withhold sovereignty in whole or in part undercut the principle of noninterference in the internal affairs of another political entity.

In the past several decades the role of sovereignty in international relations has changed again. A large number of former colonies and semisovereigns have become full independent states, and no longer is there a situation in which many states are denied sovereign rights. Instead, the proliferation of states, many of which are small or weak, has strained the principle of sovereign equality. Various arrangements for vetoes or weighted voting have been developed to assure stronger countries that they would not fall under the "tyranny of the majority."

During the same period, there has been a growing effort to limit the extent to which a sovereign may freely act within its own territory. Several arguments justify this development. In an economically interdependent world, or in a world where a local conflict could ignite a global war, what occurs inside one state affects other states as well.[7] Hence, there may be times when the greater collective interest of the community of nations might justify restricting the absolute right of a sovereign to act within its own territory. Moreover, international affairs are becoming too complex to be handled through individual decisions made by autonomous sovereigns. International rules or organizations may be needed to manage these matters in a coherent and efficient manner. On a moralistic level, the concept of international human rights also would attempt to create minimum standards of state behavior that cut across national boundaries. All these considerations point toward an effort to subordinate municipal law to international, world, or transnational law.

## II. China and Sovereignty

Two favorite Chinese phrases are "the affairs of a country should be handled by the people of that country" and "the affairs of the world should be handled by all countries of the world, big and small." These ideas are similar to the international law concepts of territorial sovereignty and sovereign equality. China, however, arrived at these positions by a path unlike the one travelled by Western philosophers. This difference in historical development has led to divergent views both about the role of sovereignty in contemporary international relations and about specific issues involving the law of the sea.

In particular, for the past hundred years, China has tried to use the principles of sovereignty and noninterference in internal affairs to ward off foreign intrusions when it lacked the military might to do so. That struggle is deeply imbedded in Chinese political consciousness. There exists, across the entire political spectrum, a general apprehension about any policy that would weaken China's sovereign rights and permit reassertion of foreign interests in China. Of course, China has adopted the Western concept of sovereignty only recently. One should at least inquire whether China would continue to hold tenaciously to this relatively new idea even after it becomes a militarily and economically strong nation. The February 1979 effort to "teach Vietnam a lesson" suggests that under appropriate circumstances, China will attempt to directly and forcefully influence the actions of nearby states.

The traditional Chinese world order was, at least in theory, hierarchical, with the emperor at the top of a pyramid of successively lower ranks of political entities and officials.[8] The emperor had absolute powers subject to certain religious and moral constraints — after all, he was the Son of Heaven ruling all under Heaven — and in that sense was sovereign. But he was not a sovereign in the post-Bodin sense of being one, among a number of equal heads of state, who had absolute power within his own territory but could not interfere in the affairs of other states.

This is not to suggest that the traditional Chinese world order was completely unfamiliar with the Western concept of sovereign states. China certainly knew that there were other empires such as the Indian, Persian, and Roman. It had a clear concept of territory; the character for country, *guo*, consists of a spear protecting the population within the confines of a territory. During various periods in Chinese history, there coexisted a number of small feudal entities that operated as independent states, although in theory paying homage to an emperor at the top of the political pyramid.[9] The rules governing relations among these "states" resembled many aspects of Western international law.[10] However, the international concept of sovereignty remains distinctively Western.[11]

For the past century China has been concerned with how to recover and preserve control over its own affairs. International law provided a way to resist Western and Japanese intrusion.

In the late nineteenth century, W.A.P. Martin translated portions of Wheaton's *Elements of International Law* into Chinese. On several subsequent occasions, Qing officials successfully invoked Western international law against Western powers. For example, Prince Gong cited the rule regarding the inviolability of the territorial waters of a neutral to obtain release by Prussia of a Danish ship captured in a Chinese port.[12] Chinese officials quickly saw that the principles of sovereignty and noninterference in internal affairs could be used to support the demand that foreigners give up their special privileges and stop trying to control Chinese affairs.

Throughout the Republican period (1911-49), the need to regain full sovereignty received strong emphasis. At first the approach was somewhat subdued, with China promising to carry out a series of reforms in "the hope of being admitted into the family of nations."[13] Later, however, the demand for full sovereign rights became louder and more strident,[14] until the onset of World War II elevated China's stature to that of a full member of the allied powers.

The demand for full sovereign rights has been one of the foundation stones in the PRC's view of the world order, both in theory and in rhetoric. The terms sovereignty and noninterference in internal affairs appear in virtually every important document dealing with international affairs, from the Common Program to the Shanghai Communiqué.

China has particularly favored the concept of peaceful coexistence, the principles of which were first enunciated by China and India in 1954:[15]

1. Mutual respect for each other's territorial integrity and sovereignty;
2. Mutual nonaggression;
3. Mutual noninterference in each other's internal affairs;

4. Equality and mutual benefit; and
5. Peaceful coexistence.

While this concept does not add anything new to classical international law, it does have two significant features. First, it is a formulation developed by non-Western states, and thus underscores the idea that all states have a say in creating international law. Second, of the many rules of international law, the principles of sovereignty and noninterference in internal affairs are especially emphasized.

Over the past three decades, China has asserted its sovereignty over a broad spectrum of activities. It has gone to great lengths to prevent foreign interference in its affairs, even to the point of excluding foreign involvement of any kind. Attitudes shaped by pre-1949 efforts to gain and preserve national sovereignty were intensified by the danger of new foreign military threats: the Korean War, periodic clashes with Taiwan forces in the 1950s, the U.S.-Vietnamese War, and the Brezhnev doctrine of limited sovereignty coupled with the buildup of Soviet troops along the Chinese border and the border clashes in the 1960s. Throughout this period, the legal principles of sovereignty and noninterference have remained important adjuncts to military might in China's defense policy.[16] Currently, the threat of foreign invasion has diminished, but these principles continue to augment China's weak military position relative to those of the Soviet Union and the United States. Moreover, because the Taiwan problem is cast as an internal affair, and American involvement with Taiwan is viewed as an effort to interfere in internal matters, the sovereignty issue remains highly salient despite the normalization of diplomatic relations with the U.S.[17]

For example, sovereignty was invoked to justify proscription of joint ventures and direct foreign investment until promulgation of a new joint venture law in 1979. Following a policy of limited economic contact with other countries, for many years the level of China's foreign trade was only about four billion dollars annually.[18] There has been a threefold increase in the level of foreign trade in the last decade, but the absolute volume remains quite small, especially when adjusted for inflation. Few Chinese trade delegations went abroad, and foreign businessmen visiting China faced restrictions on where and with whom they could deal.[19]

Similarly, since the mid-1950s, China's international cultural contacts have been very limited. Except for certain specialized topics, foreign publications are not available in China. Few government leaders travel abroad. Scholarly exchanges and tourism involve only small numbers of persons traveling in a circumscribed manner. The recent increase in travel and exchanges is highly dramatic, but in absolute terms is still miniscule.

Over the years, China has also developed intellectual positions and political attitudes that stress maintaining control over one's own affairs and limiting contacts with the outside. Chinese legal scholars have criticized the concept of transnational law or world law as a new means by which imperialist countries can interfere in the domestic affairs of other states. Although direct military intervention can no longer be used with impunity, imperialist countries could try to translate their preferences into rules of international law, and then insist that these rules are universally applicable.

Chinese commentators once denounced the United Nations and other international organizations for being creatures of the imperialist countries.[20] Such denunciations were much more common when Peking was excluded from participation.[21] Now that the PRC is a member of the United Nations and Third World countries are becoming more influential through voting coalitions, China may be more receptive to both international organizations and international lawmaking. However, China continues to criticize "unrepresentative" bodies such as the International Monetary Fund.[22] More important, China remains opposed to United Nations activities that might infringe on the territorial sovereignty of individual states, such as the formulation of international population control policies,[23] education policies,[24] or the conduct of a world housing survey.[25] In addition, there remains a lingering feeling that international organizations and lawmaking still favor the developed countries.

At least part of China's stress on "going-it-alone" reflects its attempt to make a virtue of necessity. The Western embargo imposed during the Korean War and later disruptions in trade and scientific exchanges accompanying the Sino-Soviet split meant that China had little choice except self-reliance. At the same time, there is a strong intellectual and emotional commitment to this idea. The post-Opium War century brought out all the dangers of foreign political and economic interference. The Communists' pre-1949 experiences and the developmental successes of the first three decades provided evidence that self-reliance was the best way to achieve political and economic independence.[26] This belief is reinforced by China's traditional attitudes of self-confidence and dislike for foreign contamination.

As the Chinese often state, self-reliance does not mean autarky. There is room for considerable flexibility so long as one maintains control over one's own lifelines and destiny. Thus, depending on actual conditions, a state might be able to accept some foreign loans and investment as well as have considerable scientific and commercial contacts abroad, and yet remain self-reliant. From the early years of Mao to the time of the "gang of four," the decision to seek cooperation with the outside on the basis of equality and mutual benefit has never been disputed. For example, some of the largest increases in trade volume occurred in the early 1970s, when the influence of the "gang of four" was at its peak. What has been debated are the extent and the terms of such contacts.

During the past year, China has increased its international economic activity by purchasing more foreign goods, sending a number of trade and technical missions abroad, and encouraging Western and Japanese businessmen and tourists to visit China. These activities stretch even further the bounds of self-reliance. At the same time, one should not exaggerate the extent of China's involvement in the international economic system and thereby foster the reemergence of the myth of the China market with its billion customers. Despite the immense press coverage of new sales and purchases, China's total foreign trade volume of $20 billion is about the same as Taiwan's. Foreign trade as a percentage of gross national product is only slightly higher in the 1970s than it was in the 1950s.[27] Trade with the United States was $1.1 billion in 1978. This amount constituted only about one percent of total U.S. foreign trade and was less than one-fifth the volume of U.S.-Taiwan trade.

These figures are cited not to deprecate the current growth of China's international economic activity, but rather to caution against overly optimistic and unrealistic expectations of trade and investment possibilities with China. Foreign contacts are unlikely to grow to great proportions; if they do, later retrenchment seems inevitable. Economic constraints operate to limit the quantity of such interaction; and the intellectual and emotional roots of self-reliance still run deep.

## III. Sovereignty and the Law of the Sea

In traditional international law, a sovereign had jurisdiction over the land he possessed plus a thin maritime belt along the sea coast.[28] In the areas beyond national jurisdiction, the principle of sovereign equality produced two legal regimes. Land that did not belong to a recognized sovereign was considered *terra nullius* and might be claimed by any sovereign on the basis of discovery and occupation.[29] Nonsovereigns, of course, could make no claims. The high seas beyond the maritime belt could not be claimed by anyone; they were open to all sovereigns. Through the "four freedoms of the high seas"—navigation, fishing, overflight, and the laying of cables and pipelines—international law attempted to establish the legal basis for equal access to the high seas.[30]

The principle of equal access applied far better in theory than in practice. The more advanced and wealthier states had much greater ability to exploit the high seas; only they could maintain extensive commercial and military fleets and engage in long-distance fishing. It would be in the interest of these states to keep the maritime belt of territorial sea as thin as possible so

*China and the Law of the Sea Conference*                                                                                    233

that they could continue to freely use the rest of the ocean. For each mile that the territorial sea or exclusive economic zone is widened, another 300,000 square miles of ocean, much of it prime fishing grounds, is closed to foreign fishermen.[31] Similarly, the expansion of the territorial seas to 12 miles would convert more than 100 international straits into territorial waters.[32] An important part of UNCLOS has been to balance the interests of the developing coastal states wishing to protect their fish and other resources with those of maritime states wishing to preserve free navigation.

The mineral resources of the seabed pose a new problem. Absent other constraints, one could by analogy to the existing four freedoms of the high seas add a fifth, freedom of mining,[33] and perhaps a sixth, freedom of research.[34] In this way, states possessing the requisite capital and technology could legitimately collect mineral nodules from the ocean floor. UN General Assembly Resolution 2749, however, declared that seabed resources were "the common heritage of mankind." The specific legal consequences of this general principle were to be worked out at UNCLOS; this task remains the major obstacle to reaching an overall agreement at the conference.[35]

## IV. China and the Law of the Sea

The high seas and the seabed present a different issue for China with respect to the concept of sovereignty. It would have been logically consistent with China's views on territorial sovereignty if it had adopted a position, similar to Western international law, that the ability of a sovereign state to act in areas beyond national jurisdiction should be constrained as little as possible. China would suffer a short-term disadvantage since the developed countries could exploit the high seas and seabed more quickly, but later would be able to participate actively as its own technology and resources increased. Such a stand, however, would create serious economic and political problems. The gap between developed and developing states would widen further since freedom of the high seas and freedom of the seabed are tantamount to awarding control of these resources to the developed states.[36] It may be an overstatement that "a country which first gains control of the seabed will control the whole world";[37] nevertheless, resources, such as the mineral nodules, might indeed be exhausted before the less developed countries have the capability to engage in deep-sea mining. For China and other developing countries to get a share of these resources, the ability of the developed states to act unilaterally will have to be limited, either by delaying exploitation by anyone or, more practically, by placing exploitation under international control.

Consequently, China sees the attributes of sovereignty to be very different in the areas within and the areas beyond national jurisdiction. In the former, sovereignty means control over one's own affairs and non-interference by outside forces. In the latter, sovereignty does not mean freedom to act, but rather the right to participate in decision making and to share in the benefits. Viewed in this way, China's support for a strong ISA that would handle all exploitation of seabed resources does not constitute the surrender of a sovereign right to engage in unilateral seabed mining; rather it reinforces a state's sovereign right to fully participate in international affairs.[38]

For at least several hundred years, the Chinese distinguished between *neiyang* (inner ocean) and *waiyang* (outer ocean) in a manner somewhat similar to the territorial seas/high seas distinction of Western international law. It was not clear, however, just where the line was drawn between the two areas, although distances of ten *li*, about 3.6 statute miles, were used at the end of the nineteenth century.[39]

The Republic of China (ROC) government officially adopted the three nautical mile rule in 1921. It also signed the 1930 Hague Treaty on Territorial Seas which used the same limit. In the 1930s and 1940s, various proposals were made by the military and by fishing interests to extend national jursidiction to twelve miles. At the International Law Commission meetings preparing for the 1958 Law of the Sea Conference, the ROC made a tentative proposal for a twelve-mile limit. Finally, the ROC extended its jurisdiction to twelve miles for fishing in 1968; on other matters it took a "flexible" stance. In draft position papers for UNCLOS, the ROC again stated that it favored a twelve-mile limit.[40]

For a number of years, the PRC did not deal with the law of the sea in a systematic manner. The few scholarly writings available generally said that the limit of the territorial sea was "undetermined." Beginning in 1957, probably in anticipation of the Geneva Conference on the Law of the Sea (in which the PRC did not participate), some writers argued for a twelve-mile limit. When Indonesia proclaimed a twelve-mile limit in December 1957 and applied the archipelago principle of connecting the outermost islands by baselines, the PRC declared its support.[41]

During the 1958 Taiwan Straits crisis, the PRC issued a major statement claiming twelve miles of territorial sea (measured from baselines connecting the mainland to coastal islands) and naming the bays and straits within Chinese national jurisdiction.[42] Thereafter, China issued a series of warnings to the United States—which were ignored—not to come within twelve miles of Quemoy.

The Chinese positions departed from traditional international law, but were not especially radical or different. In 1958, a majority of countries claimed only three miles of territorial sea. There was no general agreement on this limit, however, and many countries claimed from 4 to 200 miles. Similarly, the use of baselines to connect coastal islands was a known technique, although it usually applied to well-defined fringes of islands such as exist in Norway.[43] There was some concern at the time that China might make extravagant claims by drawing baselines to islands far off the coast, but such claims failed to materialize.[44]

After the 1958 crisis, China again said little about the law of the sea, except for protests against the creation of combat zones in the South China Sea by the United States and South Vietnam. When some South American states extended their maritime claims to 200 miles in 1970, China voiced its strong support.[45]

UNCLOS presented a highly favorable opportunity for China to help change the law of the sea both to protect its own interests and to consolidate Third World cooperation against the superpowers. Peking argued that customary international law was developed by the imperialist countries and reflected the latter's interests.[46] These powers also dominated the 1958 Conference on the Law of the Sea.[47] By restricting the size of territorial seas, the Western powers were better able to exploit the fish and coastal resources of weaker states.[48] Freedom of navigation in the high seas meant freedom for the superpowers to send their navies everywhere and to carry out illegitimate activities in coastal waters.[49] More recent efforts to establish the "freedom of research in the high seas"[50] and to apply the "freedom of the high seas" concept to seabed mining[51] were viewed by China as new attempts to plunder the world's resources.

China, together with others, urged the creation of a new law of the sea that would reflect the interests of the weaker states. Their resources would be protected by a 200-mile limit and an ISA with extensive powers that would ensure an equitable distribution of resources located in areas beyond national jurisdiction. The complete revamping of the law of the sea was seen as part of the Third World's "historic task of combating colonialism, neo-colonialism, and great-power hegemonism,"[52] including the establishment of a New International Economic Order.

While calling for the creation of a new law of the sea, China has shown some hesitancy about being bound by international rules, even where it plays an active role in formulating these rules.[53] Part of this attitude reflects a feeling that the superpowers are likely to continue dominating the international rule-making process. For example, China argues that coastal states must be given extensive powers to impose pollution controls since "international standards" are inadequate,[54] presumably because the major maritime powers set these standards and are unlikely to favor more stringent controls.

China also is unwilling to entrust dispute resolution to an international body; it favors bilateral negotiations between the parties. Thus, in trying to delimit the territorial sea between adjacent or opposite states, the parties should negotiate "on the principle of mutual respect for sovereignty and territorial integrity, equality and reciprocity."[55] Similarly, in delimiting the exclusive economic zone or continental shelf, the parties should "jointly determine the [boundary] through consultations on an equal footing."[56] China may think it can achieve a more favorable result by negotiating individually with its neighbors, or it may just feel uncertain about submitting to the jurisdiction of a tribunal applying Western-style procedures and rules.

Finally, on a more abstract level, China contends that a single uniform rule is often inappropriate because natural conditions differ greatly around the world.[57] Thus, in determining the limits of the territorial sea:

> [T]he length and curvature of the coastal countries, the depth and inclination of the seabed along their coasts, the specific conditions of their coastal resources and the joining of neighboring countries in the same sea area are diversified. Moreover, the needs of economic development and national security differ for the people of each country. It is, therefore, entirely proper, legitimate and irreproachable for coastal countries to delimit in a reasonable way their own territorial seas according to their specific natural conditions, taking into account the needs for the development of their national economy and for their national security. To require uniformity and deny particularity on this matter will lead to a dead end.[58]

China's first efforts to deal with the law of the sea at the United Nations were somewhat tentative. An Zhiyuan's speech in March 1972 at the Committee on the Peaceful Uses of the Seabed set forth several basic principles but was vague about how these principles should be implemented.[59] Two working papers submitted to UNCLOS, dealing with the seabed[60] and with the sea area with national jurisdiction,[61] were brief and lacking detail. As the negotiations proceeded, the Chinese delegation both amplified its views and addressed additional issues such as pollution control.

The positions China favors with respect to the law of the sea are generally consistent with those of the Group of 77[62] and contain few unusual features.[63] A coastal state, as an exercise of sovereignty, may "reasonably define the breadth and limits of its territorial sea according to its geographical features and its needs of economic development and national security and having due regard to the legitimate interests of its neighbouring countries and the convenience of international navigation."[64]

In addition, a state may claim all resources in the water column and seabed of an exclusive economic zone. No uniform size is set for these zones. There is an outer limit of 200 nautical miles measured from the baseline of the territorial sea; presumably, this distance also is the outer limit of territorial sea claims.

A coastal state also "may reasonably define, according to its specific geographical condition, the limits of the continental shelf . . . beyond its territorial sea or exclusive economic zone,"[65] and thereby claim the resources on the shelf (but not the water column). No depth or distance criterion is suggested for delimiting the extent of the shelf, but it is clearly seen as extending beyond 200 miles where conditions warrant.

China asserts that all resources in the area beyond national jurisdiction (i.e., beyond exclusive economic zone and shelf) "are, in principle, jointly owned by the people of all countries."[66] This includes not only mineral resources in the seabed, but in theory also the fish in the high seas.[67] China supports the creation of an international authority that would hold the rights to seabed resources on behalf of all mankind, and would regulate not only mining but also other activities such as research.

Traditional freedom of navigation rules are maintained with two major exceptions.[68] First, the extension of the territorial sea to twelve miles will change the status of many straits from international to territorial waters. China argues that there is no right of free transit through such straits; instead, the coastal state may promulgate rules governing passage. Second, China holds that the regime of innocent passage through territorial waters does not apply to warships.[69]

China's positions are tailored to maximize its own interests. One important problem facing China is the eventual need to determine its marine boundaries with Japan. The Informal Composite Negotiating Text (ICNT) provides that opposite states should delimit their exclusive economic zones and continental shelves "by agreement in accordance with equitable principles, employing where appropriate, the median or equidistance line, and taking into account all the relevant circumstances."[70] Japan favors the median line rule which would divide the exclusive economic zone in the East China Sea equally between the two countries. The division of the continental shelf also would be equal if the shelf's extent is defined by a specific distance such as 200 miles from the territorial seas baseline.[71] If a depth criterion is used, however, the Ryukyu Trough cuts Japan off from most of the East China Sea. The situation is further complicated by the dispute concerning sovereignty over the Diaoyutai islands, several uninhabited islets located just west of the Ryukyu Trough midway between the Ryukyus and the China mainland.[72] If these islands belong to Japan, and if such islands also possess shelves, then Japan's claim would extend beyond the Ryukyu Trough to a substantial portion of the continental shelf in the East China Sea.

The rules proposed by China greatly reduce Japanese claims in this area.

A state is allowed to claim an exclusive economic zone "in accordance with its geographical and geological conditions, the state of its natural resources and its needs of national economic development."[73] While the term "geographical" might suggest using a median line to delimit the Sino-Japanese boundary, the phrase "geological conditions" implies that a reasonable boundary line might be the Ryukyu Trough.

China carefully defines the continental shelf as "the natural prolongation of the *continental* territory."[74] It is implicit in the Chinese phrasing that the shelf belongs to the continental state, thus reducing or cutting off island states such as Japan and the Philippines from economic exploitation of the shelf.

The Chinese draft specifies that islands possess territorial waters, but does not define what constitutes an island.[75] No explicit statement is made concerning whether islands possess exclusive economic zones and continental shelves. The language suggests that any area, including an island, that is entitled to a territorial sea is also entitled to an exclusive economic zone.[76] At the same time, islands, not being "continental," arguably have no shelves. In contrast, the ICNT provides that an island possesses a territorial sea, an exclusive economic zone, and a shelf, but that "rocks which cannot sustain human habitation or economic life of their own" have only territorial seas.[77]

The lack of clarity in the Chinese formulation may be due to poor drafting; on the other hand, it may be due to concern over the Diaoyutai islands. If the islands are later determined to belong to Japan, under the Chinese proposal such ownership would not be the basis of any shelf claims and may not be the basis of exclusive economic zone claims. At the same time, territorial sea claims alone would give China sovereignty over large portions of the South China Sea around the Spratly, Paracel and other islands.

On other issues as well, China's interests are well protected. China has only a coastal navy and is highly concerned about Soviet naval presence in the Pacific and Indian oceans.[78] The denial of innocent passage for military vessels would obstruct Soviet and U.S. naval movements without affecting its own. The generation of Russian and American opposition to this principle substantiates Chinese assertions of conspiracy between the two superpowers. In addition, while foreign trade is important to China, it is limited in quantity. Commercial navigation does not play the critical economic role it does in major maritime countries like Japan. Again, granting coastal states considerable authority to regulate navigation, research, pollution, and laying of cables is of far more benefit than harm to China.

China does not engage in extensive long-distance fishing since most of its fishing grounds are within coastal waters.[79] Its activities in the East China

Sea already are subject to fishing agreements with Japan and North Korea.[80] Much of the South China Sea fishing takes place in the territorial seas and exclusive economic zones of the Paracel and Spratly islands. Long-distance fishing will not expand significantly in the near future. Fishing is still organized by communes, and no single commune would have the financial resources to purchase the necessary equipment. Moreover, the development of aquaculture in lakes and ponds, which now supply a substantial proportion of Chinese fish needs, appears to be the principal focus of Chinese efforts.[81] Thus, empowering coastal states to control all fishing in the exclusive economic zone enhances China's control over nearby fisheries without unduly restricting its own fishing activities. In contrast, Soviet policy favors permitting foreign fishermen to fish up to the maximum sustainable yield where local fishermen have not done so. China criticizes this policy as the plundering of the resources of weaker coastal states by major long-distance fishing states such as the Soviet Union.[82]

China proposes that landlocked and shelf-locked states share a "certain portion of ownership" in the exclusive economic zone, the extent of which is to be determined through bilateral or regional "consultations on the basis of equality and mutual respect for sovereignty."[83] China can afford to be quite generous in defending the rights of such geographically disadvantaged states since it is unlikely to lose many resources to them. In fact, only Mongolia would be given rights in the Chinese economic zone under this proposal. Its small population and long distance from the coast, however, suggest a minimal claim to maritime resources. Moreover, negotiations with Mongolia over possible sharing of such resources and access to the sea may provide China with an opportunity to reduce Soviet influence in that country.

Finally, the creation of a strong ISA with extensive powers to exploit seabed and high seas resources would enable the less developed countries, including China, to get a larger share of these resources than would be possible under a free-for-all system. To induce the highly developed countries to agree to set up an ISA, the principle of "one-state one-vote" was relaxed. The weighted voting schemes proposed for the ISA Council, politely described as "geographical representation," gave the developed countries a larger share of power than their numbers alone warranted.[84] The willingness of China to agree to something less than equal voting power for all states is an important concession with major ramifications for other international issues and forums.

A strong emphasis on territorial sovereignty pervades the Chinese positions on the law of the sea. Coastal states are given wide powers to control fishing, vessel-source pollution, and scientific research in not only their territorial seas but also in their exclusive economic zones. Similarly, the interests of the coastal states are paramount in defining innocent passage and in imposing limits on the right of transit through formerly international straits.

China specifically cites as an attribute of sovereignty the power to claim territorial sea (and presumably an exclusive economic zone and continental shelf). Customary international law plays only a minor role in determining the permissible extent of such claims. Instead, each sovereign decides what is reasonable, given its own specific conditions and needs, or, through a multilateral treaty process such as UNCLOS, groups of sovereigns agree to particular limits, such as 12 nautical miles for territorial sea and 200 miles for the exclusive economic zone.

The Chinese stress on sovereignty is strikingly evident in its approach to dispute resolution. The general approach of UNCLOS is to suggest a rule from which the disputants could vary if circumstances warrant. Where the disputants cannot arrive at an amicable agreement through negotiations, the problem is handed over to an international tribunal for arbitration or adjudication. Thus, the delimitation of the exclusive economic zone and continental shelf is done by agreement "in accordance with equitable principles, employing, where appropriate, the median or equidistance line, and taking account of all the relevant circumstances."[85]

The Chinese approach to dispute resolution emphasizes bilateral negotiations rather than some presumptive rule. China may feel that some rules of ICNT, such as the use of the median line, do not support Chinese interests. It might also believe that it can exert the most leverage on neighbors in Southeast and East Asia by dealing with them on an individual basis. At the same time, the stress on bilateral dispute resolution reflects the Chinese view of sovereignty: Each state is in full control of its affairs and settles its own problems. China will have serious difficulty dealing with the shape and role of the proposed sea tribunal.[86] Accepting compulsory jurisdiction for the tribunal might violate the principle of sovereignty and might also set a precedent for other matters. In addition, China may feel uncomfortable or unfamiliar with the tribunal, which is likely to follow Western legal concepts even though many of the members are from non-Western states. At the same time, however, China is in an awkward position since many Third World states favor compulsory jurisdiction. A possible compromise is to limit compulsory jurisdiction to matters concerning the seabed or the interpretation of treaty clauses.

## V. Conclusion

Many political changes have taken place in China during the past six years, yet Chinese positions on the law of the sea have remained the same. Law of the sea issues generally did not impinge upon specific domestic interests and consequently were not affected by domestic changes.

A strong emphasis on sovereignty runs throughout the Chinese positions regarding the law of the sea. The power of the coastal states to assert jurisdiction over nearby waters is stressed. The willingness of China to grant considerable powers to the ISA is not a retreat from the concept of state sovereignty. Instead, under China's view of sovereignty, the area beyond national jurisdiction should be governed by all states, perhaps acting through an international organization. The issues arising at UNCLOS do not confront China with the need to yield some aspect of its sovereignty. Consequently, only limited analogies can be made from UNCLOS to other international forums such as the United Nations Conference on Trade and Development, where the subject matter affects activities of a sovereign within his own territory.

## Notes

1. Ying Dao, *Recognize the True Face of Bourgeois International Law from a Few Basic Concepts*, in JEROME COHEN & HUNGDAH CHIU, eds., PEOPLE'S CHINA AND INTERNATIONAL LAW 36, 71 (1974) [hereafter COHEN & CHIU].

2. Another aspect of sovereignty that involves assertion of personal jurisdiction over persons by virtue of their nationality will not be dealt with here.

3. RESTATEMENT (SECOND) OF THE FOREIGN RELATIONS LAW OF THE UNITED STATES §§ 6, 11, 17-19 (Proposed Official Draft 1962).

4. LASSA F. L. OPPENHEIM, INTERNATIONAL LAW 120, 286 (8th ed. 1963) [hereafter OPPENHEIM].

5. *Id.*, 259-85. *Cf.* U.N. Charter, Art. 2, Para. 1, stating, "The Organization is based on the principle of the sovereign equality of all its Members."

6. OPPENHEIM, *supra* note 4, at 120-23. See also Kong Meng, *A Criticism of the Theories of Bourgeois International Law Concerning the Subjects of International Law and Recognition of States*, in COHEN & CHIU, *supra* note 1, at 88-100.

7. *But see* Jiang Yang, *The Reactionary Thought of Universalism in American Jurisprudence*, in COHEN & CHIU, *supra* note 1, at 42-6; Yang Xian and Qin Qian, *Expose and Criticize the Imperialists' Fallacy Concerning the Question of State Sovereignty*, *id.* at 110-18.

8. JOHN K. FAIRBANK, ed., THE CHINESE WORLD ORDER: TRADITIONAL CHINA'S FOREIGN RELATIONS 5-14 (1968).

9. *See, e.g.,* Yung Wei, The Division and Unification of the Chinese Political Systems (Mar. 1975) (International Studies Assn., Working Paper no. 35).

10. RICHARD L. WALKER, THE MULTI-STATE SYSTEM OF ANCIENT CHINA 73-95 (1953).

11. Until the twentieth century there was no generally accepted Chinese term for sovereignty. The present term for sovereignty is *zhuquan*. Earlier terms used included *zuigao* (highest), *duli* (independent), *ziyou* (free), *tungzhi* (controlling), and *zizhu* (self-ruling).

12. IMMANUEL HSU, CHINA'S ENTRANCE INTO THE FAMILY OF NATIONS 132-45,

199-210 (1960). *See* COHEN & CHIU, *supra* note 1, at 1-12.

13. Sun Yat-sen, *The Manifesto from the Provisional Government of the Republic of China to All Friendly Nations,* North China Daily News, Jan. 5, 1912, *reprinted in* IMPORTANT DOCUMENTS RELATING TO CHINA'S REVOLUTION, 1912, at 78, 78-81 (1912).

14. *E.g.,* CHIANG KAI-SHEK, CHINA'S DESTINY 138-47 (Wang Chung-Hui trans.,1947).

15. Agreement on Trade and Intercourse between Tibet Region of China and India, Apr. 29, 1954, India-People's Republic of China, *reprinted in* COHEN & CHIU, *supra* note 1, at 119. *See also* JAMES HSIUNG, LAW AND POLICY IN CHINA'S FOREIGN RELATIONS 31-47 (1972).

16. *See* Qi Xiangyang, *Smash the New Tsars' Theory of Limited Sovereignty, in* COHEN & CHIU, *supra* note 1, at 153-55; J. HSIUNG, *supra* note 15, at 48-88.

17. U.S. DEPT. OF STATE, BULL. NO. 66, at 435, 437 (1972). The Shanghai Communiqué states in part: "the liberation of Taiwan is China's internal affair in which no other country has the right to interfere."

18. *See* Chapter 4 in this volume.

19. *See* Ilsa Sharp, *No Carnival in Canton,* FAR EASTERN ECONOMIC REVIEW, May 29, 1971, at 6-8. *See also* Stanley Lubman, *Trade with the United States, in* VICTOR LI, ed., LAW AND POLITICS IN CHINA'S FOREIGN TRADE 220-46 (1977); Randle Edwards, *The Old Canton System of Foreign Trade, id.* 360-78.

20. *See supra,* note 7.

21. Dong Biwu, *The Tenth Anniversary of the United Nations, in* COHEN & CHIU, *supra* note 1, at 1291-98.

22. *China's Principled Stand on Monetary Problem,* PEKING REVIEW [hereafter PR], Oct. 20, 1972, at 11.

23. *China's Position on the Population Problems Expounded,* PR, Mar. 22, 1974, at 8-9.

24. *China's Principled Stand Explained,* PR, Nov. 8, 1974, at 13.

25. 57 U.N. ESCOR (1918th plen. mtg.) 155. For the text of the proposed survey, see 57 U.N. ESCOR, Supp. (No. 1) 22.

26. *Speech by Deng Xiaoping, Chairman of the Delegation of People's Republic of China,* PR, Apr. 12, 1974, Supp. at 1; *Speech by Zhou Huamin, Head of Chinese Delegation,* PR, May 21, 1976, at 17.

27. *See* Chapter 4 in this volume.

28. OPPENHEIM, *supra* note 4, at 255-56.

29. *Island of Palmas Case,* 2 U.N. R. INT'L. ARB. AWARDS 829 (1928); *Clipperton Island Case,* 2 U.N. R. INT'L. ARB. AWARDS 1105 (1931).

30. *Convention on the High Seas,* Art. 2, 13 U.S.T. 2312, T.I.A.S. 5200, 450 U.N.T.S. 82 (1958).

31. Statement of Arthur Dean at Geneva Law of the Sea Conference, Mar. 11, 1958, *reprinted in* WILLIAM BISHOP, INTERNATIONAL LAW CASES AND MATERIALS 596 (3d ed. 1971); *see also No Superpowers' Control of the Sea Is Allowed,* PR, Aug. 18, 1972, at 13-15.

32. U.S. DEPT. OF STATE, PUB. NO. 8764, U.N. LAW OF THE SEA CONFERENCE 1974 (1974).

33. *See, e.g.,* H.R. REP. NO. 12988, 95th Cong., 2d Sess. (1978). (A proposed Congressional bill to develop seabed resources states that "deep seabed mining is a

freedom of the high seas, subject to a duty of reasonable regard to the interests of other States." This bill would enable American corporations to begin mining pending action at UNCLOS which would "give legal definition to the principle that the mineral resources of the deep seabed are the common heritage of mankind.")

34. *Second Session of UN Sea-Bed Committee in 1973 Concludes,* SURVEY OF CHINA MAINLAND PRESS [hereafter SCMP], Aug. 1973, at 170-73.

35. U.S. DEPT. OF STATE, BULL. NO. 77, at 389 (1977) (statement of Elliot Richardson).

36. *Chinese Delegation Leader Ch'ai Shu-fan's [Zhai Shufan's] Speech,* PR, July 12, 1974, at 11-14.

37. *China's Stand on the Question of Rights over Seas and Oceans,* PR, Mar. 10, 1972, at 14 [hereafter *China's Stand*].

38. *NCNA Correspondent Views Session,* reprinted in FOREIGN BROADCAST INFORMATION SERVICE, DAILY REPORT: PEOPLE'S REPUBLIC OF CHINA [hereafter FBIS], July 19, 1977, at A2-4; *Sea Law Conference Enters Final Stage,* PR, Aug. 30, 1974, at 17-18; *On Governing International Sea-Bed Areas,* PR, Aug. 25, 1972, at 10-12.

39. For a thorough discussion of historical and contemporary Chinese views on the territorial sea, see Hungdah Chiu, *China and the Question of Territorial Sea,* 1 INTERNATIONAL TRADE LAW JOURNAL 29 (1975).

40. *Id.*

41. *Sovereignty over Territorial Sea and "Freedom of the Sea,"* Renmin Ribao [hereafter RMRB], Dec. 28, 1957, at 5.

42. *Declaration on China's Territorial Sea,* PR, Sep. 9, 1958, at 21. *See also* Fu Ju, *Concerning the Question of Our Country's Territorial Sea,* in COHEN & CHIU, *supra* note 1, at 470-87, 529-34.

43. *Fisheries Case* (United Kingdom v. Norway), Judgment of Dec. 18, 1951, I.C.J. Reports of Judgments 116 (1951).

44. U.S. BUREAU OF INTELLIGENCE AND RESEARCH, DEPT. OF STATE, NO. 43, STRAIGHT BASELINES: PEOPLE'S REPUBLIC OF CHINA, (1972).

45. *Support Latin American Countries' Struggle to Defend Their Territorial Sea Rights,* PR, Nov. 27, 1970, at 7-8.

46. *Upsurge of Third World's Struggle in Unity Against Hegemonism,* PR, July 26, 1974, at 6-7; *Struggle Against Hegemony over Maritime Rights, id.,* June 28, 1974, at 14-15; *China's View on Convening Law of the Sea Conference, id.,* Dec. 22, 1972, at 13-14; *U.N. Sea-Bed Committee Ends Session, id.,* Aug. 25, 1972, at 10.

47. *Support for a New Convention on the Law of Sea,* PR, Apr. 13, 1973, at 13-15.

48. *Superpowers' Plunder of Fishing Resources Opposed,* PR, Aug. 2, 1974, at 11-12.

49. *Third World Countries Oppose Superpower Stand on "Free Passage Through Straits,"* 76-39 SURVEY OF PEOPLE'S REPUBLIC OF CHINA PRESS, Sep. 15, 1976, at 163-65; *Developing Countries Combat Maritime Hegemony,* PR, May 21, 1976, at 21-23; *Debate on the Question of Straits for International Navigation, id.,* Aug. 2, 1974, at 9-10; *No Superpowers' Control of the Seas is Allowed, supra* note 31.

50. *Second Session of the U.N. Sea-Bed Committee in 1973 Concludes,* SCMP, Sep. 4-7, 1973, at 170-74.

51. *Debate on the Regime and Machinery Governing International Sea-Bed Area,* PR, Aug. 2, 1974, at 11-12.

52. *Chinese Delegation Leader Zhai Shufan's Speech, supra* note 36, at 14.

53. In the maritime area, China has previously signed the 1930 International Load Line Convention (*NPC Standing Committee Holds 82nd Meeting,* SCMP, Oct. 29, 1957, at 2), and the 1948 Convention on Prevention of Collisions at Sea *(NPC Standing Committee Decisions,* SCMP, Dec. 31, 1957, at 1). *See also* Anthony R. Dicks, *Some Aspects of Maritime Law and Practice, in* VICTOR LI, *ed.,* LAW AND POLITICS IN CHINA'S FOREIGN TRADE 249-69 (1977).

54. *Chinese Representative on Marine Pollution,* PR, July 26, 1974, at 7-8.

55. Working Paper on Sea Area Within the Limits of National Jurisdiction (July 16, 1973), Art. 1(4), U.N. Doc. A/AC.138/SC.II/L.34, *reprinted in* 12 INTERNATIONAL LEGAL MATERIALS 1231 (Sep. 1973) [hereafter Sea Area Paper, *in* ILM].

56. Sea Area Paper, Art. 2(8), 3(6), *in* ILM at 1233, 1234.

57. *See* Mao Zedong, *On Practice, in* 1 SELECTED WORKS OF MAO TSE-TUNG 295 (1967). (The effort to keep rules flexible and to adapt them to meet differing situations is one that applies to all matters, not just international law.)

58. *The Struggle in Defense of Maritime Rights,* PR, Mar. 30, 1973, at 9.

59. *China's Stand, supra* note 37, at 14-16.

60. Working Paper on General Principles for the International Sea Area (Aug. 2, 1973), U.N. Doc. A/AC.138/SC.II/L.45, *reprinted in* 12 INTERNATIONAL LEGAL MATERIALS 1262 (Sep. 1973).

61. *See* Sea Area Paper, *supra* note 56.

62. Edward Miles, *Introduction,* 31 INTERNATIONAL ORGANIZATIONS 152 (No. 1, 1977). (Introductory notes to the articles in this volume are collectively titled *Restructuring Ocean Regimes.*)

63. This is what China advocates rather than what it may eventually agree upon as part of a Third World package.

64. Sea Area Paper, Art. 1(2), *in* ILM at 1231.

65. *Id.,* Art. 3(1), *in* ILM at 1233.

66. *Id.,* Art. 1, *in* ILM at 1262.

67. *Id.,* Art. 6, *in* ILM at 1262. (China says only that "fishing in the international sea area shall be properly regulated to prohibit indiscriminate fishing and other violation of rules and regulations for conservation of fishery resources.")

68. *Id.,* Arts. 1(7), 1(8), 2(4), 3(3) *in* ILM at 1232-3; *see also supra* note 49.

69. Informal Composite Negotiating Text, Arts. 17-36, 29-32, Third Conference of the Law of the Sea (6th Sess.) 50, U.N. Doc. A/CONF. 62/WP 10 [hereafter ICNT]. *See also Id.,* Arts. 34-45, at 32-6.

70. ICNT, Art. 74, at 50.

71. ICNT, Art. 76, at 52.

72. *See* Victor Li, *China and Off-Shore Oil,* 10 STANFORD JOURNAL OF INTERNATIONAL STUDIES 143 (1975).

73. Sea Area Paper, Art. 2(1), *in* ILM at 1232.

74. Sea Area Paper, Art. 3(1), *in* ILM at 1232. *Cf.* ICNT, Art. 76, at 52 (defining the continental shelf as the natural prolongation of "land territory").

75. Sea Area Paper, Art. 1(5), *in* ILM at 1232.

76. *Id.,* Art. 2(1).

77. ICNT, Art. 121, at 68-9.

78. *See* Chapter 3 in this volume.

79. Choon-ho Park, *Fishing Under Troubled Waters: The Northeast Fisheries Controversy,* 2 OCEAN DEVELOPMENT AND INTERNATIONAL LAW JOURNAL 110, 123 (No. 2, 1974). Other aspects of China's maritime capability also are limited, though growing. *See* Stephan Uhalley, *China in the Pacific,* OCEANS, July 1978, at 32.

80. Song Yook Hong, *The Sino-Japanese Fisheries Agreements of 1975,* UNIVERSITY OF MARYLAND SCHOOL OF LAW, OCCASIONAL PAPERS/REPRINTS SERIES IN CONTEMPORARY ASIAN STUDIES, No. 6 (1977); Choon-ho Park, *supra* note 79; Choon-ho Park, *Fisheries Issues in the Yellow Sea and the East China Sea,* UNIVERSITY OF RHODE ISLAND, LAW OF THE SEA INSTITUTE OCCASIONAL PAPER, NO. 18 (1973).

81. *See* H.V. HENLE, REPORT ON CHINA'S AGRICULTURE 125-26 (Food and Agricultural Organization of the United Nations, 1974). *See also Aquaculture: Hearings on H.R. 1833 and H.R. 4739 Before the Subcomm. on Fisheries and Wildlife Conservation and the Environment and the Subcomm. on Oceanography of the House Comm. on Merchant Marine and Fisheries,* 95th Cong., 1st Sess. 297, 593-97 (1977).

82. *See* J.K. FAIRBANK, *supra* note 8.

83. Sea Area Paper, Art. 2(3), *in* ILM at 1232; *see also* ICNT, Art. 69, at 48.

84. *Debate on the Regime and Machinery Governing International Sea-Bed Area, supra* note 51; ICNT, Art. 159, at 65. (The willingness of China to make this concession has major ramifications for other international issues in other forums.)

85. ICNT, Art. 74, at 50, 55.

86. ICNT, Arts. 279-97, at 142-50.

# Index

ABM Treaty, 156
Actual policies, 27, 28-29, 55, 60
Advocates, 136
Agriculture, 37-38, 67, 111
  and foreign trade, 220
  and national defense, 179
  radicals and, 53
Air raid shelters, 156-157
Albanian view of China, 98, 101, 102, 131
Appeasement charge, 104, 116, 123
Aquaculture, 239
Arab oil embargo, 37, 204
Armed forces. *See* Military policies; People's Liberation Army
Arms control, 185-188, 189
Arrangements, informal, 28-29
Aspaturian, Vernon, 134

Balance of payments deficit, 205, 215, 219, 220
Balluku, Bequir, 98
Barnett, A. Doak, 207-208
Beaufre, Andre, 153
Bodin, Jean, 227
Border, Sino-Soviet, 30, 102-105, 110, 111, 125, 158, 163, 230
Brezhnev Doctrine, 30, 103, 230
Brown, George, 151-152, 174
Brzezinski, Zbigniew K., 16
Budgetary linkages, 10-11, 12, 13. *See also* Spending

Cambodia, 182
Canton Trade Fair, 215, 216
Capitulationism charge, 107, 110, 113, 116, 123, 134, 209
CCP. *See* Chinese Communist Party
Centralization of policymaking, 8-9, 30, 31, 35-36
Chai Shufan, 207, 215
Chinese Communist Party (CCP), 3, 29, 31, 35, 41, 43. *See also* National Party Congress; Politburo
  and cultural policies, 39-40, 57, 65, 68, 69, 70
  and economic development, 6, 35-36
  and military policy, 41, 113, 114, 116, 121, 122, 127
  National Party Congress: Ninth, 32, 41; Tenth, 46-47, 96-98, 99, 100, 102, 103, 108, 110; Eleventh, 128, 182
  rectification of, 18-19, 32-36, 60, 65, 208
  and self-reliance, 200, 220
Clusters, policy, 11-12, 13, 14, 26. *See also* Linkages, policy; Packages, policy
Coal, 207, 210, 213, 217
Coalitions, 12-13, 19, 26, 28, 135-136, 179-180. *See also* Efficiency maximizers; Moderates; Radicals
Colby, William, 172
Colonialism, 96, 100
Committee on the Peaceful Uses of the Seabed, 236
Conference on the Law of the Sea, United Nations (UNCLOS), 225 233, 234, 235, 236-240, 241

*247*

Confucius, campaign against (*Pi Kong*), 47, 53, 95, 100, 104, 106-107, 111, 163, 204
Congresses. *See* Chinese Communist Party; National Party Congress; National People's Congress
Conservatism, 16-17, 28-29, 61, 72-73, 175
Conservative-radicals. *See* Defenders of the Cultural Revolution
Constitution
  Party, 97, 128, 137
  State, 51, 100, 181
Contenders, 136-137
Continental shelf, 237, 238, 240
Cultural policies
  independence of, 4, 6, 7, 230-231
  and 1970-71 Program, 38-41, 53, 55-60, 67-71
Cultural Revolution, 42-47, 73, 111, 118. *See also* Defenders of the Cultural Revolution; Rehabilitation of discredited officials
  and cultural policies, 38, 39, 40-41, 45-46, 53
  and economic policies, 30, 35, 205
  foreign policy during, 93, 109
  and military policy, 112, 115, 120, 133, 167, 173
  organizational forms of, 30, 34, 41, 65-66
  and planning, 10
  and socialist transformation, 5, 16

Daqing Conference, 127-128, 179, 219
Dazhai models, 45, 53
Debates, 7, 13, 17, 20, 28, 73, 179-180, 199
  on global posture, 94-137
  on military policy, 102-130, 131, 149, 157, 166, 175
  and 1970-71 Program, 32, 38, 42-43, 44-45, 51-52, 55
  and *Pi Deng*, 205

Defenders of the Cultural Revolution, 17, 18, 43, 44, 46. *See also* Radicals
  and economic construction, 36, 37
  and education, 40, 45-46, 58
  Mao and, 31, 49
  and military modernization, 133
  and *Pi Deng*, 53-54
  and *Pi Lin Pi Kong*, 111
  propaganda war by, 51-52
  and rules of the game, 18-19, 44-45, 49, 73
Defense, national, 4, 5, 6, 52, 150, 179. *See also* Military policies
Defense Department (U.S.), 165
Democratic centralism, 18-19, 36, 50
Deng Xiaoping, 109
  campaign against (*Pi Deng*), 7, 13, 53-54, 95, 111, 120-121, 199-220
  and independence, 3-4
  and law of the sea, 226
  and military modernization, 95, 114-115, 117, 118, 119, 120, 121, 122, 123, 180
  and nuclear proliferation, 186
  and rehabilitation of discredited officials, 50, 119, 208
  and science, 69-70
  and self-reliance, 201
  and theory of three worlds, 94, 99, 101, 131, 182
Deployment, military, 162-163, 164-165
Deterrence, nuclear, 151-158, 163, 171, 185, 188
Diaoyutai islands, 237, 238
Disrupters, 137
Doctrines. *See* Ideology; Military policies, doctrines in
Domestic policy, 25-74. *See also* Cultural policies; Economic construction; Military policies; Organizational policies; Politics
  and foreign policy, 13-14, 26, 27, 29, 30-31, 60-61, 72, 93-137,

199-220, 226, 240-241
Durability of policy, 3, 15-20

Economic construction, 5-6, 7, 15, 29-30, 35-38, 66-67. *See also* Modernization
  efficiency in, 7, 17, 18, 31-73 *passim,* 133
  and foreign trade, 36-37, 94, 202, 209, 210-211, 213-215, 216, 218-219, 220, 231-232
  independence in, 3-4, 6, 200, 202, 231
  and military modernization, 7, 41-42, 67, 118, 128-130, 133, 179
  speed of, 7, 36-37, 55-56, 62, 63, 68, 179
Economic expenditures. *See* Spending
Education, 38-41, 54, 55, 56, 60, 67-71
  and foreign trade, 209, 220
  radicals and, 39, 40, 45-46, 53, 57-59, 60, 67-68, 70
Efficiency maximizers, 7, 17, 18, 31-73 *passim,* 133
*Elements of International Law* (Wheaton), 229
Elitism, 41, 59
Engels, F., 151
Equality, sovereign, 227, 232-233
Equity, social, 5, 7, 16, 43
Establishment, 136
Europe
  and military policy, 93, 99, 108, 125, 132, 149, 183-184
  and theory of three worlds, 99, 101, 183-184
European Economic Community, 184
Expenditures. *See* Spending

Factionalism. *See* Coalitions
Fang Hai, 107
Fang Yi, 70, 176-177
Feint to the East slogan, 108, 110, 183
Fenwick, Ann, 6, 7, 10-11, 12, 13, 14, 17

Fingar, Thomas, 17, 133, 134, 135
Fishing, 232-233, 234, 238-239
Five-Year Plan
  First, 128
  Second, 128
  Fifth, 52, 95, 216
Flexibility in foreign policy
  and military deployments, 162-163
  and self-reliance, 200, 201-202, 207, 231
  toward Soviet Union, 104-106, 107, 109, 110, 122, 132, 162-163
  and trade, 200, 201-202, 207, 219-220
Force, military, 132-133, 148-161, 228
Foreign policy, 7-8, 15-16, 27, 55. *See also* Military policies; Trade, foreign
  and domestic policy, 13-14, 26, 27, 29, 30-31, 60-61, 72, 93-137, 199-220, 226, 240-241
  and law of the sea, 13, 225-241
Formal policy, 26-27, 55, 60, 72, 136
Functional linkages, 11-12, 13

"Gang of four," 17, 51-52, 94, 97, 98, 137. *See also* Radicals
  criticisms of, 61-62, 95, 98, 127, 149
  and cultural policies, 40, 68, 69
  and foreign trade, 204, 210, 217, 218, 231-232
  and law of the sea, 226
  and military policy, 117, 118, 123, 127, 137, 149, 151, 179
  and *Pi Deng,* 54, 204, 217, 218
  purge of, 18, 54, 63, 73, 137
  and theory of three worlds, 101-102
Geneva Conference on the Law of the Sea, 234, 235
Global posture, 93-137, 149. *See also* Foreign policy
Godwin, Paul, 95
Going against the tide, 17, 33, 46, 47, 50, 137

Goldman, Merle, 95
Gong (Prince), 229
Good Eighth Company of Nanking Road, 120-121
Group of 77, 236
Gu Mu, 215

Hague Treaty on Territorial Seas, 234
Harding, Harry, 6, 7, 10, 12, 13, 14, 17
Hegemonism, 93, 96, 97, 99, 100, 101
Helicopter crew, Soviet, 105, 106, 108, 109
Hong Cheng, 117
Hua Guofeng, 54
  and domestic policy, 62, 68
  and foreign policy, 109, 124, 128, 150, 155-156, 182-183, 184
Huang Hua, 98, 186, 187
Huntington, Samuel P., 16

ICNT. *See* Informal Composite Negotiating Text
Ideology, 6. *See also* Leninism; Mao Zedong
  and foreign policy, 7, 98, 113, 131, 132, 220
Imperialism, 97, 98, 133
  and international law, 225-227, 231, 235
  and military force, 148, 149
  surprise attack by, 97, 126-127, 128
  and theory of three worlds, 99, 100, 131, 132
Implemented policy, 27, 28-29, 55, 60
Independence, national, 2, 3-8, 18, 19, 202. *See also* Security, national of Third World countries, 96, 182
Industry, 36-37, 67. *See also* Economic construction
  and foreign trade, 209, 212, 213-215, 216
  and military modernization, 114, 116, 123, 179
Informal Composite Negotiating Text (ICNT), 237, 238, 240

Institute of World Economy, 125, 126
Intellectuals, 38-39, 40-41, 54-65 *passim,* 68
Intended policy, 26-27, 55, 60, 72, 136
International law, 13, 225-241
International Law Commission, 234
International Monetary Fund, 231
International Seabed Authority (ISA), 226, 234, 235, 239, 241
International situation, 16-17, 19-20, 131, 163
Investment funds, 36, 37. *See also* Loans, foreign; Spending
ISA. *See* International Seabed Authority
Islands, and law of the sea, 238

Japan, 149
  and law of the sea, 237-238, 239
  and Soviet threat, 93, 99, 101, 108, 125-126, 132, 183
  trade with, 37, 184, 204, 205-207, 216, 217, 219
  and U.S. nuclear umbrella, 172
Jiang Qing, 18, 51, 61, 149. *See also* "Gang of four"
  and MAC, 118
  and theory of three worlds, 100-101
Joffe, Ellis, 95
Joint Institute of Nuclear Research, 166
July 21 Workers' Universities, 59, 71
Justice, social, 5, 7, 16, 35, 43

Kim Il-sung, 182
Korea, 148, 162
  North, 182, 185, 217, 239
Kosygin, A., 103, 104-105, 110

Launch-on-warning, 165
Law, international, 13, 225-241
Legalists, 95, 119
Leninism, 32-33, 98, 131
Lewis, John, 6, 7, 8, 10, 11, 12, 13
Li, Victor, 11, 12, 13

Lieberthal, Kenneth, 95, 108
Li Hongzhang, 212
Limited response, in deterrence theory, 155, 156, 157
Lin Biao, 44, 102, 226
  campaign against (*Pi Lin*, 45, 47, 95, 100, 104, 106-107, 111-113, 119, 172
  death of, 35, 43
  and people's war, 112, 113, 117, 119, 181
Linkages, policy, 2-3, 8-14, 199. *See also* Clusters, policy
  in cultural policies, 55-56
  with economic construction, 121, 218
  with foreign trade, 209, 218
  with law of the sea, 226
  with military modernization, 121
Li Qiang, 215
Liu Guangtao, 127
Liu Xiyao, 71
Li Xiannian, 9, 127-128, 177
Loans, foreign, 7, 209-210, 212, 220, 231
Luo Ruiqing, 112, 115

MAC. *See* Military Affairs Commission
Mao Zedong, 208, 218
  and Cultural Revolution, 31, 49
  death of, 54, 55, 60, 226
  and economic construction, 179
  Lin and, 35, 112, 113
  and navy, 115
  and nuclear weapons, 123, 150-151, 154, 163, 166, 167, 171, 179
  *On the Ten Major Relationships*, 62, 124, 126, 128, 129, 166, 179
  and people's war, 111, 113, 123, 181
  and PLA, 114, 118, 124
  and radicals, 17, 31, 46, 48-49, 52, 54
  and self-reliance, 201
  and Soviet Union, 109
  and strategic defensiveness, 164

and strategy with opponents, 104, 155
  and theory of three worlds, 94, 99, 101, 131, 182, 183
  war preparedness, slogan of, 156
Mao Zedong Thought Propaganda Teams, 58-59
Martin, W.A.P., 229
Maxwell, Neville, 106
May 7 Colleges, 71
Media, 45, 48, 137
  on air raid shelters, 156-157
  and cultural policy, 56-58, 68
  and foreign trade, 210, 211-212, 213-216
  on "gang of four" errors, 61-62, 95, 123, 127
  and Party discipline, 33-35, 47, 49-50
  and people's war, 117, 119, 123, 151, 180
  and *Pi Deng*, 54, 95, 120-121, 200, 204
  and *Pi Lin Pi Kong*, 45, 95, 112-113, 117, 119-120
  and PLA rectification, 116-117
  and Soviet Union, 103, 105, 106-108, 123, 124, 125-128
  and theory of three worlds, 101, 126
  on weapons, 116, 117, 119-120, 123, 151, 176
Middle East
  war in, 111, 175, 184
Military Affairs Commission (MAC), 111, 114-116, 117-124, 133, 135, 167
Military policies, 20, 41-42, 93, 102-137, 147-189. *See also* People's Liberation Army
  debates on, 102-130, 131, 149, 157, 166, 175
  doctrines in, 112, 114-115, 117, 132-133, 147-189. *See also* People's wars
  and economic construction, 7, 41-42, 67, 118, 128-130, 133, 179

and foreign trade, 116, 117, 122, 176, 177, 212
for modernization, 5, 6, 52, 93, 94, 95, 110-130, 133, 134-136, 137, 173-181
and 1970-71 Program, 31, 41-42, 51
nuclear, 123, 149-158, 163-179, 182, 185-188
operational elements in, 158-165
radicals and, 54, 117, 118, 123, 127, 135, 137, 149, 157, 179
and sovereignty, 4, 8, 149-150, 230
and Soviet surprise attack, 97, 113, 122-123, 126-127, 128, 132, 133, 149, 164, 183
spending for, 7, 42, 109, 120, 125, 126, 128-130, 133, 136, 172, 177-179
and U.S., 97, 113, 148, 162, 165, 171-187
Mineral resources, seabed, 233, 234, 235. *See also* Natural resources
Moderates. *See also* Efficiency maximizers
on domestic policy, 109, 111, 134
on foreign policy, 104-106, 107, 108, 109, 110, 123-124, 133, 134, 135-136
Modernization, 3, 5-7, 20, 63. *See also* Economic construction; Technology
of defense, 93, 94, 95, 110-130, 133, 134-136, 137, 173-181, 205
and foreign trade, 209, 211, 219
of science and technology, 38, 55-56, 69
Mutual assured destruction (MAD), 154-155, 156

National betrayal charge, 107, 109, 110, 134
National Conference on Education Work, 71
National Conference on Learning from Daqing in Industry, 63-64, 179
National Council for U.S.-China Trade, 215
National Dazhai Conference, 53
National Defense Scientific and Technological Commission, 167
National People's Congress (NPC)
Fourth, 6, 50-51, 52, 100, 101, 110, 111, 114, 205
Fifth, 94, 95, 129
Standing Committee of, 104-105
National Science Conference, 69, 174
NATO, 183-184
Natural resources, 205-207, 210, 213, 217. *See also* Mineral resources, seabed; Oil exports
Navy, 115, 117, 118, 119, 212, 238
1970-71 Program, 29-73 *passim*
and cultural policies, 38-41, 53, 55-60, 69, 70, 71
and economic policies, 35-38, 51, 67
and military policies, 41-42, 51, 67
and organizational policies, 32-35, 64-66
and political policies, 32-35
Nixon, Richard M., 37, 97, 183
Noninterference principle, 227-230, 234
NPC. *See* National People's Congress
Nuclear weapons, 123, 149-158, 163-179, 182, 185-188

Oil exports, 37, 210, 213, 219
and Arab embargo, 37, 204
to Japan, 204, 205-207, 217, 219
and *Pi Deng,* 204, 213, 217
*On Certain Problems in Speeding Up Industrial Development,* 209
*On the Ten Major Relationships,* 62, 124, 126, 128, 129, 166, 179
Operational linkages, 9-10
Organizational policies, 30, 32-35, 64-66. *See also* Chinese

*Index* 253

Communist Party
"Outline National Plan for the Development of Science and Technology," 70
"Outline Report," 59

Packages, policy, 26, 109–110, 122–124, 135, 136–137. *See also* Clusters, policy
Paracel Islands, 110, 121, 148, 162
Party. *See* Chinese Communist Party
Party Constitution, 97, 128, 137
*Party Exercises Leadership in Everything, The,* 49–50
Peaceful coexistence, 102, 189, 229–230
People's Liberation Army (PLA), 95, 104, 109–130, 133, 158–181. *See also* Military policies
  CCP authority over, 41
  and people's war, 122, 123, 180–181
  training programs in, 111, 112–113, 114–115, 116, 117, 119, 130, 180
  and Vietnam, 163, 182, 184, 185, 228
  weapons of, 111–123, 150–179, 182, 185–188
People's wars, 122, 123, 124, 151, 180–181, 182
  and Lin, 112, 113, 117, 119, 181
  Mao and, 111, 113, 123, 181
  and military spending, 179
Petroleum. *See* Oil exports
*Pi Deng. See* Deng Xiaoping, campaign against
*Pi Lin Pi Kong. See* Confucius, campaign against; Lin Biao, campaign against
PLA. *See* People's Liberation Army
Planning, comprehensive, 9–10, 28–31, 35–36, 63, 66–67, 133
Policy. *See* Domestic policy; Foreign policy
Policymaking. *See* Clusters, policy; Coalitions; Debates; Planning, comprehensive; Politics

Politburo, 25, 26, 33, 109, 110. *See also* Chinese Communist Party; Radicals and foreign policy, 101, 110, 117, 118, 122, 134
  and *Pi Lin Pi Kong,* 111
Politics, 17, 151. *See also* Coalitions; Debates
  independence in, 3–4, 6, 231
  linkages of, 12–14
  maneuver in, 13, 17–18, 28, 32, 42–54, 73, 133–137, 218
  in *Pi Deng,* 208, 218
  policies on, 17–19, 32–35
Pollack, Jonathan, 95, 126
Pollution controls, in seas, 235, 236
Predictability of policy, 3, 15–20, 64
Press. *See* Media
Propaganda. *See* Media

Qian Xuesen, 173
Qi Jiguang, 117
Qing dynasty, 212, 229

Radicals, 9, 17, 31, 45–54, 55, 73. *See also* Defenders of the Cultural Revolution
  and agriculture, 53
  criticisms of, 61–62, 95, 98, 123, 127
  and cultural policies, 39, 40, 45–46, 53, 57–60, 67–68, 69, 70
  and foreign policy, 94–137 *passim,* 204
  and foreign trade, 204, 210, 217, 218, 231–232
  and law of the sea, 226
  Mao and, 17, 31, 46, 48–49, 52, 54
  and military policy, 54, 117, 118, 123, 127, 135, 137, 149, 179
  and *Pi Deng,* 53–54, 111, 120–121, 199–220
  and *Pi Lin Pi Kong,* 45, 47, 53, 100, 104, 106–107, 111–113, 117, 119, 204
  purge of, 18, 54, 63, 73, 137
  and rehabilitation of discredited

officials, 50, 57-58, 111, 119
and theory of three worlds, 101-102
Rehabilitation of discredited officials, 33, 34-35, 47, 50, 64
   for military modernization, 111, 115, 119
   and radicals, 50, 57-58, 111, 119, 208
   in sciences, 39, 40-41, 55-56
Ren Guping, 101
*Renmin Ribao*
   and *Pi Lin Pi Kong*, 47, 119
Republic of China (ROC) and Law of the Sea Conference, 234. *See also* Taiwan
Research and development (R&D) methodologies, 174-175. *See also* Science; Technology
Revisionism, 98, 132
   domestic, 47, 53, 107, 121, 122, 133
Revolutionary movements, foreign, 96-102 *passim,* 131, 132, 133
Rhetorical policy, 27, 55
Rolls Royce Spey engines, 115-116, 212
Rounds in foreign policymaking, 94-96, 134-135. *See also* Debates; Politics
   One (1973-75), 94, 96-102, 131
   Two (1973-75), 94-95, 102-110, 122, 132, 133
   Three (1974-77), 95, 110-124, 133
   Four (1977-78), 95, 124-130, 133
Rules of the game, 17, 28, 42, 44-49 *passim,* 72-74
Rural policy. *See* Agriculture
Ryukyu Trough, 237-238

Safire, William, 125
SALT, 185-188, 189
*Sanhe yishao,* 132
Schlesinger, James, 151, 155
Science, 6, 40, 52, 55-60, 64-65, 67-71. *See also* Technology
   and education, 38-39, 56, 57, 59, 60, 67-68, 70-71

and foreign policy, 94, 189
military, 173-177
radicals and, 39, 53, 57-60, 70
Sea, law of the, 13, 225-241
Second World, 99, 101, 102, 182-183
Security, national, 3-8, 12, 15, 18, 20
   and domestic policies, 30-31, 37, 39, 42, 54, 55-56, 60, 64, 72
   and foreign policy, 30-31, 72, 127, 132, 151, 162-163, 172, 184-185, 188-189, 200
Segal, Gerald, 95
Self-reliance, 4, 7
   and economic construction, 35, 202, 209, 210, 211, 218, 220, 231-232
   and foreign trade, 7, 116, 200-202, 204, 207, 209, 210, 211, 218, 220, 231-232
Shanghai Communiqué, 189, 229
Shipbuilding industries, 212, 213-215
Shipping industries, 212, 213-215, 216
Social equity, 5, 7, 16, 43
Social-imperialism, 97, 99, 128, 148, 149
Socialist camp, international, 99
Socialist construction. *See* Economic construction
Socialist transformation, 3, 5, 7, 16
Social justice, 5, 7, 16, 35, 43
Sovereignty, 4, 6, 8, 96, 149-150, 225-241
Soviet Union, 14, 94, 95, 102-110, 131, 149
   border of, 102-105, 110, 111, 125, 158, 163, 230
   Cultural Revolution and, 93
   flexibility toward, 104-106, 107, 109, 110, 122, 132, 162-163
   and Japan-China relations, 93, 101, 132, 149, 183
   and law of the sea, 225, 238, 239
   and military modernization, 93, 113, 117, 120, 122-123, 124, 125-128, 129-130, 132, 133, 136
   and military spending, 109, 120,

125, 126, 128-130, 136, 177-178
and self-reliance concept, 200, 202, 231
surprise attack by, 97, 113, 122-123, 126-127, 128, 132, 133, 149, 164, 183
technocratic elite in, 41
and theory of three worlds, 99, 101-102, 126, 135, 183
Third World and, 93, 96, 97-98, 132
and U.S.-China relations, 93, 96-106 *passim*, 113, 132, 172, 183-184, 188-189
U.S. détente with, 30, 49, 183-184
and Vietnam, 149, 163, 182, 184
and weapons, 149, 164-167, 171, 176, 177-179, 185-187
Spending
on foreign trade, 202-204, 213-214, 219-220
military, 7, 42, 109, 120, 125, 126, 128-130, 133, 136, 172, 177-179
*Spirit of Going Against the Tide,* 46
Stability, 3, 15-20, 64
State bureaucracy, 34, 35
State Constitution, 51, 100, 181
Strategic defensiveness, 151, 162, 164
Structural linkages, 8-9
Sulzberger, C. L., 103
Surprise attack, 97, 126-127, 128
by Soviet Union, 97, 113, 122-123, 126-127, 128, 132, 133, 149, 164, 183
Su Yu, 127, 181

Tactical offensiveness, 151
Taiwan, 148, 150, 162, 184, 230
foreign trade volume of, 232
and law of the sea, 234
UN and, 15
"Talk at an Enlarged Working Conference Convened by the Central Committee of the Communist Party of China" (Mao), 18

Technical efficiency, 7, 17, 18, 31-73 *passim*
Technology, 38-39, 53, 55-57, 68-69, 71. *See also* Science
foreign, 5, 15, 37, 54, 67, 116, 117, 122, 176, 177, 204-219 *passim*
military, 115-116, 117, 121, 122, 124, 130, 132, 135, 150-157, 173-180, 189, 212
nuclear, 149-158, 163-179, 182, 185-188
Theory of the intermediate zone, 182-183
Theory of three worlds, 14, 94, 99-102, 131, 135, 136
Deng and, 94, 99, 101, 131, 182
Hua and, 182-183
Mao and, 94, 99, 101, 131, 182, 183
and Soviet threat, 99, 101-102, 126, 135, 183
Zhou and, 99, 100, 131, 183
Third World, 93, 99, 100-101, 102, 182
and law of the sea, 235, 240
and nuclear weapons, 185-186
reactionary governments of, 98, 132
at UN, 231
Zhou on, 96, 100-101, 183
"Three Big Poisonous Weeds," 54
Tiananmen Square Incident, 54, 108, 121, 217
Tibet, 148
Trade, foreign, 36-37, 94, 231-232
and *Pi Deng,* 7, 13, 199-220
in technology, 7, 15, 37, 54, 67, 116, 117, 122, 165-167, 176, 177, 204-219 *passim*
volume of, 203, 230, 231-232, 238
Training, military, 111-119 *passim,* 130, 180
Treaty for the Prohibition of Nuclear Weapons in Latin America, 186
Treaty of Westphalia, 227
Turnkey plants, 202-204
*Twenty Points,* 209, 211

UNCLOS. *See* Conference on the Law of the Sea, United Nations
United Nations (UN), 15, 231
  Deng at, 4, 99, 101, 182, 201
  and law of the sea, 225, 233, 234, 235, 236–240, 241
  and nuclear weapons, 165, 186, 187
United States, 99
  during Cultural Revolution, 93
  and law of the sea, 225, 234, 235
  and military policies, 97, 113, 114, 125, 126, 148, 149–156, 162, 163, 165, 171–187
  rapprochement with, 37, 93, 94, 96–98, 101, 184–185, 188–189
  and Sino-Soviet relations, 93, 96–108 *passim*, 113, 125, 126, 132, 183–184, 188–189
  Soviet détente with, 30, 49, 183–184
  and theory of three worlds, 99, 101, 126, 183
  trade volume with, 232
  and Vietnam, 96–97, 131, 148, 179, 230, 235
Universities, 39–40, 56, 57–59, 68, 70, 71. *See also* Education

Vietnam, 149, 162
  China's attack on, 148, 163, 182, 184, 185, 228
  U.S. and, 96–97, 131, 148, 179, 230, 235
Vladivostok summit meeting, 106, 184

Wang Hongwen, 18, 47, 149. *See also* "Gang of four"
  and foreign policy, 97–98, 99, 100
  and MAC, 118
Watergate, 183–184
*Water Margin,* 53
Weapons, 111–123, 149–179, 182, 185–188

Wei Yuan, 116, 117
Whiting, Allen, 132

Yao Wenyuan, 9, 18, 118, 149. *See also* "Gang of four"
Ye Jianying
  and economic construction, 179
  and military modernization, 114, 117, 118, 122, 124, 128, 166, 179
Yu Qiuli, 67, 128, 179
Yu Zhan, 105, 109, 125, 127

Zeng Guofan, 212
Zero-sum policies, 10–11, 12, 17
Zhang Chunqiao, 18, 47, 149. *See also* "Gang of four"
  and military modernization, 118, 119
  and theory of three worlds, 100, 101
Zhang Tiesheng, 46, 57
Zhang Zhidong, 212–213
Zhaoyang Agricultural College, 59
Zhenbao Island, 121, 158
Zhou Enlai
  and cultural policy, 68
  death of, 53, 60, 208, 226
  and foreign trade, 205
  and four modernizations, 5, 6, 51, 52, 114
  and Japan, 183
  and military modernization, 114, 150, 166, 167–171
  and *Pi Deng,* 53–54, 121
  and Soviet Union, 97, 103, 104–105, 108, 110, 162–163
  and theory of three worlds, 99, 100, 131, 183
  Third World formula of, 96, 98, 101
  and U.S., 96–97, 98
Zhou Peiyuan, 56

## Date Due